'Good people always crackney in heaven.'

GRANT FINLAY

'Good people always crackney in heaven.'

Mythic conversations in *lutruwita* / Tasmania

GRANT FINLAY

Published by Fullers Publishing Pty Ltd

Fullers Bookshop
131 Collins Street Hobart TAS 7000
www.fullersbookshop.com.au

First published 2019

Copyright © Grant Finlay

All rights reserved. This book is copyright. Apart from any fair dealing for the purposes of private study, research, criticism or review, as permitted under the Copyright Act, no part may be reproduced without written permission. Enquiries should be addressed to the publisher.

Series Editor Professor Henry Reynolds

Designed by Julie Hawkins, In Graphic Detail

ISBN 978-0-6484179-3-4

 A catalogue record for this book is available from the National Library of Australia

CONTENTS

INTRODUCTION	1

CHAPTER 1 'Fertile not fallow spiritual lives'	8
CHAPTER 2 'Motti (one) Nyrae (good) Parlerdi (God)'	35
CHAPTER 3 Wybalenna — 'Black Man's Church'	62
CHAPTER 4 'Cracks in the Catechism'	88
CHAPTER 5 'Always crackney in Heaven'	111
CHAPTER 6 'Neglecting the simplest duties'	138
CHAPTER 7 'They think we have got no souls now'	164

BIBLIOGRAPHY		195
APPENDIX A	Church baptism records of Aboriginal children	202
APPENDIX B	Aboriginal children listed in Hobart Orphan School Register	210
APPENDIX C	Bible translation by Wilkinson at Wybalenna 1833	214
APPENDIX D	Sermons by Aboriginal people, other than Walter Arthur and Thomas Brune	218
APPENDIX E	The Aboriginal or Flinders Island Chronicle and other writings by Walter Arthur and Thomas Brune	231
APPENDIX F	Wybalenna Chronology	252
INDEX		273

Naming protocols

During the first generations of contact, many Aboriginal people had multiple names. In the colonial archives there is often more than one way of spelling them. I adopt the protocol of using the spelling and capitalisations used when quoting directly from sources. Some names of people and clans have been given new spellings by the Tasmanian Aboriginal Corporation *palawa kani* language program. These are used where they are publicly available. In all other instances the most common spelling is used.

INTRODUCTION

COLONISATION disrupts people's lives. People's outward behaviours and inner beliefs are dis-located from their earlier contexts. The historic displacement of Aboriginal people from their lands in Australia has intergenerational legacies whose effects continue today. Simultaneously with these dislocations and legacies Aboriginal people have adapted to the experiences of colonisation by learning the many social, cultural and political practices of the colonisers. They have reinterpreted their own languages and lives through the varied relationships with colonisers. Some legacies and reinterpretations profoundly affected the foundational stories through which Aboriginal people had previously shaped their identities and sense of belonging to each other and their world.

On the Aboriginal islands of *lutruwita*, an English colony was established and named Van Diemen's Land. It was later renamed Tasmania, and became part of Australia. In the first generations of colonisation, Tasmanian Aboriginal people suffered profoundly. Colonisers made concerted efforts to exterminate Aboriginal people. They almost succeeded. This dramatic and often violent disruption to Aboriginal people's lives not only disconnected many relationships, but also Aboriginal people's beliefs about their world.

The colonisers' efforts to rid the islands of their original custodians did not succeed. Tasmanian Aboriginal people survived through a mix of resistance, adaptation and reinterpretation of their world. The capacity to undertake this resistance, adaptation and reinterpretation was part of Aboriginal people's lives before any colonisers landed on these shores.

For many years Aboriginal people on the islands of *lutruwita* / Tasmania were considered to be extinct, consigned to the past with the death of *Trukanini* in May 1876. Since that time the colonising community has wrestled with conflicting narratives of Aboriginal extinction and survival. The 1970s witnessed a resurgent

Tasmanian Aboriginal political activism that confronted and disrupted these colonising narratives. Since then an increasing number of books have been written about the Tasmanian Aboriginal community, colonial history, the Black War and some of the cultural accommodation and adaptation that has occurred. However, very little has been written about the religious-mythic-spiritual lives of Aboriginal people. Some of the indications of those lives can be glimpsed when reading surviving documents, and some of those documents are published here.

The majority of Aboriginal people in colonial Van Diemen's Land did not identify with the Christian faith at all. There were no mass conversions; no large-scale attendance at Christian church services. Aboriginal people did not give up their beliefs about the world in favour of the religious narratives and practices of the colonisers. Those Aboriginal people who did engage with the Christian faith were few. Among this minority were people from various clans, roles and cultural practices. Women and men, people of different ages, experiences and identities connected with the Christian faith through relationships with various colonists and, importantly, other Aboriginal people.

The Europeans who colonised *lutruwita* lived their own identity-forming narratives. The Christian faith was their predominant mythology. There were, and continue to be, various denominations of the Christian church in Tasmania. The Anglican Church (previously known as the Church of England) was the predominant church in the nineteenth century. The Anglican Church was closely entwined in senior government positions and processes for much of that time.

From the middle of the eighteenth century in England, prior to establishing the colony in Van Diemen's Land, many Christians in England experienced what is broadly known as the Evangelical Revival. The revival inspired the 'methodist' movement within the Church of England and others beyond, such as the Independent or Congregational Church and the Religious Society of Friends (Quakers). The Presbyterian Church formed as a particularly Scottish expression of the Protestant Reformation, akin to the Church of England in England. The Catholic Church had been the predominant form of church in Europe from the time of the Roman Empire until the Protestant Reformation in the sixteenth century. In the colony of Van Diemen's Land, it was influenced by Catholics from Ireland, many of whom arrived as convicts.

The evangelical awakening also inspired missionary endeavours as Christians sought to convert others to their faith. These endeavours were undertaken by zealous individuals, as well as denominational and interdenominational mission societies.

The 'methodist' movement grew as a para-church phenomenon within and beyond the Church of England for fifty years and only formally separated from

Aboriginal Christian faith in nineteenth century Tasmania is also not restricted to documents of the church or various missionary societies or individuals at the time, but in how particular Tasmanian Aboriginal people engaged with the faith initially presented to them orally in dialogue, and subsequently textually and orally in multiple forms and through multiple people. For many, Christian faith was integral to the transitional roles they played as they adapted to the irrevocable changes wrought by the colonising context. Today's Aboriginal Christians and wider Aboriginal community have a rich heritage to draw upon.

ENDNOTES INTRODUCTION

1. *Church News*, 20 April 1864, p. 307.
2. Harris, J., 1990, *One Blood*. Sutherland: Albatross, pp. 25–27.
3. In Attwood, B., 1989, 'Reading Sources in Aboriginal History: Mission Station Visitors Books', *La Trobe Journal*, 43, pp. 21–28.
4. Attwood, B., 1989, *The Making of the Aborigines*. Sydney: Allen & Unwin.
5. Van Toorn, P., 2006, *Writing Never Arrives Naked*. Canberra: Aboriginal Studies Press.
6. Johnston, A., 2004, 'The Little Empire of Wybalenna: Becoming Colonial in Australia', *Journal of Australian Studies*, 81, pp. 17–31.
7. Plomley, N.J.B., 1966, *Friendly Mission*. Kingsgrove: Halstead Press, p. 483.
8. Gunson, N., 2002, 'Reality, History, and Hands-on Ethnography: the Journals of George Augustus Robinson at Port Philip 1839–1852', *Aboriginal History*, 26, pp. 225–237. http://press.anu.edu.au/wp-content/uploads/2011/05/ch0937.pdf accessed 14.5.2014.
9. Plomley, 1966.
10. Plomley, N. J. B., 1987, *Weep In Silence*. Hobart: Blubber Head Press.
11. Johnston, A., & Rolls, M., 2008, 'Reading Robinson in the Twenty-First Century: An Introduction', in Johnston, A., & Rolls, M., (eds.), *Reading Robinson*. Hobart: Quintus.
12. Douglas, B., 2001, 'Encounters with the Enemy? Academic Readings of Missionary Readings on Melanesians', *Comparative Studies in Society and History*, 43 (1), pp. 37-64.
13. Miller, R. S., 1985, *Thomas Dove and the Tasmanian Aborigines*. Melbourne: Spectrum.
14. Stevens, L., 2017, *'Me Write Myself'*. Melbourne: Monash University Press.
15. Stevens, 2017, pp. 16, 61.
16. Stevens, 2017, pp. 19–20.

CHAPTER ONE

'Fertile not fallow spiritual lives'

ABORIGINAL people of *lutruwita* were, and are, a people formed by a religious or spiritual worldview. In order to understand the ways in which Aboriginal people engaged with the Christian religion brought by the colonists, it is important to appreciate that Aboriginal people already lived in a world imbued with religious significance in meaning, rituals and ceremonies. These shaped their engagement with, and interpretation of, the Christian stories and rituals to which they were exposed and which some Aboriginal people incorporated into their own lives in the context of colonisation.

There are no recordings of pre-colonial Aboriginal religious practices and beliefs. Everything that is known of pre-contact Aboriginal religious life is read from sources created in the midst of post-contact relationships. Most of the surviving documents were written at least a generation after the colony began. What we have are some pointers and indicators of a number of features of the pre-existing religious lives of Aboriginal people.

Some earlier colonists writing about Tasmanian Aboriginal religious life explicitly imported descriptions of Aboriginal people's religious life from other colonies. These writings often suggest that practices elsewhere were superior or were a benchmark for assessing the legitimacy or veracity of Tasmanian Aboriginal people's religious lives. While comparative studies can be useful conversations, it is not the focus here.

During the nineteenth century when the British established their colony in Van Diemen's Land, it was widely believed by colonists that Aboriginal people lived without any religious or sacred relationship with each other or creation. Later, occasional individuals such as George Robinson described, though in somewhat disparaging ways, some of their religious beliefs. Nonetheless the more dominant view was that Aboriginal people's spirit was a vacuous place, a void, and an uncultivated land of the spirit. James Bonwick wrote in the 1880s that

> the laws of the universe would at times plough up the fallow ground of their sterile souls; but there was no sower to drop a seed of spiritual truth into the gaping furrow.[1]

The sower image used by Bonwick alludes to the 'Parable of the Sower' in the Gospel of Matthew, Chapter 13, in the Christian Bible's New Testament. The different soils represent different capacities and responses to the seed of the word of God being planted by the sower, who in the parable is identified as Jesus. While acknowledging the existence of a soul within an Aboriginal person was a somewhat progressive thought compared to those who regarded the Aboriginal people as less than human, there is, however, a double-edged fateful inevitability. In this 'fallow ground' there is both no internal existence of spiritual truth or potentiality for spiritual fruitfulness, nor an external agent necessary to impregnate their souls.

For many years among historians,[2] archaeologists[3] and anthropologists there has been a prevailing belief that earlier so-called pre-colonial *lutruwita* Aboriginal society was somehow derived from what occurred in other parts of Australia, but in diminished or atrophied form. Several writers remark on the lack of evidence of the Aboriginal people's cultic life and yet make categorical statements about its paucity and inferior quality.[4] For example, their dances were often described superficially as 'bounding and prancing' while they 'yelled and shrieked' around a fire,[5] with little consideration being given to the existence of a cosmology, let alone its possible complexity.

Others[6] have responded by discussing the complex religious systems elsewhere in Australia and invoked that complexity as present in *lutruwita*, but these views still presume the defining quality exists elsewhere, away from *lutruwita*. While comparative studies of Yolgnu, Wurundjeri, or Pitjantjatjara or other clans within and beyond Australia may reveal commonalities, it is important to also consider them in their own contexts, languages, histories, and cultural and colonial adaptations. This is particularly relevant when it is known that *lutruwita* was physically separated from those other contexts for the past 12,000 years.

Rhys Jones, writing in *The Tasmanian Paradox*,[7] took for granted the inferiority in Aboriginal people's religious life in the parallel he made between technological and religious complexity. While Jones later amended his view, the earlier perspective continues to linger in debates.

These double-charged criticisms, that *lutruwita* Aboriginal people possessed both a simpler technology and a rudimentary religion when compared with Aboriginal people in other parts of Australia, have not been based on close engagement with the people or examination of their practices. As the variety of Christian and many other religious beliefs and expressions that abound throughout the world demonstrate, simplicity of form does not necessarily indicate simplicity of religious belief.

Archaeologist and writer David Horton proposed that the very simplicity of the Aboriginal peoples' technological tool kit might in fact have achieved the same results as the supposedly more elaborate technologies used elsewhere, expressing one response to these assumptions. The time gained through simpler and easier-to-make tools and weapons may then have been used for matters of 'the ego, the mind and the soul'.[8]

While we may take issue with the culturally conditioned cosmology implicit in a focus on 'ego, mind and soul', nevertheless Horton argues that 'it is quite clear that some evidence for communal religious activity is indeed present in George Robinson's journals'.[9] Robinson's journals contain most of the available descriptions of Aboriginal religious life. He wrote copious notes as he travelled throughout Van Diemen's Land with a range of Tasmanian Aboriginal people in the late 1820s and early 1830s.

Ryan, in her important work *The Aboriginal Tasmanians*, briefly noted some of the misguided expectations when she wrote '… their religious beliefs were recorded by people who expected the Tasmanians to conform to notions of nationalistic animalism.'[10] In her overview of the religious beliefs and practices of the Aboriginal people across the island she wrote:

> Thus the men were associated with the sun spirit and the women with the moon. Their religion was thought to be based upon 'star gods' and good and bad spirits that could be compared to classical European mythology. Their spiritual practices were apparently based upon the idea of a good spirit (Moiheener or Parledee), who governed the day, and the bad spirit (Wrageowrapper), who governed the night. These and other spirits were associated with the creation, fire, river, trees, and the dead. As an uncircumcised people they can be compared with the 'older' uncircumcised tribes of mainland Australia.[11]

Despite comparing Aboriginal people with those of 'mainland Australia', Ryan avoids the hierarchical rankings of other writers. This summary by Ryan suggests a common religious worldview and consistent cultic practice among all of the Aboriginal clans on this island, without considering possible variations among them. However, regional variations in religious beliefs and practices did exist. Moiheener and Parledee (good spirit) did not necessarily have identical meanings in their different religious or linguistic locations. The Moiheener–Dromerdeene creation story is not the only one. A more regional focus to Aboriginal people's beliefs and practices is evident in the recent contributions from Cameron[12] regarding the northeast, and MacFarlane[13] regarding the northwest. McFarlane describes cultural traits specific to clans in the northwest that included 'cicatrice body patterns, dances, language, songs, sacred trees, myths, astronomy, [and] different "deities".'[14] He helpfully notes:

> the idea of a Tasmanian Aborigine is, of course, a European construct, blind to the rich cultural diversity to be found in the patchwork of mini-states that made up pre-contact society.[15]

Reynolds brought more attention on Aboriginal people as thinking subjects, political activists and negotiators with the colonist authorities of Van Diemen's Land. Yet he did not consider Aboriginal people's religious perspectives as a factor in their behaviour, particularly as part of their negotiations and 'agreement' with the colonist authorities.[16] If Aboriginal people can be seen as active political agents in their engagement with colonist authorities, then their engagements with Christian faith ought to be considered as inter-religious encounters.

This question of the role of the Aboriginal peoples' religious life in their interactions with the colonisers has been raised by Greg Lehman in his Honours thesis, *Narrative and Identity*[17] and by James Boyce in *God's Own Country?*[18] Boyce, writing of the history of the Anglican Church's relationships with Aboriginal people, raised the question of religious beliefs as a motivating factor for Aboriginal people in their interactions with colonists. An example from the 1830s of one Christian Aboriginal leader is Walter Arthur, who was involved in preaching and writing Christian exhortations at the Wybalenna settlement on Flinders Island and who had a key role in framing a petition to Queen Victoria. While Arthur was the leading petitioner, Boyce does not explore the detail of Arthur's Christian faith, or that of the other petitioners, since the focus of his book was on the role of the Anglican Church.

Although the religious beliefs and practices of Aborigines and colonists were quite different, both were fundamentally shaped by their religious worlds. Their religious lives shaped their interpretation of the other, their engagement with that other, and their willingness and capacity to adapt their own religious life through that encounter and adopt something of the other's religious life, albeit it with new interpretations.

Until the late 1990s little had been written about Aboriginal religious life in Tasmania. It is a sobering starting point to acknowledge that there is a total absence of 'primary source' material in terms of oral or written material produced by Aboriginal people themselves about their cosmology and religious practices prior to, and during, the early years of colonisation. All surviving records about *lutruwita* Aboriginal cosmologies emerged in the context of colonist interactions and are, to some extent, an engagement with, or expression of, those contexts and intercultural or interreligious exchanges.

The available information comprises a relatively small number of journal writings, letters and reports mostly by Christian churchmen, or those employed to 'liaise' with or 'conciliate' the Aboriginal people. And what little is known is largely unexamined. While there are word lists, including a corpus of over a hundred sentences and phrases and a handful of songs, the Aboriginal worldview, in which those words had particular meanings, has only recently begun to be examined. It seems paradoxical that the existence of languages, perhaps eight or nine in total, are acknowledged, yet little is known of the worldview within which those languages evolved and were practiced.

George Robinson

As noted earlier, George Robinson's writings are crucial to any consideration of *lutruwita* Aboriginal religious life. Robinson began his employment with Governor Arthur on 21 March 1829. His self-identification as a Christian missionary is integral to his interactions with Aboriginal people. Therefore before discussing his work with Aboriginal people it is necessary to examine his experience and roles.

Robinson has often been described as a 'Methodist'. This is important not just for its biographical detail but also more importantly because of how it might have influenced the theological and denominational aspects of his interactions with Aboriginal people. In 1976 Franklin described Robinson as a 'bricklayer-turned-missionary'.[19] Rae-Ellis in 1988 argued that Robinson became a Methodist when travelling from England to Van Diemen's Land with a Samuel Mansfield.[20] Harris, following Rae-Ellis, merged the two descriptions to describe Robinson as 'a Methodist, often described as a "bricklayer-turned-missionary".'[21] However, this may not have been the case.

As mentioned earlier, 'Methodism' began as part of the broader Evangelical Revival in the eighteenth century, with the conversion of Church of England clergyman Reverend John Wesley. It was a movement within the Church of England and among 'non-conformist' churches. Methodist people continued to be part of the Church of England for almost fifty years[22] before the particular denomination of the Methodist Church was formally established in 1794. There were, therefore, no sharp differentiations between being 'methodist' and being part of the broader evangelical movement inspired by the revival, at least not until the mid-1790s.

Furthermore, Christians of the evangelical revival were members of a range of denominations. Some were involved in mission societies, others continued membership of their existing denomination, and others were involved in new denominations. The question here is, did Robinson join one of the divisions of the Methodist Church?[23]

Robinson was a confirmed member of the Church of England.[24] He married Maria Amelia Evans in the Church of England at Christchurch, Newgate on 28 February 1814.[25] By 1823, there were five children: George Augustus, Charles Thomas, Maria Amelia, Henry Thomas, and William Thomas.[26] All were baptised in the Church of England at St Bride's Church, London.[27] Robinson set out for Van Diemen's Land on 7 September 1823 aboard the *Triton*.[28] On board church services were conducted each Sunday in accordance with the form of the Church of England by the captain. Religious books were distributed by the 'Edinburgh Seamen's Friend Society'.[29]

Robinson arrived in Hobart Town in January 1824.[30] Maria and the children, George, Charles, Maria, William and Henry arrived on 23 April 1826, and their first vandemonian child, Eliza, was born a year later[31]. Alfred Walter was born on 29 November 1828 and baptised in the Church of England, Hobart Town, on 28 December 1828.[32] Cecilia was born on 30 December 1835 and she and elder sister, Eliza, were baptised in Church of England, Parish of St David's Hobart Town on 22 April 1836.[33] It is clear that Robinson's public denominational affiliation was with the Church of England. There was a Wesleyan Methodist Church in Hobart at the time[34] but no record of Robinson being involved there at all. It may have been advantageous for his work prospects with the Governor to publicly affiliate with the Church of England but there would need to be stronger evidence of Methodist involvement in order to demonstrate a meaningful shift away from Robinson's Anglican roots and family baptism practices.[35]

Robinson's involvement in mission societies in London is not as emphatic as the marriage and baptism records, but is important to consider nonetheless. Darcy explores the relationships that are most likely to have shaped Robinson's missionary and humanitarian endeavours. The presiding vicar at George and Maria's marriage was Reverend Crowther, a founding member of the Church of England's Church Missionary Society (CMS).[36] A close friend was Thomas Northover, CMS clerk and accountant from 1819 who also liaised with evangelical abolitionist MPs Brougham and Buxton.[37] Darcy examines links between the Brevet Lieutenant-Colonel of Honduras, George Arthur, later Governor of Van Diemen's Land, and the CMS, both locally in Honduras and in London,[38] and suggests Robinson knew these networks and used them when he arrived in Van Diemen's Land, especially in choosing CMS missionary Reverend James Norman to endorse his application for the post at Bruny Island.[39]

In Hobart Robinson did not begin his evangelical humanitarian work immediately, but by the beginning of 1828 he helped form the Seamen's Friend Society and Bethel Union and was elected secretary.[40] His loyalty seems strongest to the Bethel Union, as shown in his hoisting the Bethel flag during Sunday services while on his travels around Van Diemen's Land.[41]

Later that year he was providing pastoral care alongside Anglican Archdeacon Bedford to some of those being hanged,[42] and was secretary of the Mechanics Institute[43] though this was not an exclusively church organisation. He was a member of the Auxiliary Branch Bible Society of Van Diemen's Land[44] where, in 1828, Reverend Knopwood was Chairperson and Archdeacon Bedford secretary (both Anglican); Macarthur (Presbyterian), Carvosso (Methodist), and five others including Robinson were members.[45]

Rae-Ellis suggests Robinson was a member of the British and Foreign Bible Society[46] but Hobart newspapers do not seem to report Robinson as a member. Likewise he is not listed as a member of the Wesleyan Missionary Society. Robinson also held several memberships simultaneously, as secretary of Bethel Union and Mechanics Institute.[47] This was not unusual for evangelically minded churchmen.[48]

As Darcy argues, the evidence suggests that Robinson, both in his earlier years in London, and then in Hobart, was not a non-conformist or Methodist as some have argued. He explicitly identified himself with the Church of England, even though he worked closely with Methodists and Presbyterians in the multi-denominational Bethel Seaman's Union[49] and Auxiliary Bible Society in Hobart. As she states emphatically, 'There is no evidence in the records of the Hobart Methodists that Robinson was involved in their organization.'[50] In January 1830 when he first wrote of sending Aboriginal people to a church service, the Church of England is described as 'church' and the methodist gathering the following evening is described as 'the Wesleyan meeting'.[51]

In considering the available documents it would be more accurate to describe Robinson as an evangelically minded member of the Church of England. This is also important when interpreting his later descriptions of performing 'divine service' in the bush and at Wybalenna. The use of the Church of England's *Book of Common Prayer* in these services forms the background to his practice of 'English-only' church services at Wybalenna.[52] It also explains his excitement on the occasion of finding pages of the prayer book smeared with ochre that will be discussed later in this chapter.

Under the direction of Governor Arthur, Robinson's purpose was 'to employ himself wholly in the service of the natives, and … to instruct them and their children.'[53] He began an establishment near what is now called Missionary Bay on the northern end of Bruny Island in March 1829. Over the subsequent three years he circuited the island of Van Diemen's Land negotiating, on behalf of the Governor, for Aboriginal people to leave their country, thereby effecting the cessation of the 'Black War' with the colonists. Robinson's journals, as edited by Plomley, provide substantial amounts of text, but often frustratingly brief or oblique references to the religious world of the Aboriginal people with whom he travelled.

His writings therefore are an important though problematic source. It is only through writings such as Robinson's that we glimpse, even opaquely, the religious world of some Aboriginal people at that time. The immediate context of their conversations indicates that dynamic interactions were under way between Aboriginal people and Christian colonists.

These interactions occurred within the broader colonist context. Robinson began his work more than thirty years after the first temporary European visitors, and more than twenty-five years after the English colonists landed at Risdon Cove. By this time Aboriginal life had adapted significantly. The disintegration of clans and of many inter-clan relationships through the Black War was noticeable. Aboriginal life was surviving and adapting through a range of relationships and conflicts with various colonists.

Furthermore, much of Robinson's writings about the Aboriginal religious world were written several years after beginning his travels. So not only are his descriptions made almost a generation after the beginnings of broader colonial interactions, but they are also several years after the beginning of his own personal involvement. This 'distance' also occurred within Robinson's own writing. For example, much of his writings about the *Nununi* (Bruny Island) stories, as told by *Wurati*, were written while *Wurati* and Robinson were in the north-east of *lutruwita*, several linguistic and religious boundaries removed from *Wurati*'s and the stories' location in the south.[54] Most of what is known of the religious life of Aboriginal people only came into Robinson's journal away from the storyteller's clan location and context, and beyond the story's communal ritual context. This remoteness is an important consideration when interpreting Robinson's writings.

An additional element of the conversations and therefore what Robinson wrote is that Robinson had been 'instructing' Aboriginal people in aspects of the Christian faith. This had begun on Bruny Island and continued through his travels. The topics of discussion were sometimes in response to particular questions from Robinson,[55] his own comparisons between the Aboriginal stories and his interpretations of the Bible[56] and in response to his instruction.[57] The storytelling was part of an ongoing conversation and relationship that was evolving over time and across several contexts.

While Robinson described his own contribution as 'instructing', he did acknowledge that he was also learning from *Wurati*, *Trukanini* and others.[58] Robinson's goal was primarily 'instruction' but the Aboriginal people's goals ought to be acknowledged even if Robinson did not explicitly name them. This learning on Robinson's part is indicated by changes in his own theological perspectives. His perceptions and interpretations of the Aboriginal people's religious beliefs and practices, and theirs of his, altered and developed through the growing understanding of each other over time and the changing socio-political context. Robinson's initial respectful appreciation at Bruny Island[59] and during the travels around the south and west coasts and in the north-east evolved into more disparaging dismissal as 'superstition' when the expeditions moved into the central highlands after the 'agreement' with the Governor, and this continued through the rest of his travels and his time as commandant at Wybalenna.[60]

It seems Robinson's changing role from storekeeper to conciliator to negotiator to settlement superintendent contributed to the changes in his interpretation of Aboriginal beliefs and practices. Therefore a more nuanced interpretation of Robinson is needed when considering his writings. The location and timing of both the conversations and the writing are as important as Robinson's role in that context, the theological topics discussed, and the other conversation participants with their roles, gender and religious beliefs at the time. Most of these conversations were among a small number of Aboriginal people from diverse clans. Some, such as Tom, also known as *Kikatapula* and who travelled in the 'roving party' of Gilbert Robertson, had lived extensively with colonists, and some had not, such as *Manalakina*, clan leader of the northeast area.

Aboriginal people were not a homogenous group. The political relationships between the small numbers who travelled with Robinson influenced what was shared, to whom he listened and what he wrote. One way of beginning to clarify variations in beliefs and practices is to note the particular Aboriginal storytellers, or informants, if they are specifically identified, and to note the geographical and clan location in which the story is sourced and the one in which the telling occurs. These varieties of sources together with linguistic differences suggest multiple Aboriginal religious beliefs and practices.

While there is a continually evolving appreciation of the range of linguistic and cultural practices across the island, the degree of religious diversity is unclear. On occasions there appeared to be some degree of commonality. According to Robinson, 'the natives assured me that the same tradition was believed by the whole of the natives in the island'[61] — though what 'same' meant in this context is not known.

There were also acknowledged variations, such as the particular powers of particular stars:

> As far as this conversation went, it corresponded with the account given by woorrady, that (according to the Cape Portland natives) the fire was first made by porm.pen.er, the two stars in the Milky Way — the Brune natives call them law.way, but do not ascribe to them the same powers as the others — and that they made it by rubbing their hands together; and that they also made the river.[62]

There were more substantive differences between the clans, such as the presence or absence of a devil:

> Woorraddy says they have no devil at Brune like the eastern natives, which their devil whistles and makes a noise like thunder and by and by he comes and stops with them.[63]

Without a comprehensive analysis of all the common and varied elements written by Robinson, and the fewer written by others, one cannot make definitive assessments. Yet religious differences are not surprising when also considering the socio-cultural and linguistic diversity between the clans. It was perhaps not dissimilar to the range of beliefs and practices among Christians from Orthodox, Catholic and Protestant churches and the various streams within each.

Creation stories are significant in religious communities. At Wybalenna the biblical creation story given in Genesis Chapter One was the first topic where a translation into a Tasmanian Aboriginal language was attempted between June and September 1833. Two years before this Robinson wrote an extensive journal entry about a creation story told by one of the *Nununi* (Bruny Island) clan. It is necessary to quote it in full in order to highlight important points about aspects of the religious worldview through which they interpreted the Christian stories.

> 7 July 1831 I proposed a question to my sable friends — how and where the first black man came from — to which question WOORRADY gave in very full detail the traditional account of this and other subjects, as believed by all the natives along the southern and western coasts of the island, and the natives assured me that the same tradition was believed by the whole of the natives in the island. The animated manner in which WOORRADY related the several incidents gave considerable effect to the story, and the profound silence and attention of the rest and the assent to the veracity of his statements by two of the natives belonging to the south coast, rendered it still more interesting.
>
> He stated that ... [unclear in original but thought to be 'Moihernee'] made the black man first, that on his first formation he had a tail like a kangaroo and no joints in his knee; that DROE.MER.DEEN.NE he never could lay [sic] down and always had to stand up, and was obliged to sleep standing; that DROE.MER.DEEN.NE cut off his tail and rubbed grease on the wound and made joints

to his knees. He then for the first time sat on the ground and expressed his approbation of the comfort.

He said LALLER made all the rivers; he cut little streams and thus made big rivers.

Said that he made the kangaroo out of the ground and that they run [sic] away: he described it by putting his hand on the ground and shewing how they came out and run away.

Said that two black men was asleep when a DROEGERDY came at night and scraped fire on them, that they called out 'be quiet', that he came again and again, and that at last they awaking caught hold of his leg, and after examining him and being much pleased they put him in the ground; and that afterwards they used to catch him and eat him. This was the first intimation of the badger.

Said that MOIHERNEE, who dwelt off Louisa Bay (Cox's Bight) used to fight with the devils, that plenty of devils dwelt at the TOOGEE Low. WOORRADY said that MOIHERNEE made natives, that the devils stopped in the ground and that MOIHERNEE took him out of the ground and made PARLEVAR; that when he was first made he had a tail and no joints in his legs, that he could not sit down and always stood erect, that DROMERDEENE saw him in this situation and came to him and cut off his tail, rubbed grease over the wound and cured it and made joints to his knees and told PARLEVAR to sit down on the ground, that PARLEVAR sat down and said it was NYERRAE good, very good.

Said MOIHERNEE made all the rivers, that he cut the ground and made the rivers.

DROMERDEENER is the bright star seen in the south; WOORRADY says he comes out of the sea, because seen from Brune which is on the south part of the island he must necessarily do so.

Said that DROEMERDEENNE made kangaroo rat, that some natives was [sic] asleep when this animal made its appearance and that the rat came and threw stones at the natives, that the natives partly awoke and again slept, when he came again and threw more stones and repeated these visits till at length the natives caught him and put him in the ground, that by and by he came out and stopped in the bush and that afterwards the natives eat [sic] him.

WOORRADY says there is a large tree at Recherche Bay on which is cut the head of a man in large size and also children, that the natives call it WRAEGGOWRAPER and that the children cry when they see it, that the native men destroyed it, and that this was done by the first white men. WOORRADY said that MOI.NEE and DROME.MER.DEEN.NE fight in the heavens and that MOI.NEE tumbled down at Louisa Bay and dwelt on the land, that his wife came after him and dwelt in the sea, and that by and by the MOI.NEE children came down in the rain and went into the wife's womb and that afterwards they had plenty of children.

Said that MOI.NEE fight the WRAEGEOWRAPPE. There is a great similarity between this and Milton, where Lucifer is hurled down from heaven.

> Said that MOI.NEE cut the ground and made the rivers, cut the land and made the islands.
> Said that WRAG.GE.O.WRAPPER is like a black man only very big and ugly, and that he travels like the wind, that he comes and watches the natives all night and before daylight comes he goes away like swift wind.
> Said that the TARNER, i.e. boomer kangaroo, made the LY.MEEN.NE, i.e. lagoons, that he sit down and make it.
>
> NOTE: The natives like the animals of the forest feed during the night as well as the day.[64]

A further reference occurs in Robinson's journal a few days later on 12 July 1831:

> Tonight explained to the natives the Creation-of God, of the Flood &c which I had frequently done when an opportunity afforded. They were very attentive.
> In conversation with them on the same subject: WOORRADY said that when the natives first saw the porcupine that two of the natives was [sic] asleep and that the porcupine came and threw stones at them and hit them on the head, the forehead.
> Said that LAL.LER the small piss ant perforated the penis.
> TRUGERNANNA said that the black women learn the girls to make baskets, to swim &c, and that the father puts a spear in the boy's hand and learns him to spear and to hunt.
> They say that MOINEE was hurled from heaven and dwelt on the earth, and died and was turned into a stone and is at Coxes Bight, which was his own country. The natives say that there is a large stone standing up which is MOINEE and that he was a native and turned into this stone.
> Also say that LALLER a small ant first made the natives (query).[65]

The following month Robinson wrote of a conversation with *Manalakina* from the northeast area:

> 16 August 1831 In conversation with the chief and other natives on the creation of man. The chief said that (1) pum.per.ne.owl.le (2) pine.ter.rin.ner, the two stars in the Milky Way made man, made rivers, gave the fire &c.
> The Cape Portland natives believe the same.
> I explained to them the being of a God, how man was created, the fall, Christ coming to save man; and if they believe not they will not be saved.
> These conversations lasted for some time, Tom taking an active part. He said he believed what the white people said. The chief said that he only knew what his father told him.
> I told them one God made black man and white man. When I spoke of heaven and how the good spirits live without food, Tom said how could they live without eating; and I explained.[66]

From these stories it is noticeable that rather than having a 'sterile soul', *Nununi* people and those of the south coast recognised two creator beings. Each being fulfilled a different role in the creation of the first person. One creator being, Moihernee, used to fight with the devils and these lived in the ground. From these devils in the ground Moihernee created the first person. The word 'devil' is ambiguous and problematic in Robinson's writings, to say the least, as will be discussed a little later.

In the first creation, after taking 'him' out of the ground Moihernee made the first person with a tail and no knee joints. These two characteristics appear to be what distinguished this first person from *Wurati* and his contemporaries. The presence of a tail, specifically that of a kangaroo, indicates an association between person and kangaroo that is closer than the relationships presented elsewhere, such as between clan and trees.[67] Kangaroo tails were prized by the Aboriginal people and on several occasions after hunting trips Robinson is presented with a kangaroo tail as an honoured gift.[68] While out hunting kangaroo the tails, together with the hind legs, were kept for eating while other parts were usually discarded.[69] Robinson himself describes kangaroos looking human-like even before he wrote the above summary of the creation story.[70]

Aboriginal men were involved in regular, almost daily, hunting of kangaroo for the primary meat protein source so their familiarity with the animal's movements and characteristics was intimate. Early colonist records note the large numbers of kangaroo, particularly through the more open woodland and grassland areas. For some years the early colony functioned as a 'kangaroo economy'[71] with the hunting dogs highly prized and their thefts making regular news.[72] In one week in 1808 convicts provided more than 100 kangaroo to the government store.[73] This suggests that in pre-colonial years the kangaroo population was abundant. It is therefore not surprising that people would develop a close religious association with the creatures they saw most often, which comprised a desirable food source and who substantially outnumbered the human population.

The second creator being, Dromerdeenne, interpreted the person's permanently erect position as unhelpful, though without any reference to malicious intent by Moihernee in creating him this way. The first person initially had a tail, but this prevented him fulfilling something integral to being a person in this religious world, namely to sit down. The act of separation wounded the person thus requiring further action from the creator being to effect the healing. The means of wounding remain unspecified (stone tool, shell, or fire, perhaps), but the healing process was familiar. It was common practice to rub grease, sometimes mixed with ochre[74] and to rub ash from various sources onto their bodies.[75] Wounding or marking of the body occurred in some ceremonies.[76] The response to the primal wounding contrasts with the bloodletting response to illnesses that Robinson noted elsewhere,[77] including the use of the blood of a kangaroo.[78]

Sitting down was 'very good'. Robinson's language here is probably reminiscent of the conclusion of one of the biblical creation stories when God saw everything he had made and it was 'very good'.[79] While we would benefit from further details of this and all other stories, we can be reasonably confident that this summary signals some of the important aspects of the Aboriginal religious world, specifically the presence and activity of several creator beings, their interactions with each other, people and some creatures.

Other creation stories involving kangaroo

As well as the identification with the first person the kangaroo appears in other stories. In *Wurati*'s story the kangaroo was created out of the ground by a small ant, Laller. Laller also made the rivers. Tarner the kangaroo was involved in creating lagoons. The reference does not indicate how Tarner did this, but it does suggest interplay of creatures as creators. It also has the repeated theme of creatures, like people, being created out of the ground. The creature/creator dynamic is also present in other creation stories. Cameron has suggested that in the northeast at least, rivers marked clan boundaries.[80] Therefore to cross a river may have had religious elements interwoven with political and social relationships.

Dromerdeene, a particular star, is named as creator of the kangaroo rat,[81] Robinson's description for one of the smaller marsupials. This creature is more active at night, when people are usually asleep, and the story tells of the rat coming to people and throwing stones to awaken them. Another explicitly night time sleeping context for creation was Drogerdy (wombat) scraping fire on two men.[82] Like the kangaroo rat's stone throwing, the two initially rejected the sleep interruption, but finally awoke and put the wombat in the ground, later catching and eating him. The importance of the land is again present. It seems there were some creations occurring explicitly at night while people are sleeping, perhaps dreaming, and some where no 'day' or 'night' are mentioned.

Gendered speakers

The reference to Laller perforating the penis suggests it may be more related to men's rather than women's stories. Each of the creator beings mentioned by *Wurati* as written by Robinson, are male. Moihernee, Dromerdeene, Tarner, Drogerdy, Laller, and the waking people putting creatures in the ground, are all male. It may be a universal aspect that all creators are male, or simply that a male storyteller is telling the stories he is able to tell and a male writer is summarising them.

The gender differentiation between Moihernee's location on land and his wife's location in water may be expressed in human gender roles. The religious identification of children coming from the sky in the rain prior to their mother's pregnancy, could at least indicate a link between children sourced in water, the woman in the water and the waters of birth. However, a simplistic identification of men = land and women = water is clearly insufficient, with the second male creator being, Dromerdeene, coming out of the water to the south. Without more records it is difficult to know of any religious link between rain and the birth of children.

There are obviously many more creatures around the land and waters of *lutruwita*, and it is almost certain there are more stories than those Robinson wrote about. One can only speculate as to what 'Mrs Robinson' may have been told if she was 'conversing' with the Aboriginal women.

Most storytellers mentioned in Robinson's writings were men, particularly *Wurati* and *Manalakina*, and only occasionally did he write about women's contributions. While Robinson does not report explicitly about women's stories, the indication from the men's stories is that the essential aspects of life were shaped by religious stories. It is likely, therefore, that other aspects not explicitly mentioned by Robinson also had religious elements. It stands to reason that these formed the interpretive paradigm through which these Aboriginal people heard the Christian gospel and saw church practices. The predominant male leadership in the church was noticeable to Aboriginal people and probably affected how Aboriginal women and men interpreted Christian faith.

This gender bias will also be seen in later chapters at Wybalenna where records of writing, sermons and exhortations are almost exclusively from men. The gendered bias of Christian churches at the time was not an exclusively Tasmanian experience. The limited range of extant sources of Aboriginal religious practice suggest that a feminist-oriented reading of those sources would be a significant challenge.[83]

Trees

The identity association between humans and other elements of creation also included plants. Particular plant species were associated with particular clans. An example is 2 July 1831, when Robinson wrote a *Note on the amusements of the natives:*

> The natives make small spears that they throw at and stick into the different
> trees. Those of Oyster Bay spear the stringy bark trees, peppermint trees,
> honeysuckle trees. The gum trees they claim as theirs and call them countrymen.
> The stringy bark trees the Brune call theirs, as being their countrymen,
> the peppermint the Cape Portland call theirs, and the Swanport claim the

> honeysuckle. Thus, if the natives of Oyster Bay spear the tree of another native
> they are much annoyed and go and pull them out.[84]

While Robinson interpreted these associations as 'amusement', there does appear to be particular identity-forming relationships between specific clans and specific species of tree. This affected how each clan saw themselves and how other clans recognised that identity and engaged in inter-clan relationships, including conflict. Each clan's naming of particular tree species as 'countrymen' indicates a totemic, or totemic-like, relationship between their whole clan and the particular species of tree.

There appears to be widespread agreement among the clans as to the trees with which each clan is identified. Therefore, depending on the climate and soil type in each clan's area, there might be countrymen/women of other clans present in the form of trees.[85] One can only speculate as to the degree to which this presence of another clan's tree-kin affected the local clan's religious world, but it does suggest openness, even normality to the near presence of others. This may have shaped the ways in which Aboriginal people tolerated and incorporated the presence of other Aboriginal people, or even the colonists and their Christian faith, into their own religious world. If Aboriginal people's religious life had the flexibility to accommodate multiple and various clans simultaneously present in home country, it was perhaps not so difficult to incorporate Christian faith into it.

Sun and moon

As well as identification with particular tree species, Aboriginal people, particularly women, marked their bodies with representations of the sun or moon. For example,

> the aboriginal females on the islands have round circles cut in their flesh in
> imitation of the sun or the moon. Some are much larger than this outline. I have
> seen a woman with four of them on her body; others I have seen with two or
> three. They are very fond of them, are generally placed on each side of the
> backbone and about the hips.[86]

This again indicates their practice of exercising multiple simultaneous connections not only with people, creatures, and plants, but also celestial bodies. The identification of the creator beings Moihernee and Dromerdeene with particular stars is one of many indications of familiarity with and importance of individual stars, constellations, planets and other extra-terrestrial bodies in the religious world of the Aboriginal people.

Although there are no references to stars or star stories in Robinson's journals until 1830, when he was in the north-west area almost a year into his travels, he was aware early on that the *Nununi* (Bruny Island) people's 'good spirit' was located in the sky.[87] Robinson describes a range of stories that different clans ascribed to particular stars, including resemblances to men and women, conflicts, family relationships between people and/or creatures and creators. Clans often had different names for the same stars, or sometimes the same clan would have multiple names.[88]

The whole cluster of stars the colonists knew as the 'milky way' was known to the Aboriginal people as a track that creators walked along. Rather than being in only one direction at the beginning of creation, this road connecting stars and land/water was traversed in both directions going down to the sea[89] and coming out of the sea into the sky.[90] The nearness of such travel contrasts with Robinson's and many other Christians' perspective at that time, who perceived Providence from a somewhat remote place in the heavens that affected life on earth. Aboriginal Christian preaching at Wybalenna regularly referred to God coming down from heaven and it is likely that these tracks from the stars were a primary interpretive analogy.

As well as a great familiarity with the stars, Robinson also describes occasions of fearfulness with particular nocturnal observations such as a 'falling star' at which they cry out and hide their heads[91] or 'electric spark', perhaps an aurora, which was thought to bring sickness if mentioned.[92] However, these occasions of apparent fearfulness are outnumbered by many more references to activities taking place during the night such as walking,[93] hunting pelican[94] or animals.[95]

Where is 'England'?

Aboriginal people made several references to 'England':

> [S]ay that the sun comes from England, that the seal comes from England, and that their people made large catamarans and went to England, that PARLEVAR sleep plenty night at sea, lost plenty of days, that there was big wind and big sea, that they see plenty of seal.[96]

Robinson was surprised to be told the deceased went to 'England' after death.

> I scarcely credited what I heard. I asked the question again, when they all replied that they went to England, that there was plenty of PARLEVAR in England.[97]

Plomley may be correct in interpreting these references to mean a place far away to the north.[98] The reference to England may describe an indefinite place a long way away, rather than the specific country in the United Kingdom. At the very least it demonstrates one way in which Aboriginal people were incorporating colonist language into their religious world. But by now it seems clear that there was no 'sterile' place in the Aboriginal religious world, that the deceased did not simply go 'far away'.

If colonist (white) people were regarded as deceased Aboriginal people returning to their country, then future deceased Aboriginal people would also go to that same place.[99] If these past deceased Aboriginal people call that place 'England', then it is not surprising that not-yet-deceased Aboriginal people would use the same word.

For the Aboriginal people the stories these returning deceased white Aboriginal people were telling about the Bible, the person Jesus, heaven, and singing songs of that country, were all occurring in a different religious context than one of 'colonisation'. As noted previously, this religious world was the interpretive context for what the Christian stories meant to Aboriginal people. It shaped how they related to each other, how they 'negotiated' the end to hostilities with colonists, and their curiosity about and engagement with the Christian faith. It is worth at least considering the idea that they saw themselves talking with their deceased ancestors.

It would have been illuminating to read of Robinson telling the biblical story of creation in the Garden of Eden and describing that 'place' in relationship to Van Diemen's Land and England in a geographic and theological sense. We do not know how these Aboriginal people may have perceived a 'garden' that was not part of their own island, nor that of the English, even though it was an important foundation to the Christian theology being presented to them at the time.

It is noteworthy that those Aboriginal people who refer to 'England' as the place of the dead are all *Nununi* (Bruny Island). Furthermore, it is one of their elders, *Wurati*, who asked Robinson for more details about England, its direction, how far it was, the animals and trees there and the size of Robinson's house there.[100] A few weeks later the women asked Robinson if his wife caught muttonfish, etc. in England before coming to this land.[101] Two years later Robinson discussed with some Aboriginal people the possibility of travelling to England, which suggests that over time, they were able to distinguish between earlier understandings of 'England' and being able to visit there and return.[102]

Birthing and naming of children

The most likely explanation for the minimal references to childbirth practices and their religious aspects are two-fold. Firstly, the rarity of children being born both among those travelling with Robinson and those gathered on the Bass Strait islands, such as Swan Island or the later settlement at Wybalenna on Flinders Island. Secondly, the white male journal writer such as Robinson was not privy to those practices that primarily belonged to women. One reference reports the after-birth was burned after sunset and the ash rubbed on people's faces.[103]

Once birthed into their parents' and ancestors' religious world, an Aboriginal child was gradually introduced to that world as they grew. It seems to have been common not to name children at their birth.[104] Rather they received the first of potentially several names when they reached two or three years of age. *Wurati*'s daughter had two names,[105] another youth from the northwest had five.[106] A person tended to have a name within their clan and a different name by which they were known to other clans. In some cases an individual might have more than two names, with the largest number recorded by Robinson being five.[107]

While no explicit explanation is given as to any religious meaning informing or shaping this practice, the very multiplicity of naming further indicates a capacity for multi-layered words and multiple meanings co-existing within a person, their closest relationships and in broader intra-clan and inter-clan relationships. This needs to be kept in mind when considering later questions about the formation of so-called *hybridized* identity as Aboriginal–Christians. The appropriation and interpretation of elements of colonial life whereby Aboriginal people were creating for themselves simultaneous and multi-layered identities needs further consideration. These 'transcultural identities'[108] grew out of existing Aboriginal religious practices that were complex and dynamic. As Attwood describes in a Victorian mission, they were 'dialectical processe[s] of the making of the Aboriginal people and their making of themselves'.[109]

It suggests people's capacity to live an intra-clan identity and a somewhat different inter-clan identity simultaneously. With this fundamental identity-forming practice it was probably not so difficult for people to live the anglicised names given to them by Robinson while they continued their own intra-clan name and identity. Robinson's later naming of people at Wybalenna with mythic names from ancient Greece and India[110] may have been an imperialistic exercise on his part, but Aboriginal people had a lifelong practice of carrying multiple names simultaneously, and Robinson's naming was not necessarily more influential on them than a naming from another clan.

Several times Robinson describes Aboriginal parents naming their child with an anglicised name. At Macquarie Harbour TOWTERER and his wife WONG.ER.NEEP named their child after Robinson, which seemed strange to him because the child was female.[111] But like the reference to 'England', this demonstrates Aboriginal people incorporating Robinson's name on their own terms and using it in their own contexts. They were not foregoing their own practices, but were incorporating these new names and places into their existing practices. It is likely this was also occurring when discussing the 'religious' stories and practices.

Wrageowrapper — Devil

Probably the most ambiguous aspect of the Aboriginal religious life is the identity and characteristics of the 'Wrageowrapper' or 'evil' spirit. Robinson initially identified it with Lucifer in Christian theology,[112] with both Wrageowrapper and Lucifer being hurled from heaven after mythic conflict with God / good spirit.[113] But even he soon recognised it as more complex than this. There was an interchangeable use of 'devil' for 'evil spirit', or a person's 'spirit', as well as for the small foraging creature named by the colonists as the 'devil'. Some of the names Robinson provides for the good and bad spirits are: TYE.RE.NO.YER.PAN.NER god (Ben Lomond),[114] PLUCK.ER.TEE.BUR.RER god (Little Swanport), and WY.ER.KAR.TEN.NER bad spirit or devil.[115] Some clans said the devil lived in the fire, others said on a big hill:

> an eastern native calls him (1) KALE.PE.NUN.NE, (2) KAR.PEN.NOO.YOU.HEN.ER, the Cape Portland natives KORM.TEN.NER: KAR.TER.NEN.NE, and the Oyster Bay MAR.KANE.YER.LORE.PANE.NER'.[116]

There are human similarities in that 'Wrageowrapper is like a black man only very big and ugly' and was thought to carry sickness in a pouch, transferring it to the rest of the tribe.[117] But there were also significant differences in that he travels like the wind, comes and watches people all night and goes before daylight.[118] The Wrageowrapper was seen by some as the cause of inner pain, treatable by cutting themselves with stones or shells,[119] or the strategic placement of the ashes of a deceased relative.[120] The women in the northwest sought to prevent interference from the devil by shaving their heads and keeping a narrow ring of hair as ornament and as a charm to keep away the devil.[121]

The identity could also be projected onto another person to curtail or end undesirable behaviour. It seems *Trukanini* used it to great effect to keep *Wurati* at some distance when she did not appreciate his interest in her.[122] This projection onto people also involved white people, particularly those who used guns.[123]

The Wrageowrapper was represented in songs[124] and dances, particularly the TYREELORE or devil dance performed by the women.[125] They performed it to persuade the devil to let them stop on the islands[126] because they were with child by this spirit or were encouraged by this devil to sing often.[127] Robinson interpreted the dance as a form of homage to the devil.[128]

Robinson mentions an occasion of performing divine service after which those Aboriginal people who had been with Robinson for some time interpreted the service to newly arrived Aboriginal people as being able to 'put away the devil'. Both Aboriginal and colonist Christians often repeat this phrase in Christian sermons at Wybalenna. It is an example of the changes in theological language that were occurring among a variety of Aboriginal and colonists.[129]

A noticeable shift occurred in Robinson's interpretation of 'devils' after the meeting of Aborigines and Governor Arthur that occurred at Launceston in October 1831, immediately prior to leaving in search of the Big River people. Prior to this his descriptions of the 'devil' or 'devils' are as more malevolent beings causing harm, sickness and death and who require homage through dance and song to assuage their harmful intentions.[130] However, it seems that as Robinson's role changed to rounding up the remaining Aboriginal people onto an offshore island, his interpretation of the 'devils' and other religious beliefs and ritual practices of Aboriginal people also changed.

The spirit whose guidance is sought by the Aboriginal people, particularly *Manalakina*, in locating the Big River people is now identified as a 'devil', sometimes with physical expressions such as heavy breathing and trembling[131] or shaking, which filled Robinson with such horror that he sought to divert *Manalakina* from 'this satanic delusion'.[132] During these months when the inexorable steps toward their removal were under way, there were an increasing number of conflicts between Robinson's preferences and those of the Aboriginal people. Robinson expressed this in conflicting guidance from his 'God' and *Manalakina*'s 'devil'.[133]

More than any other aspect of Aboriginal religious life, the 'devil' is buried under layers of unidentifiable interpretations so as to make it impenetrable. Robinson's Christian theology governed his use of the word from the beginnings of his relationships on Bruny Island, and his political, social and economic ambitions strongly influenced him — especially it seems around the meeting with Governor Arthur in October 1831 and the related land grants and generous remuneration he received. Nevertheless, there are sufficient approximations of meaning to suggest it was a regular topic of conversation and continued to have significant meaning for Aboriginal people throughout their lives.

Fire

The multiple possible interpretations and uses of the word 'devil' also affects interpretations of some stories about fire. Aboriginal use of fire was extensive and included nightly fires around which hearth groups gathered for warmth and food. They fired the land (known as 'fire-stick farming') to regenerate grasses and thereby attract grazing kangaroo. The creation of fire was linked with particular stars.[134] Fire was also involved at important life events such as burning the afterbirth and, in many clans, the deceased, as mentioned earlier. But it was also seen as a location for an 'evil spirit'.

However, we cannot be certain that this description of 'fire spirits' is not in some ways an Aboriginal interpretation and adaptation of the contemporary Christian theology of the devil and the damned members of humanity existing in the fires of hell for eternity. Robinson himself had impressed upon the Aboriginal people the association of devil, fire and the damned in his early preaching[135] and a later exchange tends to confirm this:

> 15 October 1830 Asked the one who spoke English whether she knew who God was; said he stopped up, pointing to the sky. Asked where the devil stopped; said in the fire, pointing to the fire.[136]

This conversation took place in English and began with explicit references to the Christian 'God' in the sky and Christian 'devil' in the fire. It is another example of the developing inter-religious dialogue that was occurring.

Ochre

Red ochre was particularly significant to some clans. The occurrence of ochre deposits within a tribe's country bestowed significant economic and social advantages. Valued primarily for its application as an adornment and means of exchange, it also had some religious significance. As an adornment it was used to colour hair and when mixed with charcoal and grease it was rubbed into wounds in the production of cicatrices on both men and women.[137]

Red ochre had significant symbolic potency for Aboriginal people and colonists. Aboriginal people used red ochre in hair and body colouring. Women had a particular role in acquiring it. It was traded among various clans and had limited availability. When it was unavailable Aboriginal people used substitutes.[138] Robinson was aware of its importance and went to considerable lengths to prevent its importation when he became Commandant at Wybalenna on Flinders Island.[139] While Robinson was not aware of red ochre's religious meaning[140] he was clear that it possessed significance for certain Aboriginal people.

When visiting the Toolumbunner (Mt Gog) site for the last time on 16 July 1834, the Aboriginal people showed Robinson their extensive mining activities.[141] The group was on its way back to Wybalenna, having gathered the remaining 'remnant' of the west coast clans. With no ochre sites near Wybalenna, the women's acquisitions were very valuable and demonstrate their continued practice and use of ochre in the new context. As with descriptions of creation stories and other practices it is important not to assume that one description of the role of women was universally practiced.

Nevertheless Robinson writes of more intensive singing, dancing and story telling when the Aboriginal people were acquiring ochre than he generally reported on other days.[142] Ochre was also used, like charcoal, to pigment the skin after a cicatrice scarring operation[143] and mixed with grease in successive layers on their bodies as protection from the cold.[144] Insulation effectiveness, however, would have depended on the amount of fat alone, not the pigment mixed with it.[145]

Decorating oneself with red ochre was considered the natural thing to do because as Robinson observed: 'one of the natives on being asked why he painted himself, asked the enquiring individual, "What do you wear fine clothes for?" '[146] Sagona suggests this statement indicates that 'body decoration for pleasure's sake applied to the Tasmanians too, or at least to this individual.'[147] It is noticeable that this Aboriginal person distinguished colonists' 'fine clothes' as the comparable adornment to his own ochre, and not to the clothes worn every day. Perhaps this reflected the observation that the colonists wore 'fine clothes' on special occasions — public/civic ceremonies, Sunday church services and so on — rather than as 'decoration for pleasure's sake'. The conversation about 'fine clothes' occurred after the funerals of Robert Macauley and Eumarrah on 26 March 1832, so the context for 'fine clothes' was not 'just for pleasure', but was associated with an end of life funeral ceremony.[148]

The occasional references to the varied experiences of those Aboriginal people who had not been initiated into the pre-colonial religious world are worth noting. Tom, one of the 'civilised' Aboriginal people, believed he had no devils, though Robinson disagreed.[149] Not only was there variation in mythologies among Aboriginal people from different clans, but also among the emerging generation who had not known life apart from interaction with colonists. This variation will be discussed in the next chapter when considering the range of responses to the Christian faith presented to a wide range of Aboriginal people.

ENDNOTES CHAPTER ONE

1. Bonwick, J., 1884, *The Lost Tasmanian Race*. London: Sampson Low, Marston Searle and Rivington, p. 2.
2. Clark, J., 1988, 'Devils and Horses: Religious and Creative Life in Tasmanian Aboriginal Society', in Roe, M., (ed.), *The Flow of Cultures*. Canberra: Australian Academy of the Humanities, pp. 50–72.
3. Jones, R., 1977, 'The Tasmanian Paradox', in Wright, R. V. S., *Stone Tools as Cultural Markers: Change, Evolution and Complexity*. Canberra: Australian Institute of Aboriginal Studies, pp. 189–204.
4. Clark, 1988, p. 50.
5. Clark, 1988, p. 50.
6. Kidd, M. J., 2006, *The Sacred Wound of Australia*. Nimbin: Ohlah Publishing; Miller, L., 2006, 'Isness, the Terrain of Aboriginal Being', School of Philosophy Thesis: University of Tasmania.
7. Jones, 1977, pp. 189–204.
8. Horton, D., 1979, 'Tasmanian Adaptation', *Mankind*, 12, pp. 28–34.
9. Horton, 1979, p. 32.
10. Ryan, L., 2001, *The Aboriginal Tasmanians*. Sydney: Allen & Unwin, p. 11.
11. Ryan, 2001, p. 11.
12. Cameron, P., 2011, *Grease and Ochre*. Launceston: Fullers Bookshop.

13 MacFarlane, I., 2008, *Beyond Awakening*. Launceston: Fullers Bookshop.
14 MacFarlane, 2008, p. 2.
15 MacFarlane, 2008, p. 3.
16 Reynolds, H., 1995, *Fate of a Free People*. Ringwood: Penguin.
17 Lehman, G., 1998, 'Narrative and Identity', Unpublished Honours Thesis, Hobart: University of Tasmania.
18 Boyce, J., 2001, *God's Own Country?* Hobart: ISW.
19 Franklin, M.A., 1976, *Black and White Australians*. South Yarra: Heinemann, p. 30.
20 ML Robinson Papers, Nov 1823–Jan 1824, cited in Rae-Ellis, V., 1988, *Black Robinson*. Carlton: Melbourne University Press, p. 10, f/n 6, p. 269.
21 Harris, 1990, p. 95; and Harris, J., 'Robinson, George Augustus', 1994, (ed.), B. Dickey, *The Australian Dictionary of Evangelical Biography*. Sydney: Evangelical History Association, p. 324.
22 See 'Reasons Against a Separation from the Church of England by John Wesley A. M., printed in 1758 with Hymns for the Preachers among the Methodists (so called) by Charles Wesley A. M. http://anglicanhistory.org/wesley/reasons1760.html cited 14/5/2014.
23 The primary divisions of 'methodism' were Primitive Methodist and Wesleyan Methodist, with the latter being the main form of the Methodist Church in Van Diemen's Land.
24 ML Robinson Papers, 10 August 1848, A7041, Vol. 20, cited in Rae-Ellis, 1988, p. 7, f/n 24, p. 269.
25 Christchurch Newgate Register, Marriages 1814, MS10115/6A, Guildhall Library, cited in Darcy, J., 2010, 'Child of the metropolis: George Augustus Robinson in London', *History Australia*, 7 (3), pp. 55.1 to 55.18. DOI:10.2104/ha100055, p. 55.6.
26 Rae-Ellis, 1988, p. 7.
27 Plomley, N.J.B., 1973, *An Immigrant of 1824*, Hobart. Tasmanian Historical Research Association, p. 4. The last baptism, Elizabeth, on 19 July 1795, the same year as the formal separation of the Methodist Church from the Church of England through the Plan of Pacification. It had begun in 1784 when founder and Anglican clergyman, Rev John Wesley, gave legal status to the Methodist Conference, http://www.methodist.org.uk/who-we-are/history/separation-from-the-church-of-england, accessed 16/5/2014.
28 ML Robinson Papers, 3 Sept 1823, A7022, Vol 1, part 1, cited in Rae-Ellis, 1988, p. 9, f/n 1, p. 269. See also, Plomley, 1966, p. 14.
29 Plomley, 1973, p. 18.
30 Plomley, 1966, p. 33.
31 Rae-Ellis suggests Eliza was born nine months after Maria arrived (Rae-Ellis, 1988, p. 16), but Eliza's baptism register records her birth date as 27 April 1827. This may somewhat dampen Rae-Ellis's narrative of Robinson's voracious sexual energy.
32 By Archdeacon Bedford, the last baptism for the year, TAHO RGD 32.
33 Again, by Archdeacon Bedford, baptisms 123 & 124, TAHO RGD 32.
34 The Methodist Church began in Hobart in 1820 with Rev Carvosso, TAHO NG 499.
35 Robinson's mother is buried in a non-conformist cemetery suggesting Methodist, or at least non-conformist, influence in his childhood. However, Robinson himself is buried in the Church of England cemetery at Bath. So while his early life might possibly have been in the Methodist Church or at least influenced by it, his adult life show a strong identification with the Church of England.
36 Darcy, 2010, p. 55.6.
37 Darcy, 2010, p. 55.8. In 1835, still an MP, Buxton instigated and managed the House of Commons Select Committee on Aborigines (1835) and in 1837 co-founded the British and Foreign Aborigines Protection Society, Blouet, 2004. Cited in Darcy, 2010, p. 55.9.
38 Cited in Darcy, 2010, p. 55.11.
39 Cited in Darcy, 2010, p. 55.11.
40 Other members included Presbyterian Minister, Macarthur and Methodist Minister, Carvosso, *Colonial Times*, 15 February 1828, p. 1. The *Sydney Bethel Union* continues today http://www.sydneybethelunion.com.au/milestones.htm#top, accessed 14/7/2014.

41 Plomley, 1966, p. 97, 117, 182, 187, 191, 335, 339, 352, 390.
42 *Hobart Town Courier*, 7 June 1828, p. 4.
43 *Hobart Town Courier*, 2 August 1828, p, 1.
44 Established on 8 May 1819 at the Church of England, Hobart. *Hobart Town Gazette*, 1 May 1819, p. 1, and 8 May 1819, p. 1 & 2.
45 *Hobart Town Courier*, 9 August 1828, p 3.
46 Rae-Ellis, 1988, p. 16–17, f/n 22, p. 269. The Society was founded in England in 1804 by Robinson's friend, Thornton: Darcy, 2010, p. 55.9.
47 On one occasion they had meetings on the same night, one hour apart in different venues. *Hobart Town Courier*, 17 January 1829, p. 1.
48 Rev Miller from the Independent Chapel, who conducted the marriage of Fanny Cochrane and William Smith, was a member of the Wesleyan Missionary Society, (*The Mercury*, 11 January 1854, p. 2). Van Diemen's Land Auxiliary to the London Missionary Society, (*Colonial Times*, 20 December 1854, p. 2), Mechanics Institute, (*The Courier*, 20 January 1854, p. 2), Evangelical Union, (*Colonial Times*, 2 February 1854, p. 3), Van Diemen's Land Auxiliary Bible Society, (*The Courier*, 8 March 1854, p, 2), The Tasmanian Temperance and Total Abstinence Association, (*The Courier*, 17 March 1854, p. 2), and Hobart Town City Mission, (*Colonial Times*, 9 December 1854, p. 3).
49 Darcy, 2010, endnote 3, p. 55.12.
50 Darcy, 2010, endnote 3, p. 55.12.
51 'Their attention was not so riveted here as at the Protestant church, not only because there was less pageant but because it bore a resemblance to my own family worship', Plomley, 1966, p. 94. It would appear that Robinson saw the Church of England as 'church' and the Methodist services and meetings as somewhat different.
52 Six weeks after his arrival at Wybalenna Robinson wrote in his journal, 'Abridged the church form of prayer and directed the whole service to be continued not longer than one hour. This service appeared more satisfactory than any of the former', Plomley, 1987, p. 325.
53 Plomley, 1966, p. 51.
54 Plomley, 1966, p. 118.
55 For example, 'I proposed a question to my sable friends — how and where the first black man came from...'. 7 July 1831, in Plomley, 1966, p. 373.
56 For example, 'There is a great similarity between this and Milton, where Lucifer is hurled down from heaven.' Plomley, 1966, p. 373.
57 'Tonight explained to the natives the Creation of God, of the Flood, &c.' in Plomley, 1966, p. 376.
58 Plomley, 1966, pp. 55, 59, 63, 140, 205, 217, 248, 255, 266, 280, 316, 376.
59 Plomley, 1966, p. 63.
60 Plomley, 1966, pp. 527, 561.
61 Plomley, 1966, p. 373.
62 Plomley, 1966, p. 399.
63 Plomley, 1966, p. 566.
64 Plomley, 1966, p. 373.
65 Plomley, 1966, p. 376.
66 Plomley, 1966, p. 403.
67 Plomley, 1966, p. 369.
68 Plomley, 1966, pp. 419, 420, 515.
69 Plomley, 1966, pp. 487, 489, 540, 557.
70 Plomley, 1966, p. 310.
71 Boyce, J., 2008, *Van Diemen's Land*. Melbourne: Black Inc, pp. 24, 44, 45–60.
72 For example, *Hobart Town Gazette*, Friday 30 July 1824.
73 Boyce, J., 1996, 'Journeying Home,' *Island*, 66, pp. 39–63.
74 Plomley, 1966, pp. 278, 283, 418, 501, 895.
75 Plomley, 1966, pp. 638, 640, 649, and MacFarlane, 2008, *Beyond Awakening*. Launceston: Fullers Bookshop, p. 9.
76 Plomley, 1966, pp. 59, 60, 67, 263.
77 Plomley, 1966, pp. 57, 60, 67, 285, 542, 581.
78 Plomley, 1966, p. 419.
79 Genesis Chapter 1, Verse 31.
80 Cameron, 2011, pp. 25–27.
81 Plomley, 1966, p. 374.
82 Plomley, 1966, p. 373.
83 Cameron, 2011, is one recent attempt to give greater emphasis to the role of women in Aboriginal life.
84 Plomley, 1966, p. 369.
85 There do not appear to be other tree-specific associations in regard to the types of wood each clan used to make

86 Plomley, 1966, pp. 542, 581.
spears, burn in their fires, construct their catamarans, or burn on funeral pyres.
87 Plomley, 1966, p. 61.
88 Plomley, 1966, pp. 366, 464.
89 Plomley, 1966, p. 368.
90 Plomley, 1966, p. 373.
91 Plomley, 1966, p. 186.
92 Plomley, 1966, p. 397.
93 Plomley, 1966, p. 362.
94 Plomley, 1966, p. 393.
95 Plomley, 1966, p. 845.
96 Plomley, 1966, p. 377.
97 Plomley, 1966, p. 62, also p. 230.
98 Plomley, 1966, p. 465.
99 At Wybalenna in 1837 Walter Arthur expressed something of this when he wrote, '[W]e skin black people died then arose from the dead became white men we begin to make friends of them call them father or Brother', ML Robinson Papers, A7074 CY825. While it is a common belief well documented on mainland Australia this is the only reference I have found of this view in *lutruwita*. The idea may have come from contact with Aboriginal people from New South Wales, who travelled with John Batman before joining Robinson, Plomley, 1966, pp. 427, 428, 429, 430, 484, 597, 598, 599, 605, 609, 633.
100 Plomley, 1966, p. 617.
101 Plomley, 1966, p. 625.
102 Plomley, 1966, p. 880.
103 Plomley, 1966, p. 779.
104 Plomley, 1966, p. 362.
105 Plomley, 1966, p. 155.
106 Plomley, 1966, p. 216.
107 Plomley, 1966, p. 216.
108 Peyer, B., 1997.
109 Attwood, 1989, p. 150.
110 Plomley, 1987, p. 337, 344.
111 Plomley, 1966, p. 741.
112 In the King James Bible (also known as Authorised Version), the most common translation available to Robinson in the 1830s, the only explicit mention of 'Lucifer' is in the book of Isaiah, Chapter 14, Verse 12, 'How art thou fallen from heaven, O Lucifer, son of the morning! How art thou cut down to the ground, which didst weaken the nations!'
113 Plomley, 1966, p. 373.
114 I will return to this clan when discussing the Bible translation at Wybalenna in Chapter Three.
115 Plomley, 1966, p. 281.
116 Plomley, 1966, p. 403.
117 Plomley, 1966, p. 141.
118 Plomley, 1966, p. 373.
119 Plomley, 1966, pp. 57, 60.
120 Plomley, 1966, p. 65.
121 Plomley, 1966, p. 594.
122 Plomley, 1966, p. 83.
123 Plomley, 1966, p. 181.
124 Plomley, 1966, p. 469.
125 Plomley, 1966, p. 282.
126 Plomley, 1966, p. 249.
127 Plomley, 1966, p. 301.
128 Plomley, 1966, p. 300.
129 Plomley, 1966, p. 627.
130 Plomley, 1966, pp. 249, 281, 282, 285, 287, 300, 347, 374, 403. There are only two references prior to the meeting with the Governor where Robinson describes the 'devil' telling *Manalakina* where to travel, Plomley, 1966, pp. 413, 414.
131 Plomley, 1966, p. 413.
132 Plomley, 1966, pp. 414, 488.
133 Plomley, 1966, pp. 488, 491, 493, 494, 518, 524, 526, 528, 539, 541, 545, 546, 556, 564.
134 Plomley, 1966, p. 380.
135 Plomley, 1966, p. 61.
136 Plomley, 1966, p. 249.
137 MacFarlane, 2008, p. 9.
138 Plomley, 1966, pp. 286, 670.
139 Plomley, 1987, p. 228.
140 Plomley, 1966, p. 501.
141 Plomley, 1966, p. 904. This site is in the central mid-north of Van Diemen's Land.
142 Sagona, A., (ed), 1994, 'The Quest for Red Gold', in Sagona, A., *Bruising the Red Earth*. Melbourne: Melbourne University Press, p. 22.
143 Plomley, 1966, p. 283.
144 Plomley, 1987, p. 246.
145 Sagona, 1994, p. 23.
146 Plomley, 1966, p. 594.
147 Sagona, 1994, p. 26.
148 Plomley, 1966, p. 594. Robert Macauley will be discussed in more detail in chapter two.
149 Plomley, 1966, p. 541.

CHAPTER TWO

'Motti (one) Nyrae (good) Parlerdi (God)'

ABORIGINAL people of *lutruwita* were living in a multilayered religious world when they encountered Christian people among the colonists who were spreading throughout their lands. Quite varied relationships developed from the first generation of contact from 1803 through to the removal of most Aboriginal people from the main island of Van Diemen's Land by 1835.

The first explicitly religious encounter of an Aboriginal person with the Christian faith occurred in the aftermath of a violent incident within the first year of contact. In subsequent decades some Aboriginal people learnt about Christian faith through colonist families with whom they lived on farms and islands. Others were introduced to this new religious world through organised government programs such as the Hobart Orphan School, or the appointed 'conciliator' George Robinson.

Each Aboriginal and colonist person and group interpreted the other from their existing religious perspectives, and within each group there was a variety of responses. There was no single or uniform Aboriginal response to the Christian faith. Nor was there a uniform presentation of Christian faith from among the colonists. Among the responses by Aboriginal people were occasional attendance at church services, baptisms of adults and children, engagement in ongoing conversations, and integrating Christian and Aboriginal religious artefacts in activities beyond the involvement of a Christian person or church denomination.

First Christian baptism

The initial contact between Aboriginal people and colonists occurred on the shores of the River Derwent in the south, the Tamar River in the north and the sealing community among the Bass Strait islands. The initial interactions in the south were reportedly friendly in most cases.[1] At this time most Aboriginal people were not affected in any significant way by the presence of colonists in their land. Those who were affected still continued their own religious practices and interpreted and incorporated the presence of the colonists from those perspectives.

The first reported performance of Christian 'divine service' in this Aboriginal land was led by the colonist chaplain Reverend Robert Knopwood on 26 February 1804, some five months after the colonists arrived.[2] Like the Aboriginal ceremonies, these explicit ritualisations of the colonial Christian world were performed outdoors.[3] The first formal interaction between Aboriginal people and a representative of the Christian church was the baptism of an Aboriginal child on Friday 11 May 1804.[4]

In the week preceding the baptism Knopwood wrote in his diary that he heard a cannon from Risdon on the eastern shore of the River Derwent several kilometres upstream and on the opposite shore from the new colonist settlement at Sullivan's Cove. Later that day, Thursday 3 May, Knopwood received a note:

> Dear Sir,
>
> I beg to referr [sic] you to Mr. Moore for the particulars of an attack the natives made on the camp today, and I have every reason to think it was premeditated, as their number farr [sic] exceeded any that we have ever heard of. As you express a wish to be acquainted with some of the natives, if you will dine with me tomorrow you will oblige me by christening a fine native boy who I have. Unfortunately, poor boy, his father and mother were both killed. He is about two years old. I have likewise the body of a man that was killed. If Mr. Bowden wishes to see him dissected I will be happy to see him with you tomorrow. I would have wrote to him, but Mr. Moore waits.
>
> Your friend
>
> J. Mountgarret, Hobart, six o'clock.[5]

Following the reports of the killings Knopwood stayed in Sullivan's Cove another week. He does not appear to have had any sense of urgency to meet the child or 'oblige' Mountgarret with the christening. It is curious that the initiative for this first baptism did not come from the Christian chaplain but the surgeon. Although Jean Woolmington has discussed the apparent reluctance of many early Christian missionaries to baptise Aboriginal people,[6] any reluctance on Knopwood's part was short-lived as he travelled to Risdon and baptised the child on Friday 11 May:

> At 11 a.m., Lt. Lord and self went to Risdon with Capt. Bowen. Mr. Lord returned in the eve and I stayd there. I xtianed a young native boy whose name was Robert Hobart May.[7]

The Church of England's baptism practices are set out in the *Book of Common Prayer*. But what might have been the religious paradigm of the *Mumirimina* clan whose people were killed at Risdon? The report of a large group of *Mumirimina* moving suggests they were hunting kangaroo.[8] It is known that there was singing during the preparations for hunting,[9] its associated spear making,[10] and their walking among the trees.[11] The group was reportedly moving toward the river that marked the boundary between their lands and that of the Mouheneene on the other side of the river. The nearby middens indicate it had been visited for generations.

How might the *Mumirimina* have interpreted the irregular sounds of gunshots and cannonade that were possibly the first they had heard?[12] And beyond the sounds, how might they have interpreted the associated trauma, death and scale of the killings? What might have been their interpretation of these deaths and the subsequent absence of this child?

The child was 'found' by White, a soldier, or some other person during the afternoon, perhaps after clan members had scattered. He was kept by the surgeon Mountgarret who, it seems, sought to make immediate plans for the child to be baptised and for a deceased adult male to be dissected. Mountgarret's note expresses the first indications of the two influential elements of 'religion' and 'science' in ongoing Aboriginal–colonist relationships.

In the week between the deaths and the baptism the child was fed, presumably by Mountgarret, with the colonist's food rather than his usual diet of *tarner* / kangaroo, shellfish and such like. He probably slept in Mountgarret's tent rather than the usual bark shelter. During this time the child was beginning to be dis-integrated from his religious world through separation from parents, community and culture, even though he remained in the same geographic place. As a young infant he had only begun to be introduced to that religious world, and was probably not yet initiated into it.

Baptism was usually seen by Christian colonists as an obligatory religious ceremony, one necessary to 'save' or 'redeem' a child out of their pre-existing state. Mountgarret seemed confident that the child's mother and father were both dead and the child orphaned, at least in the colonist's sense of the word. We are not told exactly who but it seems likely to have been Mountgarret who became the boy's godfather in the baptism service.[13]

The urgency to baptise the child indicates the particular beliefs of Mountgarret, Knopwood and the soldiers involved.[14] There was no similar urgency to baptise colonist children at that time or in subsequent decades. Some children were baptised within days of their birth and others after several years. The urgency here seems provoked by the child's otherness. And there appear to have been no attempts to capture and baptise any other children or adults among those wounded or uninjured at Risdon. Their scattering after the killings may partly explain why.

The performance of this Christian sacramental act of baptism was symbolic of an incursion into the Aboriginal religious world by the Christian religious world. It was also, though not obvious to the colonists, an incursion by this vulnerable *Mumirimina* child and the religious world he represented into the colonist Christian world. This baptism marks the beginning of incorporating Aboriginal people and their religious world into the Christian church.

A week after the deaths the baptism was performed at the same site with the most senior men of the colony present, except Lieutenant-Governor Collins. The 'Ministration of Private Baptism of Children in Houses' in the 1662 *Book of Common Prayer* prescribed that after the Lord's Prayer and

> the Child being named by some one that is present, the Minister shall pour Water upon it, saying these words: I baptize thee in the Name of the Father, and of the Son, and of the Holy Ghost. Amen. Then, all kneeling down, the Minister shall give thanks unto God, and say, We yield thee hearty thanks, most merciful Father, that it hath pleased thee to regenerate this infant with thy Holy Spirit, to receive him for thine own Child by adoption, and to incorporate him into thy holy Church ..."[15]

Through baptism this child had been incorporated into God's 'holy church' but it occurred without any acknowledgement of his birth name, family or clan relationships, or cultural identity.

In a further curious aspect of the story there is no record of the baptism in the Church's baptism register. The baptism records of Hobart Town indicate that Knopwood baptised Catherine Poteskie on 25 March 1804 and George Kearly on 4 July 1804. 'Robert Hobart May' should appear in between these two but does not. Nor does his name appear in any previous or subsequent entry. We have only Knopwood's diary to inform us that the baptism ever took place. It is a reminder of the gaps in early colonist baptism records and the circumspection required by those relying upon them.

Governor Collins had been absent from the settlement when the deaths and baptism occurred. On his return from the south exploring the Huon River, he met the child:

> This child, who is with Mr Mountgarrett, has been baptized by our chaplain (without my knowledge or consent having been asked) and I understand that gentleman intended to take him with him to England ... I judged it expedient to direct that the child be returned to his own people, who might if they never saw it again, imagine we had destroyed it.[16]

Clearly, Collins did not endorse what had happened. This might explain the omission from the Church of England baptism register. He clearly felt that his consent was required. The Governor's power in the Church of England in the new colony was extensive and would continue for decades to come. He appointed and funded the chaplains and allocated land for churches to be built. He appears to prefer that Aboriginal children remain within the realm of their clan and not the realm represented by the Governor or church. In contrast, Mountgarret sought to remove the child not only from his clan but from the island altogether. This variance in theology between Collins and Knopwood, Lord and Mountgarret on the appropriateness of baptising this particular Aboriginal child and perhaps other Aboriginal people is worth noting, as later an Aboriginal child, George Van Diemen, was removed to England.[17]

The intended return of Robert to his own people did not occur.[18] Boyce identifies the boy still living in the southern settlement nineteen months later: 'Robert Hobart May, native of Van Diemen's Land' was listed among the children inoculated with the smallpox vaccine in November/December 1805. The last we seem to know of him is that he, along with other children, had 'taken the infection in the most distinct and favourable manner'.[19] There is no surviving record of Robert's adult life, death or burial. If Mountgarret continued as his guardian, Robert may have moved to Port Dalrymple when Mountgarret became the surgeon there. There are records of baptisms and marriages for Port Dalrymple from 1811 onwards but not of deaths until 1824, by which time Robert would have been about twenty-two years old. Aside from Robert's baptism and inoculation, all other details of his life are unknown.

Cultural and religious adaptations — kangaroos and dogs

The violent event of May 1804 at Risdon, while significant, was not the defining interaction between colonists and Aboriginal people in the first decades of the colony. Other relationships formed, particularly around food gathering, and kangaroos in particular. In the first decade of the colony the mutual interest in eating kangaroo as the primary source of meat led to trade in the dogs used to hunt them. Given the importance of kangaroo in the religious world of at least some Aboriginal people, their adoption of hunting dogs is significant. It demonstrates another aspect of the cultural adaptations in which Aboriginal people were engaged, and also the ways these experiences affected relationships and religious practices.

Rhys Jones was perhaps the first to write about the relationship that developed between Aboriginal people and dogs in Van Diemen's Land. As Jones notes,

> within a few years of seeing their first dogs, the Tasmanians had recognised the potentiality of the animal, formed close bonds with it, and had incorporated it fully within their culture.[20]

Jones, then more recently, Boyce,[21] suggested dogs were crucial in early colonist life and in particular in the cross-cultural exchanges. 'For two decades the dog was central to a rapid change in the way of life of both British and Aboriginal people.'[22] What is of interest here is the relationship that developed between the religiously significant kangaroo and that of the introduced dogs. Dogs were used by colonists and Aboriginal people alike primarily to hunt kangaroo and there are examples, as Jones noted, of dogs being incorporated into Aboriginal cultural life. This cultural adaptation was in some sense reciprocal, as colonists used kangaroos for their primary food source and clothing for some years.

Large numbers of kangaroo were reported in the early days of the colony. One of the convicts recalled 'there were hundreds and hundreds of kangaroo about Risdon then.'[23] Within months of establishing the colonists' camp the senior leaders, including the chaplain Knopwood and others who possessed dogs, were sending hunting parties of convicts and dogs into the areas surrounding the settlements of Hobart Town in the south and Port Dalrymple in the north.[24]

In September 1804, a year after the colony began, Governor Collins ordered the first purchase of kangaroo meat by the government store for the benefit of patients in the hospital.[25] This led to a rapid increase in the numbers of kangaroo killed, up to two to three thousand pounds weight per week,[26] and by mid-1805 it had become an essential part of the colonists' diet.[27] The price of dogs escalated to more than the annual income of most people in the colony.[28] This hunting activity and its effect on the kangaroo population did not go unnoticed by Aboriginal people. They began attacking the colonist hunting parties and seizing the kangaroos. Initially Aboriginal people speared the hunters, killed the dogs, and kept the kangaroo. But a turning point occurred reasonably quickly when Aboriginal people stopped killing the dogs and began to use them themselves.[29]

This change to incorporate dogs into Aboriginal life went beyond hunting practices. Jones made reference to Aboriginal people incorporating dogs into their religious life.[30] He cited four descriptions in Robinson's journal[31] of Aboriginal people incorporating dogs into dances,[32] a fierce dog on the west coast feared by people who wore clothes,[33] a warning not to criticise dogs because a 'devil' would ensure they took on the characteristic of the criticism,[34] and a dog perceived to be influenced by its deceased master.[35]

The dogs in the dance had a peripheral role as part of the 'horse dance'.[36] The dog thought capable of eating people who wore clothes is an intriguing contrast to the dogs that usually hunted kangaroos, the earlier primary clothing source of Aboriginal people. This dog was perceived to hunt people who wore or had adopted colonial dress.[37] The final two references indicate the Aboriginal people's awareness that a dog's behaviour could be influenced by the people around it.

To Aboriginal people, kangaroos supplied more than food. Kangaroo skin was tanned using the bark of the blue gum and the black wattle and used for clothing. Likewise among the colonists, as early as 1804 Governor Collins had issued a pair of shoes, locally made with kangaroo hide, to every prisoner.[38] And within a few years, as a result of shortages and the inadequacy of imported clothing, many colonists' clothes were made from kangaroo fur.[39]

Knopwood suggested a potential 'ritual killing' associated with kangaroo.[40] When seen through the awareness of the religious role of the kangaroo in the Aboriginal creation story described earlier, these uses of kangaroo skins and meat by colonists and the interaction of Aboriginal people with the dogs becomes more intriguing. If Aboriginal people had religious interpretations of kangaroo, they were likely to also have religious interpretations of the colonists' interaction with the same kangaroo.

Within a few years the dog had been transformed within the Aboriginal worldview from threatening predator to an integral part of their social and conceivably their religious world. It seems there were religious elements to this and other adaptations that were occurring. The dance and story of close connection between dog and master suggest the beginnings of a new 'proto-myth'. Dogs continued to be integral to Aboriginal people's lives, and in some later situations they outnumbered Aboriginal people, such as at the Aboriginal settlements of Wybalenna[41] on Flinders Island and Oyster Cove south of Hobart.[42]

The widespread hunting led to a dramatic decline in the number of kangaroo in the 1820s. The numerical decline of a creature with such religious significance is likely to have affected the religious interpretations made by Aboriginal people. This decline was linked with the dramatic increase in colonist land grants throughout the 1820s that led to an explosion in sheep numbers.[43] By then the Aboriginal population was greatly reduced and more sparsely dispersed, including among colonist families.

Baptism of other Aboriginal children

Like Robert Hobart May who lived with the surgeon Mountgarret, other Aboriginal people, particularly children, began living with colonist families, at least from 1810. Through these relationships some were baptised in Christian churches, or admitted to the Orphan School in Hobart from the mid 1820s. Some of the adults were living on the Bass Strait islands and elsewhere with people such as Gilbert Robertson and John Batman. Some of these adults were engaged in 'roving parties' in search of other Aboriginal people. Others travelled with George Robinson from 1829 when he was appointed conciliator by Governor Arthur. The range of contexts, particularly the personal relationships, indicates the variety of Aboriginal people's interactions with the Christian faith.

The Aboriginal children living with colonist families had minimal formation in their pre-contact Aboriginal religious life due to the young age at which they were acquired by colonists. In the forty years following the baptism of the *Mumirimina* boy, 'Robert', in 1804, more than forty other Aboriginal people, mostly children, were baptised by Christian clergy. While the absolute number is not large, on average about one each year, they were a sizeable proportion of Aboriginal children born after the beginnings of colonial contact. In the early years Governor Collins opposed the capture and acquisition of Aboriginal children. Colonists seem to have heeded this, as no baptisms of Aboriginal people, aside from Robert Hobart May, are reported until April 1810, after Collins died. The situation changed, but not dramatically, when Murray and others were subsequently in charge. There were never any mass baptisms of Aboriginal people, even with the occasionally large numbers visiting Hobart Town.

Church records of Aboriginal children baptised up to 1811 list only a first name. Three Aboriginal people were baptised on 4 November 1811 when two adult women, Mary and Anne, were baptised, and Anne's daughter, Lucy, was given a family name, Murray, seemingly in line with the name of the colony's recent commandant. This practice of acquiring a colonist family name seems to have become the norm quite quickly as all but two subsequent entries include a name in the 'Family' column. However not all family names listed for these Aboriginal people can be associated with a known colonist family. Of the early ones, according to Fels, Mary Fitchett Farnum (14 January 1811), George Weston (15 July 1811) and Sarah May (23 September 1811) do not seem to share a 'family' name with any listed convict, settler, or recently arrived Norfolk Islander. Fels suggests the most likely possibility is that they are names of soldiers of the 73rd Regiment that came to Van Diemen's Land with Murray to replace Collins' Royal Marines, but there is no name list available of this regiment with which to compare.[44]

It is likely these baptised Aboriginal children were domestic servants of colonist families as several have explanatory comments in the 'parent' column, such as 'Hogan's servant girl' (Catherine Van Diemen, 8 September 1817) or 'E. Lord's boy (Charles Frederick Van Diemen, 9 March 1818).[45]

One example from among these baptism records indicates the variety of contexts in which these Aboriginal children were baptised and possibly introduced to the Christian faith.[46] Robert Macauley's story is of interest because he began in an Aboriginal family, was raised in a colonist family and then became part of George Robinson's 'conciliation' activities.

Robert Macauley

Robert Macauley was baptised on 1 January 1813 by Robert Knopwood in Hobart Town. According to Plomley, Robert (*McAlly / Macauley*) was 'found' at the Cross Marsh in 1810 by Sergeant James Macauley, whose wife, Mary, nursed the child. They thought him to be around 18 months old when he was 'found'.[47]

Sergeant Macauley and his wife are mentioned in Knopwood's diary in January 1808, receiving compensation from the government farm after suffering a house fire started by some settlers lodging there.[48] The circumstances of how they 'found' Robert are unknown. What is known is that he was a servant to the Macauleys throughout his childhood, including after Sergeant Macauley died in 1822.[49]

In the two years before he died, James Macauley was among those contracted to provide kangaroo meat, 1000 pounds, between January and April 1820, to the government store.[50] No doubt it was through these hunting expeditions that Robert became an excellent shot, for which he was later praised by George Robinson. Robert's initiation into a relationship with the kangaroo was very different from that described by *Wurati* in the previous chapter.

Mary Macauley then married Mr Busby of Muddy Plains.[51] Throughout his childhood Robert learnt the ways of this colonist family, the English language and the 'habits of industry'. We can only speculate as to how Robert may have understood his own identity as he grew up.

When George Robinson took up the government position at Bruny Island in 1829 he wrote to the colonists throughout Van Diemen's Land[52] asking them to give up Aboriginal people who were in their employ. Mrs Macauley–Busby handed Robert over to Robinson about six weeks later. It is a strange aspect of the policy that having grown up in this colonist family, and for all outward appearances to have become part of colonist society in ways the colony's leaders desired, Robert was then removed from colonist society onto the 'establishment' on Bruny Island.

Robinson seems to have wanted Robert, and others like him, for two primary purposes. First, to be an example to other Aboriginal people of how to adapt to colonist life, and second, to be a demonstration to colonist society of the capacity of Aboriginal people to live as part of that society:

> [W]hen I [Robinson] view him [Robert] ... I no longer doubt the necessity which exists that as many of the aboriginal children as possible should be brought together and by a course of proper discipline taught to imbibe those impressions which through the assistance of Almighty God will ultimately lead to their general conversion.[53]

Robinson hoped Robert would

> 'incite' his countrymen to adopt similar agricultural and boating skills and other civilized habits such as sobriety.[54]

Robert was twenty-one years old, and therefore of 'full age' when handed over to Robinson. It is another indication of the stratified nature of colonist society and the inferior rights of those in the 'employ' of others. Governor Arthur initially promised Robert ten acres of land, later increased to twenty with the addition of a boat, cart and bullock.[55] This is the first known indication to grant land from the Crown to an Aboriginal person. It raises many questions, such as who is granting whose land to whom? And why not grant the land without requiring Robert to join Robinson at Bruny Island? But the grant of land appears not to have occurred, presumably because Robert left with Robinson for Port Davey as part of the so-called 'friendly mission' in early 1830.[56]

During his travels with Robinson, Robert was noted as an excellent shot with a gun,[57] a skill probably learnt from many kangaroo hunting expeditions with James Macauley. We are not told much of Robert's interactions with other Aboriginal people. Robinson mentions one exchange between Robert and *Wurati* where Robert does not believe the malevolent spirit, the Wrageowrapper, was nearby to them.[58] Robinson occasionally mentions Robert when the younger Aboriginal man was away hunting or sent somewhere carrying messages.[59]

Despite these few references, what is of particular interest is Robert's presence in the audience when *Wurati* told the creation story mentioned in the previous chapter.[60] The range of people among the audience shows the diversity of mythologies among the Aboriginal people at that time, particularly as represented in two of the men present, Robert and *Wurati*. *Wurati* was conversant in *Nununi* language, custom and, at least to some extent, creation stories. He was telling the story of the creation of the first person. In so doing he was also telling of the religious associations between people and kangaroo.

Robert, also an Aboriginal man, was younger than *Wurati* at about twenty-two years of age. He had spent almost all of his life with a colonist family. He had learned to shoot kangaroo with a rifle and probably also with the assistance of kangaroo dogs. He had earned colonist money selling the kangaroo meat to the colonist commissary store. It is intriguing to ponder the conversations *Wurati* and Robert may have had with each other about kangaroo and their different experiences and relationships with them.

Robinson makes little other explicit reference to Robert until March 1832 when Robert was ill in the hospital in Launceston, as was another Aboriginal man, Eumarrah. On 23 March Robert died from lung inflammation, and Eumarrah died the next day.[61]

The deaths of these two Aboriginal men also provide examples of the variety of Aboriginal experiences that were occurring. Robert was buried with a Christian funeral service officiated by a Minister, Reverend Browne.[62] Robinson described the coffin, attendees, weather and 'the same rites was observed as over a white person'. Eumarrah was buried an hour later. 'He was buried the same as Robert but without the funeral rites.'[63] After Eumarrah's funeral 'One of the natives on being asked why he painted himself, asked the enquiring individual, "What do you wear fine clothes for?" '[64] It is not clear in this if the Aboriginal people who 'ochred' themselves did so for both Robert's and Eumarrah's funerals or just Eumarrah's. Also, it may be the Christian funeral was performed because of Robert's baptism but was not done for Eumarrah because he was not baptised, or there may be other reasons. But the difference itself indicates the varied lives of Aboriginal people and how colonists interpreted them and interacted with them. Both funerals are examples of the changing ways of being Aboriginal at that time.

Aboriginal children at the Hobart Orphan School

As well as individual Aboriginal people, particularly children, living in colonist families, others were subject to colonist government humanitarian activities such as the Orphan School in New Town, Hobart. Preparations for the school began in 1825 when Governor Arthur, together with the Church of England, set it up modelled on a similar school in New South Wales.[65] Meetings of the Committee of Management were held weekly, usually in the vestry of St David's Church.[66] The school was to be a 'school of industry, where labour as well as learning is taught'.[67]

In 1827 Governor Arthur sent circulars to several clergymen and magistrates requesting they provide the names of children within their districts who could be brought to the school. About 400 children were found to be of need, but only fifty were admitted in the first intake. The buildings were intended to house 300 children, and within two years of beginning the Committee of Management were turning children away due to a lack of accommodation.[68] In April 1844 there were 513 children living there.[69]

The school was primarily for illegitimate, poor or orphaned children. During the troubled years of its operation, about forty Aboriginal children were registered there. Other children were also admitted, including those of settlers and soldiers, who were required to pay.[70] The school was under-resourced and conditions were poor. Rations were minimal, and often sold to others.[71]

Of the approximately forty Aboriginal children admitted to the school between 1828 and 1850, thirty-four were explicitly identified in the register as Aboriginal, with a couple, such as Mathinna, staying more than once. About four others are identified indirectly as Aboriginal in the minutes of the Committee of Management. These were usually children of Aboriginal women and sealers in Bass Strait. Given that there were several hundred children in the school at any one time, and several thousand over the life of the school, the numbers of Aboriginal children admitted were only a small proportion. Without knowing the total number of Aboriginal children living with colonists, it is difficult to know the proportion of Aboriginal children throughout the colony admitted to the school.

According to the register, the first Aboriginal child admitted was Thomas Bunce, a seven-year-old boy whose mother was unnamed but designated as 'aborigine'. There is no entry for his father. He was probably in the first intake since his name appears on the first page of the register, 2 August 1828.[72] Minutes of the Committee of Management two weeks after his admission indicate some interest in him prior to his admission:

> The Committee received an official from the Colonial Secretary dated the 12th instant transmitting a letter from James Grant dated the 1st instant, referrable as is supposed, to the aboriginal Boy called Tommy admitted on the the 2nd instant, who, when if the boy is to leave the school, it appears Mr Grant is desirous of taking into his service. The Committee on their part will see that the wishes of His Excellency and Mr Grant are complied with.[73]

It is unlikely that James Grant is the boy's father as the correspondence indicates his desire to take Thomas 'into his service'.[74] This phrase was used consistently by those colonists who sought children from the school for domestic service or labouring work. Like James Grant, members of the public were able to make application to have a child discharged into their service. The girls were usually discharged to be domestic servants and the boys to learn a trade.[75]

According to the register, Thomas was the only known Aboriginal child at the school for four years, a period which saw the end of the Black War, the Black Line and the formation of the Aboriginal Establishment in the Bass Strait islands. In August 1832, two more Aboriginal boys, Daniel, aged 10, and Peter, aged 9, were admitted.[76] However, not every child was recorded in the register. The minutes of the Committee of Management occasionally provide further information. For example, sixteen months after Thomas was admitted, two sisters, Sarah Scott, aged 11 years, and Rebecca Scott, unknown age, were admitted on 3 December 1829. They were admitted 'on the foundation' (i.e., at government expense) as 'children of a deceased Native Woman by a Sealer who deserted them some time since.'[77]

It is worth remembering Robinson began the establishment on Bruny Island in March 1829 and desired to bring Aboriginal children together for instruction.[78] However, while some such as Robert Macauley and others were brought into Robinson's enterprise, others were not, such as Thomas Bunce, or Sarah and Rebecca Scott. Another such Aboriginal child living with a colonist family was Mary Ann Robinson. She had lived with Mrs Harriet Alwyn in Launceston for seven years, since 1826, when aged two. Alwyn applied in July 1833 and Mary Ann was admitted to the school in August 1833.[79]

Sarah and Rebecca Scott do not appear in the school register at all, yet Sarah was still at the school six months after admission when a Mrs Moore applied to have her discharged into her care to work as a domestic servant.[80] It was not until November that year that the committee granted this request due to overcrowding in the school.[81]

These absences and incomplete descriptions in the register are in some ways like the early baptism records in that the records themselves explicitly identify a number of Aboriginal children even though there were other Aboriginal children who were not labelled as such by those making the entries. To further complicate the situation there was the regular situation of Aboriginal children having multiple Aboriginal and multiple English names. Some children whom George Robinson later recorded being discharged into his care were not recorded in the register under the same names that Robinson used.[82]

One interesting aside is an application for admission on 23 October 1830. The mother of William Perry, 8 years, and John Perry, 6 years, applied for them to be admitted 'on the foundation' because her husband, a convict in the service of Lieutenant Griffiths of the Tea Tree Bush, was currently engaged in the pursuit of the hostile Aboriginal people and so she was unable to provide for her children for the present time. This 'pursuit' in October 1830 was the Black Line, so it is interesting that orphaned Aboriginal children were in the school alongside colonist children who were 'orphaned' while a parent was out pursuing Aboriginal people.

The late 1820s and early 1830s saw a number of events that further disrupted Aboriginal life. These included the Black War in the late 1820s, the Governor's inquiry into the Aboriginal children living with colonist families in Launceston in 1827, the Black Line of 1830, and the activities of Robinson from 1829 to 1834.

It is surprising in this context that there were not many more Aboriginal children admitted to the school. It seems that in the first years of its operation the school was not a primary site for incorporating Aboriginal children into colonist society even though it fitted the broader agenda of Governor Arthur and others to 'civilise and Christianise' Aboriginal people.

From the records of the Orphan School it seems those colonist farmers, families, and humanitarians who had Aboriginal children in their households preferred to keep them rather than give them to the school or to Robinson. So while the school may have been established, at least in part, to address concerns about the large numbers of illegitimate children in the colony, relatively few Aboriginal children lived there.

However, the place of the school in the lives of Aboriginal people changed significantly after 1831. From 1832 to 1835, correlating with the first years of the Wybalenna settlement on Flinders Island, more and more Aboriginal children were admitted to the school. Here again the records in the register and those in the minutes of the Committee of Management differ in the names and number of children.[83] Two or three boys arrived in August 1832 and a little over three months later, three more boys, 'one half caste and two native', were brought along with a 'native girl aged 18 years'.[84] Of the three boys, one named Friday, aged 10, grew into a significant leadership role when he returned to Wybalenna in October 1835. 'Friday' is another example of the multiple names by which a number of Aboriginal children were known. At Wybalenna in 1836, the catechist, Robert Clark, reported to Commandant Robinson, 'the clerk who assists me at the Divine service is the Native youth formerly called Friday now Walter he is the son of a Chieftain he reads the responses very well has a knowledge of the scriptural history and is a well conducted lad.'[85]

On 3 September 1834 a group of five boys from Wybalenna were admitted: Charles, Frederick, George, Samuel, and William. Five months later on 6 February 1835, the next and largest single intake of nine boys and girls were admitted. This included Pungerwalla, Mowana, Walkenny, Tully, Tina, Beamanrook, Fireboke, Mendou, and Tommerick. Like Friday / Walter, these Aboriginal children were not orphans. Walter's parents, Rolepa / King George[86] and his wife Luggernemennener[87] were living at Wybalenna at the time. One explanation for the removal of children from Wybalenna was the lack of a catechist / teacher, but most children were not returned to their parents even when the first catechist, Thomas Wilkinson, arrived at Wybalenna in June 1833.[88]

These examples indicate that there was not a single or universal experience of Aboriginal people at this time.[89] Some Aboriginal children were living with colonist families,[90] and others were part of the sealing community in the Furneaux Islands.[91]

Other children were living with their parents and other adults from their own and other clans at Wybalenna, and other children not connected to any of these families were also at the Orphan School.[92]

The cause of the sudden and short-lived increase in Aboriginal children at the Orphan School appears to be because of policies of particular commandants at Wybalenna. At the end of February 1835 there were twenty Aboriginal children at the Orphan School.[93] When Robinson became commandant at Wybalenna and left Hobart in early October 1835 to take up the position, only four boys remained at the school: Thomas Bunce, Thomas Thompson, Duke and Charles. Boyce argues that Robinson's actions in returning children to Wybalenna were probably part of the treaty or agreement between Governor Arthur, Robinson, and the Aboriginal people in ending the conflict and acceding to the colonists' desire for the Aboriginal people to be removed from the mainland of Van Diemen's Land.[94]

Christian teaching — instruction and services

Until 1844 all the children including Aboriginal children at the Orphan School were registered and taught as Protestants.[95] Prior to the construction of St John's Anglican Church at New Town in about 1833, the children walked each Sunday to St David's Church in Hobart for Divine Service. The civil engineer was requested to install sufficient seats for boys and girls in the new St John's church[96] so that the children were spared the walk into Hobart Town and the exposure to 'profane and improper language' on their way to church.

The report into the school in 1848 by the Inspector of Education, C. Bradbury, indicates religious instruction was taught on Wednesdays and Saturdays.[97] This report was after the closure of Wybalenna, when Aboriginal people were removed to *putalina* / Oyster Cove south of Hobart. Following this removal seven Aboriginal children were entered in the Orphan School register on 27 December 1847. The specific content of the religious instruction at the school was not described in the report but the method of instruction was reported as being of 'no defined character' with 'no attempt made to accuracy, parrots prayer'.[98] This ill-defined content and method were in stark contrast to the 'Madras' or 'Bell and Lancaster' method and quarterly catechetical examinations at Wybalenna that began in 1833 and continued for some years.[99]

Assessing the experience and impact

In assessing the impact of the Orphan School on the interaction of Aboriginal people with the Christian faith, it is important not to overstate the case based on later activities in Tasmania or elsewhere. According to the register, except for the years 1834 and 1835, there were rarely more than six or seven Aboriginal children in the school at one time. This is a small minority of children in the school and a small minority of Aboriginal children in the whole Aboriginal population.[100]

More Aboriginal children were living with colonist families than were in the Orphan School. Therefore the school was not a major factor in colonist policies in regard to Aboriginal people. The presence of Aboriginal children at the Orphan School during the years of the Wybalenna settlement indicate that there was not a single fixed colonist policy in regard to Aboriginal people, particularly children, at this time. On the one hand the general intention to 'civilise and Christianise' in order to incorporate Aboriginal people into colonist life would seem to be fulfilled by keeping Aboriginal children at the Orphan School until they were apprenticed out to a colonist tradesperson or household. Yet their removal to Wybalenna removed them from interaction with colonist society and gave them some limited freedom to distinguish themselves from colonist society. The stated policy of trying to incorporate Aboriginal people into colonist society contrasted sharply with the actual practice of separating them from that same society. This contradictory behaviour continued for some time.

The Orphan School was not a major site of exposure of Aboriginal people to Christian faith. For most Aboriginal children there were other experiences of colonist life that had greater impact. However, for those Aboriginal people who were at the school the experience of learning English and attending Sunday church services over an extended period of time did contribute to their understanding and practice of that particular form of the Christian faith. Those who survived beyond childhood were at a significant advantage in adapting to colonist life compared with those who had little familiarity with Christianity. They were therefore on the cusp of a fundamental shift in what being 'Aboriginal' meant in Aboriginal and colonist contexts, and particularly their religious expressions. The routines, work, literacy and education at the school did, albeit unintentionally, empower some individuals to adjust, manipulate and resist the less rigorous institutional life at Wybalenna.[101] A number of these children grew into significant leadership roles between Aboriginal people and colonists where relationships were negotiated in the English language and in its written and oral forms. However, before turning attention to those later developments it is important to consider some inter-religious dialogues that were occurring prior to the Government Establishment at Wybalenna.

Religious discussions

While changes were occurring in the lives of Aboriginal children through participation in the sealing community, colonist families and the Orphan School, Aboriginal adults were also learning more of the Christian faith through some of the same families, as well as through the government's 'conciliator' George Robinson. It is important to remember that throughout the first generations of colonisation in Van Diemen's Land there was no explicit mission to Aboriginal people by any of the Christian churches. Governor Arthur had approached the (Anglican) Church Missionary Society in 1828, prior to setting up the establishment on Bruny Island, but they declined.[102] References to conversations about Christian theology between Aboriginal people and colonists are therefore limited to those that appear in personal journals or occasional church reports. As mentioned earlier, one of the most prolific sources for these conversations is the journal of George Robinson. One such conversation was discussed in the previous chapter, but a number of others appear in his journal between the beginning of the establishment on Bruny Island in March 1829 and when he took up the position of commandant at Wybalenna on Flinders Island in October 1835.

In these conversations Robinson showed the beginnings of his own efforts to interact with the religious world of Aboriginal people, including his interpretations and attempts at translation of Christian beliefs into one local language of those with whom he was conversing. These conversations are also indicative of ways in which some Aboriginal people were interacting with Robinson and interpreting the Christian faith that he was presenting. As noted in the previous chapter, the context of those conversations was in the bush and therefore vastly different to the church services, Orphan School or later catechetical classes at Wybalenna. They were more akin to the informal conversations occurring between Aboriginal people and colonists within the families on the Bass Strait islands and other places.

At the beginning of the establishment on Bruny Island Robinson began trying to learn the language of the local *Nununi* people.[103] As already mentioned, the purpose of the establishment was to 'ameliorate' the Aboriginal people by means of 'civilization' and 'instruction in the principles of Christianity'.[104] Robinson's evangelical fervour was expressed in his preaching and reading of scripture to the colonist sawyers.[105] This was a development of his earlier preaching to seamen as a member of the Bethel Mission.[106]

His first explicitly reported theological conversation with Aboriginal people was alluded to on 25 May 1829, on the topic 'the being of God'. Robinson described his appreciation of the reality, if not the full extent, of his misunderstanding due to his unfamiliarity with their language.[107] Despite his rudimentary understanding of the *Nununi* language, a few days after these tentative beginnings Robinson 'performed divine service in the natives' hut' on Sunday 31 May 1829.[108] He says he 'preached to the aborigines in their own tongue' and describes part of the sermon:

> MOTTI (one) NYRAE (good) PARLERDI (God) MOTTI (one) NOVILLY (bad) RAEGEWROPPER (devil). PARLERDI (God) NYRAE (good). PARLERDI

(God) MAGGERER (Stop) WARRANGELLY (sky), RAEGEWROPPER (devil) MAGGERER (Stop) TOUGENNER (below) UENEE (fire). NYRAE (good) PARLERWAR (native) LOGERNER (dead) TAGGERER (go) TEENNY (road) LAWWAY (up) WARRANGELLY (sky) PARLERDI (God) NYRAE (good) RAEGE (whiteman) etc, etc. NOVILLY (bad) PARLERWAR (native) LOGERNER (dead) TAGGERER (go) TEENNY (road) TOOGUNNER (below) RAEGEWROPPER (devil) UENEE (fire) MAGGERER (Stop) UENEE (fire).[109]

We see here the basic outline of an evangelistic sermon: there is one God and one devil. God is good and is up in the sky / heaven. The devil is bad and is down in the fire. When a good Aboriginal person or white man dies he will go the way to heaven. When a bad Aboriginal person or white man dies he will go the way to the devil and stop in the fire.

It is worth considering how the Aboriginal audience may have interpreted some or all of these words, the interaction of images Robinson presented, and the different meanings they and he gave to the words. For Robinson, 'Motti (one)' was the monotheist's foundation of one God, understood as Trinitarian (Father, Son and Holy Spirit). By contrast the *Nununi* Aboriginal people had at least two creator beings, Moihernee and Dromerdene, named in the creation story told by *Wurati*. There is no indication of the Aboriginal people's interpretation of Robinson's words about the 'one good God'.

For Robinson, 'Parlerdi (God)' was the God understood as Trinity, with several centuries of church Reformation and fifteen hundred years of creeds and debates within the Christian church as background to his use of the word. The Aboriginal people without that background would have understood the word quite differently. For the local *Nununi*, 'Parlerdi' identified the specific planet known to Robinson as Saturn. More than a year later following further conversations about the stars, Robinson writes that:

> All the stars and constellations near to Saturn and the planets are figurative of men: natives fighting, courting; husband and wife; men's legs, limbs ...[110]

It is possible he may not have known the specific identification of 'Parlerdi' with 'Saturn' at the time of his sermon. It is not difficult to imagine some tentative conversations about the 'being of God' a week earlier and the Aboriginal people making reference to 'Parlerdi' (Saturn) and gesturing toward the sky, which Robinson misunderstood as 'God' (in the heavens).

From the previous chapter we know that the Aboriginal people identified particular stars with particular creator beings[111] so it is possible that Robinson's audience on Bruny Island understood his reference to 'Parlerdi / Saturn' as a reference to a particular creator being or some other religious identity. This sermon, and the previous week's discussion, were at the tentative beginning of understanding each other's religious worlds and it would seem that this involved some degree of mutual recognition and some divergence. Both acknowledged the existence of creator being(s) beyond themselves. They acknowledged some interaction between humans and these being(s). Both used human-like characteristics and language to describe these beings, such as 'natives fighting' or 'courting', or God 'judging'.

There was also divergence when looking in more detail at the myths. We lack the information about the details of interaction between the Aboriginal creator beings to know if there was a hierarchy among them, or if all were mutually equivalent, or the possibility that there are several names for the same being as there was for Aboriginal people. *Wurati*'s creation story mentions Moihernee and Dromerdene fighting in the sky and Dromerdene tumbling to the earth so in that story one is more powerful than the other, but there does not appear to be a moral difference of good and evil ascribed to either being. In Robinson's Anglo-Christian theology there is only one God who reigns supreme over all creation, including all other angelic beings. There is also a stark moral difference between God and the angelic being, the devil. This one God was also referred to using different names.

For Robinson and other nineteenth-century protestant Christians, MOTTI (one) NOVILLY (bad) RAEGEWROPPER (devil) referred to the Satan, Lucifer who fell from heaven, the tempter of Christ and Christian people. There is some resonance for the Aboriginal people, for whom the RAEGEWROPPER was a somewhat malevolent being. However, in the extant sources, there is not any reference to the kind of conflict between RAEGEWROPPER and creator beings that was the mainstream nineteenth-century protestant understanding of God and devil in conflict. The RAEGEWROPPER seems to have more of a personal nuisance role than the morally evil and anti-Christ role of the devil in Christian theology. There seems some resonance but not a dynamic equivalence.

PARLERDI (God) MAGGERER (Stop) WARRANGELLY (sky) is common Christian shorthand for God's transcendent location in heaven that was thought to be above the earth in the sky, stars, and 'heavens'. There is some resonance here in the Aboriginal myths of creator beings identified with particular stars and there being some interaction between these beings and humans, animals, and the land, but Robinson's theology did not limit God to one particular star, but rather as creator of all stars.

The sources are too limited to know if the Aboriginal people's creator beings had a similarly somewhat distant interaction with people. There do appear to be more references to immediate effects of the Wrageowrapper's activities upon people than the creator beings.

In regard to the phrase, 'RAEGEWROPPER (devil) MAGGERER (stop) TOUGENNER (below) UENEE (fire)', the precise identity and characteristics of the Wrageowrapper / devil is difficult to determine because of the multiple uses and meanings mentioned by Robinson. It seems in this sermon Robinson was presenting the common Anglo-Christian view of a three-tiered universe of God in heaven above, devil in hellfire below, and people / creation existing on the earth in between. In Robinson's writings about the Aboriginal people, 'devil' had multiple meanings. It referred to their own seemingly personal spirit, a malevolent being causing sickness and death, a being to whom the tyreelore women danced in order to please, and it was the blue flame in the fire. This being also has different names among different clans, which suggests its varying characteristics and qualities.[112]

Having announced in his sermon what he believed happens to the Aboriginal person and the white man when they die, Robinson later that same day asked *Nununi* people 'where they went to after death'. An Aboriginal man died the same day as this sermon and Robinson describes in some detail the funeral preparations, including cremating the body on a pyre. This is helpful in interpreting the context of the sermon. The response to his question startled him:

> One said to England. I scarcely credited what I heard. I asked the question again, when they all replied that they went to England, that there was plenty of PARLEVAR in England.[113]

At the very least this indicates that the Aboriginal people did not believe, as Robinson did, that following death there was a moral separation of people, good from bad, the former in the sky and the latter in the fire beneath the ground. This is a substantial point of difference in mythologies. While there were differing mortuary and funerary practices around the island, for example, cremation or entombment in hollow tree trunks,[114] there are not clear indications of the religious beliefs. About a week after this sermon Robinson wrote that he

> conversed with the natives on religious subjects. Learnt that they had some idea of a good spirit whom they called parllerde, and that he stopped in the sky (Warranggelly)'.[115]

Like the references to God as good spirit, the references to devil may have had some general approximation to the Aboriginal people's religious beliefs about the Wrageowrapper, at least enough to continue conversing and sharing different understandings and thereby gaining greater appreciation of the nuances of each other's beliefs. At the very least the Aboriginal people and Robinson began revealing to each other their own mythologies and through these conversations they developed a vocabulary with sufficiently general and somewhat mutually intelligible meanings to build on each one's understanding of the other.

Religious adaptation — ochre and prayer book

Like the spoken words and their conceptual meanings, Robinson mentions one fascinating instance of the interaction of artefacts and other physical items of each other's religious worlds. A couple of weeks after the conversations about the creation story in July and August 1831 discussed in the previous chapter, Robinson wrote about an experience he found quite startling. The group came across an Aboriginal shelter:

> All the ground in front of this habitation was thickly strewed with the feathers of the emu, and bones of this stately bird as also other animals such as the kangaroo covered the ground, which the natives had broken to pieces to obtain the marrow to anoint their head and body. In front of this domicile a row of small fires had been kindled, which were burning at the time *Manalakina* and the other natives had discovered them. On searching about, found the claw of an emu and some red ochre, but what appeared to me the most extraordinary was finding some pieces of the leaves of the Common Prayer Book, covered with red ochre. On examining these I found them to contain parts of psalms 30, 31, 32, 33 and 96, and on reading the first five verses of the 31st psalm, I found it so peculiarly adapted to me that I could not help exclaiming, 'Marvellous are thy ways, O Lord, and thy paths are past finding out'; and on reading the 33rd psalm at the 13th and 14th verses, 'The Lord looked down from heaven and beheld all the children of men' &c, I thought them peculiarly applicable to this forlorn and hapless race of human beings.[116]

Here we see the interaction of several religious artefacts from either side of the colonial exchange that have been brought together by this group of Aboriginal people who were absent from their shelter. The several fires indicate several hearth groups gathered together. Thickly strewn feathers and bones suggest a substantial feast of emu and kangaroo. The possible religious attributes of the emu are unknown, however the general significance of the kangaroo is known from the earlier creation story. The breaking of the tail (again from the creation story) to obtain marrow for nourishment and healing is also familiar.

On searching further, Robinson found an emu claw, ochre and, what are for him the most extraordinary items, fragments of psalms from the Anglican Church's *Book of Common Prayer*, which were covered with red ochre. While the particular psalms are what arouses his delight, one could first of all consider how these Aboriginal people seemed to be using these textual fragments. They appear to have incorporated these pages into their world and thereby created their own meaning, the tearing of the pages perhaps paralleling the breaking of kangaroo bones to release the anointing marrow. In her insightful article, Van Toorn suggests the pages were 'red but unread':

> Red ochre played an important part in Aboriginal ritual life, so it is probable that the people of north-east Van Diemen's Land used the pages from the Prayer Book—part of the script for Christian worship—for different ritual purposes. Although these people would not have been able to decipher the words of the text, they covered the pages with red ochre, perhaps ritually appropriating the power of what they correctly saw as one of the white man's sacred instruments.[117]

These Aboriginal people were thought to have been responsible for recent killings in the area and had confiscated these and possibly other items from their supposed victims. They may have had sufficient familiarity with the colonists to know the role of this book in the colonists' religious lives. Regardless of what these absent Aboriginal people knew or did not know about the place of the *Book of Common Prayer* in colonist life, they had retrieved these pages, kept them, and incorporated them into a substantive gathering including by the use of the much valued symbolic substance of red ochre, marrow from kangaroo tail, and possibly emu feathers. For these Aboriginal people these religious artefacts belonged together in this event and location, and as such it is a site of religious interaction and hybridity. The beliefs about the pages interact with those of the ochre, marrow and bones, as they do, though in a very different way, for Robinson.

For Robinson it seems the text, specifically the 13th and 14th verses of Psalm 33, is somehow mediating God 'looking down' upon all the children of men, including those who are now not present at the fireside but for whom Robinson is searching. These particular words are probably not the focal point for the Aboriginal people who brought together claw, marrow, ochre and pages, but the very fact of their bringing these artefacts together suggests something of the religious dialogue and interpretation in which they were engaging, largely on their own terms. There was, apparently, no colonist Christian person present. The circumstances of these people's acquisition of the pages are uncertain, as is their familiarity with the religious nature of the book, and these pages in particular. While we do not know if they possessed the entire *Book of Common Prayer* they have clearly used these pages in a dynamic relationship with ochre, marrow and bone in this particular physical and religious location.

Religious adaptation — attending church

As well as these interactions of physical artefacts and occasional conversations, Robinson made a few brief references to Aboriginal people attending church services. As mentioned, the Orphan School children attended church services each Sunday at St David's Hobart and later St John's New Town. Robinson also regularly performed 'divine service' during his travels. As well as these occasions, Robinson mentions Aboriginal people going to church services, usually while in or visiting Hobart. The first such mention is in January 1830, and the people's attraction to the pageantry of the Protestant Church (Church of England):

> The aborigines were sent to church. Their conduct through the service was surprisingly decorous and conformable to that observed by the congregation. They appeared sensible that they were in some sacred place and on their return expressed the highest delight with what they had seen and heard. They were quite enraptured with the music. When asked who the house belonged to, they replied 'The person who sat in the pulpit'; upon which I explained to them that they had visited the house of God, at which they seemed much surprised. I may without flattery to these poor creatures term them perfect models of obedience. Their behavior hitherto has given me the greatest satisfaction.[118]

One Aboriginal person, a woman, Luggenemenener / Tuery, was known by other Aboriginal people to go to church and attend prayers though it is not clear how often.[119] She was from the Ben Lomond clan and had taken a group of Aboriginal people to John Batman's house in that area for refuge from those hunting them, probably to avoid the Black Line.[120] She had earlier stayed at Robinson's home in Hobart Town, or more precisely, the 'asylum' next to Robinson's house.[121]

Luggenemenener was the mother of Walter Arthur (previously known as Friday) who was removed to the Orphan School from 1832 to 1835. As will become clear in the next chapter, she was likely involved in the first Bible translation at Wybalenna. These early references to her attending church services were part of a range of engagements with the Christian faith. What is particularly distinctive is that she was one of only a few adult Aboriginal people who had known life before the colonists infiltrated their world who then became actively involved in Christian activities.[122] There is, however, no mention of her being baptised. Nor is there any indication that her husband, Rolepa / King George, attended church services.

These examples suggest Aboriginal people were interpreting the Christian faith in their own terms both within and beyond their relationships with colonist Christians. They interpreted and adapted Christian words and artefacts from their pre-existing beliefs. The less rigorous institutional life at Wybalenna and its location as the gathering place of diverse Aboriginal clans and quite different Christian people points to it as a significant site for evolving Aboriginal–Christian identities and practices.

ENDNOTES CHAPTER TWO

1. Nicholls, M., (ed), 1977, *The Diary of the Reverend Robert Knopwood 1803-1838* Launceston; Foot & Playsted, p. 36.
2. Hookey, M., 1929, *Bobby Knopwood and His Times*. Hobart; W.E. Fuller, p. 16.
3. The first Christian funeral service occurred on Saturday 28 April 1804, (Currey, J., (ed), 2005, *Knopwood's Hobart Town Diary*. Malvern: Colony Press, p. 29), after Knopwood and Lt Governor Collins had marked out a 'burial ground at a distance from the camp' following the death of Elizabeth Edwards, aged 4, Nicholls, 1977, p. 50. Until the 'old' St David's church was consecrated in 1822, 'divine service' occurred in the store in Bathurst Street, or the Barrack grounds, or under the verandah of Governor's cottage and surrounding gum trees, Hookey, 1929, p. 131.
4. Boyce, 2001, p. 1.
5. Nicholls, 1977, p. 51.
6. Woolmington, J., 1985, 'Missionary Attitudes to the Baptism of Australian Aborigines Before 1850', *The Journal of Religious History*, 13 (3), pp. 283-293.
7. Nicholls, 1977, p. 51.
8. Plomley, 1966, pp. 487, 489, 540, 557.
9. Plomley, 1966, p. 220.
10. Plomley, 1966, p. 376.
11. Plomley, 1966, p. 369.
12. Robinson noted that some Aboriginal people interpreted gunfire as 'thunder', Plomley, 1966, pp. 196, 205.
13. The *Book of Common Prayer* states: 'For every child to be baptized there shall be not fewer than three godparents, of whom at least two shall be of the same sex as the child and of whom at least one shall be of the opposite sex; save that, when three cannot be conveniently had, one godfather and one godmother shall suffice.' It was the responsibility during the 'Private Ministration of Baptism of a Child', for the Godfathers and Godmothers to pronounce the name of the child, Church of England, 1968, *The book of common prayer and administration of the sacraments, and other rites and ceremonies of the church according to the use of the Church of England, together with the psalter or psalms of David, pointed as they are to be sung or said in churches, and the form and manner of making : ordaining and consecrating bishops, priests, and deacons*, London; W. Clowes by Eyre & Spottiswoode, pp. 154, 158.
14. *Book of Common Prayer*: 'No Minister shall refuse or, save for the purpose of preparing or instructing the parents or guardians or godparents, delay to baptize any infant within his cure that is brought to the church to be baptized, provided that due notice has been given and the provisions relating to godparents are observed'. Church of England, 1968, p. 154.
15. Church of England, 1968, p. 154.
16. Boyce, J., 2004, Robert May, *Tasmania 40° South*, 35, p. 46.
17. Lawson, Z., 2013, George Vandiemen: a Tasmanian Aborigine in Lancashire, England (1822–1827), *Journal of the Royal Australian Historical Society*, Vol 99, No 2, pp. 153-169.
18. Boyce, 2004, p. 47.
19. Boyce, 2004, p. 47.
20. Jones, 1970, pp. 256-271.
21. Boyce, J., 2004, 'A Dog's Breakfast ... Lunch and Dinner: Canine Dependency in Early Van Diemen's Land', *Tasmanian Historical Research Association*, 52 (4), pp. 194 – 213; Boyce, J., 2006, 'Canine Revolution: the social and environmental impact of the introduction of the dog to Tasmania', *Environmental History*, 11 (1) pp. 102–129; and Boyce, J., 2008.
22. Boyce, 2006, p. 102 .
23. Van Diemen's Land: Copies of All Correspondence between Lieutenant Governor Arthur and His Majesty's Secretary of State for the Colonies on the Subject of the Military Operations Lately Carried on against the Aboriginal Inhabitants of Van Diemen's Land (Including Minutes of Evidence Taken

before the Committee for the Affairs of the Aborigines, 1830), Hobart; *Tasmanian Historical Research Association*, 1971, p. 259. An officer wrote on arriving at the Derwent that 'the woods abound with kangaroos and emus' and that 'six or seven kangaroos have been killed in a forenoon with greyhounds by the surgeon at Risdon Cove', Hamilton-Arnold, B., (ed.), 1994, *Letters and Papers of G. P. Harris, 1803-1812: Deputy Surveyor-General of New South Wales at Sullivan Bay, Port Phillip, and Hobart Town, Van Diemen's Land*, Victoria; Arden Press, p. 61.
24 Knopwood claimed to have killed the first kangaroo by any of the gentlemen in the camp, Nicholls, 1977, p. 47, 51, 62, 80, 128.
25 Boyce, 2006, p. 108.
26 cited in Boyce, 2004, 'A Dog's Breakfast', p. 200.
27 Boyce, 2006, p. 110.
28 Jones, 1970, p. 260.
29 Jones, 1970, p. 261.
30 Jones, 1970, p. 269.
31 Jones, 1970, p. 269.
32 15 November 1830, Plomley, 1966, p. 278.
33 3 July 1832, Plomley, 1966, p. 626.
34 21 June 1834, Plomley, 1966, p. 888.
35 13 July 1834, Plomley, 1966, p. 900.
36 Plomley, 1966, p. 278.
37 Robinson writes that he was encouraged to 'go without clothes', Plomley, 1966, p. 626, and therefore adopt the Aboriginal dress.
38 Boyce, 2006, p. 110.
39 Boyce, 2006, p. 110.
40 Fels, M., 1982, 'Culture Contact in the County of Buckinghamshire, Van Diemen's Land 1803-1811', *Tasmanian Historical Research Association*, 29 (2), p. 57; and Boyce, 2004, 'A Dog's Breakfast', p. 205.
41 ML Robinson Papers, A7065 CY550, p. 85.
42 Correspondence, Kirwan to Colonial Secretary, TAHO CSD, 1/18/703.
43 Boyce, 2006, p. 120. See also, Kenny, R., 2007, *The Lamb Enters the Dreaming*. Melbourne: Scribe.
44 Fels, 1982, p. 65.
45 Edward Lord briefly served as Commandant of Hobart in 1810, http://www.govhouse.tas.gov.au/governor/previous-governors, accessed 10/5/2014. See also Alexander, A., 2015, *Corruption and Skullduggery*, Hobart, Pillinger Press, p. 211.
46 It would be a fascinating and worthwhile research project to trace all of these children through their later lives. Others about whom there is some information are: Fanny Hardwicke, George Van Diemen. See also Lawson, Z., 2013, *George Vandiemen: A Tasmanian Aborigine in Lancashire, England (1822-27)*, Journal of Royal Australian Historical Society, 99, 2, pp. 153-169.
47 see TAHO CSO 1/ 269/6468. There are several variant spellings of Sergeant James Macauley, such as M'Cauley, Macauley, and McAlley.
48 Hookey, 1929, p. 74.
49 James McAuley, Died 1822, Age 44, Born 1778, Location Hobart, Church of England, TAHO RGD 34/1, no. 566. See also Buchanan, A. M., 1994, *Index to Tasmanian Deaths / Burials, 1797-1840*. Hobart: A.M. Buchanan, p. 85.
50 *Hobart Town Gazette*, 1 January 1820.
51 Edward Busby, Convict/Medway(1), married Mary McAulay, 7 April 1828, Hobart Town, in McKay, T., 1992, *Van Diemen's Land Early Marriages 1803-1830*, Vol 1. Kingston; T. McKay, p. 29. Muddy Plains adjoined Clarence Plains on the eastern shore of the River Derwent, Hobart, see Widowson, H., 1829, *Present State of Van Diemen's Land comprising an account of its agricultural capabilities with observations on the present state of farming &c. pursued in that colony and other important matters connected with emigration*. London; Robinson, p. 101.
52 26 May 1829, Plomley, 1966, pp. 60, 102.
53 Plomley, 1966, p. 69.
54 Plomley, 1966, 104.
55 Plomley, 1966, p. 73.
56 Fifty years later the initial land grant to Fanny Cochrane Smith was also not

57 taken up immediately. *The Mercury*, 31 October 1884, p. 3.
57 Plomley, 1966, pp. 70, 71.
58 Plomley, 1966, p. 170.
59 Plomley, 1966, pp. 120, 162, 183, 366, 409, 565.
60 Plomley, 1966, pp. 373, 376.
61 Plomley, 1966, p. 594.
62 Plomley, 1966, p. 594.
63 Plomley, 1966, p. 594.
64 Plomley, 1966, p. 594. The discussion of 'fine clothes' in the previous chapter considered the perceived parallel between ochre and fine clothes in the report of an Aboriginal person. This discussion concerns the contrasting funeral rites used for Robert and Eumarrah.
65 Minutes of Committee of Management, 24 and 28 April 1828, TAHO SWD 24. See also letters of Superintendent Charles O'Hara Booth, TAHO CSO 24/149/1401 and reports of Inspector of Education, C. Bradbury in 1848, TAHO GO 33/68.
66 Minutes of Committee of Management, 20 April 1828, TAHO SWD 24.
67 Purtscher, J., 1993, *Infants at Queen's Orphanage, 1851–1863*. Hobart; Van Diemens Land and Norfolk Island Interest Group, unpaginated.
68 Minutes of Committee of Management, 9 January 1830, TAHO SWD 24.
69 Purtscher, 1993, *Infants*, unpaginated.
70 For example, the children of the Chief Constable of Tea Tree district were admitted and the father was required to pay £12 per half year from his salary for his two children, but most others were required to pay £6 per annum to be paid in quarterly instalments. These 'fee-paying' parents were permitted to see their children on the first Monday of each month between 11:00 am and 2:00 pm in the presence of the master or matron and all admissions required the approval of the Governor, or at least the Colonial Secretary, Minutes of Committee of Management, 20 April 1828, TAHO SWD 24.
71 Minutes of Committee of Management, 20 April and 26 July 1828, TAHO SWD 24.
72 TAHO SWD 28. George Robinson began the establishment on Bruny Island in March 1829.
73 Minutes of Committee of Management, 16 August 1828, TAHO SWD 24. Stevens is simply wrong to argue that there is no information on how Thomas came to be at the school. There is also no evidence to support the claim that Thomas was at the Bruny Island station or belonged to the *Nununi* clan, Stevens, 2017, p. 18, 63.
74 A 'James Grant' appeared in several Hobart newspapers, selling a horse (*Hobart Town Courier*, 19 July 1828), and being appointed to settle accounts for a James Gilligan who was leaving the colony (*Hobart Town Courier*, 19 July 1828). In October 1828 he bought land (Lot 69 for 5s 6d) through a tender process and was involved in the sale of a house in Macquarie Street (*Hobart Town Courier*, 25 October 1828). A James Grant Esq was involved in the sale of quantities of wool in England (*Hobart Town Courier*, 28 Oct 1828).
75 For example, Minutes of Committee of Management, 3 April 1830, TAHO SWD 24.
76 TAHO SWD 28. These two may have been the sons of *Wurati* who was travelling with George Robinson at the time. Their names were later known as Peter and Davy Bruny.
77 Minutes of Committee of Management, 3 December 1829, TAHO SWD 24. Other families from the Bass Strait Islands sought to have children admitted. John Smith, 23 February 1832, applied for his son to be admitted. The child's mother was an Aboriginal woman living at Wybalenna on Flinders Island, TAHO SWD 24. Another sealer, Lawrence Read, admitted his daughter, a child of a 'Native of Kangaroo Island', on 15 March 1832. Read was required to pay a fee and his daughter was the only Aboriginal child whose presence at the school was paid for by a parent, TAHO SWD 24.
78 Plomley, 1966, p. 69.
79 Minutes of Committee of Management, 8 August 1833, TAHO SWD 24.
80 29 May 1830, TAHO SWD 24.

81 Minutes of Committee of Management, 27 November 1830, TAHO SWD 24.
82 Plomley, 1987, Annotation 14 Sept 1835, pp. 619–620.
83 The Management Committee records three boys (all unnamed) arriving 16 August for immediate admission and requiring clothing, Minutes of Committee of Management, 23 August 1832, TAHO SWD 24. The Register records two boys, Daniel and Peter, admitted on 17 August, TAHO SWD 28.
84 The Management Committee decided it could not recommend the admission of the girl on account of her age and referred her situation to the Aboriginal Committee, 20 December 1832, TAHO SWD 24. The Register records the three boys as Luke, aged 6, Arthur, aged 11, and Friday, aged 10, TAHO SWD 28.
85 ML Robinson Papers, A7064 Vol. 43, CY550, p. 9. Walter's role at Wybalenna and *putalina* / Oyster Cove will be examined in several of the following chapters.
86 Plomley, 1987, p. 824.
87 Plomley, 1987, p. 806.
88 ML Robinson Papers, A7062 CY549, p. 79.
89 This is further indicated by the Aboriginal adults living among colonists, such as Bill Ponsonby and Catherine Kennedy who were married in St John's Church, Launceston on 16 August 1830, Plomley, 1966, p. 582. 'On Monday 16th instant, two of the Aborigines of this country were married at St John's Church, Launceston. This is the first marriage of the kind which has ever fell under our notice in this colony. They had both been domesticated for some time amongst the European population'. *Launceston Advertiser*, 23 August 1830, p. 3.
90 Such as the previously mentioned Robert Macauley, Fanny Hardwicke and Mary Ann Robinson, among others.
91 Such as the previously mentioned John Smith, and other sealing families such as James Munro, 9 November 1830, Plomley, 1966, p. 269.
92 Such as Thomas Bunce / Brune / Bruny, TAHO SWD 24. For the coalescing of Thomas' 'family' name, see correspondence Clark to Robinson, 9 November 1835, CSO 1/18798, p. 80.
93 According to the Register there were 11 in 1834; 6 in 1833; 6 in 1832; 1 in each of the years previous to that. In the subsequent years there were 4 in 1836; 3 in 1837; 3 in 1838, TAHO SWD 28/1/1, unpaginated.
94 Boyce, 2001, p 33. Sadly one of the children, Frederick, died on 30 September 1835, the day before Robinson took five other children with him to Wybalenna.
95 This irked the Catholic and Jewish communities in particular. In the 1840s the Catholic population at the school was about equal to the Protestant population, whereas in the community at large, Protestant numbers were five-times greater than Catholic. After 1844, Catholic children were instructed in their faith, had their own dormitories and cemetery, TAHO GO 33/68, Purtscher, J., 1993, *Children in Queen's Orphanage 1828–1863*. New Town; Schaffer, unpaginated.
96 Minutes of Committee of Management, 12 September 1833, TAHO SWD 24.
97 TAHO GO 33/68, see also letters by Superintendent Charles O'Hara Booth TAHO CSO 24/149/1401. Cited in Purtscher, 1993, *Children*, unpaginated.
98 TAHO CSO 24/149/1401, 311 & 320.
99 Robinson had identified this system when beginning at Bruny Island in1829, Plomley, 1966, p. 56. Catechist Robert Clark introduced Bell's Madras system at Wybalenna in 1834, ML Robinson Papers, A7062 CY549, p. 168. The earliest surviving catechetical examinations at Wybalenna are from May 1837, Plomley, 1987, pp. 858–59, ML Robinson Papers, A7062 CY549, pp. 131–141.
100 In James Barnard's paper examining the 1848 census of Van Diemen's Land, Table 23 details the working of the Queen's Orphan School. The

total number in the school at the end of 1848 was 460; of whom 396 were the offspring of convicts and 64 the children of free parents. Of these again, 3 boys and 4 girls were children of the Aboriginal people. Barnard, J., 1850, 'Observations on Statistics of Van Diemen's Land for 1848: compiled from Official Records in the Colonial Secretary's Office', *Papers and Proceedings of the Royal Society of Tasmania*, 1 (2), p. 110.
101 Boyce, 2001, p. 33.
102 'The failure was in not even trying', Harris, 1990, p. 93, 94.
103 Plomley, 1966, p. 58.
104 Plomley, 1966, p. 56.
105 Plomley, 1966, pp. 55, 59.
106 As discussed in Chapter One, *Colonial Times*, 15 February 1828, p. 1. *Hobart Town Courier*, 7 June 1828, p. 4. *Hobart Town Courier*, 9 August 1828, p, 3.
107 Plomley, 1966, p. 60.
108 If Robinson 'performed' from the *Book of Common Prayer* it was probably the first such service where a majority of participants were Aboriginal. In 1829, Easter Day was 19 April, therefore Friday 29 May was Ascension Day, forty days after Easter. The *Book of Common Prayer* had prescribed Bible readings, Collects and the requirement to read the Athanasian Creed during 'Divine Service' on the Sunday following Ascension Day, Church of England, 1968.
109 Plomley, 1966, p, 61.
110 Plomley, 1966, p. 366, 464.
111 Plomley, 1966, pp. 373, 399, 402.
112 Plomley, 1966, pp. 182, 249, 281–2, 373, 616.
113 Plomley, 1966, p. 62. See discussion of 'England' in previous chapter.
114 Cameron, 2011, p. 39.
115 Plomley, 1966, p. 63.
116 Plomley, 1966, p. 410.
117 Toorn, P. V., 2002, 'Before the Second Reformation: Nineteenth-Century Aboriginal Mediations of the Bible in Van Diemens Land', *Semeia*, 88, p. 44.
118 Plomley, 1966, p. 94.
119 21 November 1830, Plomley, 1966, p. 281.
120 Plomley, 1966, p. 281.
121 Plomley, 1966, pp. 279, 439.
122 Mary and Ann, mother of Lucy Murray, who were baptised on 4 November 1811, are others.

CHAPTER THREE

Wybalenna — 'Black Man's Church'

ABORIGINAL people had many different experiences of colonial life and the Christian faith that was an integral part of it. They were introduced to the Christian faith in various forms through colonist families with whom they lived, attending church services with those families or on their own, or in the formal setting of the Orphan School. Some experienced services of Christian worship known as 'divine service' away from colonist towns and churches. This occurred among the few who travelled with George Robinson through the bush, or as part of family prayers on the Bass Strait islands. A few acquired Christian artefacts during raids on colonist houses. The range of these contexts narrowed somewhat during the early 1830s as the largest portion of surviving Aboriginal people, about 200 in total, became concentrated at the 'Aboriginal Settlement' of Wybalenna on the west coast of Flinders Island, off the north-east coast of Van Diemen's Land.

Wybalenna is a crucial location in the experiences of Aboriginal people, from the 1830s through to today. It is pivotal when considering the interaction of Aboriginal and Christian religious beliefs and practices. It is a site of some of the earliest attempts in Australia to translate portions of the Christian Bible into an anglicised version of an Aboriginal language. These attempts happened in the midst of continuing inter-clan relationships and religious practices, and an evolving *pidgin* language among those clans.[1]

With little history of Christian mission among Aboriginal people to draw upon, Christian practices and teaching at Wybalenna were experimental rather than rigid. They were shaped by the interaction of the particular people, especially leaders, who lived there. A variety of methods was employed, with tentative conversations as well as voluntary catechetical classes. For Aboriginal people at Wybalenna, writing English text became a religious as well as political act. Some of the earliest Christian preaching by Aboriginal people in first language, *pidgin*, and English occurred at Wybalenna.

Furthermore, few of the documentary records of this period have previously been published. With such diverse Aboriginal and colonist participants, many of whom were redefining themselves and each other, the context is multi-faceted and multi-layered. In the context of Wybalenna, diverse Aboriginal–Christian theologies began to emerge. As Aboriginal people simultaneously interacted with these multiple forms of Christian faith they were also continuing to hunt, perform ceremonies, and fulfil other pre-existing social, cultural and political roles. They were also creating new ones.

It is impossible to assess the degree to which particular Tasmanian Aboriginal people integrated the Christian faith into their identities. It is possible however, through examining surviving documents, to identify particular practices in which they engaged, how often they did so, and the various contexts in which they performed them. Rather than showing a totalitarian regime indoctrinating passive and helpless victims, the documents show a wide range of experiences during the years of the Wybalenna settlement from 1832 until it closed in 1847.

At the settlement there were various Aboriginal Christian and non-Christian actors performing a variety of roles. There was not simply one Aboriginal voice, nor was there a single Aboriginal Christian voice or experience. They were actively interpreting what was occurring. They were adapting and using their new context to strengthen and expand some existing roles, clan relationships and indeed some aspects of their spiritual worldview. It makes sense in this context to speak of multiple and multi-faceted Aboriginal experiences and identities[2] and of the precarious nature of colonist, particularly colonist Christian, identities and practices.[3]

These interpretations and adaptations do not diminish the realities of the active efforts undertaken by Governors, commandants, catechists, and others to persuade and sometimes coerce Aboriginal people to cease their existing languages and practices. These efforts caused significant disruption to Aboriginal people's lives and their religious world. Nor does it ignore the significant trauma Aboriginal people experienced in sustained bereavement, particularly in those brief periods when up to ten per cent of their number died of illnesses. But in the midst of these experiences and efforts by colonists, Aboriginal people were also actively pursuing their own adaptations. For some periods there are few if any records, and for others, particularly when Robinson was commandant, there are many. In these the priorities of the commandants, catechists (Bible teachers) and chaplain can be seen, but more importantly, some of the interpretations and responses Aboriginal people were making is also evident.

Early years: removal of children, Bible translation, Sunday services

The desire among colonists for a separate settlement for Aboriginal people began as early as December 1826,[4] before Robinson was appointed to begin an establishment on Bruny Island in 1829.[5] Swan Island, located just off the north-east coast of Van Diemen's Land, became something of a *de facto* settlement in 1830[6] comprising 'captured natives' from the north-east[7] including the Ben Lomond area. In early 1831 they were moved to Preservation Island in Bass Strait, then to Gun Carriage (Vansittart) Island under the oversight of Archibald Maclachlan, a convict, and then Sergeant Alexander Wight, who oversaw the move to 'the Lagoons' on Great (Flinders) Island in mid-November 1831.[8] Around this time Aboriginal people from Big River arrived,[9] followed by those from the north-west in the second half of 1832,[10] and from Macquarie Harbour in the first half of 1833.[11]

Once on Flinders Island, and when opportunity presented, Aboriginal people continued to hunt, and in the evenings gathered for singing, dancing and storytelling.[12] In the early days of the settlement there was no catechist and therefore no organised program of Christian practices such as Sunday services or education. This changed when W. J. Darling became commandant in March 1832, with specific instructions from Governor Arthur to 'civilise' the Aboriginal people.[13] It is important to acknowledge Wybalenna was a government settlement and not a church mission station. All colonists such as the commandants (with overall responsibility), catechists (teachers of Christian faith and the Bible), other officers (medical officer, storekeeper, overseer) and convicts, were appointed by the Governor and all rations were provided from the government stores. This was not a 'mission' run by any church.

In February 1833 the settlement moved to 'Civilisation Point', despite the poor water supply and exposure to the prevailing, and often cold, westerly winds.[14] During Darling's time the site became known as 'Wybalenna'. Stevens claims the name Wybalenna was from the 'Nuenonne Bruny Island language' and states 'Use of his own language highlights the degree of seniority that Wooreddy — now commonly known as Doctor — had achieved in the VDL–European cultural exchange.'[15] However, there is no evidence to support such a claim. At least one documentary source identifies the language from which 'Wybalenna' was drawn as 'signifying in the language of the Ben Lomond Natives, Black man's houses'.[16] The naming appears to be in response to Governor Arthur's suggestion that Mr Darling 'will find some native name for it'.[17]

Removing children

Upon arrival at Wybalenna, Darling instituted weekly church services almost immediately. As noted earlier, he also removed several Aboriginal children to the Orphan School in Hobart. There are some discrepancies in records between the Orphan School register, minutes of the Committee of Management of the Orphan School and those in Plomley's edited extracts from Robinson's papers in regard to the names and the numbers of Aboriginal children removed. However, it is clear that several groups of Aboriginal children were removed on two separate occasions between August and December 1832.[18] One explanation for the removal of these Aboriginal children was the lack of a catechist/teacher at the settlement, but most children were not returned to their parents even when the first catechist, Thomas Wilkinson, arrived in June 1833.[19]

At the beginning of 1834 the visiting Quakers, Backhouse and Walker, reported there were one hundred and eleven Aboriginal people at Wybalenna, including eleven adolescents and eleven children under five years of age.[20] A few months later about ten children were returned from the Orphan School to their parents from 26 April to 18 June 1834[21] though four seem to have died of pneumonia soon after arriving.[22] These returning, and surviving, children would have increased the adolescent and infant population from twenty-two to almost thirty. A further eight or nine were returned with the next commandant, Robinson, in October 1835.[23] These returning children became a particular focus for the commandant and catechist. But simultaneously many of them were returning to parents and clan, to a context where their first language continued to be spoken and other ancestral practices continued, albeit in modified forms.

Also underlying the removal of children to the Orphan School was the ongoing conflict between successive commandants and catechists. In a letter to the Colonial Secretary, 19 February 1835, Commandant Nickolls referred to the nine children removed to the Orphan School[24] and followed this with another, on 21 February, alluding to the 'inefficiency of the catechist', Robert Clark.[25] Several children were removed even while a catechist was present.[26] Despite criticisms, Clark remained as catechist until early 1838 when Reverend Thomas Dove arrived as chaplain. But even then Clark continued teaching[27] and in fact took over from Dove, who refused to teach the Aboriginal children. The alleged 'lack' of a 'competent' teacher seems a façade to cover other interpersonal conflicts among the colonist leaders.

Bible translation

The arrival of Thomas and Louisa Wilkinson at Wybalenna in 1833 marked the beginning of some significant developments. The Wilkinsons had arrived in Van

Diemen's Land in March 1833. Thomas' appointment as catechist was on the recommendation of Archdeacon Bedford, who considered him 'very capable of instructing the natives'.[28] The *Hobart Town Courier* reported,

> We have much pleasure in announcing that the Rev. Thomas Wilkinson, the missionary appointed by the government for the Aboriginal people, has arrived at the colony on Flinders Island and commenced his arduous but interesting labors. We shall be most anxious to hear by every opportunity what success he meets with.[29]

Thomas began conversations about the Christian faith and Louisa began teaching the women 'domestic and feminine occupations'.[30]

The conversations between Wilkinson and various Ben Lomond people progressed well enough that just on three months after his arrival, Wilkinson wrote to Governor Arthur on 17 September 1833 with a sample of what he said was his translation into the Ben Lomond language of the 'principal parts of the first four chapters of Genesis'.[31] Unfortunately all that survives are the 'principal parts' from Genesis Chapter One in Arthur's papers,[32] and a mostly similar version in the diary of the Quaker, George Washington Walker.[33]

The translation conversations occurred while at the same time there was deepening conflict between Commandant Darling, Catechist Wilkinson, and the Medical Officer Mclachlan. Arthur despatched the two Quakers, Backhouse and Walker, in November 1833 to investigate the situation and seek mediation. Walker reported to Governor Arthur affirming Wilkinson's teaching and language learning:

> T Wilkinson ... has succeeded as well as could have been anticipated considering the difficulties he has to contend with. The language has never been reduced to writing and it is extremely difficult to come at the idiom ...
>
> ... but this is to be expected in the study of a language hitherto only known orally by those who speak it and of which Europeans have hitherto been almost wholly ignorant. The literal translation is almost confined in great measure to the verbs and nouns.
>
> ... T. W. has composed a considerable vocabulary of words.[34]

Translating these portions highlighted some significant challenges in communicating across the different languages and worldviews among the evolving Wybalenna community. Unlike Robinson's conversations with *Nununi* people in May 1829, Walker believed that the Aboriginal people

> seem to have had no idea of the existence of a creative presiding power implied by the word God nor any word corresponding with such sentiment in their own language[35]

and that in regard to their languages

> some of the Aboriginal terms have a very indefinite and extended meaning as in the words crackneh and pomleh.[36]

As well as the challenges, it also shows the capacity and skill of Aboriginal people in incorporating English words in the development of an evolving *pidgin*, or *lingua franca*, unique to Wybalenna such that Walker noted that 'several of [the] anglified terms [such as Godneh, grassneh] are now in such common use among the natives that they may be considered as incorporated with the language'.[37]

This development of bilingual communication between Wilkinson and certain Ben Lomond people, and a new evolving *pidgin* 'among the natives' suggests that there were multiple contexts operating simultaneously at Wybalenna. There were interactions among the various Aboriginal clans, those among various colonists (commandant, catechist, soldiers, overseer and convicts), and the few Aboriginal people and colonists interacting with each other. The documents suggest the successive catechists Wilkinson and Clark were among the few, if not the only colonists, using, or attempting to use, the evolving *pidgin*, while many, if not most, of the Aboriginal people were using it primarily with each other.

The surviving documents are written in English, yet most Aboriginal people were conversing with each other in the evolving *pidgin* and not writing in English at all. At that time the Aboriginal population was approximately one hundred and thirty, comprising people mostly from north and north-eastern parts of Van Diemen's Land, including the Ben Lomond area,[38] yet there are very few surviving documents of their interactions with each other. What have survived are documents primarily about colonists' interpretations of interactions between them and Aboriginal people. It is important to remember the larger context of Aboriginal people's inter-clan relationships. These were likely to have been more significant to Aboriginal people's daily life than relationships with colonists.

Like the earlier Aboriginal people being baptised, or conversing with Robinson, or the children at the Orphan School, the conversations between Wilkinson and Ben Lomond people opened new thoughts about their own and the other's religious world. It is arguable that the use of English and the evolving *pidgin* were contributing factors that added to rather than subtracted from their existing religious worldviews. These changes were developing *pidgin* and anglicised words and incorporating them into their existing languages. The meanings of the words developed through the conversations. In this way the context was something of a threshold which was neither wholly English nor wholly Ben Lomond (or other Aboriginal languages) but the beginnings of an exploration of something new through which each was enlarging their understanding and experience of themselves, the other, and their creation stories within their worlds.[39]

The topic of Genesis as the initial Bible translation is noteworthy. As discussed in the previous chapters, these origin stories are identity-defining meta-narratives through which all later stories are interpreted. It is unknown if Wilkinson or the Aboriginal people raised the topic of the beginnings of creation, but Wilkinson was certainly focussing exclusively on translating the foundational stories in the first four chapters of Genesis. This resonating topic of creation stories is understandable in the early stages rather than beginning with the more dissonant elements such as the person of Jesus Christ. While the content of the creation stories from Ben Lomond and Genesis Chapter One are different and the form in which they are carried, oral and written, is different, the common theme of the beginnings of land, people, and so on, appears to have had sufficient resonance to enable each to recognise the other and to interpret the other's story from within their own worldview. And though we do not have any documentary evidence, it is likely the Ben Lomond person, or people, were also doing their own oral translation of the 'principal parts' of Wilkinson's creation story into their own language.

At Wybalenna, as in churches and Robinson's travels, the Bible was read regularly during weekly divine services. Darling had been performing these for over a year, and Wilkinson since his more recent arrival, so the Ben Lomond people had some familiarity with the colonist Christian reverence for the biblical text. Wilkinson's translation suggests the printed biblical text was present in their conversations. He wrote to Governor Arthur '... I am certain they understand what I read to them and show at times a considerable interest in what they hear ...'[40] However, the exact role the written text played, and the interpretation the people formed about it, is unclear. The example in the previous chapter of the coalescing of kangaroo marrow, ochre and text suggests alternate ways of engaging with the written text.

Nevertheless, in this translation and interpretive experience we glimpse something of the different worldviews being shared in the conversation. The Coastal Plains people,[41] whose country was near the Ben Lomond people's, had stories of creation which were interpreted by Robinson in his journals. As mentioned earlier, in these stories beings came from the stars to the earth.[42] In Genesis, God (one being) made the heavens and the earth. In at least one Aboriginal story (*Nununi*, Bruny Island) the moon was female and sun male,[43] while in Genesis God, understood as exclusively male by colonist Christians, made these 'lights', a greater and a lesser one (Genesis chapter one, verse 16).

During his own language learning and conversations Wilkinson is likely to have explained something about the biblical creation stories, Genesis chapters, and their place within the larger book of the Bible. So although the formation of the translation into a new written form is important, the preceding oral dialogue from which the translation emerged is perhaps more important. For this is where the two different languages and worlds are open to each other and seek some mutual understanding and perhaps resonance in meaning. This occurred prior to the story becoming text. Through this dialogue both stories, and speakers, were changed.

For his part Wilkinson shows adaptability and flexibility, rather than a 'monologic' view. 'God' in the King James Version (KJV) text of the Bible became 'Godneh' with the meanings created through the conversations in the evolving *pidgin* that preceded the formation of the translated text. In this translated text Wilkinson introduced creatures that do not appear in the biblical text (Genesis 1:25).[44] This 'Godneh' making 'bullock' and 'bush kangaroo' may be somewhat similar to the Ben Lomond creation story, but unfortunately we do not have a copy with which to compare.[45] The reference to the kangaroo is evocative of the creation story *Wurati* told Robinson in July 1831[46] but it is unknown if the Ben Lomond clan had the same, or a similar story.

The insertion of 'bush kangaroo' may seem a minor point, but it does express Wilkinson's acknowledgement of 'Godneh' creating the animals of Ben Lomond country, and therefore 'God' is not limited to creatures appearing in the biblical narrative. These variations from the KJV text suggest an opening and expansion of Wilkinson's theological worldview, even if only for reasons of expediency. The insertion of 'Godneh' into Ben Lomond language was an enlarging of the Aboriginal people's worlds. Like the developing *pidgin*, the outcome is *not exactly* the King James Version of the Bible nor the Ben Lomond story, but an approximation taking some steps at interpreting each for the audience of the other.

It is also unclear how the Aboriginal people might have interpreted the Genesis story with its specific days of creation and people being made in the 'image' or 'likeness' of the creator. In *Wurati*'s story, Moihernee was married and his wife and children came to earth in the rain, thus indicating Moihernee is male, husband and father.[47] While Robinson noted some correspondence between *Wurati*'s and *Manalakina*'s creation stories,[48] it is unclear if the Ben Lomond stories were similar. Nor is it clear if the Aboriginal people interpreted God as supreme over all other gods or how they regarded the relationships between the various creator beings of different clans and stories from their own clan. But it does demonstrate they were willing to converse about their origin stories and hear Wilkinson at least talk, if not also read, about his.

As well as the insertions, there are many deletions from the biblical text of Genesis. About three-quarters of the words in Genesis Chapters One and Two are omitted from the translation. Words such as, 'day', 'night', 'firmament' and so on disappeared in the translation, as did the specific geographic location of Eden near the headwaters of the Pishon, Gihon, Tigris and Euphrates rivers (Genesis Chapter

Two, verses 10–14). Attempts to explain these omissions are pure conjecture, however some points can be made. One clear omission is the construction of time into seven days. This construction of time certainly became a regular part of life at Wybalenna, particularly the transference of the seventh day of rest (Sabbath) onto the first day of the week (Sunday) when divine service was performed and no work was to be done.[49] It was also incorporated into questions in catechetical examinations.[50] Wilkinson may have omitted it because at that time life at Wybalenna was not as regimented as when Robinson became commandant two years later.

The omission of 'heaven' in the 'firmament' was also only temporary. It became a regular feature of preaching by both Aboriginal and colonist preachers. Like the construction of time, these metaphors and the construction of one's spatial context are foundational to meaning-making. However, even when later Aboriginal preachers used the same words, European constructions of 'up' and 'down' should not be assumed as the only way of interpreting such metaphors as 'heaven' and 'hell'.

Another intriguing omission is the reference to people having 'dominion' over the creatures (Genesis 1:26). Like the lack of construction of time, and the spatial context, the absence — perhaps avoidance — of reference to the human relational context in the created world might have aided the beginnings of the conversation, but the contrast at the core of these worldviews could not be avoided for long. The appearance of the word 'dominion' in the earliest surviving writing tests of Aboriginal children suggest the concept was part of conversations at least from 1835 onwards when Robinson became commandant.[51]

The translation of Genesis occurred sometime between June 1833, when Wilkinson arrived, and September when he wrote to Governor Arthur. While there are no documents naming the participants, we can surmise their identities to some extent based on the language used and which speakers were at Wybalenna at that time. The Ben Lomond child Friday / Walter has been suggested because of his later writing.

Born in 1819 or 1820, Walter had been taken from his family at a young age and taught to read and write at the Orphan School in Hobart.[52] However, if the Hobart Orphan School register is reliable, Walter George Arthur was not at Wybalenna at all during Wilkinson's time as catechist. According to the register, Walter, known as Friday, was admitted to the School on 30 November 1832 and remained there until 26 May 1835.[53] It is possible that he had several separate stays at the school but this seems unlikely. The Aboriginal girl, Mathinna, had separate entries for her separate sojourns at the school, but there is only one entry for Walter. It seems unlikely that Walter was not at the Orphan School during the translation experience at

Wybalenna. As noted in the previous chapter, there are instances, however, where the dates in the Orphan School register do not synchronise with other sources, such as Robinson's journal, or catechist reports from Flinders Island.[54]

Walter is an obvious candidate for participation in the translation exercise, because of his later participation in writing the *Flinders Island Chronicle* with Thomas Bruny, and his later sermon and letter writing. He would have been 10 or 11 years of age at the time and, as will be seen in the catechism classes, children of this age could be sufficiently competent in their English to teach adults. As noted, Wilkinson was the first catechist at Wybalenna and only arrived halfway through 1833. It is possible that Walter was fluent in English before going to the Orphan School, and it is possible that Walter was at Wybalenna and participated in the translation, despite the register records. However, for this to be the case he would have had to have been removed from Wybalenna sometime after the translation (September 1833) but before Robinson became commandant (October 1835) because Walter, along with seven other children, are named as travelling with Robinson from the Orphan School to Wybalenna in October 1835.[55]

It is more likely that others from the Ben Lomond clan were involved in the translation. One can only ponder at why those involved in the translation did not talk about doing more translation later on when Walter was writing the *Flinders Island Chronicle*, sermons and letters. The 'English-only' policy of Robinson is the most likely explanation. It is possible that Walter no longer had any of his first language by the time he left the Orphan School, but this also seems unlikely since he entered the school at about ten years of age, spent a possible maximum of two and a half years there and had at least six adults at Wybalenna, including his parents, who continued speaking his first language when he arrived there in October 1835.

Identifying other Ben Lomond people at Wybalenna in 1833 who might have been involved is somewhat problematic because of reliance on Robinson's sometimes confusing records and Plomley linking multiple names. Nevertheless, some of those who might have been involved in the translation include Rolepa[56] and his wife Luggernemennener[57] who were leaders of the Ben Lomond clan and about the same age as Wilkinson. Robinson believed these two were in fact the parents of Walter, and that he was their eldest son.[58]

Luggernemennener is mentioned several times in Robinson's journal, including taking people to John Batman's in November 1830 to avoid the Black Line[59] and the previously mentioned visit to church and Robinson's house in Hobart.[60] In this she appears comfortable conversing with Robinson and Batman and so would have been a competent participant in the conversation and translation with Wilkinson.

Another possibility is the brother of Luggernemennener, Trowlebunner / Achilles[61] and his wife Toogernuppertootenner / Maria II,[62] who both travelled with Robinson in the north-east.[63] Neither is recorded with Robinson on the west coast during 1833 when Wilkinson was translating Genesis at Wybalenna. Another person, *Tanganutara* / Sarah, also travelled with Robinson in the north-east.[64] She also was not with Robinson in 1833 so is likely to have been at Wybalenna and could also have been involved in the translation.[65] A further possible participant is Margaret, who is listed in Robinson's 1832 census of the Aboriginal people at Wybalenna, but her clan identity is unclear.[66] Several other people are identified with the Ben Lomond clan in the list of those attending the school in February 1836[67] and later catechism examinations,[68] but it is not clear if they were at Wybalenna when the translation conversations were occurring from June to September 1833.

Wilkinson's letter to Governor Arthur suggests more than one Ben Lomond person was involved. He wrote,

> ... I am certain *they* understand what I read to *them* and show at times a considerable interest in what *they* hear ... [my emphasis][69]

Several of those mentioned above could have been involved, and / or others. It seems conclusive at least that Walter Arthur was not involved, and likely that two or more Ben Lomond adults were, including his mother.

Each of these people mentioned above had extensive involvement with either Robinson or other colonists such as John Batman. They demonstrated a growing familiarity with the English language and a continuing use of their own first language at Wybalenna. However, there is no evidence of Walter or any of the other Ben Lomond people, or other clans, choosing to write their own translations of their own stories into English, or of translating the Bible or other English books into their own languages. The most obvious explanation is that they were not yet literate people and continued to prefer their customary oral rather than written communications. Governor Arthur's assimilationist agenda may be the more likely explanation[70] but it may have been that they did not want to tell their stories in the language of the colonists, particularly when most Aboriginal people did not write in English at all.

A further issue is the intended audience for the written translation. If the Ben Lomond people were not literate, who was? And to whom did Wilkinson provide it? Surviving documents show Wilkinson provided a written excerpt of his work to the Governor and to Backhouse and Walker. Neither of these 'audiences' could read or speak the Ben Lomond language, but both had significant power over Wilkinson's place at Wybalenna, particularly in the context of his conflict with Darling and Maclachlan, the medical officer. His copy to the

Governor was probably to demonstrate an example of his work since arriving at the settlement and as evidence of fulfilling his primary role during the flurry of his other written correspondence complaining to the Governor about both Darling and Maclachlan.

Walker wrote his copy from Wilkinson's notes while visiting Wybalenna between November 1833 and January 1834. He visited the settlement on behalf of the Governor to try to resolve the conflict between Wilkinson, Darling and others. Walker's report would have a significant influence on the Governor's decision about Wilkinson's future.

Another possible audience is the congregation in the Sunday services at Wybalenna. As mentioned earlier, scriptures were read during the weekly Sabbath services so it is possible that the translation was read on one or more of these occasions. Given Darling's use of 'Wybalenna' (a Ben Lomond word) for the settlement site and continuing to use Aboriginal people's names in their first language, it is possible the translation could have been read during a Sunday service. But weighted against this is the depth of conflict between Darling and Wilkinson and to what degree this affected the content and practice of Sunday services. Walter Arthur is the only Ben Lomond person shown by the records from Wybalenna to be sufficiently literate to be able to read such a document, but he was not at Wybalenna at that time.

When Robinson arrived, there is no indication of any similar translation ever taking place, and he actively discouraged any use of *pidgin* in Sunday services.[71] It is therefore likely that the translation of Genesis remained an oral experience for the Ben Lomond people and it is unknown how they viewed this transformation of their spoken words into the written form.[72]

According to Plomley, Wilkinson's efforts with Genesis were not appreciated by Governor Arthur, who, in annotating Backhouse and Walker's report wrote: 'The perusal of this leads me deeply to regret that a person who can be so useful should have, unfortunately, acted so imprudently'.[73] While Plomley, and following him, Van Toorn,[74] seem to assume that Arthur's regret was specifically related to the translation of Genesis, it is more likely that the large volume of correspondence to Arthur from Darling and Wilkinson complaining about each other and making various accusations about 'bigotry', 'indiscreet language' and other behaviour[75] is much more likely to be the source of Arthur's 'regret' than the beginnings of the Bible translation. Wilkinson's translation was sent to the Governor in September 1833. Amidst several letters complaining about Wilkinson, Darling suspended him in October. In response Arthur sent Backhouse and Walker to investigate the situation during November 1833 to January 1834. In their report in January 1834 Backhouse and Walker refer to:

> the expression used by Mr Tho Wilkinson tow^d the Commandant in some of his official communications + his indiscreet conduct relative to the Surgeon ...

and

> ... intimating in his communication to the Govt that after what had passed it was impossible that the Catechist and himself could ever co-operate again.[76]
>
> T. W's chief defect appears to be a want of tact in keeping up an amicable intercourse with his brother officers with all of whom he has had some difference or misunderstanding that has led to the entire estrangement of himself and family from their society.[77]

Arthur's annotation to Wilkinson's September translation is dated 27 January 1834, following the report by Backhouse and Walker about the prolonged conflict between commandant, catechist, medical officer and storekeeper.[78] The 'reconciliation' they mediated was unable to address the underlying conflict, and within a few months Arthur removed Wilkinson.[79] The dating of the annotation in January 1834 suggests Arthur's regret is at the conflict, the irreconcilable differences between catechist and other officers, and the sooner than expected dismissal. Arthur's annotation could actually be read as appreciating the usefulness of Wilkinson's translation rather than dismissing it.

Arthur's removal of Wilkinson as catechist in early 1834 was followed by the removal of Darling as commandant in July.[80] Soon after Darling's departure, Governor Arthur appointed another catechist from the Church of England, Robert Clark, on 11 July 1834,[81] and then Henry Nickolls arrived on 24 September 1834 to become the new commandant, but for only a year.[82] Clark continued the practices of Sunday services and teaching people in his home. He did not resume any translations of biblical text into any of the Aboriginal languages. He did, however, introduce other changes, some of which were at least as controversial with the subsequent commandant, Robinson. Some of these were played out during Sunday church services.

Sunday services

Sunday church services were a regular and pivotal part of life at Wybalenna, and in the broader colonial life noted in previous chapters. During Robinson's travels he continued to perform divine service in the bush.[83] The performance of Christian worship was central to the identity and relationships among colonists, particularly those with political power. Of particular interest are the ways Aboriginal people interacted with and interpreted these religious rituals.

The earliest reference to a Sunday church service at Wybalenna seems to be on 4 March 1832 when Robinson was visiting the settlement two days after Darling arrived. Robinson described the occasion:

> Today the whole of the aborigines on the establishment (near a hundred in number) attended divine service under a large awning that was erected for the occasion. The whole of the whites also attended, likewise Ensign Darling and Captain Bateman. I read the prayers, at the conclusion of which I read the fifty-third chapter of Isiah [sic] and then concluded with an extempore prayer. It was an interesting occasion. The most marked attention was observed. Before the service commenced Tom explained to the natives the nature of the service. All the chiefs with their wives sat by themselves.[84]

The following week Darling ordered that divine service be performed 'every Sunday morning at 11 o'clock when all persons belonging to the Establishment will attend'.[85] This was while the settlement was at 'the Lagoons'. All men were to cease work at noon on Saturday in order to 'wash their clothes and make themselves clean for the following Sunday'.[86] The performance of Christian worship was therefore closely linked with the authority of the commandant, the cessation of 'work' and washing clothes and bodies in preparation. The cessation of work and requirement of bodily and clothing cleanliness was an expression of how the colonists understood 'civilise and Christianise' for their own lives. To Aboriginal eyes, the practice of preparation for the performance of ritual and sacred storytelling was familiar, as was a directive given by a clan leader. But what was clearly different here was that whereas Aboriginal people smeared their bodies with grease and ochre in their preparations, the colonists completely washed their bodies and clothes in readiness for their performance of ritual and sacred storytelling.[87] This sharp contrast between cleaning and smearing was quite different to the adoption by Aboriginal people of the colonist practice of special dress for Sunday services.

Initially the buildings at Wybalenna were rudimentary. In the earlier outdoor church services Aboriginal people are likely to have sat where and with whom they chose. The lack of architecture at the time suggests they were likely to have been on the ground, perhaps in clan groups.[88] In late 1833 the entire population comprised approximately one hundred and fifty people; one hundred and twenty of whom were Aboriginal and thirty colonists. If most Aboriginal people were at the service, they are still likely to have outnumbered the colonists by at least three to one. After two years of services performed in the open air, Backhouse and Walker reported in January 1834,

> It is highly expedient that a suitable building should be erected on the Settlement as a school room and a Chapel.[89]

The first such building adjoined the catechist's quarters soon after Clark arrived. The cramped space in the chapel was a noted factor in people being absent from services: 'the smallness of the place in which we met and the manner in which the people were wedged together ... would have produced the same effect in any congregation.'[90] It seems there was simply no room to fit them in.

When Robinson arrived in October 1835 he described the room as 'extremely damp, in want of a wooded floor and having no chimney'.[91] By then the chapel had been changed to a room adjoining a 'native hut' which Robinson described as

> incommodious and bleak and moreover without a fireplace (warmth being essential to the comfort of the natives), and it was likewise wet (the rain not only came in at the roof which is in some parts was quite flat or leanto, but run in off the ground and covered the floor).[92]

Following Robinson's survey he immediately made plans for the chapel to take over the adjoining Aboriginal hut. The renovations included a fireplace, windows and an east-facing door sheltered from the westerly winds. It was completed by the beginning of December 1835.[93]

This spatial move from outdoors to damp indoors, firstly adjoining the catechist's house, then the commandant's[94] house and then an Aboriginal family's hut, influenced how Aboriginal people interpreted Sunday services. As mentioned above when examining the Bible translation, and as will become apparent when discussing the schools, the Ben Lomond clan seem to have been the largest clan and taken a particular interest in the religious practices of the colonists. It seems the chapel–hut was among those 'upper huts' occupied by Ben Lomond and Big River people.[95] It is worth considering how they, and other clans, may have interpreted the location of the colonist's religious ceremony in what was identifiably one of their buildings. The chapel–hut remained located among Aboriginal huts for almost three more years before the brick chapel was completed in July 1838.[96]

Most Aboriginal people did not attend Christian worship at Wybalenna, though the convicts were forced to. There was strong pressure to attend[97] but not everyone did so and there does not seem to have been any punishment for not attending. Perhaps those who did attend were making a choice to do so. It is important to consider their experience of 'worship' was initially outdoors, among tree limbs, sitting down, probably on the ground (the rudimentary nature of the houses at the time suggests chairs were unlikely to have been available), and in a public group. It could be regarded as something similar to, though also clearly different from, the Aboriginal clan gatherings with people of various ages, genders, and leaders with particular roles in storytelling and ritual performance, as described earlier.

The service followed the order prescribed in the *Book of Common Prayer* and therefore was conducted in English and led by those who could read English. Sunday services were led by Wilkinson, who within a short time had completed his translation of the 'principal parts' of the first chapters of Genesis into Ben Lomond language. This is likely to have been incorporated into how Aboriginal people interpreted Wilkinson's role leading the ceremony. Other officers or visitors, such as Backhouse and Walker, read from the recognisable book (Bible) containing the colonist 'origin-story' and other stories. Some Aboriginal adults (most of the children were still at the Orphan School) had seen a form of this service in huts,[98] buildings,[99] and in the open air[100] and so are likely to have been familiar with its religious nature. It seems more likely that Aboriginal people were spectators, rather than participants, at this colonist 'corroboree'. Many were fluent in English but it seems more of them conversed with each other in the evolving *pidgin* of Wybalenna. This suggests their first languages and worldviews were their primary frames of reference for interpreting what they witnessed.

Therefore they may have interpreted Wilkinson's role as something like one of their own ceremonial leaders, such as Ben Lomond leaders, Rolepa or Luggernemenener, who are likely to have been conversing regularly with Wilkinson during the recent cold season about their respective origin-stories. Backhouse and Walker could be regarded as visiting storytellers from a neighbouring clan. They read several chapters from the New Testament, taking about 15 minutes to read, depending on the passage chosen, and if it were from a Gospel would be a narrative style probably similar to a series of stories told by a clan leader.

It is one among many unanswered questions to wonder at how Aboriginal people might have interpreted 'a reading from the Gospel of St Matthew …' of a story about the person Jesus, but written by an unknown and not present person, Matthew, for example, and being read by Wilkinson, Walker or one of the other colonists present. It is clearly a story from another place, another person's story, but known by the colonists who are now sharing it with the Aboriginal people. This practice of story sharing seems similar to story sharing referred to by Robinson where after *Wurati* told his creation story, Robinson asked the other Aboriginal people present if their creation stories were similar.[101]

Another consideration is how the Aboriginal people interpreted the person of Jesus, whom they heard about in the stories and whom the colonists sometimes addressed with the particular posturing in prayer. Was Jesus seen as a spirit ancestor like those from the stars? A returned, but not physically present, ancestor, like the 'white' people? A storyteller–lawgiver from another tribe? While the colonist distinction between scripture reading and prayer is recognisable to those familiar with church practice, it is worth considering how those Aboriginal people less familiar might have interpreted this practice of readings addressed to the people and prayers addressed to God, and to consider how they distinguished between stories to other Aboriginal people and those to their spirit beings, if they did so at all.

The later catechist, Clark, kept records of the number of services and number of Aboriginal people attending for the three months of September to December 1836. He reported that Aboriginal people averaged from sixty to eighty both forenoon and afternoon and Tuesday evening attendances varied from thirty to sixty, a cold evening and a late hour of them taking tea being cited as cause for the falling attendance.[102] Robinson's census in January 1836 indicated a population of 108 with 12 children.[103] Only four deaths were recorded that year[104] so the overall Aboriginal population was about 110 or so. This shows that between twenty and forty per cent of Aboriginal people did not attend Sunday services and between forty and seventy per cent did not attend school in those three months. It therefore seems apparent that those who did probably wanted to be there, even though the reasons for their choice may be difficult to know.

It seems, as Robinson reported, that Aboriginal people were not forced to attend church in the same way the convicts were. Different clans were regularly away from Wybalenna on hunting trips, visiting other islands or some other activity, including on Sundays.[105] Robinson wrote, 'If the people should once object to come, it would not be in my power nor would it be right had I the power to compel them against their will. They are free subjects'.[106] People may argue about what it meant for Aboriginal people at Wybalenna to be 'free subjects' but it seems clear that they were not forced to attend church services. Robinson, however, did offer a number of incentives and, it seems, gave preferential treatment to those Aboriginal people who complied with his desire for an English language Christian faith.

The content of the church services expresses much of the dynamic of Wybalenna. Superficially it appears as a site of colonist imposition. The erection of the seventy-five foot (about twenty metres) flagstaff at the end of December 1835 and the Sunday (Sabbath) day flag-raising connected Christian worship with a crucial symbol of colonist identity and authority.[107] But behind these apparent expressions of compliance or a lack of protest, successive commandants, catechists, and visitors such as Walker acknowledged that Aboriginal languages and behavioural differences continued.[108] Like the previously discussed Bible translation, the 'outer conformity' of clothing ought not be assumed to indicate 'inner' conformity.

During the earlier years services were described as beginning with 'church prayer', meaning from the Church of England *Book of Common Prayer*, and involved 'hearing Scripture' read in English by an officer of the settlement, singing hymns in English, an exhortation from an officer of the settlement, before concluding with church prayers.[109] The reference to portions from the *Book of Common Prayer* do not indicate if the whole service was followed each week or just the prayers, but it is indicative of the regular format practiced by Wilkinson, and by Clark, as instructed by the rural dean, Reverend Palmer.[110] However Clark also made a number of adaptations, most of which appear to be seeking a way that was more akin to Aboriginal gatherings, and most of which Robinson despised.

When Robinson arrived in October 1835 he was unhappy with what he witnessed and immediately began his long, but ultimately unsuccessful, campaign to change Clark's practices, especially from speaking the 'gibberish so common on the settlement'. Robinson believed the practice 'had a bad tendency by exciting ridicule in the minds of the natives, particularly as it was not the native language.'[111] This criticism was in stark contrast to Robinson's own initial practice at Bruny Island where he sought to learn and preach in the local language.[112]

Clark's practice therefore seems to have been to abide by the rural dean's instructions to 'read the church prayers'[113] but he also adapted this and sought to address Aboriginal people in the 'language of the settlement', the evolving *pidgin*. He delivered sermons without written notes and in the 'gibberish' as Robinson called it.[114] He changed his style of prayer from the more common kneeling with head bowed and eyes closed to one of opening his eyes and being 'full of gesture'.[115] Robinson's agitation about Clark's prayers was exacerbated whenever Clark failed to include particular reference to Robinson in the prayers.[116] The pettiness of this last criticism is clear in Robinson's report that in praying for the Governor, Clark prayed that God would 'preserve him that is over this colony and settlement; query F I colony?'[117] It seems Robinson was agitated that Clark did not make it explicit that 'this colony' was the settlement on Flinders Island, and the 'Governor' of that colony was Robinson. It suggests more about Robinson's pomposity than a noteworthy error by Clark.[118]

Clark's clothing during services was also a constant irritation, particularly that he did not wear a black gown like a clergyman.[119] In these examples, though, Clark could be seen to be attempting to develop something of a bi-cultural approach to the prayer book and evolving *pidgin*. In the next chapter I will examine the evolving *pidgin* records of several Aboriginal people at the evening schools but it is important to note that Clark seems to be alone among the officers of Wybalenna in speaking sermons sometimes in this evolving *pidgin* or plain English. Needless to say, Robinson was never impressed.[120] Some examples of Clark's sermons, as reported by Robinson, include:

> 28 Dec 1835 "my black brothers and sisters". He spoke about the fall of our first parents, about the Devil jumping up in the heart of Adam and making him eat the apple, but the manner and language used was altogether absurd.[121]
>
> On Tuesday (9 February 1836) last [Clark] said God did not gammon, there was no gammon with God, it was beneath him to gammon.[122]

> 9th May 1837 Mr Clark gave at this meeting another specimen of what he considers the native language. He told Louisa and Juliet they would CRACK.A.BUGYAR (meaning "dead") when they would die. Mr Dickenson remembered the catechist saying to his audience on Sunday that Jesus Christ tumbled down from his mother; I also heard the same.[123]
>
> 19th November 1837 A specimen of the catechist's sermon: he began - CARNE black woman too LUBRE what I say don't be lolling about sit up right there mind what I say to you. I am going to talk about death. You don't like to hear about death. I don't wonder of it. I seen the two woman that died, they were as well as you. Now mind what I say. What for you lost it, what for you having forgotten it?[124]

Like the Aboriginal preachers at the Saturday evenings of 'mutual instruction', discussed in the next chapter, Clark's use of the evolving *pidgin* in Sunday services was happening at the same time as the fairly regimented English language catechetical examinations and so Clark, in some ways like Aboriginal people, was performing the regimented catechetical examinations for Robinson and at the same time speaking evolving *pidgin* to Aboriginal people in Sunday Services. His reference to the Aboriginal people as 'brothers and sisters' needs to be seen in the context of the wider colonial context where Aboriginal people's humanity was not only doubted but also often rejected.

Clark's use of spatial language, at least as reported by Robinson, is also noteworthy. Humanity's first parents 'fall', Jesus Christ 'tumbled down' or 'dropped' from his mother and the devil 'jumped up in the heart of Adam'. A number of the Aboriginal clans had creation stories where creator beings first came down from the stars. *Wurati* had told a story of Moihernee tumbling down to earth and his wife and children coming down in the rain.[125] Clark's reference to Jesus Christ 'tumbling down' may be his attempt to convey the Christian teaching of the Son of God being from God who is 'up in heaven'. If 'tumbling' was simply a reference to Jesus being born from his mother, it is doubtful it would have elicited a report from Dickenson to Robinson.[126]

The reference to the devil 'jumping up' in the heart of Adam may be an attempt to connect with those Aboriginal beliefs where the devils were in the ground[127] but became more active when they jumped up. This 'jumping up' is also used to describe their expectation that after they die they would 'jump up' into the next. Several Aboriginal people used this same phrase in similar contexts in their addresses in 1838 such as Dowwringgi, 'let Jesus Christ "jump up" in your hearts',[128] and Druemerterpunner that Jesus 'jump up and went to heaven' after he died.[129] Clark's description of 'God did not gammon' is that God does not deceive or lie.[130] Exhorting people to not tell lies is a regular theme in the school addresses by Aboriginal speakers such as Noemy,[131] Drinene,[132] Druemerterpunner,[133] and Dowwringgi.[134]

Aboriginal contributors to the Sunday services

The participation of Aboriginal people in the Sunday services was very limited. Aside from congregational singing, few Aboriginal people shared in the leadership of services. Walter Arthur and Thomas Bruny were involved most often.[135] Clark reported

> the clerk who assists me at the Divine service is the Native youth formerly called Friday now Walter he is the son of a Chieftain he reads the responses very well has a knowledge of the scriptural history and is a well conducted lad.[136]

In February 1837 Robinson appointed Walter and Thomas to read prayers at the school and Walter to lead the congregational singing and receive 1/- weekly. An older man, Makeaduru, was elected verger and received 1/- each week.[137] The role of verger is usually associated with Christian worship but in this instance seems to be limited to the Saturday school. The payments may have been a 'reward' given out by Robinson to encourage attendance, particularly when twenty to forty per cent of Aboriginal people were not attending services.[138]

Later that year, 15 October 1837, one of Thomas' papers was read at the morning and evening services.[139] These papers were editions of the *Flinders Island Chronicle* and other writings by Thomas and Walter Arthur. What is unusual about this is it is the only reference to one of their papers being read during a *Sunday* service. The other four occasions, all during 1837, all occurred at school, three at a Saturday school[140] and one at a Wednesday school.[141] It is unclear if Thomas read his own papers. At the service a fortnight later Robinson was quite critical of Thomas' reading, probably from the *Book of Common Prayer*, describing it as 'very bad'. Not surprisingly he held Clark responsible.[142]

Interpretations and attendance by Aboriginal people

There were varied interpretations by Aboriginal people of what they experienced. The cessation of 'work' such as catching fish, collecting firewood or bathing was mentioned earlier.[143] Toward the end of 1836 a group informed Robinson

> that they did not hunt on God's day that they were singing hymns and repeating the Lord's Prayer.[144]

One Sunday in May 1837 Clark reported ten to twelve people in one of the native huts singing hymns and receiving catechetical instruction from Warwe.[145] A few months later Clark reported a

> party who had been out hunting informed me that on the Sabbath day they observed the settlement flag which is hoisted every Sunday and that they would not hunt but continued in their huts singing and praying and talking of God.[146]

Wurati returned from a separate trip a few weeks later and reported that while out in the bush Albert

> sung Sunday corroboree and read book and prayed to God at night but the sealing women used red ochre and grease and danced their native song and did not mind those things, Saturday 30 September 1837.[147]

These are further examples of ways Aboriginal people not only varied from each other in their responses to Christian faith but were also interpreting it from within their own world, noting the parallel between Sunday 'corroboree', book and prayer and the red ochre, grease and dancing and singing native songs. This seems to have been reciprocated in Clark's attempts to use *pidgin* and adapting his own practices in Sunday services.

But not everyone was actively engaged in these interpretations. Robinson reported soon after his arrival that the Aboriginal people seem disinterested in what happened during the services, describing them as 'listless, drowsy, careless and indifferent, and indulging in somnolency'.[148] While this is also part of his ongoing criticism of Clark and was used as some of the rationale for introducing the schools in early 1836, there is probably some truth to these observations, at least on some occasions. Clark himself reported,

> there are still a large number who do not appear to have their attention awakened, sometimes they appear to be alive to the statements made to them at other times they remain in a listless state in the same manner in which many congregations in civilized society appear at different periods.[149]

Clark noted his own fluctuating engagement:

> My mind rises and falls with that undulating interest but which frequently terminates with disappointment when on the following Monday I make enquiry relative to what they heard on the previous day.[150]

Clark interpreted the apparent listlessness as similar to many colonist attendees at church. It is important to note the contrasting behaviour recorded by Robinson and others when Aboriginal people were listening to each other. Aboriginal conversations may have been a more interactive style with story telling and the acrobatic dances rather than just sitting still.

Children at church services

One final point to note in regard to the Sunday church services is the regular separation of Aboriginal children from the adults. Aboriginal children had been removed to the Orphan School from 1832 to 1834 with most returning by October 1835. The reports by the catechist, Robert Clark, for Sunday services in 1837 indicate that for most of that year seven to ten Aboriginal children regularly attended the convicts' church services, mostly the service at 4pm.[151] This period includes the first four months of 1837 when the children had been sleeping 'at the native houses',[152] as well as subsequently when they were living in the catechist's hut, so their sleeping arrangements are not sufficient explanation. Robinson's strong abhorrence at liaisons between convicts and Aboriginal people makes this Sunday practice all the more noteworthy even if there is no obvious explanation. It may have been simply for reasons of space, given the crowded chapel during the other services, which usually had more than twice the number of people. In the next chapter I will provide more detailed examination of the school classes occurring at this time, but suffice to say at this point that children and adults were involved together in those classes.

It suggests the separation in the Sunday services, where they were less involved and more like spectators, to be for reasons of space. Considerably more flexibility and dynamism was occurring during the schools and particularly the evening schools of mutual instruction.

ENDNOTES CHAPTER THREE

1. 'Creole' and 'pidgin' are technical linguistic terms: '"Pidgin" is a contact language used among people who have no other language in common. When a nativised pidgin becomes the language of a new speech community, the process is known as "creolisation". This creolised pidgin, or "creole" is structurally more complex as it has to meet all the communicative requirements of native speakers. The structural complexity of a creole is comparable to that of other languages'. Muhlhausler, P., 1991, 'Overview of the pigdin and creole languages of Australia', in Romaine, S., (ed.), *Language in Australia*. Melbourne: Cambridge University Press, pp. 159-173. Further research into the languages spoken at Wybalenna would be helpful. The short time in which multiple Aboriginal languages were interacting at Wybalenna suggests a pidgin language was developing which had not yet evolved into a creole. Therefore I will use 'pidgin' in describing the evolving common language rather than creole.
2. Attwood, 1989, p. 150.
3. Johnston, A., 2004, 'The Little Empire of Wybalenna: Becoming Colonial in Australia', *Journal of Australian Studies*, 81, p. 19.
4. King Island was suggested. *Colonial Times*, 1 December 1826.
5. Plomley, 1987, p. 54.
6. Plomley, 1987, p. 15.
7. Plomley, 1966, pp. 479–480.
8. Plomley, 1987, p. 35, 36.
9. Plomley, 1966, pp. 585–586.
10. Plomley, 1966, pp. 701–703.
11. Plomley, 1966 pp. 741–743, 819– 21.
12. Plomley, 1987, p. 35.
13. Plomley, 1987, p. 48.
14. Plomley, 1987, p. 22.
15. Stevens, 2017, pp. 43–4.
16. ML Walker Papers, B727 CY1408 p. 310.
17. As Commandant, Robinson does not seem to have ever referred to it by its Aboriginal name, but only as the 'Settlement'. Likewise correspondence from the Colonial Secretary's Office. It is named as Wybalenna throughout this chapter as part of trying to consider

18 One group was removed between August and October, though the Orphan School Register and Darling's reports differ on the dates, and a second group between November–December, where again, the dates differ. ML Walker Papers, B727 CY1408, 9 October 1832, and Plomley, 1987, p. 63.
19 ML Robinson Papers, A7062 CY549, p. 79.
20 ML Walker Papers, B727 CY1408, p. 322. This was a little less than two years before Robinson became Commandant.
21 Purtscher, 1993, unpaginated. This is another indication that the numbers of Aboriginal children at the Orphan School were, in this peak year, a substantial proportion, but still not a majority of the overall number of Aboriginal children.
22 Plomley, 1987, pp. 940–941.
23 ML Robinson Papers, A7044 Vol. 23, CY548.
24 ML Robinson Papers, A7062 CY549, p. 161.
25 Plomley, 1987, p. 83.
26 Five boys are entered in the Orphan School Register on 3 September 1834 while James Allen was 'interim' commandant and one month after Robert Clark had been appointed as catechist following the removal of Thomas Wilkinson, Orphan School Register, TAHO SWD 28.
27 ML Robinson Papers, A7044 CY548, pp. 102–13.
28 Plomley, 1987, p. 69.
29 *Hobart Town Courier*, 2 August 1833, p. 3. Wilkinson appears in the Wesleyan Methodist Biographies, 'WILKINSON, Thomas (1799–1881) Born on 6 April 1799 at Sunderland, County Durham, England, the son of David Wilkinson, sea pilot, and his wife Elizabeth, nee Dixon. He was married on 5 November 1820 at London, England, to Louisa Price, daughter of Henry Price and his wife Charlotte, nee Frisley. Worked in the East London area for many years. Arrived at Hobart, Van Diemen's Land, in March 1833. Religious instructor to the Aboriginal people on Flinder's Island', Wesleyan Methodist Biographies, http://www.companyofangels.net/evbiomth.html, accessed 17/5/2014.
30 ML Walker Papers, B727 CY1408, p. 322.
31 Plomley, N. J. B., 1976, *A Word-list of the Tasmanian Aboriginal Languages*. Launceston; Foot & Playsted, pp. 41–42.
32 TAHO CSO 7578.
33 ML Walker Papers, 9 Dec 1833, B727 CY1408, p. 313. I do not propose to examine these translations in detail as the particular linguistics are not the focus of this chapter, but both versions and a copy of the King James Version of Genesis 1 with a ~~strikethrough~~ the words Wilkinson omitted from it, are in Appendix C.
34 ML Walker Papers, 9 Dec 1833, B727 CY1408, p. 311.
35 ML Walker Papers, 9 Dec 1833, B727 CY1408, p. 311.
36 ML Walker Papers, 9 Dec 1833, B727 CY1408, p. 311. Crackneh meant something akin to 'sit down' and pomlch akin to 'make', Plomley, 1976, p. 391, 291. Walker also gathered Aboriginal words and songs, transcribing some into literate form, Plomley, 1987, pp. 288–291.
37 ML Walker Papers, 9 Dec 1833, B727 CY1408, p. 311.
38 ML Walker Papers, B727 CY1408, unpaginated.
39 See also, Johnson, A., 2001, 'The Book Eaters: Textuality, modernity, and the London Missionary Society', *Semeia*, 88, pp. 25–6.
40 In author's possession.
41 Cameron, 2011, pp. 8 – 19.
42 Plomley, 1966, pp. 373 – 74, 376, 392, 399.
43 Plomley, 1966, p. 380.
44 ML Walker Papers, 9 Dec 1833, B727 CY1408, p. 311, and Plomley, 1976, pp. 41, 42.
45 Robinson had gone further than Wilkinson in his initial attempts translating sermons into *Nununi* language where he used 'parlerdi' for God (31 May 1829), (Plomley, 1966, p. 61), see Chapter Two, but his

initial openness closed down before, or at, Wybalenna where he maintained an English-only practice of Christian faith and discouraged the catechist, and others from using anything other than English.
46. Plomley, 1966, pp. 373-74.
47. Plomley, 1966, pp. 373-74.
48. Plomley, 1966, p. 399.
49. Settlement Order 9, 11 March 1832, ML Robinson Papers A7074 Vol 52, CY825, unpaginated. Another example was when Dray and her husband stopped their 'work' of fishing on Sundays, ML Robinson Papers, A7062 CY549, pp. 166-167. These changes to people's interpretation of time is similar to Attwood's discussion of the changing spatial context at Ramahyuck. See Attwood, B., 1994, *A Life Together, A Life Apart*. Carlton; Melbourne University Press. See also, Nanni, G., 2012, *The Colonisation of Time: Ritual, Routine and Resistance in the British Empire*. Manchester; Manchester University Press.
50. ML Robinson Papers, A7044 CY548, pp. 282-288, also A7066 CY551, pp. 105-109.
51. ML Robinson Papers, A7074 CY825, p. 55.
52. Van Toorn, P., 2002, 'Before the Second Reformation: Nineteenth Aboriginal Mediations of the Bible in Van Diemens Land', *Semeia*, 88, p. 48.
53. Orphan School Register, TAHO SWD, 28.
54. One example is that of Thomas Thompson who is entered in the Orphan School Register as arriving on 9 May 1836 (4 year old, parents unknown, half caste) and leaving 26 August 1847, Purtscher, 1993, 'Children', unpaginated. However Robert Clark's report of examinations on 9 May 1837 (exactly one year after Thomas' arrival at the Orphan School) has extensive questioning of Thomas Thompson where he is described as 'about 11 years of age and well conducted, being instructed in the trade of a carpenter. He is a teacher in the school', ML Robinson Papers, A7044 CY548, pp. 288-291, but note the age difference between Orphan School Register (4 years old in 1836) and Catechetical Examination (11 years old in 1837). It seems more likely that Thomas was at Wybalenna doing catechetical examinations rather than at the Orphan School.
55. Plomley, 1987, Annotation 14 Sept 1835, pp. 619-620.
56. Plomley, 1987, p. 824.
57. Plomley, 1987, p. 806.
58. ML Robinson Papers, A7044 CY548, pp. 278-282. See also Plomley, 1987, pp. 851, 843, 824. Their other son, Rolepana, was living with John Batman at Ben Lomond at the time with a boy from a neighbouring clan. Rolepa is listed as his father and Luggernemennene as his possible mother, Plomley, 1987, pp. 824, 910, note 4.
59. Plomley, 1987, p. 276.
60. Plomley, 1987, p. 279.
61. Plomley, 1987, p. 830.
62. Plomley, 1987, p. 863.
63. Plomley, 1987, p. 274.
64. Plomley, 1987, p. 364, 391.
65. She is also listed as 'being with child by Rew' (Plomley, 1987, p. 873), and as the mother of Fanny Cochrane, (Plomley, 1987, Appendix 2:D, p. 946). Fanny's involvement with the church will be discussed later.
66. Plomley, 1987, p. 873.
67. School list February 1836: Christopher, Philip, ML Robinson Papers, A7062 CY549, pp. 145-146 and A7062 CY549, p. 337.
68. Catechism list May 1837: Christopher, Philip and Maria, ML Robinson Papers, A7044 CY548, pp. 272, 274, 297.
69. In author's possession.
70. Van Toorn, 2006, *Writing Never Arrives Naked*. Canberra; Aboriginal Studies Press, p. 101.
71. Plomley, 1987, p. 304.
72. Hofmeyer, in writing about the story of *Pilgrim's Progress*, in African contexts, described the interplay of oral and written forms of the story. Oral forms preceded the written thereby creating a 'proto-audience' for when the text became available, Hofmyr, I., 2003, 'Portable Landscapes' in Trigger, D., & Griffiths, G., *Disputed Territories*. Hong Kong: Hong Kong University Press, p. 139. While Wilkinson's translation did not proceed,

the existence of the Genesis creation story in pre- or neo-literate form among Ben Lomond people and between them and Wilkinson was itself a significant inter-religious dialogue and probably contributed to ongoing involvement of Ben Lomond people in catechetical classes and writing.
73 Plomley, 1976, p. 69.
74 Van Toorn, 2006, p. 100.
75 ML Walker Papers, 9 Dec 1833, B727 CY1408, pp. 310-11, see also Johnston, 2004, pp. 23-31.
76 ML Walker Papers, B727 CY1408, p. 299.
77 ML Walker Papers, B727 CY1408, p. 307.
78 See for example, Johnston, 2004.
79 It may have occurred in April, Plomley, 1987, p. 70, however the *Daily Journal* records '18th February 1834 *Shamrock* returned and got under way for Green Island to carry Mr Wilkinson and family', ML Robinson Papers, A7074 Vol 52, CY825.
80 Settlement Order, 28 July 1834, ML Robinson Papers, A7074 Vol 52, CY825.
81 ML Robinson Papers, A7062 CY549, p. 79, Harris, 1990, p. 99.
82 Plomley, 1987, p. 78.
83 For example, Plomley, 1966, pp. 97, 117, 187, 195, 331.
84 Plomley, 1966, p. 593.
85 Settlement Order 9, 11 March 1832, ML Robinson Papers, A7074 Vol. 52, CY825, unpaginated.
86 Settlement Order 1, 23 March 1832, ML Robinson Papers, A7074 Vol. 52, CY825, unpaginated. The cleaning of bodies and wearing of 'fine clothes' for Christian services had already been notices by Aboriginal people and an interpretation that linked it with their practice of applying grease and ochre, Plomley, 1966, p. 594.
87 The washing of grease and ochre from the bodies of Aboriginal people was later identified as a factor in their ill health at Wybalenna, ML Robinson Papers, A7066 CY551, pp. 201–221.
88 A little over two years later Robinson describes a meal where they 'sat down on the grass to dine in true aboriginal style'. Plomley, 1987, p. 339.
89 ML Walker Papers, Report to Arthur, B727 CY1408, p. 322.
90 ML Robinson Papers, A7062 CY549, pp. 315–317.
91 TAHO CSO 1/18798, pp. 84–85.
92 Plomley, 1987, pp. 313–14.
93 Plomley, 1987, pp. 313–14.
94 There is some apparent contradiction between chapel adjoining catechist's quarters, CSO 1/18798, p. 85; or commandant's quarters, Plomley, 1987, p. 625.
95 Journal for 21 November and 4 December 1835, Plomley, 1987, p. 625, and the smaller Big River clan, Plomley, 1987, p. 495.
96 Plomley, 1987, p. 570. Miller, 1985, p. 41. A renovated version of this chapel still stands at Wybalenna today.
97 Settlement Order 1, 15 August 1833, ML Robinson Papers, A7074 Vol. 52, CY825.
98 Plomley, 1966, p. 61.
99 Plomley, 1966, pp. 94, 95.
100 Plomley, 1966, p. 98.
101 Plomley, 1966, pp. 374, 376–77.
102 ML Robinson Papers, A7064 Vol 43. CY550, p. 303.
103 Plomley, 1987, pp. 878–881 and ML Robinson Papers, A7074 Part 6, CY825.
104 Plomley, 1987, p. 941.
105 Plomley, 1987, p. 337. On one trip forty-two Aborigines were away, Correspondence Robinson to Colonial Secretary, 2 March 1832, ML CY1470 A7056, p. 99.
106 Plomley, 1987, p. 314.
107 It was also raised when a boat was sighted or in harbour, Plomley, 1987, p. 332. Robinson began his travels from Bruny Island hoisting the flag of the Bethel Union Society when conducting church services so it was not new to those who were familiar with him, Plomley, 1966, pp. 96, 97, 117, 182, 187, 191, 335, 339, 352.
108 ML Walker Papers, B727 CY1408, p. 322.
109 ML Walker Papers, B727 CY1408, 8 Dec 1833, p. 310.
110 Plomley, 1987, pp. 316, 625, note 1.
111 Plomley, 1987, p. 304.
112 Plomley, 1987, p. 61.
113 Plomley, 1987, p. 316.

114 Plomley, 1987, pp. 304, 320.
115 Plomley, 1987, pp. 319, 320.
116 Plomley, 1987, pp. 430, 436, and others.
117 Plomley, 1987, p. 501.
118 Clark referred to the 'Aborigine Colony on Flinders Island' in his return of attendances for church services, 7 May 1837, ML Robinson Papers, A7066 CY551, p. 69. The 'Prospectus' of the *Flinders Island Chronicle*, which Robinson oversaw, described it as a 'register of events of the colony Moral and religious', where the 'colony' is clearly Wybalenna. ML Robinson Papers, A7074 CY825, p. 1.
119 Plomley, 1987, p. 320.
120 Plomley, 1987, pp. 319, 328, 330, 345, 434 and many others.
121 Plomley, 1987, p. 328.
122 Plomley, 1987, p. 345.
123 Plomley, 1987, p. 440.
124 Plomley, 1987, p. 501.
125 Plomley, 1987, p. 374.
126 Similar language was used by Drinene during one of his addresses reported in 1838 that in heaven people will be with God and 'you will not fall down from him', ML Robinson Papers, A7044 CY548, p. 42.
127 Plomley, 1987, p. 373.
128 ML Robinson Papers, A7044 CY548, p. 49.
129 ML Robinson Papers, A7044 CY548, pp. 50–51.
130 Plomley, 1987, p. 200.
131 ML Robinson Papers, A7044, CY548, pp. 38, 43-44.
132 ML Robinson Papers, A7044, CY548, pp. 40, 44-45.
133 ML Robinson Papers, A7044, CY548, pp. 45-46.
134 ML Robinson Papers, A7044, CY548, p. 49.
135 The Orphan School Register records Thomas Brune being discharged on 16 November 1836, Purtscher, *Children*, 1993, unpaginated.
136 ML Robinson Papers, A7064 Vol. 43, CY550, p. 9.
137 Plomley, 1987, p. 421.
138 Though Commandant, Catechist and surgeon were all being paid for their services. Noticeably, it seems to be in 'real' rather than the 'settlement' money used in the markets. This money was placed in the 'Aboriginal Fund' to the credit of each person and could be drawn from for market purchases, ML Robinson Papers, A7044 Vol. 23, CY548, p. 63.
139 Plomley, 1987, p. 487.
140 Plomley, 1987, pp. 484, 491, 493.
141 Plomley, 1987, p. 489.
142 Plomley, 1987, p. 493.
143 ML Robinson Papers, A7062 CY549, pp. 165–67.
144 ML Robinson Papers, A7064 Vol 43, CY550, pp. 301–302. Other references to Aboriginal people singing hymns, 7 December 1836, 22 February 1837 and 24 June 1837 (note 1), Note 1, Plomley, 1987, 20 February 1837. In October 1836 during Robinson's visit to Hobart, Mr Logan set an Aboriginal song to music, Plomley, 1987, pp. 391 and 657.
145 Albert, ML Robinson Papers, A7066 CY551, pp. 95–96.
146 Plomley, 1987, p. 709 and ML Robinson Papers, A7066 CY551, pp. 247–248.
147 Plomley, 1987, p. 480.
148 Plomley, 1987, pp. 313, 314, 447, 643, note 1(c). While noting Robinson's criticisms of Clark, it ought to also be noted that Robinson only ever described his own audiences as 'attentive' and his sermons being well received even though he preached exclusively in English, some being sixty pages long and taking more than two hours to deliver, Plomley, 1987, 331, 337, 433 and ML Robinson Papers, A7074 CY825, pp. 7–24. He also gave a lecture on 'pneumatics' that would take almost three hours to present.
149 ML Robinson Papers, A7064 Vol. 43, CY550, pp. 9–10.
150 ML Robinson Papers, A7066 CY551, pp. 165–168.
151 ML Robinson Papers, A7065 CY550, p. 83. A7066, CY551, pp. 3, 17, 33, 71, 81, 97, 125, 155, 167, 179, 209, 223, 275, 351.
152 Plomley, 1987, pp. 65–67.

CHAPTER FOUR

'Cracks in the Catechism'

THE PREVIOUS chapter examined the context of the early years at the Wybalenna settlement on Flinders Island, and in particular the translation of some biblical text into the Ben Lomond language, and some of the experiences of Sunday services from 1832 to early 1839. This chapter examines the various schools, forms of writing such as the *Flinders Island Chronicle* and catechetical examinations, and various forms of Christian addresses in first languages, in the evolving *pidgin* of the settlement, and in English in oral and written forms.

These expressions demonstrate that Aboriginal people continued to interpret Christian faith from multiple and diverse perspectives. The various languages used show that they did this from their pre-existing worldviews that continued to evolve and adapt to new contexts and concepts. Through examining the surviving reports it will become evident that rather than being brainwashed into surrendering their culture, language and religious beliefs, Aboriginal people interpreted the Christian faith through their continuing and adapting worldviews.

Schools at Wybalenna

The emphasis on English language in church services and catechetical examinations constrained the documented expression and recording of Aboriginal interpretations. However, the schools provided some opportunity, albeit limited, for first language and *pidgin* addresses. These school addresses were occasionally recorded in the documents that survive of Commandant Robinson and Catechist Clark. These documents are one part of one aspect of the Wybalenna context but they give insight into ways that some Aboriginal people were interpreting and incorporating Christian faith into their lives.

As mentioned in the previous chapter, a school of sorts had begun at Wybalenna in 1833 with the arrival of the first catechist, Thomas Wilkinson. A more formal arrangement developed in 1835 as the second catechist, Robert Clark, taught colonist and Aboriginal children together.[1] Following enquiries from various Aboriginal adults, particularly from the Ben Lomond clan, Clark began regular classes instructing people in the English alphabet.[2] Following the arrival of Robinson as commandant in October 1835, a series of schools began in 1836 with Sabbath day and weekday evening schools. Clark began a catechetical lecture for Aboriginal people on Tuesday evenings (and one for the convicts on Thursdays) and a prayer meeting for the Aboriginal people on Saturdays.[3] There were also Sunday services in the forenoon and evening,[4] and a Sunday school.[5] From time to time instruction was given almost every day of the week.[6] While it is tempting to assume that in the context of Wybalenna and these services and schools that Aboriginal people simply adopted what they were told and parroted back pre-formatted catechetical answers without any reflection or critique, the records tell a different story.

Schools and catechisms

Wilkinson's school began soon after his arrival in June 1833. It was located in his house or in that of one of the Aboriginal families,[7] and was more a mutual conversation than a formal method of instruction. It appears to have involved several Ben Lomond people teaching Wilkinson their language, though some of them already knew English, and led to translating some biblical text into Ben Lomond language. As already noted, only a few Aboriginal children were at Wybalenna until the middle of 1834 so the 'school' initially involved adult Aboriginal people conversing with adult catechist and commandant. In their report in January 1834, Backhouse and Walker recommended 'that a suitable building should be erected as a school room and a Chapel',[8] indicating the close association between the performance of Christian worship and school education. Governor Arthur's role in determining the purpose of instructing Aboriginal people is set out in a letter to Commandant Nickolls on 20 December 1834. The

> most likely method of bringing the natives to habits of civilisation and industry will be by gradually withdrawing them from their former customs in doing so however much caution and circumspection is evidently necessary ...[9]

Wilkinson's omission of substantial portions of Genesis One in his translation, and the mutual language learning in his home, and also initially by Clark, could be seen as examples of this 'caution and circumspection'. As mentioned, when Clark's school class began Aboriginal and colonist children were together.[10] In later classes children and adults participated together. It seems that at Wybalenna there was not an explicit or exclusive focus on Aboriginal children[11] as developed in later 'missions' and reserves around Australia.

Whether or not it was 'caution and circumspection' or some other factor, a significant school development occurred in early May 1835, five months before Robinson became commandant. Clark wrote to Archdeacon Bedford:

> Last week one of the tribes waited on me to request I would instruct them about 26 men and the next day the remainder of the men of the other tribes did the same. I immediately commenced their education on the plan of Bell and Lancaster so far as I could carry their method in effect so far as I could having no school room the people came regularly to my own house and my room being invaded.
>
> At nine o'clock the first division comes in regular here from their huts to my house and takes their places. I have pipes and tobacco prepared for them, which they smoke. Over the fire places or on the slates I have made the letters which they have to learn ... when all have completed this task they hand me the slate to examine and tell me the name of the letters they have made. At 12 they leave me and the white children and black children come to school they leave at 2 o'clock and then the Ben Lomond attend me and are instructed in the same manner as above."[12]

It appears Clark began teaching Aboriginal adults on the invitation from one unnamed clan. This clan's identity can probably be surmised from the only clan Clark names as having a class for itself, the Ben Lomond. Given the involvement of this clan in close conversation with Wilkinson two years earlier, it is not surprising they took up the conversation with his successor, Clark. It also suggests some conversation among the clans between the initial invitation and the other clan's request the following day. While there was the initial use of pictures and plates,[13] once the classes began in Clark's home the focus turned to learning letters on slates. One can only speculate at the potential associations the men made between Christian faith, learning letters and pipe smoking, with the latter perhaps contributing to the lung inflammations suffered by so many in subsequent years.[14]

Like the Sunday services, instruction was interrupted when people were 'out hunting' or by ongoing 'hostile feeling' between clans.[15] This conflict seems to have arisen from previous disagreements prior to being at Wybalenna. The impetus for going into the bush could have been seeking some separation from one another, as well as opportunity to continue ceremonial singing and storytelling. Another interruption was the occasional outbreak of disease, such as 'affliction of the eyes'.[16] It indicates at this time some degree of 'caution and circumspection' on the part of the catechist adjusting to the comings and goings of the clans and that Christian instruction occurred when people requested it.

Arrival of Robinson

The arrival of Robinson as commandant in October 1835 marked the beginning of several new school practices as part of his, and Governor Arthur's, larger scheme to 'civilise and Christianise' the Aboriginal people. During February 1836 Robinson introduced the Sabbath School and a School Committee,[17] appointed various teachers, Aboriginal and colonist,[18] and renamed virtually every Aboriginal person.[19]

In September 1836 Robinson introduced and supervised the first edition of the journal, *The Aboriginal or Flinders Island Chronicle*,[20] which will be discussed in more detail later. He also instituted the weekly market and related 'Aboriginal Fund'.[21] Throughout his years as commandant, Robinson oversaw building work, such as the brick 'terrace' houses, the separate brick chapel and some road construction. He sought to regulate relationships among Aboriginal people in the form of 'marriages', and actively sought to abolish Aboriginal gatherings, such as 'corroborees',[22] trade in ochre,[23] and 'hunting trips'.[24] Collectively, these activities form a picture of Robinson's desire that Wybalenna become a 'model English village'[25] in its housing, food growing, trade, newspaper and central focus on an evangelical Christian life.

While this was the picture Robinson created in his journal and reports, the experiences at Wybalenna suggest a more complex situation. While Robinson's papers and reports are voluminous, he was not necessarily the primary person to whom Aboriginal people related at Wybalenna. His descriptions indicate the role and affect he thought he had, but they do not adequately describe any of the one hundred and fifty other personal perspectives at Wybalenna.

Soon after his arrival Robinson required a report from Clark on attendances at the boys' school.[26] The day after Clark made his report the school was removed from the house adjoining the commandant's to an 'upper house' on the settlement.[27] At this time the Aboriginal houses at Wybalenna were separated into two main groups, with the 'lower' occupied by west coast people and the 'upper' comprising Ben Lomond, Big River and other clans. It is likely that with most of the school participants coming from the Ben Lomond clan that the schoolhouse / chapel was among their houses.[28] It is unclear how this location influenced Aboriginal interpretations of the school and church services but it is important to note that this location lasted for several years, at least until July 1838, and the Christian teaching and services, while no longer in the open air, were in an identifiable 'Aboriginal' place and not that of a model English village. Clark also gave instruction at several native cottages.[29]

As well as moving the school Robinson expressed increasing frustration at the perceived incompetence of Clark.[30] However when the officers, commandant, catechist, surgeon and storekeeper, instituted the Sunday School for Aboriginal people in February 1836, Clark was appointed superintendent.[31] They gave it the rather grandiose title 'The Flinders Island Sunday and Evening School for the Instruction of the Aboriginal people'[32] and the usual optimistic beginnings were reported.[33]

The teachers were a mix of colonists, as well as five Aboriginal youths comprising three males, Walter Arthur, and the brothers Droierloine and Maiki, and two females, Mary Ann and Pengernoburric / Bessy Clark.[34] Robinson described it as 'a new era at Flinders'. Walter was about sixteen, the son of Rolepa[35] and his wife Luggernemennener,[36] who were likely to have been involved in the Bible translation with Wilkinson. Droierloine[37] and Maiki[38] were sons of *Wurati* who assisted Robinson on the 'friendly mission'.[39] Mary Ann was eighteen, and Pengernoburric, aged twelve, was the daughter of Tingernoop from Port Davey.[40] Another boy, Timemeniddic, was appointed a 'monitor', or assistant. His parents were from Sandy Cape–Macquarie Harbour[41] and Port Davey.[42] This highlights one of the early features of the school: Aboriginal youths were teaching adults. While these youths were more competent in writing in English than virtually all the adults, it no doubt affected the cultural and religious context of their existing family and clan relationships.[43]

Droierloine's and Maiki's father, *Wurati*, a clan leader, had travelled extensively with Robinson and conversed with him many times so he may have had a role in his sons becoming teachers. Until Robinson met *Manalakina*, *Wurati* had been his primary source for stories, particularly the *Nununi*, such as the creation story discussed in chapter one. Similarly, Walter's parents were also clan leaders, with previous experience with both Robinson and the previous catechist, Wilkinson. In the classes Mary Ann was teaching her mother, as was Pengernoburric.[44] At least four of these five Aboriginal youths were children of clan leaders. It is possible their parents actually put them forward as part of continuing their own leadership roles. It seems reasonable to suggest that these leaders saw the emerging new context requiring them to engage with the colonists in the English language and perhaps wanted their children to have a leading role.

Method of instruction — Bell and Lancaster

There appear to be no surviving records of Wilkinson's method of instruction other than Walker's report. The arrival of Clark in July 1834 introduced his educational preferences. Just twenty years earlier educational theory and methodology had been hotly contested in England as the methodology of Dr Andrew Bell's 'Madras' system and soon after the 'Lancaster' system came to prominence. This was essentially a method of 'mutual instruction' where pupils taught fellow pupils.

In England rival organisations such as the 'National Society for promoting the education of the Poor in the principles of the Established Church' (1811) and the Lancasterian alternative, 'the British and Foreign School Society' (1814,) became established.[45]

Robinson had identified 'Dr. Bell's system' when outlining his initial plans for the Bruny Island establishment in April 1829.[46] Likewise Clark when writing from Wybalenna to Archdeacon Bedford in May 1836 said, 'I immediately commenced their education on the plan of Bell and Lancaster so far as I could carry their method in effect ...'[47] Like other aspects of settlement life, this method had its local variations. Of particular interest is this method's contribution to changing relationships among Aboriginal people and between Aboriginal people and colonists. The emphasis on mutual instruction seems to have enhanced the role of Aboriginal teachers such as Walter Arthur, who opened the school with prayer and is named as particularly crucial to a number of other Aboriginal people wanting to learn.[48] This growing knowledge and familiarity with the colonist religious language, the 'God book' and 'Sunday ceremony' could have enhanced, rather than diminished, Walter's intra-clan role and that of the Ben Lomond clan among others at Wybalenna.

Wybalenna catechism

It appears that the primary tool of instruction was the catechism. While the earliest surviving reports of catechetical examinations are from May 1837, there are references to the catechism in 1836 when Robinson conducted an examination on 23 August.[49] At the end of the year he wrote that he believed Clark was diverting from the 'assembly's catechism' regarding the body of a divine person atoning for sin.[50] This reference to the 'assembly's catechism' identifies it as the Longer and Shorter Catechisms of the Westminster Assembly. The Assembly was a group established by the Parliament in London (House of Commons and House of Lords) in 1643 'to advise as to a further and more perfect reformation in the Liturgy, Discipline, and Government of the Church of England' and beyond this church to the 'Churches of Christ in the three kingdoms' (England, Scotland and Ireland).[51] The Shorter Catechism of the Westminster Assembly became the primary tool for Christian instruction in the Church of England and other English Reformed Churches. Like the Bell and Lancaster method of teaching, the catechism was one of a number of common colonial practices in use throughout the Anglican and English-speaking reformed churches introduced to Aboriginal people at Wybalenna.

While today's readers may feel offended, even violated, by the preformatted answers and rote style, the commandant and catechist were working within a context where the very humanity of Aboriginal people was not only challenged but also often strongly denied. Their methods and content were part of their response in that they believed Aboriginal children and adults were as capable of learning the Christian faith as any colonist, child or adult, and for them these were the prescribed method and content to teach the Christian faith. Robinson indicated something of this when he wrote, 'I have had no more trouble in teaching a black boy his letters than in teaching a white boy.' He then set out for Clark the plan he would adopt, were he the catechist, to which Clark conformed.[52]

Like the earlier translation of the 'principal parts' of Genesis by Wilkinson, the form of catechism used by Robinson and Clark varied substantially from the Shorter Westminster Catechism. An example is the question 'What is God?' In the Shorter Catechism the required answer was, 'God is a Spirit, infinite, eternal, and unchangeable in his being, wisdom, power, holiness, justice, goodness, and truth.' At Wybalenna the same question is answered simply as, 'A Spirit.'[53] Of the 107 questions in the Shorter Catechism, most Aboriginal pupils were only asked between seven and twelve questions during examinations.[54] The Aboriginal teachers were asked many more. For example, Thomas Thompson was asked forty-three questions[55] and Thomas Brune one hundred and twenty, which included a large number that were beyond the Shorter Catechism.[56] Another variation was the inclusion of biblical and general knowledge questions, such as those regarding Adam and Eve, Cain and Abel, and Noah,[57] and questions on geographical and maritime terms,[58] days of the week, and seasons of the year.[59]

A further variation is shown when comparing questions asked in the catechetical examination with phrases appearing in several of Robinson's sermons. Two of Robinson's sermons, delivered in December 1835 following the deaths of *Manalakina* and Nooerer, contain phrases that appear regularly in the catechetical examinations but which are not in the Assembly Catechism. Some examples are questions of the nature of soul and body, eternal destination of heaven or hell following death, questions about the Bible, and the importance of praying at home and in the bush.[60] So while at first glance the catechism examinations can appear to be regimented, they were substantially modified according to Robinson's own personal preferences and directives given to the catechist to follow. This suggests Robinson's criticism of Clark mentioned earlier — that he was diverting from the 'assembly's catechism'[61] — is more likely another instance of Robinson's petty complaint about Clark, since Robinson himself did not follow much of the full form of the catechism either.

After ten months under the regime of Sabbath and Weekday Evening Schools, Clark reported to Robinson that the school operated from ten to noon with twelve attending of whom four read the testament, three had writing lessons, two were learning arithmetic, four were beginning to read, and four were spelling words of three letters. Their progress had been interrupted by their hunting trips. Clark believed they had

> acquired a knowledge of the character of the supreme being as the creator of all things; the fall of man; a heaven for good people and a hell for bad; that Jesus Christ came into the world to save man both black and white from the power of the devil here and the punishment of wickedness hereafter.[62]

The people were examined every Tuesday evening and instructed in the calendar, counting, singing psalms and hymns, and the Lord's Prayer. He noted an increasing knowledge of English, improvement by the women in sewing under Mrs Clark's tuition and a growing regard for one another in place of tribal hatreds.[63] Robinson's census earlier in January 1836 indicated twelve children among the population.[64] In Clark's report there are twelve boys and girls attending school[65] including the five Aboriginal teachers. The report also highlights the gender separation continuing, with the women being taught 'domestic and feminine occupations'.[66]

Writing

As mentioned previously the conflict between the earlier commandant, Darling, and catechist, Wilkinson, demonstrated the importance of writing in the exercise of power in relationships at the settlement. Anna Johnston noted the important role of writing in 'becoming colonial' at Wybalenna.[67] The closely associated elements of 'civilise' and 'Christianise' meant there was a growing association between learning to write in English and learning Christian teachings for Aboriginal people as well. Therefore it is necessary to examine the earliest surviving sources of Aboriginal people writing in English as part of assessing their interaction with and interpretation of Christian faith.

While there is no documentary evidence of Thomas Wilkinson teaching Ben Lomond people to write in 1833, there are extensive reports of Robert Clark teaching people, at least from May 1835. As noted earlier Clark began teaching the alphabet using slates. The earliest surviving records of Aboriginal people writing whole words in English on paper are from an initial assessment of the children Robinson brought from the Orphan School when he became Commandant in October 1835.[68]

The first, dated 27 October 1835, is the most extensive and is identified as Friday's, that is, Walter Arthur's.

> Lesson the first
>
> In six days the Lord made the Heavens and the Earth the sea and all that there in is And on the seventh day God ended his work and he rested on that day for this

> Reason we keep the Sabbath holy because the Lord rested on that day. Six days are for working in which our Labouring is to be done but the seventh is a day of rest. And the Lord God Planted a Garden in Eden and placed there Adam whom he had formed.[69]

Other specimens are dated 1 December 1835 and name Bryan McSweeney as being present. The papers were signed by Robert Clark.[70] This explicit verification of the authenticity of the writing suggests the catechist was aware of people's disbelief in the ability of these Aboriginal children, and Aboriginal people more generally, to understand English and to write. The presence of an independent witness presumably was an attempt to add authoritative weight to the evidence.

In regard to Walter's 'Lesson the first …' it is somewhat complementary that his parents were probably involved with Wilkinson in translating the 'principal parts' of Genesis into a written form of their Ben Lomond language in mid 1833. Then within ten days of their son, Walter, being reunited with them, Wilkinson's successor, Clark, asked Walter to copy out Clark's 'principal parts' of the same part of Genesis. But unlike his parents Walter was required to copy an English — and not a Ben Lomond — translation. Again it is important to remember the documentary archive tells only part of the story, but it seems not beyond the realms of probability that Walter and his parents may have had a rather fascinating conversation about this biblical creation story. Indeed, it is possible that by requiring Walter to write this summary in English, Clark may have prompted a particular conversation between Walter and his parents in which they could have taken the opportunity to reawaken some first language words which he may have forgotten during his years in Launceston[71] and the two and a half years at the Orphan School in Hobart. It could be that what on first reading appears to be an instrument of assimilation could have been used as an instrument for strengthening first language oral familiarity.

In regard to this piece of writing, Van Toorn argues that 'in the process of reinforcing the doctrine that God created the world, the passage functions as an instrument of cultural assimilation by teaching that the Sabbath should be observed as a day of rest.'[72] However, after two and a half years in the Orphan School Walter had already experienced multiple 'instruments' of cultural assimilation, including over one hundred and twenty Sabbaths within the sandstone walls of St John's Church. Wybalenna was substantially less an assimilationist context. Walter was reunited with his parents who were still speaking his first language. At the time of writing his 'Lesson' he had experienced only two church services at Wybalenna, in two different buildings,[73] with the first held in a hut and probably among those occupied by his own Ben Lomond people. Furthermore, in that service the person leading the worship, Clark, spoke in the 'language of the settlement',[74] a *pidgin* of Aboriginal languages. This would be somewhat less of an assimilationist instrument than anything he had experienced in the previous two and a half years at the Orphan School. While Van Toorn rightly points out that 'writing never arrives naked',[75] it may be wearing several culturally and religiously diverse layers when arriving in different 'locations' simultaneously.

The varied writing contexts can be seen when considering other Aboriginal children. Droierloine's and Maiki's reunion with their father, *Wurati*, was somewhat different from Walter's. Droierloine and Maiki had been in the Orphan School longer than Walter: just over three years, according to the register. And while Walter's parents had been at Wybalenna for several years, *Wurati* had been travelling with Robinson throughout Van Diemen's Land since before his boys went into the Orphan School. It appears he was reunited with them in Hobart Town[76] prior to travelling to Flinders Island. The documentary evidence shows him to be a master builder of bark canoes, multilingual and a respected storyteller.[77] He had conversed with Robinson many times, including on biblical topics of Creation, God, and the Flood.[78] Like Walter's parents, it seems harder to imagine *Wurati* not talking with his sons about these things, including giving his opinion about Robinson and the situation of being on the island. While Walter, Droierloine and Maiki had spent the previous two and a half years in the Orphan School, their parents were from different parts of the island, spoke different languages, and for the previous several years had quite different experiences with Christian people. With such diverse relationships one cannot assume a single interpretation of their writing.

Six months later a more extensive writing sample shows further variation among the authors but also the continued coalescing of theology and writing skills. One sample dated 24 June 1836 bears Thomas Bruny's name.[79] As already noted, although the Orphan School register records him being discharged on 16 November 1836, Robinson records having to get an order from the Colonial Secretary to get him on 27 May 1836.[80] It seems more likely that Thomas was discharged, along with four others, into Robinson's care on 27 May and they arrived at the settlement on 17 June 1836.[81] Therefore the sample text, dated 24 June 1836, is probably part of Robinson's assessment of Thomas about a week after he arrived at Wybalenna.

> Protection
> Protection Protec [sic]
> 23rd Psalm
> The Lord is my shepherd therefore can I
> lack nothing. He shall feed me in a green
> pasture: and lead me forth beside the water
> of comfort. He shall convert my soul: and

> bring me forth in the paths of righteousness
> for His Name's sake
>
> Thomas Bruney 24th June 1836
> Flinders Island[82]

The headline of 'protection' expresses the teacher's primary interpretive guide for the student. Without knowing Thomas' thoughts and interpretation of the psalm, it is worth pondering the shepherd(s), sheep, pasture, and water in the context of his almost six years at the Orphan School, about half his life at that point. Thomas had only just arrived at Wybalenna. Having no previous relationship with any adults there, he was probably unaware of the settlement sheep on Prime Seal Island, so was more likely to have interpreted it from his school experience.[83]

Clark inserted 'convert' rather than the King James rendering 'restore' my soul. Whereas the biblical version is a *restoration* back to previously experienced food and comfort, the evangelical interest of the catechist directs the current psalm writer, Thomas Bruny, towards a 'conversion' of his soul into a new path of 'righteousness' expressed in written English text, submission to catechetical oversight and commandant approval. However, although probably unknown to Thomas, within the psalm there are also the anti-monarchical elements written in a context when God, rather than the kings of Israel, was seen as the 'shepherd' of the psalmist.

While at Wybalenna as a 16-year-old Aboriginal youth straight from six years at the Orphan School, Thomas was likely to interpret 'protection' as that provided in housing, rations and clothing from the commandant and storekeeper; nevertheless, there are within this psalm the potential seeds for rejecting that colonist mediated protection in favour of a direct Aboriginal experience of God. The emphasis on 'my' shepherd, together with the individualised answers to the catechism, no doubt came from the European emphasis on individual faith, and it is difficult to assess what resonance or dissonance this had with existing Aboriginal concepts of a person, or how a parent-less, and clan-less, Thomas Bruny might have interpreted it.

Nevertheless it is important to consider that Thomas, and every other Aboriginal person at Wybalenna, engaged in their own direct experience of Christian faith. Beyond the control, emphases and various influences of commandant and catechist, Aboriginal people were developing their own interpretations of Christian text, teaching and ritual, and doing so from their existing language and worldview. For some, such as Thomas, this was only in English. For others it was likely to have been multi-lingual, including first language, the evolving *pidgin* and English, and for others it is likely to have been multi-lingual Aboriginal languages together with the evolving *pidgin*. With so few Aboriginal people possessing English writing skills, these Aboriginal interpretive experiences are most commonly demonstrated in conversations and other oral forms rather than these few examples of written text.

Robinson reports one such conversation in January 1837 during an evening class. Robinson asked, 'Who made me?' and one of the pupils, Penermeroick / Milton, answered 'the Devil'.[84] Classes continued the following day, during which an unnamed woman and a man, Makeaduru, who would soon be elected verger,[85] were tested by Robinson. The woman was asked, 'Who is God?' To which she answered, 'Eve.' She was asked, 'Who made you?' To which she replied, 'Heaven.'[86] Makeaduru was asked, 'Who made you?' He replied, 'My father.'[87] Robinson's journal then says 'Davy Bruny, one of the young teachers, responded to the woman saying, 'what did you say "Eve", you should say "God", God is a spirit, is not a woman, God is a white man.'[88]

I speculated earlier on a possible conversation between Walter Arthur and his parents about the creation story in Genesis One, textually rendered in Ben Lomond language and English. This response by Maiki about 'God' as creator is a reminder both of *Wurati*'s creation story of Moihernee and Dromerdeene, and of Robinson's 'sermon' summary on Bruny Island in May 1829, discussed in chapter two. Again, it would have been a fascinating conversation between the *Nununi* father and son on this topic. As Van Toorn notes regarding these responses: 'it is difficult to know today — as it was difficult for Robinson in his time to know — precisely what the people "learned" in the classroom'.[89]

While Penermeroick, the unnamed woman, and Makeaduru may have misunderstood the questions, or misconnected their growing storage of prepared catechetical answers, it is possible that they did not misunderstand or misconnect but were giving alternate interpretations. Maiki / Davy Bruny answered the woman's question not just with the answer expected from the 'Wybalenna Catechism', 'God is a spirit', but made two additional statements that God is not a woman, and God is a white man. So although nothing in the Bible says God is a white man, Maiki had 'learned' from his lessons in the Orphan School, from catechist and commandant that God is a white man. This could mean God is a colonist[90] like Robinson, Clark and others, thereby associating God with colonisation, or that God is at least the white man's God. It could mean God is a dead Aboriginal who has jumped up into life again, thereby associating God with Aboriginal ancestors visiting clans again.[91] Like the surviving examples of writing, these dialogues suggest multiple and varied 'learning' was occurring.

Penermeroick's answer to Robinson's question 'Who made me?' could be much more disturbing. The answer 'the Devil' was one among many references to the Devil that stirred Robinson so often in his journal writing, particularly in the performance of the 'Devil dance'.[92] While Van Toorn suggests 'some Aboriginal pupils were deviating from the script'[93] there were follow-up catechetical examinations four months later which provide further information which needs to be considered. In these reports of 1 May Penermeroick and Makeaduru were in the same class, along with Moultehelargine / Ajax, another 'older man'. Penermeroick was not questioned because of illness. In this report Makeaduru is described as 'not perfect in his letters'. In response to 'Who made you?' he answered 'God'.[94]

On 9 and 21 May there were the quarterly examinations over which Robinson presided. Again, these men are in the same class as Moultehelargine and Maiki was their teacher. Makeaduru is described as 'imperfect in his alphabet'. His only question was, 'Who made you?' to which he again replied 'God'. It is reported that 'this pupil is inattentive but is a good husband and a quiet well behaved man. He holds the office of Cook[95] and Chapel keeper. Is stout made about 30 years of age from the central part of V. D. Land'. There is no report of Penermeroick being questioned.[96] The woman is unnamed so it is not possible to match her answers to any particular person's catechetical examination.

There is a degree of speculation to any explanation, but it is clear that between January and May the records of Makeaduru's answer to 'Who made you?' changed from 'My father' to 'God'. It is possible to explain this as a 'subaltern' expressing outward compliance.[97] Makeaduru was born about 1802/3[98] and was one of the generation who were older than the colony. He could be like *Trukanini* regarding 'God' as belonging to the 'white man'.[99] Against this, however, is that in early February he was elected verger / chapel keeper, for the Sunday services, for which he received 1/- per week.[100] It is possible Makeaduru performed this role for the sake of the money, or some other role, motivation or benefit. Being one of the oldest people at Wybalenna, elected by the people to the role, it may have been recognition of his seniority. Because of his age he is likely to have been in a leading role in clan ceremonies and possibly inter-clan ceremonies, so to have and be seen by his and other clans to have a role in the colonist religious ceremonies was probably also a factor. His performance as verger / chapel keeper was in an audience of various Aboriginal clans and colonists, so was a multi-faceted-performance to clans and colonists simultaneously. He therefore could have performed this role with multiple purposes and meanings, an example of multiple layers in simultaneous locales.

Post-colonial discourse on 'liminality' is relevant here. This liminal, or transcultural, space is one in which Aboriginal, colonist and Christian forms are, as yet, indefinable in this context. Makeaduru's clan and inter-clan role is being fulfilled in a new context of the chapel and simultaneously the role of verger is being fulfilled in a new context of Aboriginal clan and inter-clan relationships. It is not clear to what degree each element in the discourse is interpreting the other, as Makeaduru is engaged in a 'constant process of engagement, contestation and appropriation'[101] simultaneously.

As mentioned previously those pupils with the most extensive knowledge were questioned and recorded at greater length. The written records were also part of the performance review of the catechist, commandant, and indeed the whole enterprise of the settlement. This is perhaps why so few variant answers are recorded in the examination records. Reporting a brief list of questions is suggestive of fewer 'correct' answers from the pupil. Unfortunately Makeaduru died on 29 December 1837[102] and so no further responses are known.

Another consideration is that the 'variant answers' come from Robinson's personal journal, and not from any catechetical examination report. It is worth considering Robinson's own motivations in recording the variant answers. On 20 January 1837, immediately prior to asking the woman 'Who is God?', Robinson wrote:

> Again put questions on the first principles of religion. The catechist said I did not ask those who had regularly attended. I assured him I had, and then asked the parties he referred to. They were equally at a loss. He referred me to a woman whom he said would understand who is God. She answered 'Eve'; who made you, 'heaven'. The catechist then said she did not understand my question and he purposed asking some questions. Constantine said he, who made you; answer 'my father'. He was therefore silenced.[103]

Following Maiki's comment about God being a white man, Robinson wrote:

> The evening was concluded by singing by the natives. The parson was evidently astonished at my mode of questioning the natives.[104]

As well as suggesting variant interpretations among Aboriginal people, Robinson's journal entries of the variant answers are also part of his ongoing criticism of Clark and this needs to be kept in mind as part of the context. Nor can the possibility be discounted that the answers given by these particular Aboriginal people was a way of embarrassing Clark in front of Robinson.

As well as these indications of diverse — some would say, subaltern — responses to questions, the classes themselves were not fully attended by Aboriginal people, including those involved in the catechetical examinations. Clark's records show that Aboriginal teachers and students were absent due to influenza epidemics,[105] ophthalmia,[106] or for no apparent reason.[107] In April 1837 the results of the catechetical examination show that forty-six were present and twenty-two absent.[108] This suggests Aboriginal people were not as regimented or regular in their attendance or participation as might first be assumed, or later 'missions' practiced, but they were clearly learning Christian faith through the catechism, writing and, probably more importantly, conversations with each other. This attendance of only two-thirds of the students in April seems to have been the catalyst for an important development that actually strengthened Aboriginal voices and more diverse interpretations and expressions of Aboriginal Christian faith.

At the end of April 1837 Clark left Wybalenna for a few days to go to nearby Chalky Island. While he was away Robinson arranged the evening school on Saturday 29 April, where he says he 'playfully asked them to commence to exhort and admonish each other from the desk'. This was done by *Tukalunginta* / William, Rolepa, Philip, and Noemy. Noemy began and spoke 'partly in his own and partly in English'.[109] It is not clear if Robinson specifically asked them to use their first language, but given Robinson's emphasis on learning English and the catechetical style of set answers, this seems unlikely. The initiative for first language seems to have come from the first speaker, Noemy from the west coast.

These men and their messages will be examined subsequently because the only written records of interpreted notes are from addresses they, and others, gave in 1838. However, the timing of the decline in attendances, particularly at the catechetical examinations, seems to have stirred Robinson to try something different. Seizing the opportunity, Noemy and others spoke first of all in their own languages. Also of interest is Clark's reaction when he returned. He wrote to Robinson on 3 May 1837:

> I have the honour to state the very great satisfaction and delight I experienced on my return from Chalky last week in witnessing the native chiefs and others address their countrymen at the Saturday night prayer meeting particularly when I heard some of them introduce the name of God and our Lord Jesus Christ. To me this meeting afforded more heart felt delight than any I ever witnessed or assisted in thro the course of my life and called up the liveliest feelings of gratitude to my God for his goodness and love
>
> I take leave respectfully to request your permission to form a class of the persons who you will please to select and on such days of the week as you will appoint to instruct them more fully in the Precepts of Religion and Truth *to enable them to speak of the Truths of Revelation in their vernacular languages* on those interesting occasions. I have already spoken to one or two of the Natives and it has met their approbation subject to your approval.[110] [my emphasis]

Clark, like Wilkinson, attempted to encourage what was already occurring among the clans. Aboriginal people, particularly clan leaders, were discussing Christian faith with each other in their own first languages and the *pidgin* of the settlement. They were exploring their own unmediated experience of God and their own interpretations of the mediated experiences of school catechisms and church services. However, Robinson 'gave a negative' to Clark's request.[111]

Something seems to have changed between the April examinations and those in May. The first language sermons are at least part of the answer, and another part could be that Robinson introduced monetary rewards in 'Settlement currency' for attendance and answering questions.[112] In the April catechetical examinations forty-six of sixty-eight participated with twenty-two absent.[113] On 9 May the picture was quite different. There were twelve male classes with a total of forty-two students examined. The three female classes comprised twenty-eight students, giving a total of seventy Aboriginal people examined in the catechism.[114] While Robinson refused Clark's participation in 'vernacular language' classes, the continuation of first language addresses suggests the clan leaders were not as constrained.

The size and membership of the classes is instructive for a number of reasons, particularly the age and clan mix. Among the twelve male classes two had two pupils, seven three pupils, and three had four pupils. Only one class comprised all pupils from the same clan (the first class, all from Big River) and all others had pupils from at least two or sometimes three clans. In regard to ages all six Aboriginal teachers were under eighteen years of age while only two pupils were in the same age cohort. Fourteen were identified as being in their twenties, fourteen in their thirties, and seven in their forties. The widest age difference was thirteen-year-old Maiki teaching thirty-year-old Makeaduru, forty-seven-year-old Moultehelargine, and forty-six-year-old Penermeroick.[115]

There were only three female classes: Mrs Dickenson's with eleven pupils, Mrs Clark's with twelve and Mary Ann's with four.[116] Five pupils were under twenty-six with twelve men in the same cohort; eighteen were between twenty-seven and forty with twenty men in the same cohort; and two between forty-five and fifty with four men in the same cohort. It is difficult to know how these demographic mixes and gender separation affected the learning but it is worth noting it as an element of the context. There was real potential for gender differentiation in the interpretations of the Christian faith. Further examination of Aboriginal women's interpretations will be a significant challenge due to the scarcity of sources.

Monthly examinations were also held in June,[117] where Clark reported that the students had generally not improved.[118] So while Robinson had introduced monetary rewards for school participation it did not have any immediate impact on their adherence to the set catechetical answers. It is noticeable that Robinson made no mention of the first language, or *pidgin*, addresses in his report to the Governor of 24 June 1837. Instead he maintained the façade of compliance among the Aboriginal people. The picture he gave the Governor was that religious and other instruction of the natives were conducted in the English language and 'many speak it fluently and with a perfectly English idiom'.[119]

Robinson intensified his efforts on English language learning. In August he further separated Walter Arthur and Thomas Bruny from their cohort of young Aboriginal teachers. At a special meeting of the School Committee he annulled the rule for appointing Aboriginal boys as teachers, except for Thomas and Walter. He then appointed two of his own sons, George and Charles, as teachers, and downgraded the other Aboriginal youths to 'monitors', assistants to the teachers.[120] The attendance at the August examinations remained relatively high with eighty-nine students, forty-four males and forty-five females participating.[121] Robinson's English-only faith appeared to be in the ascendancy.

The Aboriginal or Flinders Island Chronicle

It is not surprising with these efforts of Robinson's that the regular editions of the *Flinders Island Chronicle*, the English language hand-written journal, resumed in earnest in September 1837, apparently a year after the one-off first edition.[122] There seems some confusion concerning the date of the first edition.[123] A single first edition in September 1836 with no subsequent editions for just over a year seems improbable.[124] However, Robinson left Wybalenna on 15 September 1836 for Hobart Town[125] before returning to Wybalenna, via Launceston and George Town, on 6 December 1836.[126] This temporary absence does not fully explain a year's hiatus in the production of the journal but it does suggest some restraint is required before amending original documents.[127]

Robinson's emphasis on the English language *Chronicle*,[128] intended to be published each Saturday,[129] appears to be an attempt to assert control over, or at least counter, the growing expressions of Saturday evening Christian addresses in Aboriginal first languages and the evolving *pidgin*. It was perhaps also an attempt to exert authority over a catechist who more and more spoke in the *pidgin* rather than English when preaching in Sunday services through middle to late 1837. The first edition reads in part like a 'Robinson-Settlement-origin-story':

> we date our history of events from the Month of October 1835 when our beloved father made his appearance among us dispelling the darkness and cheering us with a dawn of hope freedom and happiness.[130]

Robinson's control is clear: 'Proof sheets are to be Submitted to the commandant for correction before publishing'.[131] The *Chronicle* was to bear Robinson's — rather than Clark's — authority, at least initially.

It is difficult to see the prospectus and first edition of the *Chronicle* as anything more than Robinson's English-only faith being ventriloquised through the two youths in order to improve his reputation among colonists. One of the copyists, Thomas Bruny, an orphan, was still at the Hobart Orphan School in October 1835, when, through the *Chronicle*, he wrote that it was the time from which 'we date our history'. The 'beloved father', Robinson, visited the Orphan School at that time,[132] but left Thomas behind with much less than 'a dawn of hope freedom and happiness'. Thomas remained at the Orphan School for at least nine months after this 'beginning' of 'our history'. Robinson's visit led to Walter's removal to Flinders Island and return to his father, mother and sister, and probably a greater degree of happiness. Walter is unlikely to have known Robinson at all prior to this, having entered the school while Robinson was only briefly in Hobart between his ventures in the north-west and Macquarie Harbour at the end of 1832.[133] Walter's 'beloved father' is unlikely to have been Robinson at all but more likely to be someone from within his own Ben Lomond clan, perhaps even his own still living father.

Furthermore few Aboriginal people, other than Walter and Thomas themselves and the other Aboriginal 'teachers', were able to read much English at that time. Therefore the primary audience for the written text, like Wilkinson's Bible translation, was unlikely to have been the 'captive audience' of Aboriginal people,[134] but rather colonists, many of whom were not at Wybalenna at all, such as the Governor, church leaders, or content colonist pastoralists who had donated subscriptions to thank Robinson for ridding the island of its first people.[135]

The grandiose claims of the prospectus and first edition echo those expressed at the commencement of the Sunday and weekday evening schools in February 1836. And like the schools, subsequent editions of the *Chronicle* suggest that Aboriginal people used the experience to develop skills they valued, and they incorporated them into existing clan relationships and cultural practices. Aboriginal people adapted the school experience into opportunities for Saturday evening first languages addresses by clan leaders offering 'mutual instruction', in an apparent continuation of their existing, but changing, roles. Likewise divine service was adapted in the 'bush' to become 'Sunday corroboree' celebrated alongside dances. The *Chronicle* never became an Aboriginal language journal. The desired 'emulation' in writing did not occur. Instead Aboriginal people continued to communicate with each other primarily in oral forms and adapted colonist Christian practices into their own relationships, with their interpretations.

The practice of writing did, however, influence personal and clan relationships to a degree. While the readers of the *Chronicle*'s English text were almost entirely colonists, the 'readers' (i.e. interpreters) of the context at Wybalenna were much wider and included Aboriginal people. Thomas and Walter themselves appear to be aware that their involvement in the *Chronicle* affected their relationships with each other and with other Aboriginal people. It was not so much the particular words they used but the power they garnered through the performance of writing. They appear to have used threats of naming women in the paper to persuade several to clean themselves and their houses. Several women 'said they [Walter and Thomas] might KARNY speak but not write'.[136] Within the *Chronicle* whose audience was primarily not Aboriginal, Thomas mentions unnamed men taking books into the bush and going hunting[137] and native women carrying grass.[138] Thomas names himself and Walter 'assisting Mr Clark in the church on Sundays'.[139] Walter names Thomas, 'when we are in school I always see Mr Thomas Brune laughing and playing away in the middle of school'. He writes of 'Flora and Louisa' going to offshore islands to hunt and for skins, and of 'Natives' making their own garden ... own fruit ... own fences'.[140] Thomas names 'the Aboriginal male Noemy has got the love of God shed abroad in his heart ...'[141] Each of these written examples were of people 'emulating' colonist work and are likely to have engendered appreciation among their few colonist readers.

The beginning of 1838 marked the start of another tumultuous year among the officers at Wybalenna. Robinson's frustrations with Clark seem to have played a role in Governor Franklin's appointment of a chaplain, Reverend Thomas Dove. However Clark continued to have a teaching role due to Dove's apparent lack of interest in teaching Aboriginal people, particularly children.[142] The annual catechetical examinations were conducted between 9 and 22 February, and certified by the newly arrived chaplain. In his report Dove credited the improvement to Clark, Dickenson and the three Robinson boys and, noticeably, no Aboriginal teachers. He recommended that the method of instruction continue.[143] Robinson likewise placed credit with the teachers and saw it as 'conclusive evidence of the success of his plan and role as Commandant'.[144] A contrasting view is alluded to when, after a fortnight of catechetical examinations, some of the Aboriginal people were asked if they liked the examination. They replied that they did not like the 'damnation'. Robinson interpreted this as a 'mispronunciation'[145] but perhaps it was not.

Conflict emerged again between officers.[146] Robinson sought a report from Clark regarding the Aboriginal people, something that should have been Dove's responsibility. It was not until July, after several months of complaints and conflict,[147] that Dove finally commenced teaching at the school.[148] He reported there were several Aboriginal clans continuing to speak their first languages. His reference to the 'sealer's jargon' may actually be the *pidgin* of the Aboriginal people, but he reports a preference for using English.[149]

Among the officers, Robinson and Dove regarded colonists speaking *pidgin*, or 'bad English' as a degradation of themselves.[150] Clark desired to speak to the Aboriginal people primarily in *pidgin* but was discouraged from doing so.[151]

Aboriginal speakers spoke in first language to their own clan, *pidgin* to a mixed Aboriginal audience, and in English to colonists. This multilingual practice is indicative of a growing sophistication in interpreting Christian faith and conversing about it in multiple languages, worldviews and formats simultaneously.

ENDNOTES CHAPTER FOUR

1. ML Robinson Papers, A7062 CY549, pp. 165–67.
2. ML Robinson Papers, A7062 CY549, pp. 165–67.
3. Plomley, 1987, p. 684.
4. For example, ML Robinson Papers, A7065 CY550, p. 83.
5. For example, ML Robinson Papers, A7066 CY551, p. 265.
6. ML Robinson Papers, A7066 CY551, pp. 79–80, 125–126, 137.
7. ML Walker Papers, B727 CY1408, p. 322.
8. ML Walker Papers, B727 CY1408, p. 322.
9. ML Robinson Papers, A7062 CY549, pp. 119–126.
10. ML Robinson Papers, A7062 CY549, pp. 165–67.
11. ML Robinson Papers, A7062 CY549, pp. 165–67.
12. ML Robinson Papers, A7062 CY549, p. 168.
13. ML Robinson Papers, A7062 CY549, p. 168.
14. Regarding trade in tobacco, see Birmingham J., and Wilson, A., 2010, 'Archaeologies of Cultural Interaction Wybalenna Settlement and Killalpaninna Mission', *International Journal of Historical Archaeology*, 14, p. 22.
15. ML Robinson Papers, A7074 Part 6, CY825, unpaginated. This continuation of hunting for substantial periods of time seems partly explained by the Aboriginal people's general dislike of the rationed 'salt meat'. Major Ryan reported in March, July and August 1836 that the Aboriginal people did not like it and therefore sought fresh meat in the bush, ML Robinson Papers, A7062 CY549, pp. 213–257. Years later, at *putalina* / Oyster Cove, Aboriginal people spent considerable time in the bush getting fresh meat when the rations from Hobart were spoiled or of inferior quality, *Oyster Cove Visitors Book*, 28th March, & 27th April 1857, J. Kirwan Visiting Magistrate, TAHO CSO 89/1/1, pp. 19, 21.
16. ML Robinson Papers, A7062 CY549, p. 88.
17. ML Robinson Papers, A7064 Vol. 43, CY550, p. 295.
18. Plomley, 1987, p. 343.
19. Plomley, 1987, p. 337, 344. This re-naming was discussed in Chapter One.
20. ML Robinson Papers, A7074 CY825, p. 1.
21. ML Robinson Papers, A7044 Vol. 23, CY548, p. 63.
22. ML Robinson Papers, A7044 Vol. 23, CY548, p. 63, also Plomley, 1987, pp. 346, 468.
23. Plomley, 1987, pp. 312, 437, 468, 643.
24. Plomley, 1987, pp. 333, 334, 336, 377, etc.
25. Robinson outlined these ideas when he first went to Bruny Island, Plomley, 1966, p. 56. However, they were only partially fulfilled at Wybalenna. Some later Christian missions developed a more thorough reconstructed landscape than happened at Wybalenna. See, for example, Attwood, 1989, p. 7. See also, Birmingham, J., and Wilson, A., 2010, pp. 15–38.
26. ML Robinson Papers, A7062, pp. 291–94.
27. Journal for 21 November and 6 December 1835, Plomley, 1987, p. 625.
28. Plomley, 1987, p. 495. The brick chapel that still stands today was not completed until July 1838.
29. ML Robinson Papers, A7066 CY551,

29. p. 126. See Birmingham, J., 1976, 'The Archaeological Contribution to Nineteenth-Century History: Some Australian Case Studies', *World Archaeology*, 7 (3), pp. 311–315; and Birmingham, 2010, for archaeological evidence of continuing cultural practices and incorporation of elements of 'British' in the cottages constructed at Wybalenna in 1837–1838.
30. Plomley, 1987, p. 316.
31. Plomley, 1987, p. 342.
32. ML Robinson Papers, A7062 CY549, pp. 131–141. Plomley, 1987, pp. 343–44.
33. ML Robinson Papers, A7062 CY549, pp. 131–141.
34. While Thomas Bruny became a teacher later on, when the school began he was still at the Hobart Orphan School. Although the Orphan School Register records Thomas being discharged on 16 November 1836, Robinson records having to get an order from the Colonial Secretary to get him on 27 May 1836, Plomley, 1987, p. 355. It is more likely that Thomas arrived at Wybalenna in early June 1836 and became a teacher soon after because a sample of writing at Wybalenna that bears Thomas' name is dated 24 June 1836, ML Robinson Papers, A7074 Vol. 52, Part 6, unpaginated.
35. Plomley, 1987, p. 824.
36. Plomley, 1987, p. 806.
37. Plomley, 1987, p. 840.
38. Plomley, 1987, p. 839.
39. Plomley, 1966, pp. 241, 478, 586, 701, 819.
40. Plomley, 1987, pp. 818, 853.
41. Plomley, 1987, p. 804.
42. Plomley, 1987, p. 797.
43. Plomley, 1987, p. 346.
44. Plomley, 1987, p. 346
45. Ward & Trent (et al), 2000, *The Cambridge History of English and American Literature*, New York; G. P., Putnam's Sons, 1907–21, http://www.bartleby.com/224/1417.html, accessed 2/3/2012.
46. Plomley, 1966, p. 56.
47. ML Robinson Papers, A7062 CY549, p. 168.
48. Plomley, 1987, pp. 858–59, ML Robinson Papers, A7062 CY549, pp. 131–141.
49. Plomley, 1987, p. 377.
50. Plomley, 1987, p. 402.
51. Carruthers, S. W., 1957, *Three Centuries of the Westminster Shorter Catechism*. Fredericton; Beaverbrook Foundations/University of New Brunswick.
52. ML Robinson Papers, A7062 CY549, pp. 255–258. Also, Correspondence Clark to Robinson, 9 November 1835, TAHO CSO 1/18798, p. 78.
53. ML Robinson Papers, A7044 CY548, p. 268.
54. ML Robinson Papers, A7044 CY548, pp. 266–278.
55. ML Robinson Papers, A7044 CY548, pp. 288–291, also ML Robinson Papers, A7066 CY551, pp. 110–11.
56. ML Robinson Papers, A7044 CY548, pp. 282–88, also A7066 CY551, pp. 105–09.
57. ML Robinson Papers, A7044 CY548, pp. 287–88, also A7066 CY551, pp. 109–10.
58. ML Robinson Papers, A7044 CY548, pp. 282–88.
59. ML Robinson Papers, A7044 CY548, pp. 288–91, also ML Robinson Papers, A7066 CY551, pp. 110–11.
60. ML Robinson Papers, A7074 CY825, pp. 8–22, see also Plomley, 1987, p. 314.
61. Plomley, 1987, p. 402.
62. Plomley 1987, pp. 667–68.
63. Plomley 1987, pp. 66 –68.
64. Plomley 1987, pp. 878–81.
65. ML Robinson Papers, A7074 Part 6, CY825, no page number.
66. ML Robinson Papers, 8 Dec 1833, B727 CY1408, p. 310.
67. Johnston, 2004, pp. 17–31.
68. Plomley, 1987, p. 305.
69. ML Robinson Papers, A7074 CY825, p. 53. This is followed by Maiki / Davy Bruny, ML Robinson Papers, A7074 CY825, p. 54, Droierloine / Peter Bruny, ML Robinson Papers, A7074, CY825, p. 55, Ben, ML Robinson Papers, A7074 CY825, p. 57, and Rolepa, ML Robinson Papers, A7074 CY825, p. 59.
70. ML Robinson Papers, A7074 Vol. 52, Part 6, CY825.
71. Dammery, S., 2001, *Walter George Arthur A Free Tasmanian?* Clayton; Monash Publications in History, p. 3.
72. Van Toorn, 2006, p. 102.
73. Plomley, 1987, pp. 304, 305.

74 Plomley, 1987, p. 304.
75 Van Toorn, 2006.
76 Plomley, 1987, p. 621.
77 ML Robinson Papers, A7064 Vol. 43, CY550, pp. 169–70, and Plomley, 1966, pp. 374, 375, 376.
78 Plomley, 1966, p. 376.
79 Thomas' 'family name' is initially spelt 'Bruney' but later became 'Bruny' in reports and correspondence. It was sometimes spelt both ways in the same letter. See correspondence Clark to Robinson, 9 November 1835 CSO 1/18798, p. 80.
80 Plomley, 1987, p. 355.
81 Plomley, 1987, p. 360.
82 ML Robinson Papers, A7074 Vol. 52, Part 6, unpaginated.
83 Kenny has written of the context in Victoria of how an Aboriginal man interpreted and incorporated sheep and Christian theology into his existing religious world, in Kenny, R., 2007, *The Lamb Enters the Dreaming*. Melbourne; Scribe. Aboriginal people at Wybalenna had their own flock on off-shore islands since 1832 and sold wool in Launceston. The settlement had supplies of sheep for food and so people would have at least seen colonists killing and eating sheep even if they hadn't eaten it themselves. Among the adult generation at Wybalenna were those with religious stories of close associations between people and kangaroo/tarner that were also hunted and eaten, Plomley, 1966, p. 373.
84 Plomley, 1987, p. 417.
85 Plomley, 1987, p. 421.
86 Plomlcy, 1987, p. 417.
87 This is reminiscent of *Manalakina*'s reply to Robinson that he 'only knew what his father told him', Plomley, 1966, p. 403.
88 Plomley, 1987, p. 417.
89 Van Toorn, 2006, p. 61.
90 A few years earlier *Trukanini* had criticised Black Tom for saying he believed in the white man's God, Plomley, 1966, p. 379.
91 Walter Arthur, 'we skin black people died then arose from the dead became white men we begin to make friends of them call them father or Brother', ML Robinson Papers, A7074 CY825.
92 Plomley, 1966, p. 301. It is curious that the man, Penermeroick, carried the English name 'Milton'. Robinson refers to the author Milton and his book, *Paradise Lost*, in the notes of the creation story told by *Wurati*, Plomley, 1966, p. 373.
93 Van Toorn, 2006, p. 61.
94 A further biographical note is added, 'This pupil is a good husband and industrious — he holds the office of Clerk and Chapel Vesper is a stout man of about 30 years of age from the Central part of V D L', ML Robinson Papers, A7066 CY551, p. 146.
95 Plomley, 1987, p. 420.
96 ML Robinson Papers, A7044 CY548, p. 275.
97 A subaltern in this context is a person of 'inferior rank ... [and] denied access to hegemonic power', in Ashcroft, B., (et al), 2013, *Post-colonial Studies*. London; Routledge, pp. 244–247.
98 Plomley, 1987, p. 841.
99 Plomley, 1966, p. 379.
100 Plomley, 1987, p. 421.
101 Ashcroft, 2013, p. 145.
102 Plomley, 1987, p. 841.
103 Plomley, 1987, p. 417.
104 Plomley, 1987, p. 417.
105 Plomley, 1987, p. 680.
106 Plomley, 1987, p. 684.
107 Plomley, 1987, p. 681.
108 Plomley, 1987, p. 688.
109 Plomley, 1987, p. 439.
110 ML Robinson Papers, A7066 CY551, p. 49. Plomley, 1987, pp. 691, 692, note 1.
111 Plomley, 1987, p. 691.
112 Plomley, 1987, p. 450. Later that year Walsh made a report and reiterated this recommendation, ML Robinson Papers, A7066 CY551, p. 149.
113 Plomley, 1987, p. 688.
114 ML Robinson Papers, A7066 CY551, pp. 13–24, 129–49.
115 ML Robinson Papers, A7044 CY548, pp. 266–307.
116 ML Robinson Papers, A7044 CY548, pp. 293–307.
117 Plomley, 1987, p. 448.
118 Plomley, 1987, p. 695.

119 Plomley, 1987, p. 699.
120 Plomley, 1987, p. 467.
121 ML Robinson Papers, A7044 CY548, pp. 387–90.
122 ML Robinson Papers, A7074 CY825, p. 1-17, Plomley, 1987, Appendix 4:C, pp. 1009 – 13. There are six surviving copies of an edition which outlines the 'objects of this journal'. Three are signed by both Walter Arthur and Thomas Bruny, and three by only Thomas. Five bear Robinson's signature and the date '10th September 1836' on the reverse side of the page, and one does not have any verification. These appear to be a 'prospectus' similar to the school committee establishing its objects, naming its officers and giving itself a name. All editions of the *Chronicle* found in the Robinson Papers are in Appendix E. Stevens claims 'Walter Arthur's role in the production of the *Chronicle* is hearsay' (2017, p. 98). This requires the reader to completely dismiss the documentary archives in favour of an unsubstantiated exercise of imagination.
123 ML Robinson Papers, A7074 CY825, pp. 13-16.
124 Stevens' claim that the *Chronicle* 'appears to have been abandoned after just one issue' (2017, p. 70) is incorrect.
125 Plomley, 1987, p. 381.
126 Plomley, 1987, p. 398.
127 The first reference in Robinson's journal is on 30 September 1837 which Plomley incorrectly identifies as 'the first of a series …', Plomley, 1987, p. 713.
128 ML Robinson Papers, A7074 CY825, pp. 1–11.
129 ML Robinson Papers, A7074 CY825, p. 1.
130 ML Robinson Papers, A7074 CY825, pp. 13–16.
131 ML Robinson Papers, A7074 CY825, pp. 13–16.
132 Plomley, 1987, pp. 295, 620, 621.
133 Plomley, 1987, pp. 680, 704.
134 Rose, M., (ed.), 1996, *For the Record: 160 years of Aboriginal Print Journalism*. St Leonards; Allen and Unwin, pp. 1–19.
135 For example, *Colonial Times*, 7 October 1834, p. 3. *Hobart Town Courier*, 28 November 1834, p. 2; 20 March 1835, p. 2. See also, Van Toorn, 2006, pp. 111–12. Soon after Robinson left Wybalenna on 15 September 1836, the *Hobart Town Courier* printed a glowing endorsement of Robinson's activities, including the *Chronicle*. 'Mr. Robinson has been the means of establishing a weekly newspaper among them. It is entirely written by the Aborigines, and is published under the name of 'The Aboriginal Flinders Island Chronicle,' on half a sheet of foolscap every Saturday, price 2d each, and the profits arising from the work are equally divided among the editors'. *Hobart Town Courier*, 23 September 1836, pp. 2, 3.
136 Plomley, 1987, p. 489.
137 28/9/1837, *Flinders Island Chronicle*, ML Robinson Papers, A7074 CY825, p. 17.
138 28/9/1837, *Flinders Island Chronicle*, ML Robinson Papers, A7074 CY825, p. 20.
139 2/10/1837, *Flinders Island Chronicle*, ML Robinson Papers, A7074 CY825, p. 22.
140 2/10/1837, *Flinders Island Chronicle*, ML Robinson Papers, A7074 CY825, p. 23. Stevens' claim that all editions of the *Chronicle* are in Thomas Brune's hand (Stevens, 2017, p. 66) is not supported by the documentary evidence.
141 6/10/1837, *Flinders Island Chronicle*, ML Robinson Papers, A7074 CY825, p. 25.
142 Plomley, 1987, p. 535.
143 Plomley, 1987, p. 725.
144 Plomley, 1987, p. 535.
145 Plomley, 1987, p. 535.
146 Robinson was in conflict not just with Clark but also Dove: 'The gross effrontery of this insignificant personage exceeds all I have ever met with, and this a parson. To dare to dictate to me what I should do in command of the settlement! As well might I dictate to him the subject and method of his sermon!' cited in Plomley, 1987, p. 573. See also, Miller, 1985, p. 27.
147 Plomley, 1987, p. 563.
148 Plomley, 1987, p. 571.
149 Plomley, 1987, p. 744. Also, Miller, 1985, pp. 39, 42–44.
150 Plomley, 1987, p. 568.
151 Plomley, 1987, p. 304.

CHAPTER FIVE

'Always crackney in Heaven'

ABORIGINAL people had been conversing with each other about the Christian faith since early contact with colonist Christians. This occurred with the participation of adults and children in early baptism services, attempts by Robinson to preach in a *pidgin* at Bruny Island,[1] in discussing church services[2] and during the so-called 'friendly missions'.[3] At Wybalenna the conversations between Ben Lomond people and Thomas Wilkinson in translating parts of Genesis into a written version of their language is likely to have involved conversations among Ben Lomond people themselves in clarifying words and meanings. They had requested the later catechist, Clark, to teach them.[4] They engaged with each other in 'Sunday corroboree'[5] and sang English language Christian hymns in their cottages.[6] These indicate a variety of discussions of Christian stories and practices were occurring in multiple languages.[7]

Sermons in the context of Christian evangelicalism

In order to appreciate these writings and addresses by Aboriginal people at Wybalenna, it is important to be aware of the place and practice of evangelical Christian preaching within the context of eighteenth-century and nineteenth-century Christianity. Evangelicalism was a broad movement among Christian churches, particularly in England and America. It was not restricted to a particular denomination. One expression, 'methodism', traces its roots to 24 May 1738, when founder John Wesley felt his heart 'strangely warmed'. Methodism began as a 'method' followed by small group of Christian people. It was initially a para-church movement but primarily within the Church of England. As noted earlier, Methodism was known as a distinct stream within the Church of England, at least from the 1750s.[8]

The Methodist denomination only came into existence as a denomination formally separate from the Church of England after Wesley's death in 1791, though there was movement in this direction before then. Many of the missionary organisations that emerged in the late eighteenth century, including those in which Robinson was a member in London and in Hobart, grew out of the influence of the Evangelical Revival. What is relevant for Robinson's behaviour in the context of Wybalenna is the practices that emerged of reading, writing and speaking that 'violated prevailing rules of eighteenth-century British propriety' by authorising non-ordained preachers with limited education to speak publicly and to write extensively.[9] Many missionaries came from among 'lower' or marginal 'middle' classes. While not sponsored by any missionary society, Robinson and Clark are examples of that broader group of mission-minded evangelicals.

This, along with the 'Bell and Lancaster' school system and catechetical teaching, seems to have influenced the development of their methods among the Aboriginal people at Wybalenna. The evangelical practice of regular meetings to study scripture and provide mutual spiritual nurture was another feature introduced at Wybalenna in the form of the evening classes for 'mutual instruction'. The absence of female speakers in these classes is likely to be a consequence of the suppression of evangelical women preachers such as occurred within Methodism after John Wesley's death in 1791.[10] These were the immediate contexts in which the sermons and addresses were delivered at the settlement.

Within these broader characteristics of evangelicalism, Robinson and Clark were the more immediate influences and role models for the Aboriginal speakers. Robinson's desire for emulation among the Aboriginal people expressed in the *Flinders Island Chronicle*[11] was also seen in the classes for mutual instruction. Such role modelling by colonial powers that sought to induce emulation, or mimicry, among the colonised was common in colonial contexts. Bhabha has critiqued the practice in India of an evangelical system of mission education conducted uncompromisingly in the English language through which Indians would become outwardly 'like' the English but remain dependent and not ever become equal.[12]

In considering this type of critique in the context of the Aboriginal speakers at Wybalenna, there are several clear examples of the speakers, particularly Walter Arthur, Thomas Brune, and Noemy, mimicking Clark and Robinson in their writing and speaking styles. These mimicking characteristics include regular quoting of, and indirect references to, biblical passages, quoting Christian hymns, exhorting people to pray each day, and referring to people's sin and their need to turn away from the devil so they can go to heaven when they die. In at least two addresses Walter Arthur describes Noemy speaking 'as if he were a minister'.[13]

It is problematic to assess the extent to which Robinson desired the Aboriginal people to become 'like' him but not 'equal' to him. There are indications of aspirations to equality in the desire that Walter Arthur become a catechist[14] and therefore be equal to Clark. The production of the *Chronicle*[15] was somewhat similar to Robinson's own writing practices, describing daily life within the settlement and writing sermons and other addresses for that context. The invitation to the Aboriginal people to address the same weekday evening school as Robinson and Clark is another. In the sermons, equality is expressed in the references to 'black men and white men' being created by God and descendant from the same ancestors, Adam and Eve.[16]

But there are also elements of inequality. The first language addresses were limited to evening schools only, never in Sunday services. Robinson, as commandant, had superior authority over all others at the settlement. This suggests the Aboriginal people were encouraged to become something towards being equal, or at least less unequal, but at Wybalenna they would always remain dependent upon Robinson or any other commandant for the supply of rations and any required building works. The earlier aspiration that Walter Arthur could perhaps become catechist, the second highest paid position at Wybalenna, disappeared when Walter and Mary Ann were removed to Chalky Island.[17] Robinson's strong emphasis on an English language Christian faith[18] meant the path towards independence and equality would need to be through competency in English writing and speaking, and few Aboriginal people could write a sentence.

While this mimicry can be seen from the colonist perspective as teaching colonised people enough for them to be useful but not enough to become equal, post-colonial perspectives from the viewpoints of the colonised interpret these same sources as examples of agency or parody.[19] The context at Wybalenna can be seen as a 'contact zone'[20] or 'contested place'[21] where Aboriginal people appropriated and interpreted elements of colonist life and were in the process of creating for themselves 'transcultural identities'[22] in a 'dialectical process of the making of the Aboriginal people and their making of themselves'.[23] Therefore it is appropriate to see the addresses as examples of 'survivance narratives',[24] developed in the context of a deep rupturing of much of their previous sense of themselves, and the beginnings of new and provisional narratives, which, for some, incorporated Christian faith.

This 'mixing' of Aboriginal and Christian rhetorical styles and broader spiritual cosmologies did not constitute an adulteration or denial of Aboriginality.

Rather, they expressed creative strategies for emerging Aboriginal identities in a contested cultural and political space, particularly where Aboriginal people were at a political and economic disadvantage. The addresses are dialogical discourses that enabled adaptation, incorporation and resistance, while attending to survival. The improvisational nature of these addresses was seen as each Aboriginal writer / speaker expressed multiple speaking positions simultaneously. Van Toorn has noted the conspicuous oscillations in both Walter's and Thomas' use of first-, second- and third-person pronouns.[25] They both had uncertain and ambiguous cultural, social, and political positions at Wybalenna, being part of some groups but not others.[26] These 'oscillations' are more profound than the ambiguous speaking position of every preacher who is simultaneously addressing an audience and part of the same audience.

Walter, as a younger person, had other religious role models at Wybalenna who were likely to be at least as influential as Clark or Robinson — if not more so. Walter's father Rolepa was leader of one of the largest clans at Wybalenna, the Ben Lomond, and showed signs of continuing his father's leadership role. It seems reasonable to interpret Rolepa's behaviour as seeking to pass on his knowledge and practices through subsequent generations. To maintain family and clan narratives across these frontier generations would be invaluable. But their relationship was problematic. Walter had experienced childhood cultural disruption and dislocation from family and clan, but reconnected, to some degree, with family and clan at Wybalenna.[27] Thomas Brune, by contrast, was an orphan without any family or clan relatives at Wybalenna. Colonists had been his role models and shaped his identity for most of his childhood years. Therefore, his writing / speaking position was significantly different.

Aboriginal addresses and writings

While researchers rightly give attention to the surviving writings of the *Flinders Island Chronicle*,[28] it is important to remember there are more references to first language, *pidgin*, and English sermons and addresses of 'mutual instruction', and more participant voices, than there are editions and writers of the *Chronicle*. The voluminous writings of Robinson and the written text of the *Chronicle* can skew our perception and give rise to preference of text above voice. But Wybalenna was primarily an oral context. This variety of languages and breadth of participants are therefore much more significant in considering Aboriginal interpretations of Christian faith at Wybalenna. Indeed, the increasing number of first language Aboriginal Christian voices and addresses, particularly during September and October 1837, may have contributed to the demise of the *Chronicle*, last issued on 16 November 1837.

The largest number of surviving 'sermons' are in English, however, and belong to Thomas Bruny with twenty-four,[29] and Walter Arthur, thirteen.[30] Of the Aboriginal people at Wybalenna they were the most familiar with Christian faith and had experienced a variety of sermon presenters, including at the Orphan School. There is a marked difference in writing style and content between the English addresses of these two younger men and Clark's notes of the first language addresses given by the older men between February and April 1838.

Over the seven weeks from 24 February to 21 April 1838, Clark reported first language addresses given by seven Aboriginal men from different clans on six of the Saturday evening schools.[31] By this time it seems Robinson's 'English-only' faith was losing what support it had among the Aboriginal people. Walter Arthur fell quickly into the status of *persona non grata*. Like the demise of the *Chronicle*, the reports of first language addresses coincided with the last dated English addresses given by Walter, on 6 and 20 February 1838.[32] There are seven undated sermons bearing Walter's name so it is possible he preached again after this time, but not for at least a year. As a climax to Robinson's increasing frustration,[33] Walter and Mary Ann were married by the chaplain, Reverend Thomas Dove, on 16 March 1838[34] and within three days, purportedly with the consent of Walter and Mary Ann, the officers of the settlement agreed to send them to Chalky Island.[35] Four months later Walter and Mary Ann were moved to Prime Seal Island on 18 July[36] and did not return to Wybalenna until 25 January 1839.[37]

It is intriguing to ponder why Robinson saw it as preferable to exile Walter and Mary Ann rather than have them at Wybalenna. Both had been involved as teachers of other Aboriginal people for two years and, according to their catechetical examinations, were among the most knowledgeable of Christian teaching and most capable in writing. As a writer of the *Chronicle* Walter had been held up as someone to emulate, an example of Robinson's achievements in 'Christianising and civilising'. However for Robinson and the other officers it became more important to cease the *Chronicle* than continue it, even with Thomas Brune as sole author, and more important to remove Walter and Mary Ann entirely from the settlement.

While the exact reasons are unclear, the inter-clan relationships are another potential factor. Thomas, an orphan, had arrived later than virtually all other Aboriginal people at Wybalenna, in 1836. His youthful age and clan-less status are likely to have mitigated his influence or 'emulation' among the clans if he had continued as sole chronicler. Walter's clan, the Ben Lomond, had been a substantial portion of the Wybalenna population, but no one from that clan is mentioned giving an address during these weeks in 1838. Instead the West Coast, North and Big River clan leaders gave the most addresses. This may express a change in the inter-clan political relationships at that time.

The addresses given in this period by clan leaders total twenty-six. Most are 'in their own language' or the 'language of the settlement' but some are in English. Addresses were given by Noemy (West Coast) and Drinene (North) in each of the five reports, Dowwringgi (Big River) and Druemerterpunner (Big River) in three, *Wurati (Nununi* / Bruny) in two and *Piway* / Napoleon / *Tanaminawayt* (Cape Grim) and Robert (North-East) in one, the last. With several clan leaders and most clans involved, except it seems the Ben Lomond, these first language and pidgin addresses were likely to be more influential than the *Chronicle* or English language sermons by Walter or Thomas.

A further contrast is that the addresses by Walter and Thomas were firstly written, usually under supervision of Robinson or Clark, and later performed in the evening school, whereas the addresses by older Aboriginal men were first delivered orally in first languages and then translated into the local *pidgin* before being written by Clark in his reports to Robinson. While Johnston has noted the intricate connection between writing, identity and colonist culture and the important role of writing in construction of 'Britishness' under empire,[38] the role of writing was also shaping new forms of Aboriginal identity. As mentioned previously, Walter and Thomas were aware of their increased power in being able to name people in the *Chronicle*.[39] Dammery suggests 'Walter had observed how Robinson exercised his authority, and had made the connection between power and writing'.[40] However the absence of any evidence of Walter keeping his own writing collection with his own copies of sermons, other letters, or an autobiography suggests that writing was not a primary element in his emerging Aboriginal–Christian identity. It was only in the mid-1840s, in the post-Robinson era that, with some assistance from Clark, Walter Arthur began writing directly to the wider colonial audience of the Governor.[41]

It may be a simple coincidence but perhaps worth noting that the Christian season of Lent, which covers the forty weekdays plus six Sundays leading up to Holy Saturday (the eve of Easter day) began on Ash Wednesday 28 February 1838, with Easter Day on 15 April. The reports of sermons therefore began just prior to Lent and finished on the first Saturday after Easter. While it is unknown if this played a role in the first language sermons, nor is it known what the Lenten practices of Robinson, Dove and Clark were in 1838 (Easter is not mentioned in Robinson's journal), the season of Lent is a time for Christian people to focus on the meaning and significance of being Christian through attending to the life, suffering and death of Jesus Christ.

Conversations in first languages

The earliest surviving example of an Aboriginal person speaking about God in 'Aboriginal-English' at Wybalenna is not in an address, but earlier, 28 April 1835, prior to Robinson's arrival, when Clark reported an unnamed Aboriginal man who was very sick. Clark wrote:

> desired him to call upon God Almighty as none other could relieve him ... he told me in his own language 'meena carny God almighty to parraway menatti and neenna too an appav— [indecipherable] and meenatti a little one meena locthia God almighty' that is I prayed to God to put away my sickness and understood me or heard me and I am but little sick I love God almighty I attributed his recovery to the intervention of the Divine powers.[42]

While this is another example of the evolving *pidgin*, the report further substantiates the multi-facetted 'transcultural identities' that Aboriginal people were manifesting linguistically and religiously. In this man, previous interpretations and responses to illness were now incorporating elements of Christian prayer.

Formal addresses and 'mutual instruction'

The earliest surviving documentary references to Aboriginal people addressing each other in first languages about the Christian faith are on 29 April 1837 when Robinson wrote:

> I had long resolved when the opportunity offered to induce the male Aboriginal people to attempt the instruction of their countrymen, and during the catechist's absence from the settlement at Chalky I took the occasion to playfully ask them to commence to exhort and admonish each other from the desk. This was done by King William, King George, Philip, Nome, and was well observed and attended to by all present. I requested them to bear it in mind that they would have to speak this day. The native youth opened the school by prayer. I then called upon Mr Dickenson to read a portion of scripture, as they were the foundation of all morality. Mr Allen was then requested by me to address them; he spoke to them on the fall of man. I then asked the natives if they understood what had been said to them. Nome said he understood it. This was the reply I wanted. I then desired him to come forward and address his countrymen. He did so and spoke with great confidence and vehemence and delivered a most instructive and interesting discourse partly in his own and partly in English. Spoke against the practice of thieving and desired them to live honestly. Told them of Jesus Christ and God our Father, of heaven, of glory, of going up to heaven, of hell. Said bad people went to hell, that good people went up to heaven; Devil is in Hell. King William, King George, Philip and Alfred spoke as well. It was a most interesting meeting. Singing was introduced at intervals.[43]

The format for the evening school followed a regular pattern: A youth (unnamed, but probably Walter or Thomas)[44] began with prayer, likely to have come from the *Book of Common Prayer*.[45] An officer of the settlement followed this, in this case Mr Allen the surgeon, reading a portion of the Christian scriptures (unknown passage), and then addressing the whole group in a general exhortation.[46] Those Aboriginal people in regular attendance had witnessed this format for over a year and so were familiar with the routine. Robinson sought assurance from the people about their understanding, and then invited Noemy to speak from the 'desk'.

It is noticeable that Robinson chose only males. This is in contrast to earlier evangelicals within the Church of England, such as John Wesley, who encouraged women to preach in public gatherings of men and women.[47] Gender separation was a common practice in the classes at Wybalenna so that while Mary Ann is listed as a teacher,[48] the students in her class were also all women. Two months earlier some women expressed reluctance, or shame, if asked questions at the school in the presence of the men.[49] This gender differentiation is noteworthy. Women later became 'translators' of the men's first language addresses, at least in those surviving addresses from February–April 1838,[50] so had a significant role in reporting to Clark, and through him to Robinson. In this role they were able to provide some of their own 'interpretation' in the translation. So while it seems they were not permitted to speak to the whole group, they did have a role in translating and interpreting. There is no documentation of the women 'addressing' each other in their first language but if there were several of them in the evening school it seems unlikely that they would not have. As well as considering if the men's addresses were ventriloquised versions of what Robinson, Clark and Allen wanted to hear, we ought also consider that what these settlement documents from 1838 show are not necessarily what the Aboriginal men said, but what the women reported, and of that the documents are what Clark wrote to Robinson of what the women said.

The four Aboriginal men whom Robinson 'induced' to speak were *Tukalunginta*, Rolepa, Philip, and Noemy. A brief biographical sketch of two will illustrate their roles and status at Wybalenna and the place of these addresses within that context. Rolepa was leader of the Ben Lomond clan and father of Walter Arthur. He was probably involved in the beginnings of the translation work with Wilkinson in June–September 1833 and seems to have fulfilled a leadership role in the settlement, particularly in nominating constables,[51] arranging and celebrating marriages[52] and acting in a protective role for some others.[53] Together with Purngerpar / Alfred and *Wurati*, Rolepa welcomed Governor Franklin to the settlement.[54] He and Robinson exchanged gifts;[55] however, Robinson's generosity did not extend to writing to John Batman on behalf of Rolepa to have his other son, Rolepana, returned.[56] He did not participate in the addresses for which there are more extensive records in February–April 1838, even though he was still at Wybalenna. Perhaps the 'exile' of his son, Walter, in March that year was part of the reason. Rolepa died on 1 June 1840.[57]

It is likely that Rolepa's address in the school was an expression of his continuing leadership role at Wybalenna. He was familiar with Christian traditions and continued to speak his first language. His wife Luggernemennener had attended church services in Hobart and was likely to have been involved in the Bible translation a few years earlier. While Rolepa cultivated a relationship with Robinson, he clearly, and perhaps more importantly, involved himself in arranging marriage relationships and ordering life among various Aboriginal people within and beyond his own clan. Interestingly, like *Tukalunginta*, he was not involved in the English language catechism tests that began a week or so after his address. It seems these two older men chose to participate in the more open context of 'mutual instruction' than the narrower pre-formatted English language answers of the catechism, though Rolepa's son, Walter, performed very capably.

Noemy was a constable[58] and his wife gave birth to a daughter the day before his address.[59] Like the 'Kings' he received a coat from Robinson[60] and participated in nuptial[61] and funerary arrangements within his clan, including burial and cremations outside the 'official' cemetery.[62] The settlement journal refers to Noemy being beaten by Purngerpar and others in December 1838.[63] Both were 'constables' but Noemy for the 'upper huts' and Purngerpar for the 'lower huts',[64] so the fight was between two clan leaders and could have been about inter-clan conflict. In these examples, it seems the pre-existing practices of older men were continuing and the additional roles and meanings of 'constable', 'coat' and 'address' were incorporated into these arrangements and relationships. Noemy continued to instruct Robinson in the translation of particular words.[65] He also incorporated adaptations in the form of acquiring reading skills[66] and developing a practice of holding a book in his hand while giving his address,[67] perhaps more an indication of its symbolic power than its literary content.[68]

These men were a generation older than Walter Arthur and Thomas Brune. The two youths were fifteen to seventeen years of age in 1837–1838. By contrast, Rolepa, Walter's father, was about forty-seven or forty-eight. The age of *Tukalunginta* was unknown but being 'King' he is not a youth. Philip was thirty-three or thirty-four, the same age as Noemy. The men represented at least three different clans, Oyster Bay, Ben Lomond and West Coast. Philip's clan is unknown. It is possible that these four men used the opportunity of giving an address to (re-)assert their personal seniority among their own clan's people, and the other clans, through their use of their first language, the encouragement to focus on 'moral' teaching from Mr

Allen's general exhortation, and the newly added, and potentially authoritative, speaking position of the school 'desk'.[69]

When Clark returned from Chalky Island he sought permission from Robinson to address the natives 'in the language generally spoken by them on the settlement'. He had previously been prohibited by Nickolls from doing so, and also by Allen when acting commandant. Allen recommended Clark not use the language because his address to them 'was highly ridiculous', and Robinson refused the request.[70]

The following Saturday, 6 May 1837, Robinson reported further addresses given by Noemy who spoke, this time in English, 'about J Christ [and] put questions to the natives very pertly'; Druemerterpunner from Big River clan 'spoke in English about J Christ'; *Tukalunginta* spoke in his own language and said 'God made everything, named animals, birds' (someone must have translated his first language into this English summary); and Rolepa 'spoke partly in his own and partly in English'. 'Dr Allen spoke. Mr Dickenson read 6th Chapter of John, the raising of Lazarus,[71] and I [Robinson] spoke. Catechist concluded with prayer. Several other natives spoke on the occasion.'[72]

The absence of Philip and the presence of a new speaker, Druemerterpunner, is worth noting. Druemerterpunner from Big River was about twenty-five years old at the time and married to Drunameliyer / Caroline.[73] He nearly died in June 1837[74] but recovered sufficiently that in the following month, like the other 'Kings', he was appointed a constable '*viva voce* of the assembly'.[75] He, like many others, continued to practice cultural ways in regard to deceased relatives. For example, he gave Robinson a bone of his deceased brother on the day of the funeral.[76] Like Noemy, Druemerterpunner was involved in a conflict with a member, possibly leader, of another clan, *Piway*, about the mistreatment of his dogs.[77] He is among those Robinson writes as saying the Collect and Lord's Prayer.[78] In 1838 he is among those who gave addresses at the evening school[79] and in August he signed the declaration about accompanying Robinson to Port Phillip.[80]

After several months of 'silence' in the documents, there are occasional references to further addresses, such as 3 September[81] and Saturday evening school 7 October 1837, where four papers, two each by Thomas Brune and Walter Arthur on 'general subjects and religion', were read in English followed by addresses from Walter, Thomas, *Nikaminik* / Eugene, *Wurati*, Moultehelargine, Maccamee / Washington, Lerpullermener / Henry, Meterluererparrityer / Christopher, and a few others.[82] Clearly the number of speakers had grown since March and April.

Noemy's address, 2 September 1837 (Saturday), reported by Clark (Sunday 3 September) as being given first in his native language and then in the dialect of the settlement, is as follows:

> God noracoopa he coethee us, you coethee God — coethee plenty a big one you taplaldy weethicallee God send Jesus Christ to save us to parraway the Devil, potheae you coethe the Devil parraway, coethe God coethe Jesus Christ the son of God — you taplady lutha you coethe you norocoopa God make you good man you go top weekthiekatha.[83]

This reporting of the 'dialect of the settlement' illustrates some of the potentially varied interpretations of Christian teaching that were occurring outside of the control of catechist and commandant, a 'second Reformation' as Van Toorn describes it.[84] Linguistic translation is more approximate than exact and the lack of documentary evidence for a number of the evolving *pidgin* words, as distinct from first language words, simply adds to their tentative nature. The address in first language is likely to have flowed more smoothly with more words as it was the language most familiar to Noemy, rather than this haltingly written *pidgin* reported by Clark. These pidgin words are also likely to have been more comprehensible to the Aboriginal audience than to Clark because the pidgin was evolving from their languages rather than directly from English. An approximate translation of the address is:[85]

> Noracoopa — very good[86]
> Coethee — could be: cothe, hastily, soon, instant[87]
> Could be: koety, hole or cave[88]
> Could be: coot.er.wen, frighten[89]
> Taplaldy / taplady — could be: tabelty, go on[90]
> Weethicallee — could be: we.tick.et.ter — high up[91]
> Weekthiekatha could be a variant spelling of weethicallee / weticketter — high up[92]
> Lutha — could be: loatta — gum tree[93]
> Parraway — go away, put it away[94]
> Potheae — could be: no[95]

An approximate English translation could be:

> God *very good*, he *fear* us, you *fear* God, *fear* plenty big one, you *go on high up* God send Jesus Christ to save us *put away* the Devil, *no* you *fear* the Devil *put [Devil] away*, *fear* God *fear* Jesus Christ the son of God — you *go up a gum tree* you *fear* you *very good* God make you good man you go top *high up*.

This could then be read as something like:

> God is very good to us, if we fear (respect?) each other a lot you will go to heaven God sent Jesus Christ to save us and put away the Devil. Don't fear the devil but reject the Devil.
> If you fear God, and Jesus Christ the son of God, you will go up higher than a gum tree

> To fear God is very good and God will make you a good person and you will go to heaven

About six weeks later, 15 October 1837, the catechist reported a conversation that he had had with Kartiteyer / Hector the previous morning in the presence of Dr Walsh:

> I said to Hector 'you are very sick?' Answer 'yes me plenty manaty'. You coethee God? Hector, 'yes me coethee plenty, you coethee Jesus Christ?' 'Yes me coethee Jesus Christ the son of God'. Do you pray to him? 'Yes me pray to him plenty, me pray last night our Father which art in heaven plenty'. You very sick you krakabuka by and bye? 'Yes me tabletee werthickathe to God, me coethee'. On making this answer the poor fellow smiled. After some more conversation we departed … He died the following night.[96]

A more thorough linguistic analysis and interpretation would be beneficial. Nevertheless, these fragments are suggestive of a continuing dialogical religious identity expressed by Aboriginal people.[97]

These first language addresses of April, September and October 1837 were occurring concurrently with English language catechetical examinations, which began on 9 May 1837, and the schools, which began in February 1836. These 'addresses' occurred only in weekday or Saturday evening schools rather than Sunday services (and therefore are referred to as 'addresses' rather than 'sermons'). Several of Thomas Brune's and Walter Arthur's papers, written only in English, were read at Sunday morning and evening services. Some of these appear to be read by Robinson,[98] and other times it is not clear who read them.[99] Both youths occasionally read from the Bible at school and church service[100] and sometimes it is not clear what they were reading.[101] However it is clear that no first language addresses were delivered during Sunday services in either spoken or written form.

From these addresses it is evident that Aboriginal people continued speaking their own first languages several years into their experiences at Wybalenna. These continuing languages and cultural practices are indicative of their continuing worldviews and that these were expanding as were their mythologies through interaction with Christian teachings. Each of these men, as noticed by Robinson in his journal, were involved in behaviours that strengthened their changing cultural roles within their clans, and they were adapting in the Wybalenna context to further strengthen these roles. Rather than giving up their languages, worldviews, and cultural practices, they were translating the Christian teaching into their own changing cultural context, languages and meanings. This is not to say that these expressions of faith were not genuine or were a façade or an expression of apparent compliance to colonist masters, but that part of their experience of Christian faith was a strengthening and adaptation of existing clan leadership roles. Furthermore, this exploration may have enriched their cultural and spiritual power and to some extent confirmed — rather than overturned — their existing and adapting religious life.

Women as translators

One key difference between the first language addresses in 1837 and those in 1838 is the role of women as translators in the latter. Their involvement seems to have been linguistically unnecessary as at least some of the men did not seem to need a translator during 1837. This suggests another explanation, such as cultural practice. As mentioned previously, women in evangelical streams were active preachers but became suppressed, at least within Methodism, following the death of John Wesley. The crucial role of the women in the creation of these surviving sources from Wybalenna invites readers to consider the addresses by the older men as addresses actually given by the women, for it is their translations to Clark that became the reports to Robinson that survive. This aspect of the addresses, the theology espoused in them and the interaction of gender relationships among Aboriginal people and between Aboriginal people and colonists, is worthy of greater examination, though the brevity of the addresses limits the breadth and depth of such examinations. The strong focus of Robinson and Clark on men in catechetical classes, and in giving addresses, is clear from the written records. However, the continuing role of women within and between clans and colonists ought not be discounted or underestimated.

In 1838 the women translating were usually from the same clan as the speaker. Noemy was translated by Pengernoburric or Tedehburer / Clara.[102] The first sermon by *Wurati* was reported as translated by Pieyenkomeyenner / Wild Mary and himself,[103] and his second by Dray / Sophia.[104] Pieyenkomeyenner / Wild Mary was from a different clan, Big River,[105] and Dray / Sophia, from Port Davey,[106] whereas *Wurati* was *Nununi* (Bruny Island). *Wurati* himself was conversant in several Aboriginal languages[107] but reportedly spoke 'in his native language' during his addresses.[108] The multilingual proficiency of these three suggests there were more nuanced and multifaceted Aboriginal Christian interpretations occurring at Wybalenna. Furthermore, just as the male clan leaders were enriching their status and roles among their clan by participating in these addresses, these mostly younger women were also not only adapting to the context but enhancing their roles through their participation.

Comments about women by Walter Arthur and Thomas Brune were unmediated by women. Walter mentions women only once: 'that work that you, some of you women, was going on with other night was most abominable'.[109] Thomas mentions them twice, complementing their work ethic: 'some of the women are industrious and strong', and in one of these contrasting them to Augustus and Walter.[110]

Several older men's addresses contain criticisms of women and these may be influenced to some degree by the relationships among the women at Wybalenna. These criticisms include going 'to the bush for firewood', 'living like dogs',[111] not going to school,[112] playing too much at balls (marbles)[113] and 'putting grease and ochre on yourselves — you dirty your clothes you dirty yourselves'.[114] It is unclear if these were general criticisms of all women or only those in a particular clan. While some recent studies have examined the emergence of Australian Indigenous feminist theology,[115] the absence of any surviving writings by women at Wybalenna constrains discussion on this topic from within this context.

Addresses as emergence of pan-Aboriginal identity

The addresses enhanced the cultural and political role of the speakers and translators. They also give insight into emerging pan-Aboriginal identity across clan differences. Several speakers summarised common colonist experiences but gave different interpretations.[116] Noemy (West Coast) described their ignorance of God:

> In your own country you did not know there was a God all that you knew was to make spears and waddies and to kill one another.[117]

Drinene (West Coast) presented a moral interpretation:

> In your own country you were bad people and a great many of you died God did not love what you were doing — God sent you from your own country Why are you continuing those bad things — after a little time you will all die You ought to love God for God is very good to us all.[118]

Drinene emphasised their ignorance of Christ:

> In your own country you did not know Jesus Christ no you were like the kangaroos you went about every place the white man came to your country they kill your countrymen a great many of them you then came to live in this place and good white men came to teach you about God about Jesus Christ you are not bad now the white men does not kill you now not never.[119]

And *Wurati (Nununi)* noted their declining population:

> My brothers in our own country a long time ago we were a great many men a great number — but the white men have killed us all — they shot a great many — we are now only a few people here and we ought to be fond of one another we

> ought to love God God made everything the Salt water the bullock the horse the opossum the kangaroo and wombat Love him and you will go to him by + by.[120]

These, and other speakers, were using the opportunity to expound their interpretation of recent experiences and to advocate particular, potentially unifying, or at least collective, responses among the audience, and were using Christian theology as part of this interpretation and advocacy. The audience included most, if not all, clans at Wybalenna, though not every person, and the addresses also functioned for intra-clan and inter-clan purposes. The audience also included commandant, chaplain and catechist, and the addresses were one way Aboriginal people sought to influence those relationships. Dove commented on Noemy as an 'eloquent' and 'elegant' speaker and Robinson stated *Wurati* was not as 'advanced' as others because of his involvement with Robinson in the bush.[121] Van Toorn suggests *Wurati*'s address is a 'reclothing' of the Bible with 'meanings capable of advancing his agenda'[122] and this agenda is likely to have had different emphases for Aboriginal and colonist listeners. Interestingly, *Wurati* alone is reported using 'we' and the others 'you' in his addresses.[123] His pre-existing multi-lingual skills[124] and participation in the 'friendly mission' may have contributed to developing a stronger sense of 'pan-Aboriginal' identity earlier than others who came to Wybalenna as part of their own clan group.

Sermon forms and structures

The written addresses regularly expressed formulaic statements, 'like pieces of a mosaic that have been assembled in a variety of ways to form different configurations of the same basic picture'.[125] Van Toorn suggests the catechetical method as a likely explanation, however Robinson himself also practiced the style.[126] The 'pieces' were part of a common rhetorical device, the 'sound bites' of the era for mostly non-literate audiences. The mosaic comprised biblical quotations and allusions,[127] quotes from contemporary hymns[128] as well as the catechetical answers identified by Van Toorn. While the addresses survive today in written form it is important to remember it was a written genre designed for oral delivery.[129] In this way it is not dissimilar to earlier Aboriginal storytelling oratory.[130]

Conversion

One of the greatest literary legacies of evangelicalism, alongside its hymnody, is the plethora of conversion literature in public magazines and private letters. Behind all of these stand the oral tradition of spoken testimony in band and society meetings.[131] These are testimonies of individual, rather than collective, experiences of God, but they do follow narrative conventions. In the sermons at

Wybalenna there are aspects of collective memory and also exhortations about personal behaviour.

Hindmarsh identifies several conventions in evangelical conversion narratives. They include original prosperity, descent into humiliation, and return. As such it is a microcosm of the biblical story of Creation, Fall, Redemption, and new Creation. In these narratives a shadow was cast over the speaker's earlier life. Where they narrated an awareness of religious concerns early in life, it subsequently faded as they fell into vices and oscillated between wrongdoing and remorse. Where they had grown up in formal religious observances such as church services, these were cast as a form of pharisaic legalism. Another element was retrospective interpretations of providential deliverances that prepared them for later experiences of God's grace as steps on the way to conversion.[132]

These narrative patterns sometimes varied, as different elements were foregrounded more or less than others, but on the whole it operated within a basic pattern of biblical narrative and Reformation theology. The pattern offered an opportunity for the subjects to locate themselves personally in a spiritual and moral, social and political meta-narrative or tradition, and explored how their story uniquely reflected common broader themes. By so doing the orator articulated a narrative-self, newly enfranchised and empowered to respond to daily life.[133]

At Wybalenna the addresses by the Aboriginal men show elements consistent with these 'conversion' narratives, with some significant variations. The following is a brief discussion of several of these elements: God's Providence, sin, prayer and heaven / hell. One of the strongest similarities is in interpreting their earlier individual and collective lives. This was expressed as not knowing God 'in their own country'. This previously unrecognised providential care prepared the way for 'good white men', such as Robinson or Clark, to teach them about God and Jesus Christ in more recent times so that they now knew. An example of this narrative of ignorance changing to knowledge is by Drinene:

> You did not know God in your own country ... God sent the white man Parson/
> Catechist and he has instructed us about God and Jesus Christ the Son of God
> we now know that Jesus Christ made the trees the salt water the sun and moon
> and the kangaroo and the emu and every thing God loves every thing that is
> good and he loves good men and good men love God'.[134]

The elements of trees, salt water, sun, moon, kangaroo and emu evoke memories of the creation stories of each, and the mythic creator beings who were the active agents in creation. Drinene implies Jesus Christ did the creating previously ascribed to the creator beings, but, at least in this documentary source, he stopped short of naming Jesus Christ as the creator being. This theological point that God saw everything people did 'in their native country' is likely to be 'mimicking'

Robinson's preaching. In one of his earliest sermons at Wybalenna in December 1835 he spoke in a rhetorical exchange with God: 'I know you regard them, and this because you have lived with them'.[135] This emerges from Robinson's theology of God as omniscient (all knowing), omnipresent (all present), and omnipotent (all powerful).[136] However, this idea stops at the point of God being in the land, living with the people, and watching people's 'bad thoughts'. It does not progress to naming God as part of Aboriginal people's religious expressions. From the geographic and mythic distance of Wybalenna God is named in creation, in the land and animals, everywhere except in the people themselves. Walter Arthur wrote: 'they did not have these things in their heads before they came on Flinders now [sic, 'no'] they did not have these words in their own country'.[137]

The absence of the words suggests the act of 'naming' God, Jesus Christ, in their country was a crucial gap in their experience. Of these Aboriginal people at Wybalenna, only *Trukanini* and Dray / Sophia returned to their own, or at least nearby, country. All others at Wybalenna lived displaced from ancestral country and their evolving dialogical religious identity was adapting to that displaced context.[138] As well as 'reading' God into their country, Walter Arthur 'read' Aboriginal people into the biblical narrative.[139] An undated and unnamed sermon also links Aboriginal people with the biblical story of creation:

> My dear friends you know that God made the heavens and the earth and sea and the trees and the stones and everything that moveth and he made you and me that we might serve him he made man and put him into the garden of eden a garden of pleasant and the all animals were not savage and transgression falled upon Adam and sin came upon all men black and white and then Jesus Christ came into the world to die for our sins according to the scriptures.[140]

This dialogic 'reading' and 'speaking' between Aboriginal and Christian stories and places by Aboriginal people is an expression of a profound religious transformation that was occurring. One consequence of not knowing God in their own country is that Robinson, and the Aboriginal speakers, rarely refer to their earlier, and continuing, religious life as 'sinful' or 'evil'. Most often they describe themselves as ignorant — I / you / they 'did not know God'. They were saved from previously 'not knowing' to now 'knowing' about God and Jesus Christ. They were also 'saved' from the bad white men who were killing them.[141]

The strongest criticism of their earlier life is from Drinene:

> In your own country you were bad people and a great many of you died God did not love what you were doing — God sent you from your own country Why are you continuing those bad things — after a little time you will all die',[142] and
>
> 'You did not know God in your own country — you were evild [sic] me[n] [sic] there'.[143]

It is unclear why Drinene alone spoke so critically, but it does suggest a variety of views among the Aboriginal speakers. It would appear the rote catechetical answers and few colonist teachers did not prevent Aboriginal speakers developing their personal emphases. In some ways their narratives are not dissimilar to addresses by leaders of the early church, where Jesus is read back into the history of Israel and where specific psalms and prophetic writings were given Christological interpretations and 'ignorance' and culpability were common themes.[144]

Other words not as strong, but striking nonetheless, were from Noemy, from the west coast like Drinene: 'God sent Jesus Christ his son to bring us to his country' [emphasis added].[145] Their displacement from their own country and being brought to Wybalenna appears as a salvation motif in at least two speakers, without the 'returning' metaphor of the conversion narratives. They do not seem to perceive that God would send Jesus Christ into their own country but rather that God would remove them. However, it would be a mistake to conclude that there was a simple theme of old-own country-pre-colonial religion equals a bad-sinful-life from which God-Jesus-Robinson-Clark-good-white-men saved them and brought them to salvation-Wybalenna-white-colonial-Christian life-heaven. The phrase 'God's country' will be examined further as it most often appears in sentences about 'heaven' rather than contrasting their 'own country' with 'Wybalenna'.

'Sin'

It is somewhat surprising that the strongest critiques of pre-contact Aboriginal religious life came from the older men, and not from the younger Walter Arthur or Thomas Brune. This is in stark contrast to the common perception that Aboriginal children were more 'vulnerable' to conversion because of their impressionable psychological development. The examples in Robinson's journals of *Trukanini* and *Manalakina* seemingly rejecting Christian faith,[146] and the roles of the younger dis-located Aboriginal people such as Walter and Thomas, could give this impression. Similar theories of Aboriginal conversion can be found elsewhere:

> Anthropological literature on cultural rites of passage, in which young members of a group are initiated into the community through a process strikingly similar to that of conversion, stresses the nearly universal practice of performing rituals of initiation while the novitiates are still of an impressionable age. It is obviously much more difficult to break down pre-existing notions of the self and reaggregate the elements of selfhood into a new social persona when the individual has already achieved biological and social maturity.[147]

The surviving sources appear to show a different scene at Wybalenna. Rolepa and Luggernemennener were involved in Bible translation. Drinene's words have been mentioned already. *Wurati* criticised people's continuing practices saying, 'you make your persons too filthy by putting grease and ochre on yourselves — you dirty your clothes you dirty yourselves — put it away you women'.[148] Druemerterpunner said,

> You should not go to the bush a long way to corroberry you are to come here to learn to sing and to pray you ought to be more attentive and learn to work'.[149]

Each of these people were adult clan leaders with pre-existing notions of selfhood as a multifaceted dialogical identity. For them, it seems, Christian faith was a new dialogical experience that could be built upon previous dialogical interactions. The addresses contain exhortations to upright moral behaviour and to relationships with each other. Most often this is phrased as 'don't scold each other', 'fight', 'growl'. Here again Walter[150] and Thomas[151] have fewer references than the older men, who appear to have continued exercising their senior roles in these matters.[152] Walter's only critique of pre-colonial life seems to be a reading back into that context of behaviour happening at Wybalenna: 'God knows all the bad thoughts that you did while you was in your native woods You thought that God did not see you then and now'.[153] It may simply be that Walter and Thomas were less familiar with that life and therefore could not comment.

Heaven / Hell — 'God's country' / 'Devil's country'

Like other evangelical themes, a person's place in eternity received significant attention. There appear to be more contrasts among the writers and speakers on this theme. Walter wrote on four occasions about 'a world above the sky where you and I must go by and by when we die' where the final judgement and separation of 'good' from 'bad' will occur.[154] The 'good' will 'go to the houses of God' and to the bad 'the Devil will take you to his own country there you be tormented forever'.[155] Biblical related metaphors are mentioned in only one address and include a trumpet call[156] and 'singing to the Lamb that was slayne [sic] for us'.[157]

Thomas wrote more varied descriptions 'about the way that we should get to heaven'[158] with more written about heaven than of hell. He once used the metaphor of 'house' as Walter did,[159] but did not use 'country' like Walter and the older men. His dis-located experience may be an explanation. Thomas most often used biblical phrases and metaphors such as the parable of the sheep and goats,[160] 'singing to God and the Lamb',[161] and teachings of Jesus.[162] He is the only one to use the word 'resurrection'.[163]

The 'returning' motif of conversion narratives is present in Thomas' writings, where heaven is a place of returning to an innocence lost. Thomas described looking forward to heaven where 'I am returning unto God and to Jesus Christ'.[164] This theme of heaven as a form of 'returning' is expanded to describe people's age in heaven: 'there will be no end of you you will be young men in heaven'.[165] Several of the older men also used this metaphor.[166]

Among the older Aboriginal men the most common metaphor for heaven is 'God's country', 'a good country', 'a happy place', in contrast to hell which is the Devil's house / country, a bad place.[167] Like the younger speakers, the older men described heaven as a place where they would return to a younger version of themselves. Noemy described it as:

> if you go to heaven you will not die any more — you will be there little boys
> Angels little girls to you old women there always young forever there'.[168]

'God's country' was not at all associated with being at Wybalenna, or being displaced from their own country through colonisation. The ageing, sickness and death they experienced at Wybalenna were not heaven. Colonist life was not heaven. They will only be in 'God's country' after they die. Like their earlier, pre-contact stories of life after death, once they die they will be located in a place away from where they are living now. The reference to being younger versions of themselves seems to harken back to pre-contact time in their lives. The scarcity of sources makes it impossible to make more detailed comparisons between the earlier stories and the Christian addresses, but there are glimpses of similarities and new thoughts.

Crucial to the new thoughts is the Bible, 'God's book'.[169] However, the older men used fewer biblical references, probably because they had fewer skills in English literacy. Drinene made a general reference to the Bible — 'the Bible tells us plenty about Gods country'[170] — and only Noemy gave a specific verse.[171]

Equally crucial are their first language, and *pidgin*, interpretations. Clark's notes include occasional *pidgin* words used by other men such as Druemerterpunner:

> we die we go to heaven good people always *crackney* in heaven Mr Clark tell me
> + you Jesus Christ die was crucified — He die a little one not a long one then he jump up and went to Heaven by + by he bring you and me to Heaven if you are good people'.[172]

Crackney is translated 'to sit'[173] and was an important aspect of a creation story told by *Wurati*, when the first person 'sat down' for the first time and 'said it was NYERRAE good, very good.'[174]

Dowwringgi also used the phrase 'jump up', 'Let Jesus Christ jump up in your hearts then you are good and you are on your road to heaven',[175] and 'pray to him that Jesus Christ may spring up in your hearts You go to heaven a good place that you did not make'.[176] Druemerterpunner seems to use the phrase to describe resurrection, and Dowwringgi uses it for conversion, which itself is a foretaste of the final resurrection in Christian theology. So while biblical text, catechism, formulaic prayers and hymns were influential, continuing Aboriginal languages, adaptive *pidgin* and cultural roles continued to shape people's translations as they explored new narratives in their lives.

All people, black and white, in heaven

Another of the new thoughts was an expanding sense of the human population. Noemy, like Thomas, spoke of the universal population in heaven, 'white men and black men there they are always singing about God'.[177] The colonising experience seems to have contributed to an expanding sense of becoming 'Aboriginal' beyond the clan differentiations. Christian theology seems to have encouraged a growing experience of identifying with other 'black' people, and of 'black and white' together in heaven or hell. This idea of equality of all blacks, and of black and white before God is used by Thomas to affirm that the Aboriginal people have all they need to know:

> yes my friends ... there is black men in other countries they knows [sic] about God and Jesus Christ they don't have more instructions than what you have they can read the Bible and understand it.[178]

Drinene:

> The parson/Catechist reads it in the Bible and he tells us there are a great many black men in another country who read Gods book about Jesus Christ the son of God.[179]

These are signs of self-confidence and self-reliance at Wybalenna. They anticipate a time when Aboriginal people know they will not need colonist teachers but will continue their current emphasis on teaching each other. This appears to be stronger in Walter's writing and perhaps is a precursor to his later letters to the Governor about having their own land, their own resources and whichever colonists among them that they, rather than the Governor, chose.[180]

The addresses express a variety of individual theological and cultural emphases, biblical and cultural knowledge, as well as linguistic, literacy and oratory skills. They also express evolving interpretations of their collective experience of dispossession and removal. The responses were provisional and improvisational. The writings and addresses contain references to remembering their lives before arriving at Wybalenna. In this regard they contain elements of collective memory and on this point the words of political anthropologist John Gillis are useful:

> We need to be reminded that memories and identities are not fixed things, but representations or constructions of reality, subjective rather than objective phenomena ... We are constantly revising our memories to suit our current identities. Memories help us make sense of the world we live in; and 'memory work' is ... embedded in complex class, gender and power relations that

determine what is remembered (or forgotten), by whom, and for what end ...
National identities are, like everything, constructed and reconstructed ...¹⁸¹

The addresses exemplify a variety of subjective narratives of people articulating emerging identities and negotiating new relationships with each other and with colonists who exercised some power over them. An example of this 'negotiation' was when Walter retold commitments made by Robinson:

> The commandant told them they should have everything given to them and they should have plenty of flower [sic] plenty of tea and sugar and new trousers and new blankets rugs and everything what they want.
> And commandant did fulfilled his promises and give them as they require. The new cottages his facing to the hill [away from cold westerly winds] and Natives are nearly all got in their new houses. The commandant told them that they should have their new houses long before and when they came to Flinders they had everything given to them and they were satisfied."¹⁸²

In recounting the initial honouring of Robinson's promises of food and housing, these public oral acts of memory also created accountability. They were the antecedents for later written requests to colonial authorities to honour promises and agreements.¹⁸³ By naming the promises, Walter provided a basis for critiquing failures to fulfil them.

It is noticeable that there are no criticisms of Robinson and Clark in the sermons. The only 'bad white men' are those who sought to kill Aboriginal people. It is unimaginable that Clark would include a critique of himself or Robinson if they were ever mentioned the addresses.

Decline and closure

Robinson left Wybalenna for Port Philip in 1839. Among the fifteen Aborigines who went with him was Walter Arthur, one of the primary writers. The *Chronicle* had ceased in January 1838 and other writings seem to also have declined considerably or ceased altogether. Thomas Brune died in 1841, aged 19. When the surviving Aborigines returned from Port Philip in 1842, Walter Arthur's writing recommenced almost immediately. His focus, however, was now upon the promises made by successive Governors which had not been honoured.

Initially the letters were to George Washington Walker in Hobart.¹⁸⁴ Clark had remained at Wybalenna and was reappointed as catechist in February 1844, bringing three Aboriginal children back from the Orphan School. Walter Arthur's stream of letters continued, seemingly with the active support of Clark. The primary topic was now self-determination, that the Aboriginal people wanted to support themselves and continue living at Wybalenna and, indeed, the whole island.

The return of Jeanneret as commandant was not welcome and the stream of letters to the Colonial Secretary escalated the conflict, leading to the well-known petition to Queen Victoria in February 1846.[185] Further letters from other Aboriginal people followed including Washington, Jacky, Davey Bruny and Alphonso.[186] The earlier writing practices had some political effect, as claims and rebuttals led to successive inquiries, the removal of Jeanneret and reinstatement of Clark.

Unfortunately the aspiration of the Aboriginal people to have their own place, with whichever colonists they chose, was ignored. In July 1847 plans commenced for the final closure of Wybalenna and on 18 October 1847 the remaining Aboriginal people left for the last time.[187]

ENDNOTES CHAPTER FIVE

1. Plomley, 1966, p. 61.
2. Plomley, 1966, p. 94.
3. Plomley, 1966, p. 319.
4. ML Robinson Papers, A7062 CY549, pp. 165-67.
5. Druemerterpunner (Alexander), 14 April 1838, ML Robinson Papers, A7044 CY548, p. 48-49, and Plomley, 1987, p. 481.
6. Plomley, 1987, pp. 436, 440.
7. Plomley, 1966, p. 94-5.
8. See, Wesley, J., 'Reasons Against a Separation from the Church of England by John Wesley A. M., printed in 1758 with Hymns for the Preachers among the Methodists (so called) by Charles Wesley A. M.' http://anglicanhistory.org/wesley/reasons1760.html accessed 14/5/2014.
9. Tolar Burton, V., 2001, 'John Wesley and the Liberty to Speak: the Rhetorical and Literary Practices of Early Methodism', *College, Composition and Communication*, 53 (1), p. 67. Robinson, however, did not take up Wesley's affirmation of women as preachers.
10. Tolar Burton, 2001, p. 74.
11. ML Robinson Papers, A7074 CY825, p. 1.
12. Bhabha, H., 1994, *The Location of Culture*. London; Routledge, p. 96f.
13. 24/9/1837 & 6/2/1838, ML Robinson Papers, A7074 CY825.
14. In a catechetical examination by Robinson he described Walter: 'Is one of the Clerks to the Catechist and assists at the school' ML Robinson Papers, A7044 CY548, pp. 278-282.
15. ML Robinson Papers, A7074 CY825, p. 1.
16. For example, Thomas Brune, 4 January 1838, ML Robinson Papers, A7074 CY825, p. 127.
17. Plomley, 1966, pp. 544, 573, 776.
18. ML Robinson Papers, A7044 Vol 23. CY548, pp. 31-34.
19. Bhabha, 1994, pp. 85-122.
20. Ashcroft, 2013, pp. 62-63. See also, Pratt, M., 1991, 'Art in the Contact Zone', *Profession*, pp. 33-40.
21. McGrath, A., 1995, 'Contested ground: what is 'Aboriginal history'?' in McGrath, A. (ed.), *Contested Ground: Australian Aborigines under the British Crown*. St Leonard's: Allen and Unwin, pp. 359-97.
22. Ashcroft, 2013, p. 263; Peyer, 1997.
23. Attwood, 1989, p. 150.
24. Powell, M., 2002, 'Rhetorics of Survivance: How Native Americans use Writing', *College, Composition and Communication* 53 (3), pp. 396-434.
25. Writers/speakers also regularly used the phrase 'my friends', e.g., Walter Arthur, 6 February 1838, ML Robinson Papers, A7074 CY825, p. 97; Thomas Brune, 16 December 1837, ML Robinson Papers, A7074 CY825, p. 75; Druemerterpunner / Alexander, 14 April 1838, ML Robinson Papers, A7044 CY548, p. 48-49; Drinene

/ Neptune, 31 March 1838, ML Robinson Papers, A7044 CY548, pp. 44-45; Wurati / Alpha 14 April 1838, ML Robinson Papers, A7044 CY548, pp. 49-50.

26 Van Toorn, 2006, p. 111.
27 Dammery, 2001, p. 1-7.
28 Van Toorn, 2006. Rose, 1996.
29 Seven are undated and three have two copies, ML Robinson Papers A7074 CY825, CY979, A7044 CY548.
30 Eight are undated and one has three copies, ML Robinson Papers A7074 CY825.
31 There are written reports for five due to Clark's absence and people's deaths occurring on one weekend. Plomley, 1987, pp. 538, 549.
32 ML Robinson Papers, A7074 CY825, pp. 97, 131.
33 Robinson's daughter had found Walter and Mary Ann in bed together on 2 December 1837, Plomley, 1987, p. 506. In response, Robinson put Walter in gaol for seven days, Plomley, 1987, p. 508. In January 1838, Walter was 'tried before a jury of natives for having stolen from the government stores four knives. He pleaded guilty and was sentenced to wear irons for four days. The whole of the officers were present on the occasion and the proceedings were instituted with their concurrence', Plomley, 1987, p. 523.
34 The certificate of marriage reads — Flinders Island. 16th March 1838. The two aboriginal youths Walter and Mary Ann, having signified their desire of being united to each other in marriage, and having obtained for this purpose the consent of the Commandant, they appeared before me this day in the presence of the undersigned witnesses and others, and having solemnly declared their sense of the mutual obligations which that relation involves, and their determination through the help of divine grace faithfully to discharge them, as also their ignorance of any obstacle to their being so united, arising from consanguinity, previous contract or otherwise, were married by me agreeably to the forms of the Church of Scotland. Robert Clark Thomas Dove late catechist Chaplain of Flinders Island M Walsh M D medl officer, ML Robinson Papers, A7044 CY548, p.114.
35 Plomley, 1987, p. 544.
36 Plomley, 1987, 573.
37 Plomley, 1987, p. 776.
38 Johnston, 2004, p. 23.
39 Several women 'said they [Walter and Thomas] might KARNY speak but not write', Plomley, 1987, p. 489.
40 Dammery, 2001, p.11.
41 Ryan, 2012, p. 247.
42 ML Robinson Papers, A7062 CY549, pp. 165-66.
43 Plomley, 1987, p. 439.
44 Plomley, 1987, pp. 422, 439, 648. An example of a prayer by Thomas Brune is in ML Robinson Papers, A7074 CY825, p. 113.
45 ML Robinson Papers, A7044 CY548, p. 47.
46 Plomley, 1987, pp. 422, 424.
47 Tolar Burton, 2001, p. 67.
48 ML Robinson Papers, A7044, CY548, pp. 306-07.
49 Plomley, 1987, p. 421.
50 ML Robinson Papers, A7044 CY548, p. 38.
51 Plomley, 1987, p. 441.
52 Plomley, 1987, pp. 470, 51 -19.
53 Plomley, 1987, p. 452.
54 January 1838, Plomley, 1987, p. 524.
55 Plomley, 1987, pp. 463, 468, 490.
56 Plomley, 1987, p. 670.
57 Plomley, 1987, p. 942, or 30 June 1838, Plomley, 1987, p. 843.
58 Plomley, 1987, p. 375.
59 28 April 1837, Plomley, 1987, p. 439.
60 Plomley, 1987, p. 454.
61 Plomley, 1987, pp. 462, 470.
62 Plomley, 1987, pp. 500, 516, 568.
63 Plomley, 1987, p. 768.
64 Plomley, 1987, p. 420.
65 Plomley, 1987, p. 490.
66 Plomley, 1987, p. 482.
67 Plomley, 1987, p. 491.
68 Johnston notes a similar experience in the Pacific context, 'missionaries invested these books with such significance that native communities picked up on their importance as cultural signifiers and artefacts, potentially without also adopting the biblical message that the missionaries intended'. Johnson, 2001, p. 21.

69 It had been Robinson's desk but he gave it to the school in December 1835. Plomley, 1987, p. 319.
70 Plomley, 1987, pp. 691-92, note 1.
71 The raising of Lazarus is actually in John Chapter 11. This topic of resurrection and afterlife will be discussed in more detail later in the chapter.
72 Plomley, 1987, p. 440.
73 Plomley, 1987, p. 837.
74 Plomley, 1987, p. 448.
75 Plomley, 1987, p. 462.
76 Plomley, 1987, pp. 496, 498. For examples of other continuing cultural practices, see Birmingham, 1976, pp. 311-315.
77 Plomley, 1987, p. 495.
78 Plomley, 1987, p. 509.
79 ML Robinson Papers, A7044 CY548, pp. 45-6, 48, 54.
80 Plomley, 1987, pp. 576, 751.
81 Plomley, 1987, pp. 476, 707.
82 Plomley, 1987, p. 484. These addresses by Thomas and Walter, if they survive, must be among the 'undated' as these dates do not appear among their writings.
83 Plomley, 1987, pp. 476, 707, note 3.
84 Van Toorn, 2006, p. 118.
85 These translations are mostly from what is described in other contemporaneous documents rather than today's *palawa kani* language program run by the Tasmanian Aboriginal Corporation, which includes elements of several pre-colonial languages and additional material.
86 Plomley, 1976, pp. 240-241.
87 Plomley, 1976, p. 366.
88 Plomley, 1976, p. 255.
89 Plomley, 1976, p. 255, and email Theresa Sainty, 4 February, 2012.
90 Plomley 1976, p. 239.
91 Plomley, 1976, p. 251.
92 Plomley, 1976, p. 251.
93 Plomley, 1976, p. 436.
94 Plomley, 1976, pp. 238, 365, 426.
95 Plomley, 1987, p. 329.
96 Plomley, 1987, pp. 714-715.
97 See also, Ricoeur, P., 1992, *Oneself as Another*. Chicago; Chicago University Press, and Sandywell, 2013.
98 Plomley, 1987, pp. 484, 488.
99 Plomley, 1987, pp. 489, 491.
100 Plomley, 1987, pp. 422, 493.
101 Plomley, 1987, p. 444.
102 Plomley, 1987, pp. 250, 836, 853, 855; ML Robinson Papers, A7044 CY548, pp. 293-94.
103 ML Robinson Papers, A7044 CY548, pp. 49-50.
104 ML Robinson Papers, A7044 CY548, pp. 53-54.
105 Plomley, 1987, p. 864.
106 Plomley, 1987, p. 97.
107 ML Robinson Papers, A7064 Vol. 43, CY550, pp. 169-170.
108 ML Robinson Papers, A7044 CY548, pp. 49-50.
109 Undated, ML Robinson Papers, A7074 CY825, p. 117.
110 10 September 1837, ML Robinson Papers, A7074 CY825, p. 63, 20 April 1838, ML Robinson Papers, A7044 CY548, pp. 114-115.
111 Noemy, 10 March 1838, ML Robinson Papers, A7044 CY548, pp. 39-40, Drinene / Neptune, 17 March 1838, ML Robinson Papers, A7044 CY548, p. 42.
112 Drinene / Neptune, 24 February 1838, ML Robinson Papers, A7044 CY548, pp. 38-39.
113 Dowwringgi / Leonidas, 21 April 1838, ML Robinson Papers, A7044 CY548, p. 53.
114 *Wurati* / Alpha, 21 April 1838, ML Robinson Papers, A7044 CY548, pp. 53-54.
115 Skye, L., 2007, *Kerygmatics of the New Millenium*. Delhi; ISPCK. See also Douglas, B., 2001, 'Encounters with the Enemy? Academic Readings of Missionary Narratives on Melanesians', *Comparative Studies in Society and History*, 43 (1), January 2001, pp. 37-64, for an assessment of missionary writings about women's agency in Melanesia.
116 This recounting of colonial experience built on earlier conversations, e.g., Plomley, 1966, p. 88.
117 ML Robinson Papers, A7044 CY548, pp. 51-52.
118 ML Robinson Papers, A7044 CY548, p. 40.
119 ML Robinson Papers, A7044 CY548, p. 48.
120 ML Robinson Papers, A7044 CY548, pp. 49-50.
121 ML Robinson Papers, A7044 CY548, p. 50.
122 Van Toorn, 2006, p. 118.

123 Note the contrast in excerpts above between 'in your own country' and 'in our own country'.
124 ML Robinson Papers, A7064 Vol. 43, CY550, pp. 169–70, and Plomley, 1966, pp. 374, 375, 376.
125 Van Toorn, 2006, p. 108.
126 For example a sermon by Robinson 'On Prayer' began with part of an earlier sermon, 'Thoughts on Religion' ML Robinson Papers, A7074 CY825, Volume 53, pp. 30–72.
127 For example, Thomas Brune, 16 December 1837, Gospel of Matthew, Chapters 25 and 28, Revelation, Chapter 4, ML Robinson Papers, A7074 CY825, Volume 53, p. 73.
128 For example, Walter Arthur, quoted 'I Sing the Almighty Power of God' by Isaac Watts, Undated, ML Robinson Papers, A7074 CY825, Volume 53, p. 104.
129 Van Toorn, 2006, p. 108.
130 Plomley, 1966, p. 376.
131 Hindmarsh, B., 1999, ' "My Chains Fell Off, My Heart Was Free" Early Methodist Conversion Narrative in England' Church History, 68 (4), pp. 9–10.
132 Hindmarsh, 1999, pp. 16–20.
133 Hindmarsh, 1999, p. 26. See also, Sandywell, 2013; and Scott, J., 1990, *Domination and the Arts of Resistance*. New Haven: Yale University Press.
134 31 March 1838, ML Robinson Papers, A7044 CY548, pp. 44–45. See also, Walter Arthur, 6 February 1838, ML Robinson Papers, A7074 CY825, p. 97; Noemy, 21 April 1838, ML Robinson Papers, A7044 CY548, pp. 51–52. Thomas Brune, is the only one to say, 'I did not know…' 22 September 1837, ML Robinson Papers, A7074 CY825, p. 72, [emphasis mine]
135 27 December 1835, ML Robinson Papers, A7074 CY825, Vol 53, pp. 51–52.
136 For example, 'Thoughts on Religion', ML Robinson Papers, A7074 CY825, Vol 53, pp. 3–56.
137 24 October 1837, ML Robinson Papers, A7074 CY825, Vol 53, pp. 3–56.
138 This dis-location was also the situation of every colonist, who was also adapting to their new context, though in a different way to the Aboriginal people.
139 Undated, ML Robinson Papers, A7074 CY825, Vol 53, p. 107. Also, *Flinders Island Chronicle*, 2 October 1837, ML Robinson Papers, A7074 CY825, Vol 53, p. 23.
140 While the authorship is not stated, the handwriting is very similar to that of Thomas Brune in writings immediately prior, and subsequent, to this one. ML Robinson Papers, A7074 CY825, Vol 53, p. 113. Thomas Brune, 4 January 1838, ML Robinson Papers, A7074 CY825, Vol 53, p. 127. Drinene / Neptune, 31 March 1838, ML Robinson Papers, A7044 CY548, pp. 44–45. Dowwringgi / Leonidas, 21 April 1838, ML Robinson Papers, A7044 CY548, pp. 44–45. p. 53.
141 Thomas Brune, 20 April 1838, ML Robinson Papers, A7074 CY825, p. 130. Drinene / Neptune, 14 April 1838, ML Robinson Papers, A7044 CY548, p. 48. Alpha, 14 April, ML Robinson Papers, A7044 CY548, pp. 49–50.
142 Drinene / Neptune, 10 March 1838, ML Robinson Papers, A7044 CY548, p. 40.
143 Drinene / Neptune, 31 March, ML Robinson Papers, A7044 CY548, pp. 44–45.
144 For example, Gospel of John, Chapter 1; Acts of the Apostles, Chapter 2, Verses 17–21 and 25–28. See also, Duling, D.C., 2011, 'Memory, collective memory, orality and the gospels', *HTS Teologiese Studies/Theological Studies* 67 (1), Art. #915, 11 pages. DOI: 10.4102/hts.v67i1.915.
145 Noemy, 31 March ML Robinson Papers, A7044 CY548, pp. 43–44.
146 Plomley, 1966, p. 403.
147 Juster, S., 1989, 'In a Different Voice: Male and Female Narratives of Religious Conversion in Post-Revolutionary America', *American Quarterly*, 41 (1), pp. 34–62.
148 *Wurati* / Alpha, 21 April 1838, ML Robinson Papers, A7044 CY548, pp. 53–54.
149 Druemerterpunner / Alexander, 21 April 1838, ML Robinson Papers, A7044 CY548, pp. 50–51.
150 Undated, ML Robinson Papers, A7074 CY825, p. 109.
151 28 January 1838, ML Robinson Papers, A7074 CY825, p. 79, and undated, ML Robinson Papers, A7074 CY825, p. 95.
152 Noemy, For example, 24 February 1838, ML Robinson Papers, A7044 CY548, p. 38;

Druemerterpunner / Alexander, 31 March 1838, ML Robinson Papers, A7044 CY548, pp. 45-46; Drinene / Neptune, 14 April 1838, ML Robinson Papers, A7044 CY548, p. 48; Dowwringgi / Leonidas, 14 April 1838, ML Robinson Papers, A7044 CY548, p. 49; *Wurati* / Alpha, 14 April 1838, ML Robinson Papers, A7044 CY548, pp. 4-50.

153 6 February 1838, ML Robinson Papers, A7074 CY825, p. 97.
154 Undated, ML Robinson Papers, A7074 CY825, p. 103.
155 Undated, ML Robinson Papers, A7074 CY825, pp. 105, 109.
156 First Corinthians, Chapter 15, Verse 52.
157 Revelation, Chapter 5, Undated ML Robinson Papers, A7074 CY825, p. 105.
158 22 September 1837, Undated ML Robinson Papers, A7074 CY825, p. 67.
159 28 January 1838, ML Robinson Papers, A7044 CY548, pp. 117-118.
160 Gospel of Matthew, Chapter 25, Verses 31 to 46, 16 December 1837, ML Robinson Papers, A7074 CY825, p. 73.
161 Revelation, Chapter 5.
162 21 February 1838, ML Robinson Papers, A7074 CY825, p. 133, 20 April 1838, ML Robinson Papers, A7074 CY825, p. 134.
163 Undated, ML Robinson Papers, A7074 CY825, p. 115.
164 4 January 1838, ML Robinson Papers, A7074 CY825, p. 127.
165 Thomas Brune, 20 April 1838, ML Robinson Papers, A7074 CY825, p. 134.
166 For example, Noemy, 21 April 1838, ML Robinson Papers, A7044 CY548, pp. 51-52.
167 Noemy, 10 March 1838, ML Robinson Papers, A7044 CY548, pp. 39-40; 17 March 1838, ML Robinson Papers, A7044 CY548, p. 41; 14 April 1838, ML Robinson Papers, A7044 CY548, pp. 47-48. Drinene / Neptune, 17 March 1838, ML Robinson Papers, A7044 CY548, p. 42. Druemerterpunner / Alexander, 31 March 1838, ML Robinson Papers, A7044 CY548, pp. 45-46. Dowwringgi / Leonidas, 21 April 1838, ML Robinson Papers, A7044 CY548, p. 53.
168 Noemy, 21 April 1838, ML Robinson Papers, A7044 CY548, pp. 51-52.

Similarly, Drinene / Neptune, 31 March 1838, ML Robinson Papers, A7044 CY548, pp. 44-45, and Druemerterpunner / Alexander, 31 March 1838, ML Robinson Papers, A7044 CY548pp. 45-46; 14 April 1838, ML Robinson Papers, A7044 CY548, pp. 48-49.

169 See also Johnson, 2001, p. 25.
170 31 March 1838, ML Robinson Papers, A7044 CY548, pp. 44-45.
171 Gospel of John, Chapter 3, Verse 16. 31 March 1838, ML Robinson Papers, A7044 CY548, pp. 43-44.
172 21 April 1838, ML Robinson Papers, A7044 CY548, pp. 50-51.
173 Plomley, 1976, p. 391.
174 Plomley, 1966, p. 373.
175 This 'road' is a reminder of the 'tracks' from the stars of the 'Milky Way' mentioned in Chapter One, Plomley, 1966, p 368.
176 14 April 1838, ML Robinson Papers, A7044 CY548, p. 49, 21 April 1838, ML Robinson Papers, A7044 CY548, p. 53.
177 Noemy, 21 April 1838, ML Robinson Papers, A7044 CY548, pp. 51-52. Thomas undated, ML Robinson Papers, A7074 CY825, p. 87.
178 28 January 1838, ML Robinson Papers, A7074 CY825, p. 77.
179 31 March 1838, ML Robinson Papers, A7044 CY548, pp. 44-45.
180 The petition to Queen Victoria was dated February 1846, TAHO CSO 11/26/378. See also correspondence Walter Arthur to George Washington Walker, 30 December 1845, ML CY979 pp. 227-230.
181 Gillis, in Duling, 2011, p. 3 of 11.
182 Walter Arthur, 21 September 1837, ML Robinson Papers, A7074 CY825, unpaginated.
183 TAHO CSO 11/26/378, Plomley, 1987, pp. 148-49.
184 ML Robinson Papers, CY3695.
185 TAHO CSO 11/26/378, pp. 13-15 and TAHO CSO 24/8/824.
186 TAHO CSO 11/26/378, pp. 20-90, also Plomley, 1987, p. 151, 167.
187 Plomley, 1987, p. 134.

CHAPTER SIX

'Neglecting the simplest duties'

WHILE THE activities at Wybalenna were unfolding through the 1830s and 1840s, a distinctly different experience was occurring on the nearby Bass Strait islands before, during and after this period. Throughout the nineteenth century, the islander families with their mix of Aboriginal and colonist ancestors changed from living largely independent lives to living under strict laws closely overseen by the government by the early twentieth century. Representatives of the Christian church were involved to an increasing degree and influenced Aboriginal people's experience of the Christian faith.

The relationship between Aboriginal people on the islands and the institutional church rarely developed to their mutual satisfaction. For the most part the islanders did as they had done for decades. They did for themselves what needed to be done, at least as best they could to live a relatively comfortable life. Within the wider church the islanders and their concerns were largely ignored, aside from the interest of occasional individual clergy. The government did not regard them as 'Aboriginal' like those survivors of Wybalenna living at *putalina* / Oyster Cove in the late nineteenth century, and the church did not regard them as an 'Aboriginal mission' like the missions they developed in other parts of Australia.

The earliest introduction of Aboriginal people to the Christian faith in the north-east area of Van Diemen's Land, including the Furneaux Islands, appears to have been through sealers such as James Munro. Munro was one of a number of sealers in the islands. He lived with several Aboriginal women including Drummer.ner.looner / Jumbo, Smoker, Isaac and Little Judy. Cameron proposes that these Straitsmen and *tyereelore* developed 'endearing relationships' in which the husbands taught their wives to speak English and the women 'maintained close connections with country, their spirituality and kin'.[1] Robinson visited the islands for several months in late 1830, and from March to June 1831, as part of his conciliatory 'mission' seeking to remove Aboriginal women.[2] Robinson conducted church services, reading from the Bible and divine service of the *Book of Common Prayer*.[3]

Munro appears to have been familiar with the Bible, and possibly read it to the three women and three children with him.[4] Several sealers delivered Munro 'some Testaments and spelling books from the Mission'.[5] When Munro visited Hobart to petition for the return of women who had been removed by Robinson, he is reported to have said, 'They [the women] do not pay any attention to the Sabbath. I do read the Bible to my children I have two but they are not my own'.[6] If this is an honest description of his practice, it suggests Munro followed the style of family Bible reading rather than abiding by Robinson's 'notice' that he perform divine service from the *Book of Common Prayer* each Sunday. The sealers' expressions of Christian faith were very different from the leaders of the wider colonial society.

A similar practice is reported a few years later in November 1842 of a family on Preservation Island.[7] It is impossible to know which parts of the Bible these fathers such as Munro and Thomas Beeton read most, and what role the Bible played in their families' lives, but some fathers were clearly using the Bible in teaching their children.

These family relationships, not formal institutional relationships, were the context in which these children learned to read the Bible. It is a striking contrast to the Orphan School in Hobart and the rote learning catechetical classes at Wybalenna. In these islander families Bible passages were chosen by these fathers who had had twenty to thirty years of rarely, if ever, visiting a church building or participating in divine service. Like the Aboriginal mothers who continued to tell stories and undertake cultural practices while separated from their kin and birth country, these fathers gave their own teaching and interpretation of Christian faith without a gathered church community, without sacraments, and in some instances without a prayer book. One can only imagine how these children brought together in their own lives these stories and practices from the women and men who shaped their lives.

Lucy Beeton

One Aboriginal person among the islander families who were involved in Christian practice is Lucy Beeton's mother, Bet, or Betsy Smith.[8] Lucy's parents and other relatives lived on Gun Carriage Island until the mid 1830s.[9] They moved to Longford, near Launceston,[10] for a period of time and then returned to the islands.[11] Lucy's father, Thomas Beeton, like Munro, used petitions to Governor Arthur to counter the activities of Robinson. His literacy and active engagement with colonist leaders were probably contributing factors to Lucy's strong emphasis on education among islander families throughout her life.

Lucy's encounter with the Christian faith was firstly through her father, Thomas, and his personal endeavours reading the Bible and other tracts that he acquired from sealers and traders visiting from Hobart or Launceston. The Beeton family's knowledge, practice and experience developed without the guidance of a representative of the church and without the regular practice of communal worship. It seems they had a Bible, a prayer book and a limited number of Christian tracts.

Little is known of Lucy's childhood. After her early years at Gun Carriage, she later lived at Longford, outside Launceston in 1836 and was baptised by R. R. Davies at the Longford Anglican Church on Tuesday 9 February 1836, along with her brothers James and Henry. Her parents' names are listed as 'Beedon and Betsy Herbert', his occupation as 'Sealer, Gun Carriage Island'.[12] She was later described as 'a firm believer in Christianity'.[13]

In 1851 Thomas Beeton applied to Lieutenant-Governor Denison for the appointment of a missionary–catechist to educate their children.[14] Lucy was then twenty-two. Thomas Beeton suggested the salary for such a person be paid from the same fund as that which supported the Aboriginal Station at *putalina* / Oyster Cove. Governor Denison refused their application on the grounds that they 'could not fairly be termed Aborigines'.[15] This link between education and catechism was close and strong within colonial society, as shown in previous chapters concerning Wybalenna, as was the link at that time between the Church of England and the government.[16] Churches rarely, if ever, differentiated themselves from government decisions in regard to Aboriginal people. As will be discussed later, churches more often than not were involved in the formation of government policy, and encouraged Aboriginal people's acquiescence and compliance.

Responding to Thomas Beeton, Bishop Nixon visited the islands in September 1854 on board the government schooner, *Beacon*, as it resupplied lighthouses.[17] Nixon was uncomplimentary of Aboriginal religious expression:

> No trace can be found on the existence of any religious usage, or even sentiment, amongst them, unless, indeed we may call by that name the dread of a malignant and destructive spirit, which seems to have been their predominant, if not their only, feeling on the subject.[18]

In contrast, when visiting Gun Carriage Island, Nixon wrote:

> we came at last, to the residence of the 'greatest lady' it has ever been my good fortune to encounter. Lucy Beadon, a noble looking half-caste of some

> twenty-five years of age, bears the burden of some twenty-three stone. Good humoured and kind-hearted, she is everyone's friend upon the island. High-minded, and earnest in her Christian profession, she has set herself to work to do good in her generation. From the pure love of those around her, she daily gathers together the children of the sealers and does her best to impart to them the rudiments both of secular and religious knowledge. The daughter of one of the sealers, Lucy Beadon, takes upon herself the honourable charge of teaching day by day the younger members of the community.[19]

During this trip Nixon also baptised six children and performed the marriage of Edward Mansell and Judy Thomas, an Aboriginal woman whose English was minimal.[20] Her lack of English suggests it was not needed for daily life. But a different choice was being made for the children, who it was thought needed to learn English and receive adequate schooling. Nixon performed divine service at the sealer Tucker's house, with twenty-eight people present, which comprised the population of the whole island, plus some from nearby. He noticed that somewhat surprisingly, the people were familiar with the format, including psalm singing.[21]

These baptisms by Bishop Nixon are recorded in the register for the Anglican Church at George Town, where Reverend John Fereday was the local clergyman. The baptisms included children of John and Frances Maynard from Gun Carriage Island, Richard and Elizabeth Maynard from Long Island, John and Jane Smith from Tin Kettle Island and George and Jane Everett from Woody Island.[22] Other baptisms of islander children are also recorded in the register. It includes children baptised during Reverend W. Richardson's visit to the islands in November 1862, but also other baptisms that were independent of a visit to the islands by a clergyman.[23] This demonstrates the islanders' initiative in seeking out baptism for their children while they were visiting George Town. At least ten Aboriginal children from the Furneaux Islands were baptised at the George Town Anglican Church between 1861 and 1880 during family visits there.[24]

The purpose of these visits may have been for trade, but they were also likely to have been because of leases on various islands. Fereday was involved in brokering leases between various islander families and the Lands Department. The Beeton and Everett baptisms in January 1859 may have been at the beginning of discussions that led to Fereday applying on behalf of George Everett and James Beeton for Preservation Island and the Inner Sisters respectively in December 1862. Two years later Fereday asked the Surveyor-General to prepare leases for George Everett on Preservation Island.[25] According to Skira the George Town clergyman held money on behalf of islanders, embezzled some, but continued to act on their behalf.[26]

These families had by this time been living on these islands for several decades without any clergyman or catechist. Notwithstanding the sometimes-violent acts by several men in earlier decades,[27] it appears that some families had developed their own Christian practices and methods of teaching their children. Some of these practices, such as at Tucker's, seem to have included the *Book of Common Prayer*.[28]

Tucker's statement and Nixon's writing of it may to some extent be shaped by the desire of both men to impress their audiences: Tucker to impress the Bishop, and the Bishop to impress his parishioners reading his report. Nevertheless, the location on Gun Carriage Island where Lucy Beeton was also living at the time, and twenty-eight people filling Tucker's house, including a bedroom, for the church service, does suggest some Christian worship practice occurred in this, and other, families.

However the desire for Christian services was not universal among the islanders. At Clarke Island Nixon found 'the sacrament of baptism was declined on behalf of six children by their parents'.[29] This may have been the occasion Nixon described 'when the congregation was composed almost entirely of Wesleyans, and therefore less favourably affected toward the ordinances of the Church'.[30] But it is more likely the occasion of Dr Allen on nearby Preservation Island refusing to have his children baptised.[31]

Lucy Beeton could have become the teacher–catechist her father desired to see appointed to the islands but her identity as single, Aboriginal, and a woman, were probably factors that prevented formal training and placement within the Board of Education at that time. As an adult Lucy continued her father's interest in education and she arranged for a catechist to provide spiritual and religious instruction. Following her death an unnamed correspondent paid tribute to her:

> Lucy was a woman of fine character — generous, virtuous and deeply imbued with the highest principles of her duty to God and to her 'own people'. With me, she felt we had dispossessed 'her people' of this fair land, and banished them to die on Flinders Island, and I have often heard her say, "Why do you blessed with civilisation and Christianity, neglect to afford to us poor half-castes the simplest duties laid upon you by the requirements of Christian charity?[32]

During Nixon's tenure government financial support for the church altered significantly. The government had for several decades supported the Church of England's mission activities in Tasmania with £1800 per annum used to fund five chaplains, but this was discontinued in July 1856.[33] Previously, the government had paid for a catechist at Wybalenna, but from this time forward the church was required to provide donations from its own sources to support a catechist among the islands.[34]

In October 1861 the Tasmanian parliament debated the provision of £150 for a 'school master and catechist for the half castes and other inhabitants of the Furneaux Islands'. It was estimated there were sixty children among the 150 inhabitants. Mr Meredith spoke of Lucy Beeton, 'who had instructed the children and whose charity exceeded anything they could believe'. Where she obtained her education he could not say, but she 'devoted a good portion of her time to those who were anxious to improve'.[35]

Following this debate, Thomas Reibey, Archdeacon at Launceston, visited the islands for the first time in March 1862.[36] Like the earlier visit of Nixon, the services he conducted seem to have been well attended by most but not all of the islanders. Reibey took up the earlier request in proposing a schoolmaster and catechist and recommended Mr Mitchell.[37] Parents offered to pay for board and lodging of the children away from their homes.[38] Green and *truwana* / Cape Barren islands were considered the most accessible most of the year and *truwana* / Cape Barren was the preferred option.[39] Within the church debate continued. The government grant required that 'a like sum was contributed by a religious body inclined to take up the work'. Reibey argued that

> this important work ought to be taken up by the Church of England; the Islanders were attached to the Church, made use of her services, and were our own people.
> If we allowed the matter to drop, others would try and make terms.[40]

In September 1862 the Legislative Council resolved to increase its contribution and provide £250 for a schoolmaster and catechist for the half-caste and other inhabitants of the Furneaux Islands, provided that a like amount was raised by private subscription.[41] But church funds were lacking, as was a suitable teacher, and by the end of the year, the islanders were still waiting. Reibey wrote again, echoing Bishop Nixon a few years earlier:

> The presence of a School master and catechist will pay but the lowest measure of our duties towards them.
> In the working of the laws of God's providence we have dispossessed these poor people of this fair land. In that we may hope there was no sin, but surely sin would lie heavy at our doors if we, blessed with civilization and Christianity neglected, when opportunity was offered us to fulfil to them the simplest duties laid upon us by the requirements of Christian charity.[42]

The following month Reverend William Richardson, Anglican clergyman at Avoca, and others, visited the islands aboard the *Flying Arrow*. Richardson baptised several children and preached to those on Chappell Island.[43] Richardson suggested a monthly clergy visit to the adults, and that the children be accommodated at a school along the Tamar River.[44] Following Richardson's visit, and no doubt aware of the work of the clergymen Reibey, Fereday and Richardson in seeking someone to visit them, Lucy Beeton and others from the islands, wrote to Fereday on 26 December 1862 requesting an annual visit from a clergyman. Fereday forwarded the request to the Finance Committee of the Launceston Archdeaconry and added his parish's willingness to free him to visit the islands each year. The letter was publicised in the *Cornwall Chronicle*, a few months later on 23 May 1863:

> Rev and Dear Sir,
>
> We the undersigned inhabitants of Bass's Straits Islands, most respectfully beg of you to take into your consideration that we are left without the means of attending upon any religious ordinances, and that our children scarcely know what it is to join in the public worship of God.
>
> We very much lament this state of things for our own sakes, but we are especially anxious that our children should not grow up as if they were in a heathen land; but rather they should have some opportunities for hearing the Gospel preached to them by a Minister of Christ.
>
> We therefore entreat you to come over and help us; we have all known you long and esteem you very highly and most gratefully bear in mind the many kindnesses we have received at your hands, and we beg that if you can possibly arrange it, you will visit us more frequently than you have hitherto done, and come down regularly at certain appointed times to minister amongst us.
>
> Most humbly entreating that you will take into serious and speedy consideration our earnest request of your coming to assist us.[45]

It was signed by thirty-five islanders, and again, demonstrates a desire to link with the church community, particularly in ensuring their children learn the Christian faith and participate in worship.

Despite the letters from Reibey, Richardson and the islanders themselves, the £250 required from private subscriptions to complement the government grant was not forthcoming.[46] However, despite this lack of money, within a few months a teacher–catechist was working on Badger Island. This first teacher–catechist was not appointed by the Government's Board of Education, nor by the Anglican Church, but by Lucy Beeton herself. For two years, from May 1863 to June 1865, Mr Edwin Richardson worked as teacher on Badger Island, and later Goose and *truwana* / Cape Barren islands, teaching the two Beeton families.[47]

Richardson had been Church of England School master at Avenel, Victoria. He was eligible to receive a title deed on application at the Receipt and Pay Office, Beechworth (Victoria),[48] but it appears he did not take it up. It is not known how and why a schoolmaster in a town en route to the goldfields, and on the mail route between Melbourne and Sydney, would move to the remote Bass Strait islands, particularly without communication with the local bishop or archdeacon. It may be that Edwin Richardson, schoolmaster, was related to Reverend

William Richardson, clergyman, who visited the islands in late November 1862, but this is not known.

A month after Edwin Richardson had begun, Reibey visited the islands accompanied by Fereday.[49] They baptised children, distributed schoolbooks and tracts, conducted a funeral and examined potential sites for locating a teacher.[50] The presence of other graves at Gun Carriage Island is a reminder that the people conducted their own locally adapted ceremonies, possibly using the *Book of Common Prayer*, on the more usual days when clergy were not present. Reibey was not impressed with Richardson on Badger Island. On returning to Launceston he recommended that Richardson not continue.[51] However, Richardson did continue at least until June 1865.

In his 1863 report to Parliament Reibey noted that of the £250 sought from subscriptions, only £80 was collected. He hoped the parliament would include £250 on the Estimates for 1864 without the requirement for private subscriptions. He also asked that the six Aboriginal people still remaining at *putalina* / Oyster Cove be sent to their relatives at these islands.[52] In the following year Reibey visited England.[53] While he was there, along with former Bishop Nixon, they sought donations towards a boat to assist the church's work in the islands. Over £400 was donated from sources in England,[54] and thus began the 'fleet' that was to be built over subsequent decades.

The 'mission' to the Furneaux Islands was, in a number of ways, not unique. Within the Anglican church similar boat trips by clergymen were occurring along the D'Entrecasteaux Channel in the south. These were described in almost identical terms, and included the same activities of baptising children, distributing Bibles, prayer books, tracts and story books.[55] Some of these missions in the 'bush' (i.e., those areas outside the designated parishes) survived on donations while others were financially supported by the Diocese through the Ripon Fund.[56]

In October 1865 the first 'mission' boat, the *Gift*, was launched in Hobart. It had been built for £600 by Mr Ross, primarily from donations Reibey gained while in England.[57] The first trip in the *Gift*, and Reibey's third visit to the islands, was in March 1866. At Chappell Island on Good Friday, 30 March, he conducted an open-air service attended by fifty people, baptised four children and distributed tracts and books.[58] Despite the lack of financial support from within the church, Reibey again visited the islands aboard the *Gift* in October 1866. He baptised several children, conducted a wedding and performed divine service.[59] By early 1868 a new boat was being built to replace the *Gift*, 'which was found to be very unsuitable, she not being the class of vessel required'.[60] The *Pearl* was launched on 6 March 1868.[61]

Along with the troubles on the water, there was apparent conflict among the clergy in Launceston later that year, as Reibey was overlooked by the Bishop for the role of curate at the prestigious St John's Church in favour of a much younger man nominated by the Boards of Patronage, Reverend Marcus B. Brownrigg.[62]

Beneath these conflicts simmered a more disturbing issue that burst into the public arena at the Synod meeting in February 1870, when Mr Clark 'attempted to table petition charging Archdeacon Reibey with the grossest and most cowardly immorality'.[63] The issue came to a very public climax when Reibey launched legal proceedings against Henry Blomfield. The court case occurred 1–4 June 1870 in the Launceston Supreme Court.[64] The action was brought by Reibey claiming that Blomfield published 'false, scandalous and defamatory libel' using the words, 'The Archdeacon during my absence from home made an indecent assault on my wife'. Reibey sought damages of £1000. The events were said to have occurred in July 1868. The jury found in favour of Blomfield.[65] Reibey resigned virtually immediately as a clergyman and within weeks from school boards.[66]

The breakdown of relationship between Reibey and the church appears to have had a detrimental effect on the church's involvement in the 'Furneaux mission'. It is hard to know how many, if any, of the islanders were aware of the conflict between the 'late Archdeacon' and the Anglican church nor of how much money was being spent on the mission which amounted almost entirely, it seems, to the maintenance of the boats that sat idle in the Tamar River for about ten months of the year. It is hard to imagine the price of Bibles, prayer books, tracts, and other Christian reading material, outweighing that of the boats. Reibey's sale of the *Gift* immediately prior to the meeting of the northern Finance Committee, then claiming to be '£300 to £400 out of pocket by the mission'[67] suggests the use of the fund was almost solely on the boat. He interpreted the lack of donations from among the church members, £83 in the previous year,[68] as a vote of no-confidence in the mission, compelling him 'to abandon the attempt to benefit the half-castes of the Furneaux Group' and leaving him, on his estimation, '£300 to £400 out of pocket'.[69]

With so much denominational effort and resources put into auditing the accounts and purchasing and refurbishing the boats to carry the annual visitors, it seems the primary object of the mission, the islanders themselves, continued their usual lifestyle and expressed their Christian faith as they had been doing for years before without much interest or attention from the institutional church. It draws attention to the role of the 'Furneaux mission' within the rhetoric and the politics of the Anglican Church. This is distinct from the day-to-day faith experience of islander people, families and communities.

Following Reibey's resignation the church's processes began moving towards identifying a schoolteacher for the islands. It was now eight years since the Beetons had privately employed Edwin Richardson on Badger Island.

Bishop Bromby requested George Town clergyman, Reverend John Fereday, to visit the islands and in February 1871 he travelled in the *Freak* to several islands, conducting open air services, baptising children, conducting religious instruction, distributing books, tracts and texts, and solemnising two weddings. More than fifty people participated in these services across seven islands, including thirty at Chappell Island.[70]

Tragically, within a few weeks his return, Reverend Fereday, the islanders' longest active church supporter, died in an accident in a 'dog-cart' driven by Archdeacon Browne. A 'wheel of the carriage came into collision with the stump of a tree' and Fereday died of his injuries.[71] For all the documents by, and about, Reibey, it is important to recognise that Fereday visited the islands more often and over a longer period of time.

Following their petition in January and Fereday's visit, the islanders met Governor Du Cane on Goose Island in August 1871 to discuss leases. Du Cane reported that the government had appointed a schoolmaster with a suitable salary, and allowance for a boat and boat's crew. Money was also available for the erection of a schoolhouse on a suitable site.[72] As well as appointing Henry Collis as schoolmaster, and perhaps also in response to requests for security of leases, Lucy Beeton was given a lifetime lease of Badger Island at a yearly rent of £24 for her efforts to 'instruct and civilise' the islander children.[73] Almost ten years after the islanders first asked for a teacher–catechist, an appointment funded by the government was finally made. This appointment also marked the renewal of the partnership between the Anglican Church and the government's Board of Education in providing a schoolteacher and church catechist in the one person, as had often occurred prior to 1856.

Reibey's replacement, Brownrigg, offered to go to the islands, and the expenses, some £14 or £15, were to be charged against Archdeacon Browne's expenses.[74] Between 1872 when he first travelled to the islands and his retirement in 1887, Brownrigg undertook thirteen trips, which were each reported in the *Launceston Examiner* and the *Church News*, and have been compiled in Stephen Murray-Smith's book, *Mission to the Islands*.[75]

Brownrigg's first visit began in February 1872 aboard the *Freak*. In his report he indicated the costs of the anticipated annual trips would be 'defrayed by the residents themselves' and therefore only required identifying suitable clergymen. Islanders' contributions would be received by Lucy Beeton during the birding season and forwarded to Launceston.

> The readiness evinced by all the residents of the Islands to help in providing for their own spiritual requirements may surely be accepted as an earnest of their desire for the extension towards themselves of some spiritual care.[76]

At each place he visited, Brownrigg conducted a short service comprising Bible reading and prayer. On each Sunday he conducted morning and evening prayers.[77] As well as the prayers, Brownrigg conducted fifteen baptisms and one practice of Holy Communion. This is the first explicit mention of the sacrament of Holy Communion among a congregation comprised primarily of Aboriginal people.[78] There does not appear to have been any mention of Holy Communion being practiced at the Wybalenna settlement nor in any previous visit to the islands by Fereday or Reibey.

This may be partly explained by the Anglican Church's practice of only permitting confirmed members to be communicants in Holy Communion, and the practice of the Presbyterian Church, the denomination of Thomas Dove, chaplain at Wybalenna from 1838, of celebrating Holy Communion two to three times each year with extensive preparation for communicants. The celebration on Badger Island is therefore a significant occasion in the liturgical history of people on the islands.

Brownrigg would have followed 'The Order of Ministrations of the Holy Communion' in the *Book of Common Prayer*. This order includes recitation of the Lord's Prayer, Ten Commandments, and Nicene Creed, each of which was central to public Christian worship at that time. It is intriguing to ponder where the elements of bread and wine were sourced, whether from among the people or transported from Launceston.[79] A large number of tracts and prayer books, courtesy of the Committee of the British and Foreign Bible Society, were also distributed.[80]

The following year Brownrigg published a booklet about his visit and the profits of sale of the *Cruise of the Freak* were to go towards 'procuring books for circulation among the islanders'.[81] It is important to recognise the primary purpose of the publications was to raise funds to support his visits. The reports therefore are skewed towards representing the islanders in ways that would generate donations from church members. Brownrigg also undertook a number of visits to Hobart to raise funds for the 'Furneaux mission' in 1873,[82] 1877,[83] and 1880[84] with only relatively small amounts being donated.

Temperance

In January 1876 Bishop Bromby's visit coincided with Brownrigg's. Brownrigg reported that at Long Beach the Bishop conducted the service as elsewhere, addressing the young people on the subjects of confirmation and the Lord's Supper. There were services in the morning, afternoon and evening, the mission form being used, a baptism, confirmation of eight children, 'five of whom were half-castes', and the administration of the Lord's Supper to twelve communicants. Services were well attended, with fifty in the evening. The Sunday School classes of Mrs Collis were valuable preparations for the confirmees.[85] The role of the schoolteacher in preparing children for confirmation within the church highlights the confluence of church and state in the lives of these Aboriginal people.

Bishop Bromby's report contrasted with Archdeacon Brownrigg's in mentioning the extent of drunkenness among some adults. Brownrigg had not mentioned anything about alcohol consumption in his previous reports, but it became a regular feature from this time on. The catalyst appears to have been the wreck of the *Cambridgeshire* with its large quantity of brandy. The islanders took advantage of the availability of the cargo. Brownrigg reported that the islanders' consumption of the brandy was 'producing the greatest demoralization'.[86] Later that year Brownrigg became more active in the Temperance Society in Launceston[87] and the following year saw a new and explicit focus on the 'temperance pledge' during his visits. Thirty-five signed the pledge during his next visit. 'There is perhaps no more serious obstacle to the spread of Christianity than intemperance.'[88] In 1878,

> [a] Temperance Lecture fitly crowned the observance of the day. The
> Schoolroom was completely filled — temperance hymns were sung — and the
> utmost attention was given to the lecture, which was illustrated with diagrams.
> At the close twenty seven persons signed the total abstinence pledge, and we
> may be allowed to hope that next year there will be a branch of the Church of
> England Temperance Society established in "the Straits".[89]

Throughout Brownrigg's visits the most commonly described gathering was 'family prayers'. Larger gatherings were usually limited to Badger Island and *truwana* / Cape Barren Island at the school. There continued to be a changeover in boats and in 1881, Brownrigg travelled for the first and only time in an islander's boat when he 'took passage in ketch, *Julia*, owned by Mr Harry Armstrong, one of the half-castes.'[90]

As a sign of the increasing participation of clergy in the longer term plans of the government, Brownrigg participated in setting out the allotments for the new township on *truwana* / Cape Barren Island during his visit in 1882. These multiple roles intensified for the permanent schoolteacher, Collis, who fulfilled church, education and other government roles.[91] The schools run by Henry and Hannah Collis closed in December 1882 and did not re-open until eight years later, when Edward Stephens was appointed in June 1890.[92] With the departure of Collis, Brownrigg publicised the request for a catechist–teacher 'who would, for his part, find among the Straits Islands an interesting field of usefulness alike promoting the welfare of man and the glory of God'.[93]

The closure of the school saw the subsequent church services conducted in John Maynard's shed and cottage.[94] In 1885 Bishop Sandford conducted services on *truwana* / Cape Barren in an unfinished log hut. Due to damage to the boat the

Bishop and Archdeacon had to remain at Port Furneaux (*truwana* / Cape Barren Island township) for several days. As a result, the next day, Monday 23 February was a 'red letter' day for them as

> eighty to ninety persons attended services at Port Furneaux, services held daily and three on Sunday. Festival the following day, triumphal arch constructed and Bishop welcomed, games followed by tea and temperance meeting, with thirty to forty taking the pledge.
>
> Bishop presented to Miss Beedon, middle-aged spinster, known as the 'Queen of the Isles', who came from her royal residence on Badger Island to welcome the visitors.'[95]

The islanders' public appreciation for these visits was expressed in a statement read by Mr Summers,

> My Lord, we the inhabitants of the Furneaux beg respectfully to welcome you to this part of your diocese and to assure you that we do so with heartfelt sincerity and with gratitude for your kindness in coming to visit us, and we trust that when circumstances and your onerous duties permit we shall have the pleasure at some future period of seeing you again. We take this opportunity to mention that we receive most kind and acceptable visits from Rev. Canon Marcus Brownrigg whose kindness and advice we greatly appreciate.
>
> This address was kindly followed by one to myself [Brownrigg],
>
> Sir, we the undersigned inhabitants of the township of Furneaux tender our most sincere thanks for the interest and good you are trying to do towards us. We sincerely hope you will continue your visits to us, knowing you are trying your best to do us good. We only wish you could do a little more with us; in fact we want somebody with us that will lead us the right road and to help put down that demon — drink.[96]

The islanders' desire to have 'somebody with us that will lead us to the right road' suggests that when it was beneficial they wanted to strengthen their relationship with the church. They did not yet see themselves as willing or able to undertake church services without a church-appointed person. Events of the following decade, however, show that they were also not willing to maintain a relationship with the church if it gave little in return.

The last decade of the nineteenth century began with idealised hopes and romantic rhetoric from church leaders and concluded with conflict and hostility. Throughout this decade the Anglican clergy visits to the islands were carried out by Bishop Montgomery rather than a clergyman from the north of the state.

Montgomery followed the pattern of his predecessors in visiting the largest population centre, which had moved from Badger Island to *truwana* / Cape Barren Island with the establishment of the school. Most visits began with an initial 'community meeting' to plan the itinerary. This was followed by Sunday services in the reopened schoolroom until land was acquired and a church building constructed. Services continued to include baptisms, confirmations, celebration of Holy Communion, and the occasional wedding. These were followed by visits to homes on the smaller islands, weather permitting. Montgomery visited lighthouses and a wide range of families so his liturgical statistics include people who were not Aboriginal. Overall about half the baptisms he performed in the 1890s were of Aboriginal people.

In 1891 Montgomery visited and baptised twenty-eight, more than half of whom were Aboriginal people. While Montgomery's reports do not always indicate which families were involved, there were not sufficient Anglo families for the baptisms to have occurred only among them. In early 1892 Bishop Montgomery sought a grant of land from the government for a church building and burial ground on *truwana* / Cape Barren Island. This was initially refused.[97] Montgomery withdrew the request of a burial ground but sought an occupation licence for land on which to build a church.[98]

In early February eighty-one islanders wrote to Montgomery, as their predecessors had written to Sandford:

> We the inhabitants of the Furneaux Islands most heartily welcome your lordship to this far away part of your diocese, and we cherish the deep conviction that by your presence and wise counsels, the good work begun and carried on during the past eighteen months will be greatly assisted and blessed.
>
> We are greatly indebted to you and our late Bishop the Right Rev D. Sandford for the advantages we enjoy of regular church services and Sunday School on the Lord's Day, and would assure you that, as we are all, by baptism, members of the Church of England, we desire to remain such, by open profession and practice, and hope that the zeal of others will never inflict upon us those schisms and dissensions which have disturbed the peace of our mother church elsewhere.[99]

The 'zeal of others' and concern about 'schisms and dissensions' is probably a reference to the Methodists who were showing an interest. The islanders' identification with the Church of England was apparently strong, as Montgomery replied to schoolteacher Stephens:

> Their unity in worship is so decided that I cannot help viewing with satisfaction that an attempt by the Wesleyans to begin ministrations on the Island was seen by them to be out of the question. As Mr Masters observed after seeing the work for himself 'It would have been a crime to have intruded here'.[100]

After more than forty years of albeit only annual visits the Anglican Church had a proprietorial feeling about the islands vis-à-vis other denominations. The next chapter will provide something of a contrast by considering the experience of Aboriginal people in the Methodist Church at Irish Town, also known as Nicholls Rivulet, near *putalina* / Oyster Cove. It is unclear if Montgomery's comments are in connection to that development, or for some other reason such as the wholesale rejection by Aboriginal people at *putalina* / Oyster Cove of the services of the local Anglican clergyman, Reverend Freeman. Nevertheless, it is clear that Aboriginal people's engagement with Christian faith was occurring in the midst of denominational practices and inter-denominational relationships. The Anglican Church had been their 'default' denomination by virtue of its alignment with the colonial government, the work of Robinson and others at Wybalenna, and the visiting clergy to the Furneaux Islands. The few references to the Wesleyans such as this one, show the sensitivity to denominational relationships and that Aboriginal people were exercising their choices within this ecumenical context.

Church building

The letter from the islanders seems to have been effective in persuading the Minister for Lands to grant an occupancy licence for a church on *truwana* / Cape Barren Island. Within twelve months a site had been cleared, materials sourced from Launceston and transported by islanders who constructed the church themselves. In the words of Bishop Montgomery:

> On Wednesday Jan 24. 1893 the inhabitants of the township met me at the School room for a last Service in that building. After addressing them upon the blessings and past mercies of God, we recited 'nunc dimittis'[101] and then walked in procession to the new Church.
> On the same day Jan 24 1893, I dedicated the new Church to the uses of a Church belonging to the Church of England — setting it apart from all ordinary and common uses, and proclaiming it to be used henceforth solely as a Church of the Church of England according to her rites and ceremonies and for no other purpose whatsoever and calling it
> 'the Church of the Epiphany'[102]

During the same visit Montgomery consecrated a cemetery:

> On Thursday Feb 2, 1893, the Feast of the Purification,[103] I dedicate the Cemetery near this church according to the rites of the Church of England, as a Burying Ground for the bodies of the Christian dead. The community assembled in large numbers and walked in procession round the piece of ground which had been fenced in almost a quarter of an acre in extent.[104]

The church was consecrated in the season after Epiphany so this probably contributed to the name. Epiphany begins on 6 January, twelve days after Christmas, and continues until the Sunday before Ash Wednesday that marks the beginning of the season of Lent, the preparation for Easter. The length of the season after Epiphany is governed by the dating of Easter each year. Epiphany is a season in which the church reflects upon the manifestation of Christ to all people.[105]

The following year Montgomery described the usual practices of prayer, singing from 'Hymns Ancient and Modern' and sometimes from Sankey's hymnal. He summarised his perspective by reporting:

> baptized 16, confirmed 11, had two Celebrations of Holy Communion, and 38 communicants. The church stands firm, in spite of all the winds of heaven, but it sorely needs paint. It has never had any yet. The half-castes gave 34s 9d at the services; for this 30s goes to pay the insurance of the church; the remainder has been swallowed up in a monogram for the front of the altar cloth. The debt on the building itself is now reduced to £4. The most pressing need is the painting of the exterior of the church. Will someone help?[106]

The middle of this decade was something of a high point in people's participation in the sanctioned services of the church and in giving time to the building. It included the largest number of communicants at Holy Communion with twenty-five, celebration of a wedding,[107] nine baptisms and one confirmation who had been baptised by Stephens.[108] Preparations were being made to paint the outside of the church and build proper seats for inside,[109] however the type of seat installed still needed the approval of the Bishop.[110]

Funerals

There were relatively few deaths during this time, averaging one each year. These funeral services were conducted by the schoolmaster, Mr E. Stephens, followed by his son, Mr C. Stephens. Prior to this, families made their own arrangements for funeral services. The presence of the *Book of Common Prayer* on a number of islands, and the range of people familiar with its services, suggests people probably used the church services. Burials occurred wherever was convenient for the people at the time, so there are graves on most of the islands, and only some are marked. The consecration of land as a cemetery on *truwana* / Cape Barren Island in 1893 raised a hitherto uncontroversial issue. In the words of E. Stephens to Bishop Montgomery in 1895:

> Now is it lawful to bury on Freehold Land, when there is a consecrated Cemetery within reasonable distance? There has never been any need formerly to solve this question. As you know yourself, in years past, burials were performed anywhere, even in back yards, and we want to know whether one is compelled to bury in the cemetery or not.[111]

Montgomery was clear in his response a few years later that burials in a church cemetery required approval from church authorities.[112] But it left open the question of burials on freehold, or leasehold, land. These burials continued for those living on other islands where it was impracticable to build or transport the coffin to the cemetery on *truwana* / Cape Barren, and even on *truwana* / Cape Barren itself there are graves in various places including at Thunder and Lightning Bay.[113]

In some ways this is symbolic of the broader Christian practices among the islanders. Those closest to the church in terms of geographic and religious location joined the church through their confirmation and participation in services, and those who saw themselves as somewhat distant made their own arrangements using whatever means they chose, which sometimes included the Bible and other sources such as the *Book of Common Prayer*, hymns, pamphlets and other materials they acquired through family history and contemporary visitors.

In 1896, Montgomery reflected on the previous five years and gave his observations,

> From August 1890 to December 31 1895, there have been about 410 public Sunday services held, and Sunday-school 214 times; Other services on week days 192; total 816. For my own part it is of interest to state that I have baptised in the Bass Strait Islands (including the lighthouses) 101 children, of these 53 are half castes; and I have married two couples.[114]

The identification with the Anglican Church brought certain expectations and requirements to abide by the church's practices. The Bishop was responsible for virtually the entire conduct of the church. This included the person appointed to lead the local church. In this case it was the schoolmaster, Mr E. Stephens, followed by his son, Mr C. Stephens. The Bishop was also responsible for the church building, acquiring the necessary land, approving its materials, construction and consecration. He was the final authority for what occurred within it, the format of Christian worship, in accordance with the *Book of Common Prayer*, particularly the morning and evening prayers and other ministrations including the type of seating. It is difficult to ascertain if the islanders ever engaged in their own Christian practices beyond those of the *Book of Common Prayer* and as approved by the Bishop.

Some differentiation between islanders and church emerged as the decade progressed. Islanders increasingly asserted their own rights to leases both for island rookeries and reserve areas of *truwana* / Cape Barren Island. Increasingly the plans of the Bishop and his schoolmaster on these other matters conflicted with those of several islanders, and attendance at church declined.

By the end of the decade there was a stark contrast between Montgomery's public and private descriptions. Publicly, in the *Church News*, he wrote extensively of his new 'Bishopscourt' accommodation on *truwana* / Cape Barren Island, about muttonbirds and his travels around Flinders Island. But there are very few references to people on *truwana* / Cape Barren Island. Notwithstanding this, Montgomery reported he had baptised twenty-one children, confirmed one who had been privately baptised, had four celebrations of Holy Communion, and services in houses everywhere, besides the services in the church.[115]

Privately Montgomery seems dispirited. In writing privately and confidentially to the Premier and Minister of Education, he decried the unrealised hopes regarding people's moral condition: 'I fear the community as a whole is morally worse than it was ten years ago.' 'There is no known sin, I think, that they have not committed within the last two or three years, except murder. Every sort of immorality is common.' Three or four 'steady families' had left for Flinders Island.[116]

In his eyes the school and church were impotent in the face of the unhealthy influence of two particular individuals, Thomas Mansell and John Summers, and the legacy of the 'admixture' of 'races in these people'. Like Robinson and many others before him and since, Montgomery does not appear able to respect a way of being Christian that does not comply with his version of English-Christian-faith. All previous rhetoric from earlier bishops and other church leaders about a moral debt owed to Aboriginal people gave way to a more explicit paternalistic approach. In truth this had undergirded previous notions of a moral debt and the institutional self-indulgence in spending the pittances of donations on their own flotilla rather than engaging respectfully with the people themselves.

> It is my opinion that Government has done all it ought to have done for them. They show no fortitude but very much the reverse. The time has come to take steady measures to regulate their industry in order to save it, and to treat their petitions as though they had never been sent.[117]

Stephens, likewise, doubted the authenticity of those still attending church:

> 'Attendances at church are still keeping up, but really I cannot help thinking that there is a strong current of hypocrisy prompting them.'[118] With the representatives of the church so clearly refusing to heed the political, economic and educational concerns of local people, more and more islanders withdrew from attendance and bypassed the institution's protocols. More were writing directly to the government.[119] This may have been part of political relationships among the islander families themselves where some sought to advance their concerns through a relationship with the church, through the Bishop and schoolteacher, and others through advocating directly to members of Parliament.

However, surviving records do not sustain such an argument. One of those identified as the principal protagonists, Thomas Mansell, had children baptised in 1891, 1893, 1894, and 1898 and attended church occasionally, but was regarded by Montgomery and Stephens as an unhealthy influence.[120] The numbers of adults attending church declined significantly through most of 1899, with between two and four attending most weeks. The largest congregation for the year, which Thomas Mansell also attended, was on 10 September 1899.[121] The most regular and faithful attenders were among the women, Mrs James Maynard, Mrs Peter Mansell and Mrs Tasman Smith, bringing the children and less often their husbands.[122]

The nadir in Montgomery's assessment of the people was reached in 1900. Very tellingly, given the strong identification of being 'English' with being 'Christian', Montgomery wrote to the Police Commissioner in May and September:

> These people are not English in character — the more you know of them the less English and the more native they are in habits of work. They can never be judged as we should judge ourselves, and should therefore be firmly governed as an inferior race ... and reforms must be made gradually'.[123]

In Montgomery's eyes the islanders were clearly not 'Christian', which simultaneously meant they were not 'English'. They were 'native' and 'inferior'. In doing so, Montgomery replicated the behaviour of those of earlier generations who believed Aboriginal people needed to be 'firmly governed as an inferior race' rather than respected and engaged as equals. The unwillingness of islanders to identify with a church that was led by such a mindset is seen in the decline in the number of confirmations and Holy Communion throughout that era.[124] The people's disengagement from the church was expressed both in their absence from services and their neglect of the church building. In January 1903 it became 'utterly unsafe to stay in' and was abandoned in favour of the schoolhouse.[125]

In 1902 Montgomery was succeeded by Bishop Mercer, who appointed Reverend T. G. Copeland to visit the islands. Stephens introduced him to the perceived crisis on the islands by saying:

> Nearly all the benefits these people have had, have been derived chiefly through the exertions of representatives of the Church of England, and as matters are now approaching a crisis it is only fitting that the end should be influenced by the church.[126]

And that conflict among the islanders was split along family lines,

> Such names as Thomas, Beedon, Maynard, & Everett (who are all real Tasmanian half castes) have not appeared in connection with the Reserve, and they are all very anxious to know what the Govt is doing for them, and also what Mansell & Summers have represented to the Govt and others.
>
> I must add in justice to the true Tas. half castes that Summers & Mansell have been the ringleaders (either directly or indirectly) of nearly all the trouble

> which has occurred here during the past twelve years to my personal knowledge, and which Bishop Montgomery learnt to his cost.[127]

Even if Stephens' claims are accurate about a split along family lines, it is important to remember that involvement in the church, or Christian faith more broadly, does not necessarily result in people having similar political and social agendas. A variety of Aboriginal experiences and opinions had existed for generations, and probably for millennia.[128]

The change of building in 1903, and perhaps more importantly, the change in Bishop in 1902, seemed to prompt a change of approach in Stephens. In February it was decided that

> services are to be held for one year at 3pm at the request of the congregation. If it is found that the attendance is larger than previously, the time will be permanently adopted.[129]

This belated and small-scale respect for people's decisions seems to have had a positive response. After a hiatus of several years, confirmations began again with eleven in January 1905 with the visit of Bishop Bromby, before Stephens left in September.[130] Stephens was replaced by G. W. Knight, whose forte seems to have been singing as choir practices were held every Friday night and Sunday school from 2–3pm every Sunday. Knight described these attendances as 'satisfactory'.[131]

Bishop Montgomery's recommendation that the islanders be 'strictly governed' contributed to the development of the *Cape Barren Reserve Act*. The contrast with the islanders' own aspirations could not have been more stark when in 1911, led by George Everett, seventy-two islanders, echoing Walter Arthur and other petitioners more than sixty years earlier, wrote to their local member of the House of Assembly, Charles Howroyd:

> We would suggest that a Committee be appointed among ourselves, and that as we are quite capable of managing our own affairs, and know our requirements for the Reserve, and that any regulations we may make be submitted to Parliament and on approval be made lawful.[132]

No such 'managing our own affairs' was possible with the government, nor in the Anglican Church with its hierarchical governance structure centred on the power of the Bishop to appoint clergy, issue marriage licenses, consecrate buildings and burial grounds, and approve church furniture. Those islanders involved in church services continued to be constrained by the denominational structures and institutional culture centred around strict adherence to a prayer book and compliance with the wishes of their 'superiors'.

Cape Barren Island Reserve Act 1912

Rather than accede to the islanders' wishes, the government instituted the *Cape Barren Island Reserve Act*, which came into effect in 1912. In regard to the church, the *Act* authorised the Minister for Lands to grant any church authority a right to occupy not more than half an acre of land on the reserve for up to three years for any religious purpose. If a building was erected on the land, the Minister could issue a ninety-nine year lease at the rental sum of one pound per annum.[133]

With more people living on the reserve there was a sharp, but short-lived, increase in the numbers of children attending Sunday School, which regularly had more than fifty children.[134] However, the church's presence and influence lessened, and its focus moved toward the growing population of non-Aboriginal people on Flinders Island. As Boyce summarises the situation:

> For Cape Barren Islanders from the middle years of the first decade, this modest rebuilding of Church of England worship life ceased in 1920, when for the first time in forty years there were no regular Sunday Services held on Cape Barren Island. Services throughout the 1920s and 1930s were irregular. Cape Barren became in this time an outpost of the predominantly white church at Flinders, and visits no doubt depended on the commitment and capacity of the Minister there.[135]

Throughout this period the experience of the islanders with the church seems one of missed opportunity. Earlier generations engaged with the Bible, prayer book and other Christian materials in their own way, with family prayer times and broader gatherings for funerals they conducted themselves. There appeared a genuine desire for a growing relationship with a church denomination and the wider relationships that entailed. They identified the needs of their children and took various steps to fulfil them, sometimes well ahead of the church. At times the church was mired in its own institutional controversies and the islanders were simply a rhetorical convenience. As their interactions with the church moved from annual visits to more regular involvement, the differences between their aspirations and those of the institution became more apparent and led to significant conflict and a breakdown of relationship.

Later generations of islanders, including families of Ida West[136] and Molly Mallett,[137] show that some continued to be active Christians in the midst of ongoing institutional challenges. And there were occasional non-Aboriginal individuals, such as Ada Hudson, motivated by Christian faith, who continued to interact with Aboriginal people.

ENDNOTES CHAPTER SIX

1. Cameron, 2011, p. 106.
2. Robinson's efforts on the islands in this regard were much more active and effective than his letter to colonists in 1829 which 'netted' Robert Macauley. Robinson's dislike of the sealers is well known, Plomley, 1966, pp. 278, 294–95, and Plomley's editorial note, pp. 431–32. Several women were removed to the 'establishment', then on Swan Island, Plomley, 1966, p. 333.
3. 17 March 1830, Plomley, 1966, p. 333; 3 April, Plomley, 1966, p. 335; 29 May, Plomley, 1966, p. 357; 5 June, Plomley, 1966, p. 359.
4. 9 November 1830, Plomley, 1966, p. 269. See also, Stokes, J., 1846, *Discoveries in Australia* Vol. 2. London; T & W Boone, p. 451. The number of evangelical missions active in Van Diemen's Land at that time was noted in Chapter One in regard to Robinson and will be mentioned in Chapter Seven in regard to Rev Miller. The distribution of 'testaments' suggests the British and Foreign Bible Society. *Church News*, 1 April 1872, p. 248, or another, such as the Bethel Union which also distributed tracts, and of which Robinson was the inaugural secretary. *Colonial Times*, 18 January 1828, p. 1, and 15 February 1828, p. 1.
5. 13 November 1830, Plomley, 1966, p. 273.
6. May 1831 in Plomley, 1966, footnote 166, p. 457. It is understandable that Munro would present himself to Governor Arthur in the most favourable light, particularly when they had been removed by Arthur's appointed 'conciliator'. By presenting himself as attending to the Christian instruction of the children, just as Robinson had in 1829, Munro succeeded in regaining the women.
7. Plomley, N.J.B. & Henley, K.A., 1990, 'The Sealers of Bass Strait and the Cape Barren Island Community', *Tasmanian Historical Research Association*, 37 (2 & 3), p. 59.
8. In the documents there are various ways of spelling Beeton, such as Beedon, Beadon, and Beaton. For the sake of consistency I will use the later, and predominant form, Beeton.
9. WORE.TER.NEEM.ME.RUN.NER TAT.TE.YAN.NE alias Bet Smith had lived with Thomas Beeton since the mid-1820s. By 1831 they had two children. One died and was buried at Preservation Island, the other was Lucy. Plomley, 1966, p. 333. Beeton had extensive conflict with Robinson over the removal of Betsy and other women. He wrote several petitions to Governor Arthur seeking her return, and, like Munro, was eventually successful, Plomley, 1966, pp. 457–460. Thomas' and Betsy's move to the Longford area outside Launceston coincided with the return of Robinson to the straits as Commandant at Wybalenna. Robinson's arrival may have contributed to them leaving.
10. Plomley, 1966, p. 1011.
11. Skira, I., 1997, '"I hope you will be my friend": Tasmanian Aborigines in the Furneaux Group in the nineteenth century — population and land tenure', *Aboriginal History*, 21 (30), p. 33.
12. TAHO RGD 32/1/2. James and Henry are also listed on the petition to Rev. John Fereday, George Town clergyman, in 1862 requesting clergy visits to the islands. *Cornwall Chronicle*, 23 May 1863, p. 4. N. B. Tindale states that Beeton's family name was Herbert, Plomley, 1966, p. 1012, as does the *Cornwall Chronicle*, 19 January 1867, p. 4, although the *Chronicle* refers to him as James Herbert Beeton, not Thomas. However, Thomas Beeton is the only Beeton old enough to have been in the straits for the previous forty years, as described in the *Chronicle*. James was a son of Thomas.
13. The *Tasmanian, Supplement*, 2 October 1886, p. 2.
14. Correspondence Archdeacon Davies to Governor Denison, 22 July, 1850, TAHO CSO 24/167/4898.
15. But he suggested that the Anglican Bishop, Francis Russell Nixon, might take an interest in their welfare. Ryan, 2012, p. 279. *Tasmanian Church Chronicle*, 6 March 1852.
16. For example, 'it is the sole province of the Governor to create a parish: the utmost that the Bishop can do, is to assign to

each clergyman his own particular work'. Nixon, F. R. Charge delivered to the Clergy of the Diocese of Tasmania, 22 May 1855, pp. 8 &15 http://www.anglican.org.au/docs/archive/72.pdf accessed 14/3/2013.

17 Skira, 1997, p. 34. *The Courier*, 9 December 1854, pp. 2 & 3.

18 Nixon, Francis, R., DD, Bishop of Tasmania, *The Cruise of the Beacon, a narrative of a visit to the islands in Bass's Straits.* London; Bell and Daldy, 1857. p. 19. This was similar to the summary expressed by Backhouse and Walker when visiting Wybalenna in 1833.

19 *The Courier*, 9 December 1854, pp. 2. & 3.

20 Nixon, 1857, p. 42.

21 Nixon, 1857, p. 46. It seems James Munro and Thomas Beeton were not the only ones maintaining Christian practices.

22 TAHO NS 642/1/1.

23 On 10 September 1855 (No. 152) Amelia, daughter of Henry & Sarah Beeton, was baptised by Rev. John Fereday. On 16 January 1859 (Nos. 219–222), Lucy and Harriet, daughters of James and Rachel Beeton, and Lucy and Laura, daughters of George and Jane Everett were baptised by Rev. John Fereday, TAHO NS 642/1/1.

24 TAHO NS 642/1/1. There are several gaps in the baptism records for the years: April 1848–January 1851 [57–84]; July 1861–June 1862 [268–295]; November 1873–August 1874 [477–505]) so the actual number may be higher.

25 This correspondence also included applications for leases for Robert Dunbar on Little Green Island, Elizabeth Davis, the widow of the superintendent of the Goose Island lighthouse, on Big Green Island, and John Smith for 500 acres at Hogans Point on *truwana* / Cape Barren Island, Fereday to Surveyor-General, 9 December 1862, TAHO LSD 2/2/924; Fereday to Surveyor-General, 2 September 1862, TAHO LSD 1/51/636; Fereday to Surveyor-General, 20 September 1864, TAHO LSD 1/51/642; Boothman to Fereday, 23 May 1865, TAHO LSD 1/51/644, cited in Skira, 1997, p. 38.

26 Skira, 1997, p. 38.

27 Plomley, 1966, pp. 274, 278–79, 324, 450.

28 Nixon, 1857, p. 47.

29 *The Courier*, 9 December 1854, p. 3.

30 *The Courier*, 20 January 1858, p. 2. The sensitivity between Anglican and Wesleyan churches will re-emerge later in this chapter and the next.

31 Nixon, 1857, pp. 52–55, although five Allen children were baptised eight years later when Rev. Richardson visited Clarke Island, as recorded in the George Town Anglican Church, on 16 November 1862, TAHO NS 642/1/1.

32 The *Tasmanian, Supplement*, 2 October 1886. The 'correspondent' is likely to have been Thomas Reibey. This final quote is almost identical to a sentence in Reibey's 1863 report to Parliament, 'that there is no case which has a stronger claim upon the inhabitants of this island; and that sin will lie heavy at our doors if we, blessed with civilisation and Christianity, neglect to fulfil to them the simplest duties laid upon us by the requirements of Christian charity', Archdeacon Thomas Reibey, 'Half-Caste Islanders in Bass's Straits. Report of the Ven. Archdeacon Reibey'. *Journal of The Legislative Council*, No 48, 26 August 1863. It is also similar to his request for funds in the *Church News*, November 1862, 'In the working of the laws of God's providence we have dispossessed these poor people of this fair land. In that we may hope there was no sin, but surely sin would lie heavy at our doors if we, blessed with civilization and Christianity neglected, when opportunity was offered us to fulfil to them the simplest duties laid upon us by the requirements of Christian charity'. *Church News*, 20 November 1862, p. 95.

33 Nixon, F. R., 1855, Charge delivered to the Clergy of the Diocese of Tasmania, 22 May 1855, pp. 8 &15 http://www.anglican.org.au/docs/archive/72.pdf accessed 14/3/2013, p. 9. From 1868 it became unlawful for the Government to reserve lands for sites of places of Public Worship or for any religious purpose, or as burial grounds for any particular denomination. Correspondence, Minister of Lands to Bishop Montgomery, TAHO NS 373/214/47.

34. At this time the Government was paying Rev. Freeman £20 for 'expenses' to act as Visiting Chaplain at *putalina* / Oyster Cove.
35. *Cornwall Chronicle*, 16 October 1861, p. 2.
36. *Church News*, 21 May, 1862, pp. 4 & 5.
37. *Church News*, 21 May, 1862, p. 4.
38. This was similar to the Orphan School in Hobart and at Wybalenna where children sometimes lived with the catechist's family.
39. *Church News*, 21 May 1862, pp. 4 & 5.
40. *Church News*, 21 May 1862, 20 October 1862 p79. The 'rivalry' with other evangelicals is again evident.
41. *The Mercury*, 19 September 1862, p. 5.
42. *Church News*, 20 November 1862, p. 95.
43. *Cornwall Chronicle*, 10 December 1862. p. 4. These baptisms are recorded in the Baptism Register of the George Town Anglican Church, TAHO NS 642/1/1.
44. *Cornwall Chronicle*, 24 July 1869, p. 7.
45. *Cornwall Chronicle*, 23 May 1863, p. 4.
46. *Church News*, 20 January 1863, p. 125.
47. *Cornwall Chronicle*, 5 November 1870, p. 4. Lucy Beeton applied to occupy Badger Island in December 1857. Together with her brother, James, they placed a deposit and eventually paid off fifty acres each on Badger Island beginning in 1868. TAHO LSD 209/2/227; Fereday to Surveyor-General, 9 December 1862, TAHO LSD 2/2/924; TRE 21/2,21/2/49; DELM Dorset 7/70,71, cited in Skira, J., 1997, p. 37.
48. *Ovens and Murray Advertiser*, 7 June 1862, p. 2.
49. Murray-Smith, and following him Boyce, name a Rev. George Fereday travelling with Reibey Murray-Smith, S., (ed.), 1987, *Mission to the Islands*. Launceston; Foot & Playsted, p. 3; Boyce, 2001, p. 55. However Reibey's reports only mention Rev. John Fereday, from George Town, travelling with him, in Reibey, 1863, p. 3. The Register of the Clergy within the Diocese of Tasmania also only names a Rev. John, and not a George, Fereday, TAHO NS 3588/1/1, p. 27.
50. *Church News*, 19 August 1863, pp. 208 & 209.
51. *Church News*, 19 August 1863, pp. 208 & 209, also Reibey, 1863, p. 5.
52. Reibey, 1863. Only a couple of Aboriginal people at *putalina* / Oyster Cove, such as *Wapati*, had family relatives on the islands.
53. *Church News*, 21 September 1864 p. 365.
54. *Church News*, 20 March 1866, p. 231. A fundraising effort among 'independent' churches had raised £3600 for a mission boat to the Pacific, the *John Williams*, which visited Hobart, and *putalina* / Oyster Cove, in March and April 1861. *Oyster Cove Visitor's Book*, TAHO CSO 89/1/1, p. 16, *The Mercury*, 28 March 1861, p. 2, and 20 April 1861, p. 2.
55. *Church News*, 21 November 1864 p. 389–393.
56. The Ripon Fund began when £10 000 was bestowed by a lady in the Diocese of Ripon (near Leeds in England) to maintain 'Missions in the Bush', *Church News*, 18 December 1863 p. 256.
57. *Church News*, 20 October 1865, p. 149.
58. *Church News*, 4 May 1866, p. 261.
59. *Cornwall Chronicle*, 31 October 1866, p. 7; 24 November 1866, p. 1.
60. *Church News*, 1 April 1868, p. 57.
61. *Church News*, 1 April 1868, p. 57.
62. *Church News*, 1 August 1868, p. 121.
63. *The Mercury*, 28 February 1870, p. 2.
64. *Launceston Examiner*, 16 June 1870, p. 3.
65. *Launceston Examiner*, 16 June 1870, p. 4.
66. *Launceston Examiner*, 5 July 1870, p. 5.
67. *The Mercury*, 29 April 1873, p. 3.
68. *The Mercury*, 29 April 1873, p. 3.
69. *The Mercury*, 29 April 1873, p. 3.
70. *Church News*, 1 April 1871, pp. 58–60.
71. *Church News*, 1 April 1871, p. 74.
72. *The Mercury*, 7 August 1871, p. 2; *Launceston Examiner*, 8 August, 1871, p. 3.
73. Ryan, 2012, p. 281.
74. *Church News*, 2 January 1872, p. 200. Rev. Freeman was being paid £20 to visit *putalina* / Oyster Cove, also by boat. Correspondence Freeman to Colonial Secretary, TAHO CSD 1/18/703.
75. Murray-Smith, 1987.
76. *Church News*, 1 April 1872, p. 248.
77. Murray-Smith, 1987, p. 11.
78. Brownrigg celebrated Holy Communion among a non-Aboriginal gathering in the Kent Group on 18 February 1872. Murray-Smith, 1987, p. 43.

79 Years later, Bishop Nixon brought the 'communion vessels', chalice and paten, on each visit. On one occasion he left the vessels at home. The 'improvised paten and chalice were the homeliest description'. *Church News*, 1 August 1894, pp. 124–5.
80 *Church News*, 1 April 1872, p. 248.
81 *Church News*, 1 March 1873, p. 425.
82 *Church News*, 1 August 1873, p. 504.
83 *Church News*, 5 March 1877, p. 44.
84 *Church News*, 1 December 1880, p. 185.
85 *Launceston Examiner*, 8 February 1876, p. 3; and *Church News*, 1 March 1876, pp. 424-425.
86 *Launceston Examiner*, 8 February 1876, p. 3; and *Church News*, 1 March 1876, pp. 424-425.
87 *Church News*, 1 August 1876, pp. 502–503; 1 September 1876, pp. 518–519.
88 *Launceston Examiner*, 6 February 1877, pp. 3 & 4; and 6 February, 1878, p. 2.
89 *Church News*, 1 March 1878, p. 226.
90 *Launceston Examiner*, 9 February 1881, p. 2; see also West, 1987, pp. 6 –69.
91 Morgan, A., 1986, 'Aboriginal Education in the Furneaux Islands (1798–1986)', University of Tasmania; Department of Education, p. 117.
92 Morgan, 1986, p. 118.
93 *Launceston Examiner*, 15 March 1882, p 1.
94 *Launceston Examiner*, 3 March 1883, p. 1.
95 *The Mercury*, 3 March 1885, p. 3. Lucy Beeton died the following year, 7 July 1886, at Badger Island, aged 57, *Launceston Examiner*, 13 July 1886, p. 1. She was listed among the most prominent people who died that year, 'Miss Lucy Beedon, of Badger Island, aged 57, known as "The Queen" of the Straits Islands'". *Launceston Examiner*, 1 January 1887, p. 3.
96 *Launceston Examiner*, 7 March 1885, p. 1. This was Brownrigg's final visit to the islands. His resignation, due to ill health, was announced to the Anglican Synod in May 1887. *The Mercury*, 4 May 1887, p. 3.
97 As mentioned above, from 1868 it became unlawful for the government to reserve lands for sites of places of Public Worship or for any religious purpose, or as burial grounds for any particular denomination. Correspondence, Minister of Lands to Bishop Montgomery, TAHO NS 373/214/47.
98 Correspondence Minister of Lands to Bishop Montgomery, 14 January 1892, TAHO NS 373/214/47.
99 Correspondence Minister of Lands to Bishop Montgomery, 5 February 1892.
100 Correspondence, Montgomery to E. Stephens, 15 February 1892, TAHO NS 373/214/47.
101 Named after the first words of the Canticle of Simeon, in the Gospel of Luke Chapter 2, Verses 29–32. It is a regular part of morning and evening prayer in the *Book of Common Prayer*.
102 Anglican Church Register of Services, Cape Barren Island, TAHO NS 373/1/11.
103 The presentation of the child Jesus at the Temple in Jerusalem, Gospel of Luke, Chapter 2, Verses 21–38.
104 Anglican Church Register of Services, Cape Barren Island, TAHO NS 373/1/11.
105 In August 1896, Minister of Lands approved 'the rent for the licence to occupy Ð acre of land on Cape Barren Island being reduced from £1 to 1/- per annum', Correspondence, Sec. Lands to Montgomery, 17 August 1896, TAHO NS 373/214/47. The church on *truwana* / Cape Barren is one of a small minority of Anglican churches not named after a saint, 'all saints' or Trinity, and is the only 'church of the Epiphany' in Tasmania.
106 The first marriage in the new church was between 'the daughter of the schoolhouse' and Mr Henry Briant, from Flinders Island, with 'eight bridesmaids (seven girls being half-castes)', *Church News*, 1 August 1894, pp. 124–5. Debt was also to be an ongoing issue (see next chapter) for the Methodist Congregation at Irish Town / Nicholls Rivulet where Fanny Cochrane Smith and her family were members.
107 Mr William Brown and Miss Emily Everett. *Church News*, 1 October 1895, p. 351
108 Montgomery had baptised ninety children in the previous five years, *Church News*, 1 October 1895, p. 351.

109 *Church News*, 1 October 1895, p. 351.
110 Correspondence 23 November 1900, C. Stephens to Montgomery, TAHO NS 373/214/47.
111 Correspondence 23 November 1900, C. Stephens to Montgomery, TAHO NS 373/214/47.
112 Correspondence, 27 December 1899, Bishop Montgomery Letter Book, 23 September 1896-11 August 1902, TAHO NS 373/1/74.
113 Personal communication.
114 *Church News*, 1 April 1896, pp. 445–6.
115 *Church News*, 2 October 1899, pp. 1123–1125.
116 Correspondence, Montgomery to Premier and Minister for Education, 26 August 1899, TAHO NS 373/214/47.
117 Correspondence, Montgomery to Premier and Minister for Education, 26 August 1899, TAHO NS 373/214/47.
118 Correspondence, C. Stephens to Montgomery, 9 October, 28 November 1899, TAHO NS 373/214/47.
119 Correspondence, C. Stephens to Montgomery, 15 October 1900, TAHO NS 373/214/47.
120 T. Mansell was recorded as attending church, 10 September 1899, Anglican Church Register of Services Cape Barren Island, TAHO NS 373/1/11. Correspondence, Montgomery to Premier and Minister of Education, 26 August 1899, Correspondence re: Cape Barren Island NS 373/214/47.
121 Anglican Church Register of Services Cape Barren Island, TAHO NS 373/1/11.
122 Anglican Church Register of Services Cape Barren Island, TAHO NS 373/1/11.
123 Correspondence, Montgomery to Richardson, 31 May 1899; Bishop Montgomery Letter Book 23 September 1896-11 August 1902, TAHO NS 373/1/74, pp. 187-188. Correspondence, Montgomery to Premier, 17 September 1900, Letter Book, p. 341, TAHO NS 373/214/47.
124 There were no services of Holy Communion in 1897, 1902, 1908, 1909, 1913, 1914, 1917–1920, Cape Barren Island Church Register, TAHO NS 373/1/11.
125 TAHO NS 373/1/11.
126 Correspondence, C. Stephens to Rev. T. Copeland, 11 December 1902, NS 373/214/47.
127 Correspondence, C. Stephens to Rev. T. Copeland, 11 December 1902, NS 373/214/47.
128 This was also noted by J.E. Lord in his report to Parliament in 1908, Lord, J. E. C., 'Report upon the state of the islands, the condition and mode of living of half-castes, the existing mode of regulating the reserves, and suggesting lines for future administration', *Parliament of Tasmania, Journal and Printed Papers of the Parliament of Tasmania*, 59, No. 57, p. 12.
129 Cape Barren Island Church Register, TAHO NS 373/1/11.
130 Cape Barren Island Church Register, TAHO NS 373/1/11.
131 Cape Barren Island Church Register, TAHO NS 373/1/11.
132 Correspondence, 21 November 1911, Islanders to Mr Charles Howroyd, in Furneaux Is., Cape Barren Is. correspondence 1902/1928 [microform], Hobart, Royal Society of Tasmania, University of Tasmania, Morris Miller Library. See also *The Mercury*, 29 November 1911, p. 3.
133 *Cape Barren Island Reserve Act 1912*, section 9, http://www.austlii.edu.au/au/legis/tas/num_act/tcbira19123gvn16334/tcbira19123gvn16334.pdf, accessed 8 February 2014. When the Act was amended in 1945, the Minister was permitted to sell the portion of the Reserve occupied by a church authority by private contract, *Cape Barren Reserve Act 1945*, section 8, http://www.austlii.edu.au/au/legis/tas/num_act/cbira19459gvn14312/ accessed 8 February 2014.
134 Cape Barren Island Church Register, TAHO NS 373/1/11.
135 Boyce, 2001, p. 77.
136 West, 1987.
137 Mallett, M., 2001, *My Past — Their Future*. Hobart; Blubber Head Press, p. 13.

CHAPTER SEVEN

'They think we have got no souls now'

FROM THE closure of the Wybalenna settlement on Flinders Island in 1847 until the end of the nineteenth century the Aboriginal people's experiences with the Christian faith moved from the government-controlled settlement to a local church congregation in the south of the island. This congregation was one in which Aboriginal people were significant Christian leaders and their church building built upon land one of them had donated specifically for that purpose. It is important to remember the experiences described here were happening simultaneously with those on the Bass Strait islands.

Through the 1840s there was intensifying conflict among the leading people at Wybalenna on Flinders Island. This included extraordinarily serious actions and allegations, particularly under the superintendence of Dr Jeanneret. Jeanneret had placed Aboriginal leader Walter Arthur in gaol[1] and contrived allegations of cruelty toward Aboriginal children by the catechist Robert Clark. These may have been in retaliation for Clark's involvement in the petition to Queen Victoria the previous year.[2] The investigation by Jeanneret's replacement superintendent, Joseph Milligan,[3] and then Mr Friend, determined the imprisonment of Walter Arthur illegal and the allegations against Clark unfounded.[4] Jeanneret was immediately suspended by the Governor.[5]

The closure of Wybalenna on 15 October 1847[6] saw the transfer of the surviving forty-six Aboriginal people to *putalina* / Oyster Cove, a recently sold and repurchased former convict probation station in the D'Entrecasteaux Channel.[7] It brought these Aborigines, comprising fourteen adult males, twenty-two adult females, five boys and five girls into closer proximity to colonial society in Hobart and particularly its southern areas, and closer to the range of opportunities and conflicts therein. They were also, at least theoretically, in closer proximity to Christian missionary endeavours. During the ensuing twenty-six years until the station was essentially abandoned in September 1873[8] Aboriginal people were for the most part ignored by Christian colonists and their churches.

Unlike islander families in eastern Bass Strait who were more difficult to visit, the Aboriginal people at *putalina* / Oyster Cove were close enough to colonial society to receive three visits from the Governor[9] and be the occasional objects of passing missionary curiosity. The Aboriginal people spent their first post-Wybalenna Christmas day at Government House, New Norfolk, eating roast meat, plum pudding, and playing rounders,[10] and later that afternoon attended the theatre.[11] But behind the initial polite interest of Governor Denison and the residents of New Norfolk, the Aboriginal children were at that time in the process of once again being removed from their parents to the Orphan School at New Town on the northern edge of Hobart.

Children and the Orphan School, again

Seven of the children — the three youngest boys, Moriarty, Adam and Billy, and four youngest girls, Hannah, Nannie, Martha and Mathinna — were registered at the Orphan School on 28 December 1847, where Walter Arthur and Mathinna had been previously. The eldest boy, Charley, was to be placed with a 'respectable settler or apprenticed' and Fanny Cochrane and George were to be kept at the *putalina* / Oyster Cove Station under the care of Walter and Mary Ann Arthur.[12]

Of the children at the school, Nannie lived there for eighteen months before dying of 'inflammation of the lungs'.[13] Martha lived there for two years, from twelve to fourteen years of age, before being discharged into the care of her mother.[14] Hannah lived there two and a half years before being discharged into the care of Dr Smith, surgeon, near *putalina* / Oyster Cove, in May 1850.[15] Mathinna lived there for almost four years, from the age of twelve to sixteen, before being discharged into the care of Dr Milligan.[16] In 1851, when she was about 16, she returned to *putalina* / Oyster Cove.[17] According to one account, on 1 September 1852 she was one of four Aboriginal people drinking at an inn at North West Bay, fell into a puddle while drunk and was found dead the following morning.[18] Mathinna is believed to have been buried in the *putalina* / Oyster Cove Aboriginal cemetery.[19] The three boys were younger than the girls and so stayed at the school for longer. Moriarty was there for four and a half years before dying of 'inflammation of the lungs'.[20] Billy / William and Adam were discharged together on 13 January 1853 to Milligan, just over five years after their registration. They lived with Mary Ann and Walter Arthur at *putalina* / Oyster Cove.[21] As mentioned previously, the Orphan School children were required to regularly attend church services at St John's Anglican Church in New Town, as well as daily classes.

putalina / Oyster Cove

At *putalina* / Oyster Cove, as at Wybalenna, the Aboriginal people outnumbered colonists by about five to one. The only colonists living at *putalina* / Oyster Cove in the first few years were Robert Clark, his wife, their five children, and John Russell, who had been a servant at Wybalenna.[22] Within months of their arrival, as part of cost-saving measures, the roles of superintendent, catechist, and storekeeper were combined into one person, Clark.[23] Clark was given a salary of £130,[24] although Milligan, based in Hobart, continued giving oversight. Clark's tenure as 'superintendent' was never secure. He was not authoritarian like others, and the Aboriginal people lived as they chose, sometimes at the station, and sometimes away.

With George and Fanny the only children at the station it is unclear if Clark continued the day and Sunday schools that had been the practice at Wybalenna. Among the already deteriorating buildings was a chapel, but it is not clear if it was used, nor what form of service, if any, Clark performed.[25] The condition of the other huts was also very poor. They were open to the sky and substantial work was needed to renovate them. The colder, damp climate and valley location with minimal sunshine in the winter months, along with the thirty dogs,[26] exacerbated people's vulnerability to disease.

There were also challenges surrounding the station. A government notice sought to allay fears of the Aboriginal people among the local community.[27] For the leaders of colonist society the presence and duties of the catechist were in large part expected to be like that as for the lower classes, a constraining influence on Aboriginal people's base 'native' or 'primitive' desires, and to allay the fears of the upper echelons of society. Without surviving records of any church services or catechetical classes at *putalina* / Oyster Cove during Clark's time it is speculative to draw any definitive conclusions, other than to recognise that Clark did not comply with the expectations that he constrain Aboriginal people.

The surviving documents show Clark caught in an impossible situation of encouraging, or at least not stifling, Aboriginal people's freedom as they developed relationships with others in the area, and at the same time trying to allay the fears of influential neighbours and the Governor. Complaints soon appeared in newspapers claiming 'their dogs have committed depredations upon the sheep in the neighborhood of the station'.[28] Clark, responding to anonymous allegations, wrote to Governor Denison, 'I felt to be an imperative duty on my arrival here to prevent the Aborigines from falling into temptation and ultimately causing trouble to His Excellency'.[29] With a public house close by in North West Bay, few single Aboriginal men on the station and few single colonist women in the area, it was impossible to constrain the alcoholic intoxication and casual sexual relationships that inevitably developed, including the involvement of labourers working at the station.[30] Before long Milligan regained the position of superintendent, at an annual salary of £300, even though he was hardly ever there. Clark was relegated to the position of storekeeper at a salary of £100, but only after his pleas of destitution and ruin if dismissed, and recognising his long and faithful service to the Aboriginal people.[31]

In October 1848 Clark was reprimanded for not getting timely medical treatment for Maiki,[32] but he was a convenient scapegoat for the absent superintendent, Milligan, and a largely disinterested government. The only other colonist at *putalina* / Oyster Cove, besides Clark and his family, was John Russell, a known alcoholic[33] and known to be providing sly grog to the Aborigines.[34] Plomley, and others at the time, criticised Clark for not enforcing strict discipline, industriousness, and compliance upon the Aboriginal people. However, these impositions are not those imposed on people whom one regards as equals. They are the behaviours that 'superiors' exert upon people regarded as 'inferiors'. Clark courted such criticism because he did not regard the Aboriginal people as inferior.

Sadly, a little over two years after arriving at *putalina* / Oyster Cove, Clark's wife died in late 1849. Clark himself was ill at the same time and died of heart disease a few months later, also at *putalina* / Oyster Cove, on 29 March 1850.[35] In the stratified relationships of colonial society, Clark had been much closer to the Aboriginal people than to the upper echelons of white society. When he died he had been living with Aboriginal people for seventeen years — longer and more intensively than anyone, including from any church, before or since in Tasmania. More than any other Christian teacher he had attempted to learn to speak the *pidgin* at Wybalenna and attempted to translate biblical stories and Christian faith into Aboriginal people's own languages and conceptual meanings.

At Wybalenna he had worked with Aboriginal women in translating Christian addresses given by Aboriginal men. All the Aboriginal people at Wybalenna who had learned to write in English had done so through Clark's teaching, including the petition they wrote to Queen Victoria.[36] Clearly he was not perfect, but he was more respectful of Aboriginal people than virtually every other colonist person relating to them at the time. He made serious efforts in respecting Aboriginal people's own languages and rights, and the radical theological viewpoint at the time that one could be Christian without being English. Following Clark's death, religious instruction appears to have ceased. It was the topic of correspondence from a *putalina* / Oyster Cove neighbour, Mr Walter, to the Governor. The Colonial Secretary replied that services were conducted 'pretty regularly', but it is unclear who was responsible for them.[37]

Alcohol and temperance

Whether through medicinal uses or relationships with neighbours, the Aboriginal people consumed quantities of alcohol. This raised serious concerns for those people responsible for them.[38] Their responses involved attempts to restrict the sale of alcohol and through linking the temperance movement with a more 'Christian' lifestyle. In February 1856 the government amended the *Licensing Act* to specifically prohibit the sale of alcohol to Aboriginal people at *putalina* / Oyster Cove.[39] This did little to suppress people's practices, and at the end of 1857 they continued to 'express a strong desire to have an allowance of beer to drink daily'.[40]

These moves were similar to those of Brownrigg on the Furneaux Islands. As noted in the previous chapter, several people on *truwana* / Cape Barren Island took the 'pledge' to abstain from alcohol for the ensuing twelve months. By contrast at *putalina* / Oyster Cove there is only one reference to anyone taking the 'pledge' — Walter Arthur, in 1858, as a requirement for consideration to receive a land grant.[41]

There were other changes at the station. In 1854 the young Aboriginal woman, Fanny, now about twenty years old, was granted a Government pension just prior to her marriage to William Smith on 27 October 1854. The pension was in lieu of the cost of her rations if she had remained at the station.

By the middle of 1855, government spending was declining due to a combination of the declining numbers of Aboriginal people at the station, the economic challenges at the end of the era of transportation of convicts and the exodus from Tasmania of adult male workers in search of gold in Victoria. In response, the roles of superintendent and storekeeper were again combined into one person resident on the station. Milligan (superintendent) and Davis (storekeeper) were both sacked.[42] It appears that little, if any, effort was put into Christian faith development between the time of Clark's death in 1850 and the appointment of Reverend Edward Freeman, from the nearby Brown's River Parish[43] of the Anglican Church in July 1855. The contrast between Clark and Freeman was significant.

The Governor outlined the duties required of Freeman as Visiting Clergyman:

> Should visit regularly at least once a month; Endeavour to obtain influence over the minds of the Natives and admonish them against drunkenness and immorality. He may at his option, use the Chapel of the former Convict Establishment as the location for the assembly of such persons of the neighbourhood as may be induced to attend.[44]

Freeman's appointment was alongside that of J. S. Dandridge to replace Milligan as superintendent. Freeman was paid £20 a year to cover 'trifling expenses'.[45] In the early days of his appointment he wrote to the Colonial Secretary, 'A Scheme for the Amelioration of the Moral and Religious condition of the Aboriginal people now stationed at *putalina* / Oyster Cove by rewards and punishments'. It included fortnightly visits, individual and class catechisms, explanation of doctrine, and memorisation of the Lord's Prayer and other prayers and hymns. The Lord's Prayer was to be repeated day and night in the hearing of the superintendent, who would issue rewards.[46] This English-only emphasis was reminiscent of Robinson at Wybalenna. But unlike Robinson's approach, there was not to be the slightest variation to the set form of the *Book of Common Prayer*. This repetition of prayers and the reading of services were to become the bane of people's and the superintendent's lives.

During his regular routine Freeman assembled people in the chapel[47] and said the divine service from the *Book of Common Prayer*, including reading and explaining passages from the New Testament and encouraging people in repeating the Lord's Prayer. Freeman's primary responsibilities were to the parish at Brown's River so the services at *putalina* / Oyster Cove were on a weekday rather than Sunday.[48] He offered instruction to people in their huts, though sometimes unsuccessfully: 'I am sorry to say could not make myself at all understood by her.'[49]

Freeman often commented upon people's appearance,[50] and the cleanliness or lack thereof of people's huts and clothing.[51] Visiting Magistrate Kirwan complained of the filthy state of people's houses, and the '... 30 dogs about the place'.[52] However, despite having a reputation as an entrepreneurial timber merchant around Port Cygnet,[53] Freeman did not actively do anything to change the conditions of the timber huts at *putalina* / Oyster Cove.

The Aboriginal people's response to the new clergyman was emphatic. Within months the Aboriginal people avoided him and his services. From the middle of 1856 Freeman more often left comments in the visitor's book, such as '... Aborigines all out hunting, except two ...'.[54] In what turned out to be Freeman's final service in January 1858 he noted, '... beside the Aboriginal people twenty-six white persons attended divine service. The best congregation that has yet attended at this place.'[55] Like *truwana* / Cape Barren Island in 1900, Aboriginal people were voting with their feet and not participating in many church services or even conversations with the clergyman, or he with them. Freeman appears to have done little to change the situation and, as happened on the Furneaux Islands, his attention turned away from the Aboriginal people toward the neighboring colonist families. During his three years visiting the station he baptised several colonist children, including Superintendent Dandridge's daughter[56] and children of various labourers and farmers, but he wrote minimal references to Aboriginal people participating in church services.⁵⁷

Hunting excursions

When they were not at the station for the clergyman's visits, Aboriginal people were out in the bush. While it would be tempting to explain these 'bush excursions' of the Aboriginal people as a direct avoidance of the church services, other factors were also contributing. The Aboriginal people regularly went away from the station, sometimes while repairs were done to their huts,⁵⁸ and other times to gain fresh meat when the meat supplied from Hobart either did not arrive or was of inferior quality.⁵⁹ Sometimes the period away extended for several weeks, with only two or three present at the station.⁶⁰

Ryan suggests the Aboriginal people performed ceremonies during these trips.⁶¹ While this is possible, given that at least two people, *Trukanini*, Dray, and, before his death, Maiki, were at or near their home country, it is not very likely. There is not any explicit reference to this occurring. If ceremonies were performed, they would have been significantly different from earlier practices. By now there were only a small number of people from each pre-contact clan. Few were familiar with these earlier structures or with the dances, songs and stories. It seems likely that these practices, like other aspects of life, adapted each time they were performed because of the changing number of participants and the changing geographic, social, and mythic contexts in which they were occurring. Continuing ceremonies, and their songs, stories, dances and myths, like the development of the *pidgin* at Wybalenna, were responses to the colonial experience and contributed to a more collective, or pan-Aboriginal, identity beyond the previous clan differentiations.

Ryan distinguishes between those Aboriginal people at *putalina* / Oyster Cove who were engaged in making and using stone tools, and others, specifically Walter, Mary Ann, Fanny and Pengernoburric, who engaged in a more 'British lifestyle'.⁶² It would be convenient to argue that the older women, such as *Trukanini*, *Wapati*, and *Tanganutara*, hunted, made stone tools, and conducted ceremonies, and thereby continued or rejuvenated as much of their pre-colonial lifestyle, including their religious practices, as they could, and that these four younger ones whose childhoods were entirely, or mostly, formed in the Orphan School or at Wybalenna, adopted a more 'British lifestyle' of gardening, temperance, and church. However, as previous chapters have shown, the actual lives these people lived, and the choices they made, were much more complex and multi-layered.

Those who went out into the bush included these four, who were now middle-aged. The ones who remained at the station were those who were sick,⁶³ which usually included older ones, all women. These older women were the primary holders of many aspects of Aboriginal cultural and religious knowledge. But they were not the only ones. As the son of the chief of the Ben Lomond clan, Walter's leadership at Wybalenna continued the role of his father, which included cultural and religious knowledge.

The hunting trips were not the only reason for people's absence from the station. Each of the men was at different times sent, or went, as crew on whaling expeditions. They were sometimes away for several months.[64] It would appear from the *putalina* / Oyster Cove records that it was sickness that prevented particular women from joining the excursions into the bush, and whaling that prevented particular men, rather than a choice for a more 'British lifestyle'.

Furthermore, the 'bush excursions' also included the consumption of alcohol, a clearly identifiable part of 'British lifestyle'. Dr Smith reported that he 'treated Polly [who was] suffering from exposure and partly the effects of beer whilst out on hunting excursion'.[65] Furthermore, the songs Fanny was still singing in first language in the 1880s could only have been learnt from her mother, *Tanganutara*, or other older women, such as *Wapati* or *Trukanini*. These songs were never regarded as part of a 'British lifestyle', and by continuing to sing these songs throughout her life, Fanny was choosing a decidedly Aboriginal practice, as well as Christian faith. So there were aspects of 'Aboriginal' and 'British' lifestyle interacting and coalescing on both the station and the 'bush', and being Christian was not limited to only one of these locations.

Mission curiosity

In spite of their excursions to the bush, the Aboriginal people continued to be an object of curiosity to locals and visitors alike, including among the churches. *putalina* / Oyster Cove was a site of 'pleasure cruises' for various steam ships visiting Hobart, such as the *Tasmania*[66] and *Culloden*.[67] Governor Denison made one of his occasional visits in September 1856.[68] Two months later 'a large number of children belonging to various Sunday Schools in Hobart Town proceeded on board the missionary ship *John Williams* to visit the station.'[69] The visit was something of a public relations exercise where the local clergy accompanied the visiting missionaries in their missionary ship to visit the closest approximation to a 'mission' the locals had, though their interest in the welfare of the Aboriginal people who lived there never led to further visits.

This visit of the *John Williams* identifies the broader context of the boats mentioned in previous chapter for the Anglican Church's 'Furneaux mission'. Such fundraising to purchase boats for evangelical missions to islands populated by 'natives' was occurring among different churches at the time. Perhaps it was this visit in 1856 that contributed to the Anglican Bishop, Nixon, seeking donations a few years later for a boat to assist that church's work in the Furneaux Islands. The response to Nixon's letter was a donation of just over £400.[70] Whether it was denominational differences, comparative missionary fervour, the skills of the proposers in gaining subscriptions, the different attraction of the South Sea islands compared with the penal colony of Van Diemen's Land, or some other reason, the contrast in amounts raised for the Furneaux Islands and the South Seas activities is stark.

Walter Arthur

By 1858 the number of Aboriginal people at *putalina* / Oyster Cove had declined to fifteen, ten women and five men.[71] One of the striking features of these numbers is that the Ben Lomond clan that had been the second most numerous at Wybalenna now had a sole survivor, Walter Arthur. The large number of the clan at Wybalenna was one of the reasons Walter had followed his father as clan leader, and through his education in reading and writing in English he had grown into a leader of the whole community.

Just prior to the appointments of Freeman and Dandridge in 1855, Walter began a campaign to improve the situation for himself and his wife Mary Ann. They had initially cared for Fanny and George,[72] and were now looking after William Lanney.[73] Fanny's marriage to William Smith seven months earlier, and her departure from the station, may have prompted Walter to write to Governor Young seeking permission to also live elsewhere.[74] Frustratingly for Walter and Mary Ann, permission was not forthcoming. Nevertheless Walter and Mary Ann were granted permission to occupy part of the station land separate from the main buildings.[75] Walter and William Lanney cleared it, hoping this would one day lead to him becoming owner, which he eventually did. Walter gained sufficient income as station boatman and from selling vegetables to employ a labourer — a white person — at 18/- per week.[76] This was probably the first such situation of an Aboriginal employer and white employee in the history of Tasmania.

Walter and Mary Ann were sometimes on site when Freeman visited. In these church services Aboriginal participation was limited to the required responses set out in the *Book of Common Prayer*. It was more like Walter's years at the Orphan School, and in stark contrast to his experience at Wybalenna writing sermons, the *Flinders Island Chronicle*, and participating in the leadership of the Sunday services there. These had all ceased after his apparent conflict with Robinson, which resulted in Walter and Mary Ann being exiled to Chalky Island in 1838.[77]

However, in early 1858 the situation at *putalina* / Oyster Cove deteriorated significantly, as Walter and Mary Ann both became violent toward each other and other Aboriginal people. In March, Dandridge wrote to the Colonial Secretary about the 'continued misconduct of Walter George Arthur & his wife Mary Ann' and their relapse into 'old habits of drinking, neglecting their duty and exhibiting a violence of conduct impossible to describe' including a 'disgraceful scene of drunken violence towards the other Aborigines'.[78] Dandridge recommended

> that Walter be informed that he will not be allowed to receive anymore pay, or to retain his position as coxswain of the boat, until himself and Mary-Ann have taken the pledge against drinking.
> Walter should also I respectfully submit receive a severe censure from yourself, and a caution for the future.[79]

Walter received his censure about five weeks later. In the conversation Walter expressed his great desire to leave *putalina* / Oyster Cove and live with Mary Ann along the Huon River and cultivate a garden. Assistant Secretary Solly told him

> that before his application would be even listened to he must take the pledge for 12 months, & then if at the expiration of the first 3 I received a favourable report of the behaviour of himself, his wife, I would mention his wishes to the Govt though I could not assure him that they would be complied with.[80]

For a month nothing changed[81] but then during May and June the situation improved significantly. Although Walter and Mary Ann had not taken the pledge, Dandridge reported 'an entire change in their behaviour'[82] and by July Visiting Magistrate Walpole reported: 'Walter appears to have settled down to industrious habits and has taken the pledge against using strong drinks'.[83] As Dammery notes, most of Walter's life had been on Aboriginal establishments, each an authoritarian structure with only variations in rigidity.[84] Colonist society itself was authoritarian and there were many who desired to be free from it. Walter's and Mary Ann's experience also suggests that those who had some involvement in the church were not immune from the traumatic effects of colonisation, nor the frustrations of being constrained by limitations imposed by others who were more powerful.[85]

Christian instruction

As mentioned earlier, Reverend Freeman's last visit to *putalina* / Oyster Cove was in January 1858. In April that year Bishop Nixon visited the station and found everything under Dandridge's careful supervision in 'excellent order'. Nixon celebrated divine service[86] but Visiting Magistrate Walpole noted there were 'no Aborigines at home'.[87]

Nixon's visit in 1858 was four years after his first visit to the Furneaux Islands. It does seem strange that the Aboriginal people who were more remote received greater attention from the Bishop. In contrast to the Aboriginal people on the Bass

Strait islands who seemed to appreciate the visit of Bishop Nixon, those at *putalina* / Oyster Cove showed no desire to meet him, probably because of Freeman's legacy. This reference in April 1858 is the last mentioned visit by a clergyman, including any bishop, to *putalina* / Oyster Cove. The reason becomes clearer through correspondence in 1859.[88]

On 31 May 1859 when James Bonwick visited *putalina* / Oyster Cove he was

> deeply grieved to find that no means are adopted by Government to provide any religious instruction or amelioration and no efforts made to protect them from the vicious influence of bad white men, nor to keep them from the destructive effects of strong drink. The remnant should at least be prepared for death and eternity.[89]

Bonwick reported a comment from an unnamed Aboriginal person who spoke of the neglect of their spiritual well-being in these words: 'They think we have got no souls now.'[90]

Freeman had stopped visiting *putalina* / Oyster Cove eighteen months earlier in January 1858, when Superintendent Dandridge stopped the pay of £20 a year for expenses.[91] Archdeacon Davies suggested Mr Smales be appointed as catechist at a salary of 'not less than £100 per annum'.[92] Smales demanded £150, including a servant to cook his meals and clean his house.[93] Solly, Assistant Colonial Secretary, perhaps somewhat facetiously, replied that in 'regard to a servant it is considered the Natives may properly be induced to render what attendance may be required'.[94] Smales responded that no 'gentleman' would place himself in such a dependant situation and that without the £150 he would not take the job.[95]

Soon after Bonwick's visit Walter Arthur left the station on a whaling trip in October 1859 on the *Sussex* for an expected voyage of eighteen months.[96] His job as boatman meeting the steam ship that supplied the station was now vacant.[97] Seizing the opportunity for a change not only in religious instructor but the whole approach, Dandridge wrote a scathing report on Freeman's activities, and the rigid institutional methodology inflicted on the Aboriginal people:

> When I was appointed 4 years ago I was directed after having mustered and inspected the Natives to call them with prayers night and morning; the result of all this was that in a very short time the natives hated the very name of prayer, detested myself and finally bolted into the bush; such I am convinced will again happen if the same system be attempted to be carried out now; again whenever Mr Freeman visited the Station (he being then the Visiting Chaplain) if the Natives or any of them caught a glimpse of him before I did, by the time he arrived the place would be deserted and not one of them would be found or would make their appearance until he was gone; so that frequently he was obliged to go away without performing any services at all. In my opinion reading

any set form of prayer or having any set time for instruction (excepting upon Sundays) is productive with these people of more harm than good; the way in which they may be most benefited is to catch them as opportunity offers, either singly or in groups in their own hut, tell or read to them interesting stories upon miscellaneous subjects, particularly such as bear upon their own former history, or that of Natives of other countries (in whom I find they are always much interested) and during the reading or after the reading of their stories found religious instruction upon them, which may be thus conveyed to them in such a way as shall be both interesting and productive and good to them.[98]

Dandridge was similar to Clark in eschewing the *Book of Common Prayer* as a means of communicating or practicing the Christian faith, other than Sunday services. As superintendent he had more authority than Clark and followed his critique with a radically different method and recommended combining the roles of catechist with that of gardener. The gardener could keep the Aboriginal people supplied year round with fresh vegetables, as well as providing the older Aboriginal women with firewood.[99]

It is worth noting the contrast to the Bass Strait islands where the roles of teacher and catechist were combined, and the roles of clergy often fulfilling oversight roles handling people's pensions, negotiating leases, staking out the reserve, and making reports to Parliament about Aboriginal people. As Dandridge noted at the end of Trapper's appointment: 'His duties have been of a most opposite character; on the one hand of the highest order, imparting religious instruction; on the other, performing manual labour; few with capacity for the first would condescend to undertake the latter'. The contrast between Smales demanding a domestic servant and regarding the Aboriginal people as beneath even this role, and Dandridge's recommendation that the catechist ought to serve the Aboriginal people in practical ways, particularly the elderly women, is stark, to say the least. The combination of his sharp critique of the regimented daily office and its proponents, together with the recommendation of a wood-carrying catechist serving Aboriginal Elders, marks Dandridge as one of the very few insightful colonist Christians of the era.

Walter Arthur had experience writing Christian sermons and other exhortations and had led singing in the school and chapel at Wybalenna. He was experienced in tending sheep, growing vegetables and working the *putalina* / Oyster Cove station boat. But Walter also had a history of alcoholic intoxication and violence toward other Aboriginal people. The intoxication and violence may have lessened or been absent if his aspirations had been more effectively addressed earlier on. It is unlikely that Dandridge gave any thought to Walter fulfilling this role.[100] Walter returned from the whaling voyage in January 1861 looking much worse.[101] His death a few months later on 14 May 1861 was 'untimely' to say the least.[102] No body was ever recovered and there appears to be no record of his funeral.

In rejecting Freeman, Dandridge's preferred candidate for catechist was a white man, Francis Trappers, who lived near *putalina* / Oyster Cove. He had experience with Aboriginal people at *putalina* / Oyster Cove and parts of Australia and, importantly for the government, was willing to do the job for less than Smales, at '£100 with quarters and rations for himself and family'.[103] He began in 1859, though the details of what he did are unknown.[104]

With declining numbers of Aboriginal people, the continued poor quality of buildings, and very damp living conditions, in early 1862 Dandridge sought alternative locations for the Aboriginal people and his own family. While he examined potential locations at New Town, Glenorchy, Sandy Bay, Kangaroo Point and Rokeby,[105] other people in the *putalina* / Oyster Cove area were also submitting similar 'tenders' for the work, including Mr Worley[106] and Mr Pybus.[107] Under threat of this new competition, Dandridge provided the government with a new estimate of costs, in early May, to move the Aboriginal people and his family to the vicinity of Hobart Town. It included the 'reduction' of Trappers as catechist[108] and his appointment concluded at the end of May.[109]

The lack of a catechist, or chaplain, from 1862 probably also grew out of the government decisions of the mid-1850s mentioned in the previous chapter to not financially support religious instruction, and from May 1862 there was no government or church sponsored religious activities among the Aboriginal people at *putalina* / Oyster Cove.

Marriages between Aboriginal people and colonists

Aboriginal people at *putalina* / Oyster Cove were interacting early on with workers and some of their colonist neighbours. Some of this was during their regular hunting 'excursions', whaling expeditions, and bartering or selling ration items such as blankets. Some formed close relationships and at least three of the Aboriginal women married colonist men from the local area. The first was Fanny, who married William Smith in 1854.[110] Pengernoburric married an unnamed carpenter in April 1863,[111] and Mary Ann Arthur married Adam Booker[112] in January 1866,[113] after her Aboriginal husband Walter Arthur died in May 1861. The superintendent was required to make application to the government to sanction the marriage.[114] Pengernoburric and Mary Ann Arthur continued living at the *putalina* / Oyster Cove Station after their marriages,[115] but Fanny and William did not.

Ten years after her marriage, Mary Ann became ill in 1871. She was brought from *putalina* / Oyster Cove to the hospital in Hobart with her husband and Mrs Dandridge.[116] She died there two days later[117] and was buried the following day in St David's Cemetery.[118] The *Mercury* reported that 'Not a single mourner followed the hearse. The funeral service was conducted by the Rev. Mr. Gellibrand in the presence of the undertaker, and Mr. D. C. Jones'.[119]

Fanny and William Smith

As mentioned, one person who had left the *putalina* / Oyster Cove Station for a quite different life was Fanny, daughter of *Tanganutara*[120] and *Nikaminik*.[121] Her siblings were Mary Ann, about ten years older, and Adam, a couple of years younger.[122] A deposition by Jeanneret suggests the name 'Cochrane' was linked with Fanny while at Wybalenna.[123]

At times during her life the identity of Fanny's father was the topic of speculation among some parliamentarians,[124] anthropologists[125] and newspaper correspondents.[126] It was felt crucial at the time because of the important difference in the minds of colonists in what they had constructed as a 'full-blood' and a 'half-caste' Aborigine. The Tasmanian government accepted that she had two Aboriginal parents in 1854 in granting her pension, in 1864 in approving the first land grant,[127] in 1882 in increasing her pension,[128] and in 1884 in extending her land grant.[129]

As mentioned earlier, Fanny was part of the group that moved to *putalina* / Oyster Cove in October 1847. She was part of the most intact family arriving at *putalina* / Oyster Cove with both her parents and her two siblings. She was too old for the Orphan School, though she had been there earlier for two months from 9 December 1842 to 8 February 1843, after which she was discharged back into the care of Robert Clark at Wybalenna.[130]

There is no reference to Fanny in the surviving documentation at *putalina* / Oyster Cove from 1847 to 1854[131] so it is speculative to construct a biographical sketch. If she was temporarily in Hobart, as Plomley suggested,[132] it is likely she continued living with Mary Ann and Walter when she returned to *putalina* / Oyster Cove. Her daily life is likely to have included domestic work with the other young women, and probably some catechetical classes with Robert Clark. She would have been too young to be admitted to the public houses in the neighborhood, including at North West Bay, if she went with the other Aboriginal women on their excursions and liaisons there. Nevertheless, at some point in time in circumstances unknown, Fanny met William Smith, a sawyer, probably from the area around *putalina* / Oyster Cove given that the only available means of transport from the station were by foot and boat.

In early 1854 arrangements began for Fanny and William to be married, including approval from Parliament for Fanny to receive a pension 'in lieu of her maintenance at the establishment'.[133] What was unusual was that they clearly intended to live away from the station. Fanny was the first Aboriginal adult to be granted such a request.[134] Fanny was one of only a few Aboriginal people provided with a pension by the government.[135] Fanny's pension was listed in the government's publication of pensions.[136] The later superintendent at *putalina* / Oyster Cove, Dandridge, was responsible for the pensions provided to *Trukanini* and Mary Ann in about 1868.[137]

Fanny Cochrane married William Smith on 27 October 1854, in the Murray Street home of the Independent Minister, Reverend Miller. The marriage register reads:

> Wedding No. 297, October 27th Minister's House, Murray Street, Hobart, William Smith and Fanny Cochrane, Of full age, Sawyer, [*both William and Fanny put an 'X' as their signature*], William Smith '*his* mark' and Fanny Cochrane '*her* mark'. Rev. Miller.
>
> Married in the Minister's house aforesaid according to the Rites and Ceremonies of Independent, by License.
>
> This marriage was solemnized between us William Smith '*his mark*' and Fanny Cochrane '*her mark*'
>
> In the presence of Joseph Milligan, and John Hales.[138]

Reverend Miller visited *putalina* / Oyster Cove in 1853. This may have contributed to Fanny and William linking with him to conduct their wedding in 1854, though the Anglican Bishop Nixon also participated in this visit.[139] There was no catechist or visiting chaplain at *putalina* / Oyster Cove until Freeman was appointed in June 1855. The involvement of Miller was likely to have been through superintendent Milligan. It would not have occurred without his permission.

A newspaper article in the *Mercury* in 1882 described William as living at North West Bay at the time of their marriage.[140] There was a William Smith who was a member of the Anglican Parish at Brown's River (present day Kingston), and was living at North West Bay, which lies between Brown's River and *putalina* / Oyster Cove. However, two baptisms of children of William and Maria Smith at Brown's River Mill, on 2 April 1858 and 24 February 1861 by Reverend Edward Freeman, suggest this was a different William Smith to the man Fanny married. There may have been two William Smiths, both sawyers, in the same area at the same time, one an Anglican, and the other an Independent. William's denominational membership is unknown. There was widespread conflict in the Anglican parish with the entrepreneurial Reverend Freeman.[141]

The newspaper article in 1882 by 'One who knows' goes on to suggest William and Fanny Smith remained at North West Bay for six or eight months after their marriage and then moved to Hamilton under an engagement to Mr William Clarke, of Norton Mandeville.[142] Here they remained for two years. From Hamilton they came to live in Hobart, where they opened a board and lodging house in Liverpool Street, two doors above the well-known premises of Perkins and Nephew.[143]

Things not going on satisfactorily in this business, they removed again to North West Bay where they remained six months.[144]

If the dates in the newspaper article are accurate, William and Fanny could have been living back at North West Bay by the middle of 1857. If so, they may have been part of a petition by fifty-two members of the Anglican Parish at Brown's River, to the Bishop regarding:

> ... in consequence of the late feeling exhibited by the Rev. E. Freeman, referred to in the early part of this memorial, the Church at Kingston will again be almost deserted, and many of Your Lordship's Memorialists will have either to attend the Wesleyan Chapel, or to abandon altogether the Public Worship of their Maker, for so long a time as the present incumbent is permitted to retain his pastoral care of the parish ...[145]

The 'Memorialists' included a G A Robinson, a William Smith and fifty others[146] but it is unknown if this William was married to Fanny, and if they were part of the Anglican congregation. There was a Wesleyan Methodist Congregation at Brown's River that was part of the Sandy Bay Circuit until it separated in 1860 but membership lists are not known.[147] It is a significant but unanswered question in ascertaining the background to Fanny's and William's membership in the Methodist Church at Nicholls Rivulet thirty years later.

Funerals

In 1857 while Fanny and William were living at North West Bay, Fanny's brother Adam was living with them. Fanny gave birth to the first of her eleven children on 1 August 1857.[148] A little over five weeks later her brother, Adam, became ill, died and was buried at *putalina* / Oyster Cove.[149] Ryan speculates that 'the entire Oyster Cove community arrived next morning, camped nearby and performed ceremonies to ensure that he properly went to the next stage of his life'.[150] What 'properly' means in ceremonial terms and so far from his ancestors' country is not known and not explored. It could be argued that Mary Ann's and Fanny's involvement in the church led to a Christian ceremony of some kind. Their mother, *Tanganutara*, could represent the continuing Aboriginal ceremonial practice. However, as with other examples, such as the hunting trips, people's actual practices are likely to be more complex.

There were fifteen Aboriginal people at *putalina* / Oyster Cove, including Adam's mother and two sisters. Most were avoiding the visits of Reverend Freeman and the prayer book services, so it is difficult to determine the kind of funeral ceremony that occurred. A burial at the *putalina* / Oyster Cove cemetery required the permission of superintendent Dandridge and authority to authorise the location of the grave and gravediggers to undertake the work. Therefore the most likely scenario rests on balancing Dandridge's obligations, his dislike of Freeman, Freeman's knowledge of Adam's death and his availability to perform the prayer book service, and *Tanganutara*, Mary Ann and Fanny requesting particular funeral rites to be performed. The choice of funerary rites would rest primarily on these relationships.

Fanny and Adam were living away from the station at that time. She had had her first child five weeks earlier and Adam died at her and William's house. Fanny's separation from Anglican practices had perhaps already begun. Mary Ann and Walter were living on the station but were somewhat removed from the main buildings. Given Dandridge's dislike of Freeman and his more respectful behaviour toward the Aboriginal people it is possible that more than one service/ceremony occurred prior to, or after, the burial. Without more details any definitive conclusion is speculative.

Other funerals for Aboriginal people are also instructive. Aboriginal children who died at the Orphan School were buried there and not brought to *putalina* / Oyster Cove. The proximity of St John's Anglican Church meant the funeral service in the *Book of Common Prayer* was followed there. When Pengernoburric died at *putalina* / Oyster Cove in February 1867,[151] the few remaining Aboriginal people were all out 'hunting'[152] and Dandridge arranged the ceremony. Although the final form is unknown, it is unlikely to have contained Aboriginal ceremonial elements without any Aboriginal people present. A version of Christian funeral is more likely but the final form is unknown. When Mary Ann died in July 1871 she was buried in the St David's Church cemetery in Hobart with no one from *putalina* / Oyster Cove present. The funeral was performed by an Anglican clergyman and would have followed the prayer book.[153] Walter drowned in the River Derwent in 1861 and his body was never recovered. There is no record of his funeral so the type of ceremony is also unknown. It is clear that there was not a consistent funeral protocol occurring even for the influential people at *putalina* / Oyster Cove. The timing and circumstances of a person's death, and the availability and relationships of those looking after their bodies were the primary influences in the ceremony that was performed. It is unlikely that the death of nineteen-year-old Adam would have been afforded something akin to a full cultural ceremony but some first language songs and other religious expressions seem probable.

Pension and land grant

In 1858 according to 'One who knows', William and Fanny Smith moved to Irish Town in the district of Port Cygnet.[154] Later that year, on 3 October 1858, *Tanganutara*, mother of Fanny, Mary Ann and Adam, died at *putalina* / Oyster

Cove.[155] In the following ten or so years Fanny and William appear to have focussed on working and raising their family. Their church involvement is unclear, but given their significant later involvement in the Methodist Church, it seems more likely that this grew out of earlier and ongoing participation in a local church, probably Methodist. As well as raising their family and working in sawmills, Fanny and William again came to the attention of members of Parliament, particularly as they became less able to work. In October Fanny's pension was increased from £24 to £50 per annum.[156] Two years later, Thomas Reibey proposed Parliament grant 500 acres of land to Fanny Smith.[157] The Committee of the House of Assembly resolved to grant 300 acres including 'the 100 acres of Land she now occupies, and 200 acres more'.[158]

In 1885 the issue of a further land grant to an Aboriginal person was again raised in the House of Assembly, this time by Mr Hartnoll, who sought '£320 for the benefit of Mary Ann Smith, an aboriginal, or permission to select 320 acres of waste land in the colony'.[159] Mary Ann Smith was the 'daughter of Trollinaloona, an Aboriginal of Tasmania'. Hartnoll gave a biographical sketch of her, but this is not in the parliamentary records. The application was denied on the basis that Mary Ann Smith was deemed a 'half-caste' and as such was not entitled to a pension or land grant. The Minister for Lands feared 'similar claims would be made by all the half-castes on the Straits islands.'[160]

Nicholls Rivulet Methodist Church

It is unclear how Fanny's and William's participation in the Methodist Church began. The two most likely scenarios are firstly that William was already a member of the Methodist Church, probably at Brown's River, when he and Fanny met and married, and they simply continued attending there after their marriage until they moved to Irish Town. The second most likely possibility is that they were both involved in the Anglican Church at North West Bay with the controversial Reverend Freeman, and decided to leave and join the Methodists as threatened in the letter to the Bishop about Freeman's behaviour. Although the initial circumstances are unclear, it is clear that by the end of the 1880s they were actively involved in the Methodist Home Mission Circuit of Port Cygnet, which included congregations at Port Cygnet, Wattle Grove and Irish Town / Nicholls Rivulet. The Port Cygnet Methodist Home Mission Station held its first quarterly meeting in June 1889, five years after Parliament granted land to Fanny and about eleven years before she granted land to the Circuit. In the time between the formation of the congregation and the construction of the building, the congregation met, possibly in the Smiths' home. The quarterly membership register reports 3–5 members at Irish Town with financial contributions of approximately £10.[161]

Ten years later in 1899 Fanny gained further publicity when with the involvement of Horace Watson, she gave a number of public performances speaking about her life and singing in her first language.[162] On 30 October, under the promotional heading of 'Last of the Mohicans'[163] another benefit for Fanny Smith was held in the Temperance Hall in Hobart. The report, the following day was headed ' "The Last of the Aborigines", An interesting entertainment for the benefit of Mrs. Fanny Cochrane Smith'. It was reported:

> she said she was 60 years of age, had 11 children, who were all still living, and that, for many years past, her husband (who is a white man) had been disabled by paralysis. She speaks three native languages or dialects, and sang two songs in her own particular tongue, which were simple and melodious.[164]

Clearly her lifestyle, including involvement in the church, had not suppressed her first language. It is possible the central place of collective singing in church had strengthened her singing voice and complemented the continuation of her first language songs, or more likely vice versa. One can only wonder if she ever sang her first language songs in church. She had somehow continued speaking and singing in her first language forty years after her mother's death and more than twenty-eight years after her only remaining sibling had died, and twenty-three years after *Trukanini* died. The 'three native languages or dialects' are likely to be her own from her mother, sister and brother, that of *Trukanini* and Dray [*Nununi*], and that of *Wapati* [North-east]. These were the oldest women at *putalina* / Oyster Cove and among the longest-lived, having learnt their language prior to much interaction with colonists.

Whether it was the public performances, a change in the congregation, or more likely the example of a neighbouring Methodist landowner, the turn of the century saw movement toward a building for the Nicholls Rivulet congregation. There is no documentary evidence of why Fanny donated the land for the church, but in January 1900 Frederick Henry Thomas granted a portion of land to the Port Cygnet Methodist Home Mission Circuit for a church to be built, probably the one at Wattle Grove. The Thomas land grant was finalised on 1 August 1900.[165] Around the same time Fanny also donated some of her land to the Circuit and it was finalised on 5 November 1900.[166] At Nicholls Rivulet the construction of the church commenced immediately. The foundation stone was laid on 6 November 1900. It took six months to complete and the first service was held on Sunday 5 May 1901. So while at that time on *truwana* / Cape Barren Island people were withdrawing from the church, at Nicholls Rivulet Aboriginal people were increasing their engagement and were leading the congregation.

The Certificate of Title Vol. 121, Folio 70, for the three roods and four perches of land records the owners as:

Robert Manning Harvey of Port Cygnet, Storekeeper
Charles Batge of Wattle Grove, Farmer,
Samuel Joseph Cato of Port Cygnet, Orchardist,
William Henry Smith of Irish Town, Farmer,
Fanny Cockrane [sic] Smith of Irish Town, Married Woman,
Joseph Thomas Sears Smith of Irish Town, Farmer,
Tasman Benjamin Smith of Irish Town, Farmer and
Robert Langdon of Gardners Bay, Mining Manager

Dated this 20th day of June 1901.[167]

A perusal of the 'Methodist Church Model Deed for Wesleyan Church Properties in Tasmania'[168] reveals an extraordinary element to the context at Nicholls Rivulet. Unsurprisingly for the time there is an in-built assumption that members of a Methodist Board of Trustees will be men.[169] A check of every grant deed of every board of trustees in Tasmania up to 1905 gives a strong indication of the absence of women as trustees. It is not possible to say conclusively if Fanny was the only woman who was a member of a board of trustees in Tasmania at that time, given the number of names which have recorded only a first initial rather than a first full name, however, most lists of trustees begin with the title, 'Messrs'. Because some have just the initials of the person, some of these could be women. However, there is no other trustee listed from the year of the model deed, 18 May 1888, up to 1905, who is identifiably a woman other than Fanny Smith. It is therefore likely that Fanny was either the only woman in Tasmania on a board of trustees of the Methodist Church, or one of very, very few.

The congregation at Nicholls Rivulet had formally existed for twelve years prior to construction of the building. But the inaugural service in this building was an historic occasion, particularly when considering the range of places, styles and languages through which Aboriginal people had experienced Christian worship services in the preceding century. Fanny's personal experience of Christian worship throughout her lifetime began in a wooden hut at Wybalenna among the Ben Lomond huts, the brick chapel with a mix of Robinson reading the *Book of Common Prayer*, and Clark's *pidgin*.

This was followed by the St John's Anglican Church New Town when she lived at the Orphan School, the regimented prayer book by Freeman in the dilapidated chapel at *putalina* / Oyster Cove, and various churches with William. She then hosted church services in her own home at Nicholls Rivulet before finally a chapel was built on land she herself had donated with wood likely to have been sourced by her own family or neighbours.

It was likely to have been a momentous day for her and her family. It is only speculative but curious nonetheless to ponder what she might have sung. This was the first time Aboriginal people had had primary responsibility in deciding to have a church building — procuring the materials, constructing it and taking a leading role in the ongoing services.

Fanny and William instilled Christian faith in their children and participated in the congregation to such an extent that one of their sons, William, became a lay preacher and two other sons, Joseph and Tasman, were on the Board of Trustees. As well as property and financial affairs the Board of Trustees was responsible for appointing 'Protestant' people to preach as well as those appointed by the superintendent preacher.[170] Therefore Fanny, William, Joseph and Tasman would have participated in the appointment of William as a lay preacher. This shows something of the strength of Fanny's commitment to the church, and also demonstrates their sons' personal engagement with the faith. William's choice to become actively and publicly involved in preaching identifies him as the first Aboriginal preacher in a church service since Walter and Thomas at Wybalenna in the 1830s.[171] At Nicholls Rivulet Aboriginal people exercised greater leadership participation than at Wybalenna or the Bass Strait islands.

In this congregation, an Aboriginal person had donated some of her own legally secure freehold title land on which the church building was built. At Wybalenna it was a government establishment, and on the islands the gatherings were on 'waste' land, leasehold land, or a government reserve. Fanny's donation of some of her own land for a church is historic, and demonstrates a very personal, strong and lasting legacy that some in the succeeding generations of her family would continue.

Eighteen months after the first service in the building, Fanny's husband, William, who had been an invalid for the previous thirty years, died in December 1902, aged 81.[172] Three years and three months later Fanny also came to the end of her life. The *Mercury* reported,

> THE LAST OF THE TASMANIAN ABORIGINALS. FUNERAL OF FANNY SMITH.
>
> The closing scene in respect to the Tasmanian aboriginal race took place at Wattle Grove, Port Cygnet, on Friday, when Mrs. Fanny Cockern [sic] Smith, the last half-caste survivor, passed away. The deceased at the time of her demise was in her seventy-fourth year.
>
> Dr. Bernard Thomas was unremitting in attendance, and did all medical skill could do. The immediate cause of her death was pleurisy, followed by an acute attack of pneumonia. Deceased was held in high respect and esteem by all who knew her. She leaves a large grown-up family. Deceased was in receipt of an annuity of fifty pounds per year from the Tasmanian Government. Her funeral took place this afternoon, when about four hundred followed her remains. The Rev. Thomas officiated at the grave.[173]

Her funeral was also reported in other newspapers around Tasmania[174] and following her death the local clergyman, Reverend Roberts, held memorial services at Irish Town and Port Cygnet. It was reported he said:

> her character proved that Tasmanian aboriginals were capable of taking on a high degree of civilization. The grace of Christianity in her life was beautifully exemplified. He took his text from Genesis iv. 31. These were large congregations.[175]

Despite the strong participation of a number of families in the congregation, the Port Cygnet Methodist Home Mission Circuit was often struggling financially. In the first financial report, the Nicholls Rivulet congregation contributed about a quarter of the financial contributions of the Circuit, with ten out of thirty-eight pounds. In 1895 they contributed thirteen out of £320, and in 1900 it was ten and a half out of a total of just over £270.[176] It was not a wealthy congregation. The Home Mission Society gave an annual grant that contributed one quarter of the income of the Circuit, and from the middle of 1897 the Circuit minister forfeited one quarter of his stipend each year to help limit the debt. These two contributions comprised half the income of the Circuit. The stipend was £50 per quarter and together with the £70 loan on the minister's parsonage,[177] comprised most of the expense.[178] In 1898 a special effort raised £79 19s 0d, including a donation of ten shillings from W. Smith, the only donation from Nicholls Rivulet, and cleared most of the deficiency. Successive ministers, Reverend Beckett, Reverend Atkinson and Reverend Roberts, continued to contribute between one quarter and half their stipend to keep the Circuit financially viable.[179]

William Smith, Fanny's and William's eldest son, continued as lay preacher and church steward until 1920, and thus had a longer involvement in a leading role in the church than his mother. Unfortunately there are few records available. It would be invaluable to compare William's sermons to those of Walter Arthur, Thomas Bruny and the other Aboriginal men at Wybalenna. By 1909 the congregation's membership was listed as four: William H. Smith, Lena Smith, Flora Stanton and Mary Miller.[180] The membership reached a peak of eight in 1914–15, before settling at three members in 1920 and between five and ten during the subsequent twenty years. The Sunday School had five listed scholars through most of the 1920s. By the mid 1930s the Sunday School experienced something of a 'boom', reaching forty-one listed scholars, twice the number as at Cygnet at that time. There were five baptisms in 1934 and from the early 1940s the number of Sunday School scholars averaged between five and ten.[181]

While the transfer from Wybalenna to *putalina* / Oyster Cove brought Aboriginal people geographically closer to colonial society and Christian missionary endeavours, Aboriginal Christian people continued to develop their own form of faith with the support of rare respectful colonists and in spite of the narrow regimented forms inflicted on them by government-appointed clergy. Few Aboriginal people continued to associate with the church in this context. But when opportunity arose for them to create a different context more of their own making, some Aboriginal people became strongly engaged in Christian faith as they continued Aboriginal–Christian dialogue and adapting their practices and identities through successive contexts across generations.

These questions and challenges continue to resonate for some Aboriginal and non-Aboriginal people today. The recent reflections of Garry Worete Deverell provide one such example.[182] From January 1995 to December 2015 I was a minister with the Uniting Aboriginal and Islander Christian Congress (UAICC) in Tasmania. Aboriginal Elders have always been central in the work among the Tasmanian Aboriginal community, particularly Aunty Ida West, Aunty Girlie Purdon, Lennah Newson, and Eva Richardson. Regular discussions occurred during Sunday services and Regional Committee meetings about Aboriginal cultural practices, the legacies of colonial history, and the interactions with people's personal Christian faith. These practices and legacies shaped people's questions and interpretations of the Christian Bible, church traditions, and our contemporary collective gatherings.

Colonisation disrupts and changes mythology. The complicity of Christian churches in the colonisation of *lutruwita* profoundly affected the ways past Aboriginal people engaged with the Christian faith and how contemporary Aboriginal people question and interpret it and use it in shaping their own cultural and spiritual practices and sense of connection to country. Religious stories, mythologies and rituals influence how stories of colonisation are some of the threads in our contemporary conversations. It affects how we remember and re-present our past and how we negotiate current relationships. It shapes how and what we envision the kinds of futures we want to create. For just as the Aboriginal people discussed in this book are the ancestors of today's Tasmanian Aboriginal community, so too the legacies of non-Aboriginal individuals and institutions linger in our contemporary conversations and politics.

There has not ever been a single, or unified, Aboriginal or non-Aboriginal response to the questions and experiences of colonisation and particularly the mythic dialogues. And yet the experiences of ancestors will continue to be important partners in our ongoing conversations and transformations.

ENDNOTES CHAPTER SEVEN

1. Correspondence Walter Arthur to Colonial Secretary, 22 May 1847, TAHO CSO 24/7/101. Robinson had also gaoled Walter in early 1838, Plomley, 1987, p. 508.
2. February 1846, TAHO CSO 11/26/378, Plomley, 1987, pp. 148–49, and Correspondence Jeanneret to Colonial Secretary, 8 March 1847, TAHO CSO 24/7/101, p. 30. The series of 'depositions' against Clark are found in TAHO CSO 24/7/101, pp. 294–323.
3. Correspondence Colonial Secretary to Jeanneret, 5 May 1847 TAHO CSO 24/7/101, p. 5. Correspondence Penny to Colonial Secretary, 19 June 1847, TAHO CSO 24/7/101, pp. 37, 41.
4. Correspondence Milligan to Colonial Secretary, 22 October 1847, TAHO CSO 24/7/101, pp. 328–330, Correspondence Friend to Colonial Secretary TAHO CSO 24/7/101, pp. 91–118.
5. Chief Police Magistrate at George Town to Colonial Secretary, 6 June 1847, 'The explanation given by Mr Clark is satisfactory. Dr Jeanneret has been suspended from his office and is not I think to be trusted looking generally at his conduct as regard to Clark and others. Dr Milligan will I trust be able to settle all the matters', CSO 24/7/101.
6. Correspondence Milligan to Colonial Secretary, CSO 24/7/101, pp. 173–176. It was essentially to save the Government £300 per annum, CSO 24/7/101, pp. 333, 337–350, but once there the abandoned buildings would cost more than £300 to repair, Correspondence Kay to Colonial Secretary, TAHO CSD 1/18/703.
7. Correspondence Kay to Colonial Secretary, July 1847, TAHO CSO 24/7/101, pp. 350–355; Correspondence Colonial Secretary to Milligan, 7 August 1847, TAHO CSO 24/7/101, p. 77. 'I have this day shipped on board the schooner 'Sisters' the whole of the Aborigines consisting of 14 adult males, 22 adult females, 5 boys and 5 girls', Correspondence Milligan to Colonial Secretary, 15 October 1847, TAHO CSO 24/7/101, pp. 173–176. One Hobart newspaper reported forty-seven, adding an extra adult male, *Colonial Times*, 22 October 1847, p. 2.
8. Correspondence Colonial Secretary to Dandridge, 2 September 1873, TAHO CSD 1/33/D450.
9. *Cornwall Chronicle*, 20 January 1849, pp. 316, 317. *Launceston Examiner*, 3 May 1855, p. 2. *The Mercury*, 19 September 1856, p. 2. *Oyster Cove Visitor's Book*, TAHO CSO 89/1/1, p. 15. For a discussion of the role of the 'Visitor's Book' in later Christian missions, see Attwood, B., 1989, 'Reading Sources in Aboriginal History: Mission Stations Visitors Books,' *La Trobe Journal*, 43, pp. 21–28.
10. Davis, R., & Petrow, S., (eds.), 2004, *Varieties of Vice-Regal Life*. Hobart; Tasmanian Historical Research Association, pp. 74–78.
11. *Launceston Examiner*, 1 January 1848, pp. 5, 6.
12. Correspondence Milligan to Colonial Secretary, 29 October 1847, TAHO CSO 24/7/101, pp. 185–188. Fanny was Mary Ann's sister. At thirty years of age, Walter and Mary Ann were the youngest married couple at the Station and were later described as the 'adopted parents' of Billy (William Lanney), Correspondence 3 November 1855, TAHO CSD 1/18/703. See also Davis, R., & Petrow, S., 2004, p. 74.
13. TAHO SWD 28/1/1, unpaginated.
14. TAHO SWD 28/1/1, unpaginated. Her mother was Catherine. Plomley, 1966, p. 997.
15. Dr Smith attended *putalina* / Oyster Cove at least from 1858 onwards. *Oyster Cove Visitors Book*, William Smith, Surgeon, TAHO CSO 89/1/1, p. 31–32.
16. TAHO SWD 28/1/1, unpaginated.
17. McGoogan, K., 2005, *Lady Franklin's Revenge*. Melbourne; HarperCollins, p. 213.
18. TAHO CSD 1/51/1009, and SC 195/31/2798.
19. McGoogan, 2005, pp. 211–13. Perkins, R., & Langton, M., (eds.), 2008, *First Australians An Illustrated History*. Melbourne; Miegunyah Press, p. 101.

20. TAHO SWD 28/1/1, unpaginated. The location of the cemetery and identification of graves is unknown.
21. TAHO SWD 28/1/1, unpaginated, also TAHO CSD 1/18/703.
22. Plomley, 1987, p. 176.
23. Correspondence Colonial Secretary to Milligan, 30 October 1847, TAHO CSO 24/7/101, pp. 178–179.
24. *Colonial Times*, 21 September 1847, p. 3.
25. Correspondence Superintendent Kay to Colonial Secretary, 3 August 1855, TAHO CSD 1/18/703.
26. Correspondence, Kirwan to Colonial Secretary, 3 August 1855, TAHO CSD 1/18/703.
27. *Colonial Times*, 12 November 1847, p. 4.
28. *The Courier*, 25 December 1847, p. 3.
29. Correspondence Clark to Colonial Secretary, 31 March 1848, TAHO CSO 24/42/1331.
30. Correspondence Kirwan to Colonial Secretary, 17 April 1855, TAHO CSD 1/18/703.
31. Plomley, 1987, p. 176.
32. Plomley, 1987, p. 176.
33. Plomley, 1987, p. 177.
34. One of the labourers named was John Russell who was employed at the Station, Dandridge to Colonial Secretary, 1 November 1859, TAHO CSD 1/1/126/4656.
35. Plomley, 1987, p. 176. Three of Clark's orphaned children, William, Sandford and Alexander, were admitted to the Orphan School, 20 April 1850, and discharged between July 1851 and November 1852, TAHO SWD 28/1/1, unpaginated. During this time they would have been reunited with several Aboriginal children they had known at *putalina* / Oyster Cove and Wybalenna.
36. TAHO CSO 11/26/378, Plomley, 1987, pp. 148–49.
37. Plomley, 1987, p. 178.
38. Correspondence Kirwan to Colonial Secretary, 17 April 1855, TAHO CSD 1/18/703.
39. *Colonial Times*, 1 February 1856, pp. 2, 3.
40. *Oyster Cove Visitors Book*, 14 December 1857, E. Walpole, TAHO CSO 89/1/1, p. 25.
41. Correspondence Assistant Colonial Secretary Solly to Dandridge, 13 April 1858, TAHO CSD 1/1/126/4656. The isolated context of the islands contrasted the nearness of the Public Houses at *putalina* / Oyster Cove.
42. Correspondence Colonial Secretary to Milligan, 1 May 1855, TAHO CSD 1/18/703. Milligan immediately enlisted the help of Walter Arthur in an attempt to prevent Visiting Magistrate Kirwan being appointed to oversee the Station, Correspondence Arthur to Milligan, 1 May 1855, TAHO CSD 1/18/703, but to no avail, Correspondence Colonial Secretary to Milligan, 23 May 1855, TAHO CSD 1/18/703.
43. Present day Kingston.
44. Correspondence Colonial Secretary to Freeman, 6 June 1855, TAHO CSD 1/18/703. It is worth noting that at this point in time Rev. Freeman was visiting the station by boat from Brown's River, since there was no road to *putalina* / Oyster Cove.
45. Correspondence Colonial Secretary to Freeman, 6 June 1855, TAHO CSD 1/18/703, also *Oyster Cove Visitors Book*, 27 July 1855, TAHO CSO 89/1/1, p. 2.
46. Correspondence Freeman to Governor, 1 May 1855, TAHO CSD 1/18/703.
47. *Oyster Cove Visitors Book*, 19 October 1855, TAHO CSO 89/1/1, p. 5.
48. *Oyster Cove Visitors Book*, 27 July 1855, 31 August 1855, 19 September 1855, 24 December 1855, 7 March 1856, 29 March 1856, 25 July 1856, TAHO CSO 89/1/1, pp. 2, 3, 5, 8, 10, 11, 14.
49. Unnamed Aboriginal woman, *Oyster Cove Visitors Book*, 27 July 1855, TAHO CSO 89/1/1, p. 2.
50. *Oyster Cove Visitors Book*, 30 November 1855, TAHO CSO 89/1/1, p. 6; 24 December 1855, TAHO CSO 89/1/1, p. 8.
51. *Oyster Cove Visitors Book*, 31 August 1855, 19 September 1855, 21 November, TAHO CSO 89/1/1, pp. 2, 3, 6; and 29 March 1856, TAHO CSO 89/1/1, p. 11.
52. Correspondence, Kirwan to Colonial Secretary, TAHO CSD 1/18/703.
53. *The Courier*, 2 October 1857, p. 3. Freeman also found himself in economic difficulties. He was known as the 'Trading

Parson' and appeared in the Hobart Insolvent Court in 1860. The court was told he was out of debt in 1852, but had been in debt ever since. He engaged in sawing and shingle splitting speculation and defrauded his creditors. There had been nineteen cases of summonses and sixteen warrants of Attorney in a two-year period. *Cornwall Chronicle*, 14 March 1860, p. 5.

54 23 May, 11 June, 26 August, 18 and 31 December 1856, *Oyster Cove Visitors Book*, TAHO CSO 89/1/1.

55 *Oyster Cove Visitors Book*, 22 January 1858, Edward Freeman, TAHO CSO 89/1/1, p. 27.

56 29 August 1855, Baptism Register, Anglican Parish, Browns River, TAHO NS 2020/1, No. 258.

57 See baptisms numbered 286, 307, 318, 419, and 499. This last numbered baptism was the son of Freeman's successor, Francis Trappers, 13 December 1867, Baptism Register, Anglican Parish, Browns River, TAHO NS 2020/1.

58 *Oyster Cove Visitors Book*, 18 and 23 May 1856, TAHO CSO 89/1/1, p. 12.

59 *Oyster Cove Visitors Book*, 28 March and 27 April 1857, J. Kirwan Visiting Magistrate, TAHO CSO 89/1/1, pp. 19, 21. 18 July 1857, Edward Freeman, TAHO CSO 89/1/1, p. 23. 22 January 1858, '… Superintendent reports returning 80lbs of beef to the contractor as being foul and unfit …' E. Walpole, Police Magistrate, TAHO CSO 89/1/1, p. 27.

60 *Oyster Cove Visitors Book*, 26 August 1856, TAHO CSO 89/1/1, p. 14.

61 Ryan, 2012, p. 258.

62 Ryan, 2012, p. 259.

63 *Oyster Cove Visitors Book*, 18 July 1857, TAHO CSO 89/1/1, p. 23. 24 March 1858, TAHO CSO 89/1/1, p. 28. 18 November 1858, TAHO CSO 89/1/1, p. 35.

64 *Oyster Cove Visitors Book*, 31 January 1857, J. Kirwan, TAHO CSO 89/1/1, p. 18. Also 14 October 1857, Edward Freeman, TAHO CSO 89/1/1, p. 24. 10 July 1858, TAHO CSO 89/1/1, p. 29. '[Terminope] Augustus one of the Aborigines has just returned from a whaling voyage', E. Walpole, 23 April 1859. TAHO CSO 89/1/1, p. 37. 14 January 1860, 'four men are still about whaling', Walpole. TAHO CSO 89/1/1, p. 43.

65 *Oyster Cove Visitors Book*, 30 October 1861 W. Smith TAHO CSO 89/1/1, p. 62.

66 *The Courier*, 22 February 1853, p. 2.

67 *The Courier*, 6 December 1853, p. 2.

68 *The Mercury*, 19 September 1856, p. 2.

69 *Oyster Cove Visitors Book*, TAHO CSO 89/1/1, p. 16. £3600 was raised. *Colonial Times*, 22 November 1856, p. 2. It had sailed from England in October 1855. *Cornwall Chronicle*, 24 October 1855, p. 4. This vessel had been purchased by subscriptions raised by Sunday School children from Methodist, Congregational and other 'dissenting' churches in England for the purpose of supporting mission ventures in the Pacific Islands. *The Mercury*, 28 November 1856, p. 2. The *John Williams* sailed for the South Sea Islands in 1861. *The Mercury*, 28 March 1861, p. 2, supported by £195 donated to the work by churches in Hobart. *The Mercury*, 20 April 1861, p. 2.

70 *Church News*, 20 March 1866, p. 231.

71 *The Mercury*, 11 April 1882, pp. 1, 2.

72 Correspondence Milligan to Colonial Secretary, 29 October 1847, TAHO CSO 24/7/101, pp. 185 – 188.

73 Correspondence 3 November 1855, TAHO CSD 1/18/703.

74 Correspondence Walter Arthur to Governor Young, 23 May 1855, TAHO CSD 1/18/703.

75 Land Title 5115.1 Correspondence Colonial Secretary to Dandridge, 3 August 1855, TAHO LSD 2/1/3, p. 530.

76 Correspondence Henry John Porter to Colonial Secretary, 3 November 1855, TAHO CSD 1/18/703.

77 19 March 1838, Plomley, 1987, p. 544.

78 Correspondence Dandridge to Colonial Secretary, 6 March 1858, TAHO CSD 1/1/126/4656.

79 Correspondence Dandridge to Colonial Secretary, 6 March 1858, TAHO CSD 1/1/126/4656.

80 Correspondence Assistant Colonial Secretary Solly to Dandridge, 13 April 1858, TAHO CSD 1/1/126/4656.

81 Correspondence Walpole to Colonial Secretary, 28 April 1858, TAHO CSO 89/1/1, p. 29.
82 Correspondence Dandridge to Assistant Colonial Secretary Travers, 15 May 1858, TAHO CSD 1/1/126/4656, and *Oyster Cove Visitors Book*, TAHO CSO 89/1/1, p. 28.
83 *Oyster Cove Visitors Book*, 10 July 1858, TAHO CSO 89/1/1, p. 29.
84 Dammery, 2001, p. 45.
85 Land Title 5115.1 Correspondence Colonial Secretary to Dandridge, 3 August 1855, TAHO LSD 2/1/3, p. 530. In June 1857 he had sought land at Molly's Point, TAHO LSD 2/1/3, p. 530.
86 *Oyster Cove Visitors Book*, TAHO CSO 89/1/1, p. 28.
87 *Oyster Cove Visitors Book* TAHO CSO 89/1/1, p. 28. Walpole's comment is odd, because there is a series of photos of the Aboriginal people, taken by Nixon, dated '1858', held by the Tasmanian Museum and Art Gallery, and reproduced in Rae-Ellis, 1976, pp. 108, 110. Following the death of *Trukanini*, *The Mercury*, reported she had been baptised by Bishop Nixon, (*The Mercury*, 12 May 1876, p. 2), so it could only have occurred at the time of the photos. Rev. Freeman baptised several children at *putalina* / Oyster Cove, including Superintendent Dandridge's daughter, noted earlier, as recorded in the Baptism Register of the Brown's River Anglican Parish, but there is no record of *Trukanini* being baptized at *putalina* / Oyster Cove.
88 It seems the first member of parliament to visit *putalina* / Oyster Cove was J. D. Balfe in September 1859. He described the treatment of the Aboriginal people as 'parsimonious and ungenerous'. He recommended a trebling of the rations provided to the Aboriginal people and an increased remuneration for the Superintendent, *Oyster Cove Visitors Book*, TAHO CSO 89/1/1, p. 40.
89 *Oyster Cove Visitors Book*, TAHO CSO 89/1/1, p. 38. 'The Royal Kalendar and Guide to Tasmania from 1859', had a different view, 'Uncleanly, unsober, unvirtuous, unenergetic and irreligious with a past character for treachery, and no record of *one* noble action, the race is fast fading away, and its utter extinction will hardly be regretted', Hull, H. M., 1859, *The Royal Kalendar and Guide to Tasmania from 1859*. Hobart Town; William Fletcher, p. 13.
90 Correspondence Bonwick to Governor, 10 June 1859, TAHO CSD 1/1/136/5015.
91 Correspondence Freeman to Archdeacon Davies, 17 June 1859, TAHO CSD 1/1/136/5015. While Freeman had said at the time of his appointment 'I should without inducement have gladly performed that duty, yet I beg to acknowledge with thanks, His Excellency's kind consideration in allowing me £20 as remuneration for incidental expenses', Correspondence Freeman to Colonial Secretary, TAHO CSD 1/18/703. His gladness was clearly absent two and a half years later.
92 Correspondence Davies to Colonial Secretary, 20 June 1859, TAHO CSD 1/1/136/5015.
93 Correspondence Smales to Henty Colonial Secretary, 22 July 1859, TAHO CSD 1/1/136/5015.
94 Correspondence Colonial Secretary to Smales (Snr), 26 August 1859, TAHO CSD 1/1/136/5015.
95 Correspondence, Smales to Solly Assistant Colonial Secretary, 28 September 1859, TAHO CSD 1/1/136/5015.
96 Augustus, one of the Aboriginal people, had been whaling earlier and returned around 23 April 1859, E. Walpole, *Oyster Cove Visitors Book*. TAHO CSO 89/1/1, p. 37. For Walter, 'His pay, is the 90th share of Sperm oil, upon which he has received an advance of £3 from the Owner, Mrs. Seal', in Correspondence Shipping Master to Solly Assistant Colonial Secretary, 21 October 1859, CSD 1/1/126/4656. See also, Walpole, *Oyster Cove Visitors Book*, 20 October 1859, TAHO CSO 89/1/1, p. 42. The *Sussex* returned to Hobart in July 1860 with 40 tons sperm oil. *The Mercury*, 21 July 1860, p. 2.
97 Correspondence, Dandridge to Col Sec, 29 October 1859, TAHO CSD 1/1/136/5015.

98   Correspondence Dandridge to Solly, Assistant Colonial Secretary, 12 July 1859, TAHO CSD 1/1/136/5015.
99   Correspondence Dandridge to Colonial Secretary, 29 October 1859, TAHO CSD 1/1/136/5015. Correspondence Dandridge to Colonial Treasurer, 3 July 1862, TAHO CSD 4/19/200.
100 There are some parallels with Lucy Beeton being overlooked for the role of teacher/catechist on the Furneaux Islands. Employing an Aboriginal person does not seem to have been a consideration by those making the decisions.
101 Walpole, *Oyster Cove Visitors Book*, TAHO CSO 89/1/1, p. 56.
102 *Oyster Cove Visitors Book*, TAHO CSO 89/1/1, p. 58.
103 Correspondence Dandridge to Colonial Secretary, 29 October 1859, TAHO CSD 1/1/136/5015. Dandridge had considered Trappers for the role of Coxswain for the Station boat when Walter Arthur left on a whaling expedition, but employed John Russell at that time, Correspondence Dandridge to Colonial Secretary, 1 November 1859, TAHO CSD1/1/126/4656.
104 In late 1861, with the support of Dandridge, Trappers was given a leave of absence during which he applied unsuccessfully for the job of catechist and school master on the Furneaux Islands. Correspondence, Dandridge to Colonial Secretary, 29 October 1861, TAHO CSD 1/1/136/5015.
105 Correspondence Dandridge to Colonial Secretary, 22 April 1862, TAHO CSD 4/19/200.
106 Correspondence Worley to Colonial Secretary, 24 April 1862, TAHO CSD 4/19/200.
107 Correspondence Pybus to Col Sec, 3 June 1862, TAHO CSD 4/19/200.
108 Correspondence Dandridge to Colonial Secretary, 5 May 1862, TAHO CSD 4/19/200.
109 Correspondence Assistant Colonial Secretary to Dandridge, 28 May 1862, TAHO CSD 4/19/200.
110 Independent Chapel, Marriage Register, TAHO NS 650/1/2, No. 297. Their intended marriage was reported in one Hobart newspaper. See *The Courier*, 5 June 1854, p. 2.
111 Walpole requested the Government sanction Pengernoburric / Bessy's marriage to an unnamed carpenter, *Oyster Cove Visitors Book*, 17 April 1863, TAHO CSO 89/1/1, p. 77. Pengernoburric / Bessy died 11 February 1867, TAHO CSD 4/1/77 B231.
112 Adam Booker had been working as a gardener at *putalina* / Oyster Cove since 1862. Dandridge to Premier, 8 July 1867, TAHO CSD 4/1/77/B231.
113 The declaration of Banns is recorded in the Register of St. David's Church Hobart, on 17, 24 and 31 December, TAHO NS 282/9/2, but their marriage is not recorded in the Marriage Register of St David's Church, nor is there an entry for a Marriage License nor a marriage record in the register of All Saints Church, South Hobart. The Marriage Register for the Anglican Church at Browns River is not present in the Tasmanian Archives and Heritage Office (TAHO).
114 Henry Daldy sought permission for Mary Ann's and Adam's wedding in September 1865, *Oyster Cove Visitors Book*, 25 September 1865 TAHO CSO 89/1/1, p. 92. Correspondence Dandridge to Colonial Secretary, 20 December 1865, TAHO CSD 4/1/77 B231. The circumstances for Fanny and William were quite different, being married in Hobart in the house of the Independent clergy, and they never lived at *putalina* / Oyster Cove after they were married.
115 Correspondence Colonial Secretary to Colonial Treasurer, 16 April 1869, CSD 7/1/26 D215. *Oyster Cove Visitors Book*, TAHO CSO 89/1/1, p. 92. 'The Superintendent complained of Adam Booker having made use of obscene and threatening language on the Station to Mrs. Dandridge,' Henry Daldy, 13 December 1867. *Oyster Cove Visitors Book*, TAHO CSO 89/1/1, p. 109. 'The hut occupied by Adam Booker and Mary Ann was broken open in 1869, and two blankets and some rugs were stolen'.

    Oyster Cove Visitors Book, TAHO CSO 89/1/1, p. 115.
116 Correspondence Dandridge to Colonial Secretary, TAHO CSD 7/1/33/B450; *The Mercury*, 26 July 1871, p. 2.
117 Correspondence Dandridge to Colonial Secretary, 24 July 1871, TAHO CSD 7/1/33 D450.
118 Burial Register, St David's Hobart 1871, No. 80 Mary Anne Booker, Abode: Oyster Cove; When Buried: July 27th; Age: 50 years; Ship's Name 488; Quality or Profession: *blank*, J. Gellibrand, TAHO NS 282/11/1.
119 *The Mercury*, 28 July 1871, p. 2. Following her death it appears Booker was reluctant to leave *putalina* / Oyster Cove, Various correspondence 12, 16 and 17 October 1871, CSD 7/1/33 D450. It is unlikely Mary Ann's friends at *putalina* / Oyster Cove, including *Trukanini*, or her family, Fanny or Adam, had sufficient time to hear the news, probably from Mrs. Dandridge, and then travel to Hobart for the funeral. It does seem strange that her body was not returned to *putalina* / Oyster Cove where her current husband was living, where her brother was buried and her sister, Fanny, was living nearby.
120 Plomley, 1966, p. 985.
121 Plomley, 1966, p. 992.
122 *The Mercury*, 14 September 1882, p. 2.
123 TAHO CSO 24/7/101, pp. 294–329. Forty years later it was reported 'Cochrane' was Mrs Clark's maiden name and became attached to Fanny during her time with the Clarks at Wybalenna.
124 *The Mercury*, 25 August 1882, p. 3.
125 Ling Roth, 1898, 'Is Mrs. F. C. Smith a "Last Living Aboriginal of Tasmania"', *The Journal of the Anthropological Institute of Great Britain and Ireland*, 27, pp. 451–454. Published by: Royal Anthropological Institute of Great Britain and Ireland, http://www.jstor.org/stable/2842841 Accessed: 25/04/2013.
126 *The Mercury*, 15 June 1882, p. 3. *The Mercury*y, 23 June 1882, p. 3.
127 See Reibey speech in Parliament. *The Mercury*, 31 October 1884, p. 3.
128 *Parliament of Tasmania, Journals of the House of Assembly, Votes and Proceedings*, Thursday 5 October 1882, p. 171.
129 *Parliament of Tasmania, Journals of the House of Assembly, Votes and Proceedings*, Thursday 6 November 1884, p. 216.
130 Orphan School Register, TAHO SWD 28/1/1.
131 Fanny's father, *Nikaminik*, is not listed in the census of 1855 and therefore died at some unrecorded time, between 1847 and 1855.
132 Plomley, 1987, p. 858.
133 *The Mercury*, 8 September 1882, p. 3.
134 Note the contrasting treatment of Walter and Mary Ann Arthur, a married Aboriginal couple who were repeatedly refused permission to leave the station.
135 Reibey managed two pensions for women on the Bass Strait islands, Margery Munroe, mother of Polly Bligh and grandmother of Emma Bligh, was from Western Port and received a pension of 1 shilling per day from the government administered by Reibey since January 1862. *Church News*, 19 August 1863, pp. 208 & 209. In his 1863 report to Parliament, Reibey also called attention 'to the fact that a pension was voted to Maria Scott, an old woman, native of Tasmania and now residing on Tin Kettle Island, but she has never received it. I think it desirable that this pension should be paid through the Archdeacon of Launceston, who will take care that it is appropriated as intended', Reibey, T., 1863, Report of the Ven. Archdeacon Reibey, *Journal of The Legislative Council*, 48, 26 August 1863.
136 *Launceston Examiner*, 3 November 1860, p. 2. The £24 was equivalent to the annual wages of a servant at *putalina* / Oyster Cove.
137 Colonial Treasurer to Dandridge, undated, TAHO CSD 4/1/77/B231. This was increased to £60 per annum for *Trukanini*, and £30 for Mary Ann, in 1870. Correspondence Colonial Secretary to Dandridge, 24 December 1869, TAHO CSD 7/1/33 D450. In Parliament in 1882, Mr Burgess, member for East Devon,

noted a reference by Mr. Dooley, to an unnamed Aboriginal man with wife and nine children who sought a pension when the debate about Fanny's pension was occurring. The man's pension does not appear to have been approved. *The Mercury*, 8 September 1882, p. 3.

138 Independent Chapel, Marriage Register, TAHO NS 650/1/2, No. 297. The Independent Chapel, later known as the Congregational Church, was on the corner of Elizabeth and Brisbane streets, Hobart. Rev. Miller was Minister there, (*The Courier*, 14 August, 1854, p. 3), and Chairman of the Congregational Union, (*Colonial Times*, 23 December 1854, p. 2). He was a very active evangelical and attended meetings of the Wesleyan Missionary Society, (*The Mercury*, 11 January 1854, p. 2), and several other similar organisations, (*Colonial Times*, 2 ebruary 1854, p. 3, 9 December 1854, p. 3, *The Courier*, 8 and 17 March 1854, p. 2).

139 Aboard the *Tasmania*. *The Courier*, 22 February 1853, p. 2.

140 *The Mercury*, 14 September 1882, p. 2.

141 *The Courier*, 2 October 1857, p. 3.

142 William John Turner Clarke, of Norton Mandeville, freehold grazing farm, listed as entitled to vote in House of Assembly Electoral District of Cumberland. *The Mercury*, 14 September 1882, p. 2. He was one of the largest landholders in the district with 45,000 acres. *The Courier*, 13 February 1857, p. 3.

143 *The Mercury*, 14 September 1882, p. 2. Perkins and Nephews' Emporium was at 135–137 Liverpool Street, on the corner of Watchorn Street, Hobart http://trove.nla.gov.au/work/36699062?q=Perkins+and+Nephew+Emporium+Hobart&l-availability=y&l -australian=y&c=picture&versionId=47644210 accessed 11/2/2014. This would locate the Smith's board and lodging house in the vicinity of 139–143 Liverpool Street, between Watchorn and Harrington Streets, Hobart, noting that some street numbers in Hobart changed from time to time up to the early 1900s.

144 *The Mercury*, 14 September 1882, p. 2.

145 *The Courier*, 2 October 1857, p. 3.

146 *The Courier*, 2 October 1857, p. 3.

147 March 28 1860, Methodist Church Minutes of Quarterly Meeting 1851–1885, TAHO NS 499/1/121. Minute Book of the Australasian Wesleyan Missionary Society, TAHO NS 499/117.

148 *The Mercury*, 14 September 1882, p. 2.

149 *The Mercury*, 14 September 1882, p. 2.

150 Ryan, 2012, p. 262.

151 Bessy Clark, Plomley, 1966, p. 990.

152 Correspondence Dandridge to Colonial Secretary, 14 February 1867, TAHO CSD 4/1/77 B231.

153 Burial Register, St David's Church Hobart 1871, No. 80 Mary Anne Booker, Abode: Oyster Cove; When Buried: July 27th; Age: 50 years; Ship's Name 488; Quality or Profession: *blank*, J. Gellibrand, TAHO NS 282/11/1. *The Mercury*, 28 July 1871, p. 2.

154 *The Mercury*, 14 September 1882, p. 2. It is unclear where they lived between 1858 and 1883 when William purchased fifty acres of land at Nicholls Rivulet on 27 December 1883 for sixty-seven pounds, *Land Titles Office*, Volume XLI, Folio 44.

155 *Oyster Cove Visitors Book*, TAHO CSO 89/1/1, p. 35. *The Courier*, 6 October 1858, p. 3. Although 'One who knows' claimed she died at the home of Fanny and William. *The Mercury*, 14 September 1882, p. 2.

156 *The Mercury* 8 September 1882, page 3. See also *Parliament of Tasmania, Journals of the House of Assembly, Votes and Proceedings*, Wednesday 30 August 1882, p. 99, Thursday 7 September 1882, p. 115, and Thursday 14 September 1882, p. 122. *Parliament of Tasmania, Journals of the House of Assembly, Votes and Proceedings*, Thursday 5 October 1882, p. 171.

157 *Parliament of Tasmania, Journals of the House of Assembly, Votes and Proceedings*, Thursday 30 October 1884, p. 192. This was thirteen years after the granting of a lifetime lease to Lucy Beeton on Badger Island by Governor Du Cane. *The Mercury*, 7 August, 1871, p. 2. *Launceston Examiner*, 8 August, 1871, p. 3. *The Mercury*, 31 October 1884, p. 3.

158 *Parliament of Tasmania, Journals of the House of Assembly, Votes and Proceedings*,

Thursday 6 November 1884, p. 216. In contrast to the explanation for providing the lifetime lease to Lucy Beeton on Badger Island, for her efforts to instruct and civilise the children, no such mention was made to explain the land grant to Fanny, other than her being deemed to be a 'full-blood' Aborigine. Fanny's land grant bounded land that William had purchased in December 1883, *Land Titles Office*, Volume XLI, Folio 44. Also, Fanny and William mortgaged portions of the purchased and granted lands in the 1890's, *Land Titles Office*, Volume XLI, Folio 44. It appears that she and William had been unable to work since the early 1880s and the land sales were to provide income for them to complement the pension of £50 per year.

159 *Launceston Examiner*, 17 October 1885, p. 3.
160 *Launceston Examiner*, 6 November 1885, p. 3. See also *Parliament of Tasmania, Journals of the House of Assembly, Votes and Proceedings*, Thursday 5 November 1885, p. 197.
161 Port Cygnet Circuit Quarterly Meeting Balance Sheets, TAHO NS 499/1/2120.
162 *The Mercury*, 13 August 1899, p. 3. See also, Watson, B., 2011/12, 'The Man and the Woman and the Edison Phonograph: Race, History and Technology Through Song', *Australasian Journal of Ecocriticism and Cultural Ecology*, 1, pp. 1–8.
163 *The Mercury*, 31 October 1899, p. 2.
164 *The Mercury*, 31 October 1899, p. 2.
165 Minute Book of Trustees, Port Cygnet Methodist Circuit, TAHO NS 499/2115.
166 Minute Book of Trustees, Port Cygnet Methodist Circuit, TAHO NS 499/2115.
167 *Land Titles Office*, Vol 121, No 70.
168 TAHO NS 3329/1/1.
169 TAHO NS 3329/1/1. In 1854 the Yearly Conference in the United Kingdom created 'The Australian Wesleyan Methodist Connexion' which constituted the Australasian Conference. In 1873 the Australasian Conference constituted four annual Conferences, including the Victoria and Tasmania Conference. 'The Methodist Conferences Act 1876' in the Imperial Parliament confirmed all admissions, appointments and expulsions by the Australasian Conference. In 1884 the Australasian Conference resolved that properties '… should as far as practicable be held upon the same trusts and for this purpose a model deed be prepared which should be made applicable to the circumstances of each colony and the several annual Conferences were authorised to procure Acts of the legislature of the several colonies for the settlement of church properties on the trusts of such model deed.' TAHO, NS 3329/1/1.
170 TAHO, NS 3329/1/1.
171 Port Cygnet Methodist Home Mission Circuit Preaching Plan 1894, in author's possession.
172 *The Mercury* reported, 'The deceased was buried in the Wesleyan churchyard, the Rev. Mr. Atkinson officiating, this funeral being largely attended, many residents coming from long distances to pay their last respects.' *The Mercury*, 1 December 1902, p. 6.
173 *The Mercury*, 27 February 1905, p. 6.
174 *North Western Advocate and Emu Bay Times*, 1 March 1905, p. 2. *Zeehan and Dundas Herald*, 1 March 1905, p. 2.
175 *The Mercury*, 6 March 1905, p. 5.
176 Port Cygnet Circuit Quarterly Meeting Balance Sheets, TAHO NS 499/1/2120.
177 Methodist Church Church Building and Loan Fund, TAHO NS 499/58, pp. 29, 31.
178 Port Cygnet Circuit Quarterly Meeting Balance Sheets, TAHO NS 499/1/2120.
179 Port Cygnet Circuit Quarterly Meeting Balance Sheets, TAHO NS 499/1/2120.
180 There were forty-three members across the circuit, Port Cygnet Circuit Members Roll 1909, TAHO NS 499/1/515.
181 TAHO NS 499/1/515.
182 Deverell, G., 2018, Gondwana Theology, Reservoir, Morning Star Publishing.

BIBLIOGRAPHY

Abbreviations

CSO	Colonial Secretary's Office
TAHO	Tasmanian Archive and Heritage Office
ML	Mitchell Library, State Library of New South Wales

ARCHIVES
Mitchell Library, State Library of New South Wales

ML Robinson Papers, State Library of New South Wales, A7044, Vol. 23, CY548
ML Robinson Papers, State Library of New South Wales, A7062, CY549
ML Robinson Papers, State Library of New South Wales, A7064, Vol. 43, CY550
ML Robinson Papers, State Library of New South Wales, A7065 CY550
ML Robinson Papers, State Library of New South Wales, A7066, CY551
ML Robinson Papers, State Library of New South Wales, A7074 CY825
ML Walker Papers, State Library of New South Wales, B727, CY1408
ML Walker Papers, State Library of New South Wales, CY979

Tasmanian Land Titles Office

Land Titles Office Vol XLI, Folio 44
Land Titles Office Vol 121, No. 70

Tasmanian Archive and Heritage Office

TAHO CSD 1/1/126/4656
TAHO CSD 1/1/136/5015
TAHO CSD 1/18/703
TAHO CSD 1/33/D450
TAHO CSD 1/51/1009
TAHO CSD 1/126/4656
TAHO CSD 1/136/5015
TAHO CSD 4/1/77 B231
TAHO CSD 4/19/200
TAHO CSD 7/1/26/D215
TAHO CSD 7/1/33/B450
TAHO CSD 7/1/33/D450
TAHO CSO 1/18798
TAHO CSO 1/269/6468
TAHO CSO 11/26/378
TAHO CSO 24/7/101
TAHO CSO 24/42/1331
TAHO CSO 24/149/1401
TAHO CSO 24/167/4898
TAHO CSO 7578
TAHO CSO 89/1/1
TAHO GO 33/68
TAHO LSD 1/51/636
TAHO LSD 1/51/642
TAHO LSD 1/51/644
TAHO LSD 2/1/3
TAHO LSD 2/2/924
TAHO NG 748/1
TAHO NS 282/8/1/1
TAHO NS 282/9/2
TAHO NS 282/11/1
TAHO NS 349/1/1
TAHO NS 373/1/11
TAHO NS 373/1/74
TAHO NS 373/214/47
TAHO NS373/214/47
TAHO NS 499/1/121
TAHO NS 499/1/515
TAHO NS 499/58
TAHO NS 499/117

TAHO NS 499/2115
TAHO NS 499/1/2120
TAHO NS 642/1/1
TAHO NS 650/1/2
TAHO NS 2020/1
TAHO NS 3329/1/1
TAHO NS 3588/1/1
TAHO RGD 32/1
TAHO RGD 34/1
TAHO SC 195/31/2798
TAHO SWD 24
TAHO SWD 28

University of Tasmania

Cape Barren Is. correspondence 1902/1928 [microfilm], Hobart, Royal Society of Tasmania, University of Tasmania, Morris Miller Library

Newspapers

Colonial Times
Cornwall Chronicle
The Courier
Hobart Town Courier
Hobart Town Gazette
Launceston Advertiser
Launceston Examiner
The Mercury
North Western Advocate and Emu Bay Times
Ovens and Murray Advertiser
The Tasmanian, Supplement
Tasmanian Church Chronicle
Zeehan and Dundas Herald

Parliament of Tasmania

Report of the Ven. Archdeacon Reibey, Journal of The Legislative Council, No 48, August 26th, 1863.
Parliament of Tasmania, Journals of the House of Assembly, Votes and Proceedings, Thursday 5th October 1882.
Parliament of Tasmania, Journals of the House of Assembly, Votes and Proceedings, Wednesday 30th August 1882.
Parliament of Tasmania, Journals of the House of Assembly, Votes and Proceedings, Thursday 7th September 1882.
Parliament of Tasmania, Journals of the House of Assembly, Votes and Proceedings, Thursday 14th September 1882.
Parliament of Tasmania, Journals of the House of Assembly, Votes and Proceedings, Thursday 5th October 1882.
Parliament of Tasmania, Journals of the House of Assembly, Votes and Proceedings, Thursday 30th October 1884.
Parliament of Tasmania, Journals of the House of Assembly, Votes and Proceedings, Thursday 6th November 1884.
Parliament of Tasmania, Journals of the House of Assembly, Votes and Proceedings, Thursday 5th November 1885.
Lord, J. E. C., 1908, 'Report upon the state of the islands, the condition and mode of living of half-castes, the existing mode of regulating the reserves, and suggesting lines for future administration,' Parliament of Tasmania, Journal and Printed Papers of the Parliament of Tasmania 59, No. 57.
Cape Barren Island Reserve Act 1912.

Periodicals

Church News

Bible

All quotes from the Bible are from Division of Christian Education of the National Council of the Churches of Christ in the United States of America, 1989, *The Holy Bible, New Revised Standard Version*. Nashville; Thomas Nelson Publishers.

Books and Journals

Andrews, D., 2012, 'Was the Friendly Mission to the Aboriginal People of Van Dieman's Land in the 1830s an Evangelical Enterprise?' *Integrity*, 1, pp. 57–80.

Ashcroft, B., (et al), 2013, *Post-colonial Studies*, London; Routledge.

Attwood, B., 1989, 'Reading Sources in Aboriginal History: Mission Stations Visitors Books,' *La Trobe Journal*, 43, pp. 21–28.

Attwood, B., 1989, *The Making of the Aborigines*. Sydney; Allen & Unwin.

Attwood, B., 1994, *A Life Together, A Life Apart*. Carlton; Melbourne University Press.

Backhouse, J., 1843, *A Narrative of a Visit to the Australian Colonies*. London; Hamilton, Adams & Co.

Barnard, J., 1850, 'Observations on Statistics of Van Diemen's Land for 1848: compiled from Official Records in the Colonial Secretary's Office', *Papers and Proceedings of the Royal Society of Tasmania*, 1 (2), pp. 102–134.

Bhabha, H., 1994, *The Location of Culture*. London; Routledge.

Bingham, J., 1992, *Wybalenna: The Archaeology of Cultural Accommodation in Nineteenth Century Tasmania*. Sydney; The Australian Society of Historical Archaeology.

Birmingham, J., 1976, 'The Archaeological Contribution to Nineteenth-Century History: Some Australian Case Studies', *World Archaeology*, 7 (3), pp. 306–317.

Birmingham J., and Wilson, A., 2010, 'Archaeologies of Cultural Interaction Wybalenna Settlement and Killalpaninna Mission', *International Journal of Historical Archaeology*, 14, pp. 15–38.

Bonwick, J., 1884, *The Lost Tasmanian Race*. London; Sampson Low, Marston, Searle, and Rivington.

Boyce, J., 1996, 'Journeying Home,' *Island*, 66, pp. 39–63.

Boyce, J., 2001, *God's Own Country?* Hobart; ISW.

Boyce, J., 2004, 'A Dog's Breakfast ... Lunch and Dinner: Canine Dependency in Early Van Diemen's Land', *Tasmanian Historical Research Association*, 52 (4), pp. 194–213.

Boyce, J., 2004, 'Robert May', *Tasmania 40° South*, 35, pp. 45–47.

Boyce, J., 2006, 'Canine Revolution: the social and environmental impact of the introduction of the dog to Tasmania', *Environmental History*, 11 (1), pp. 102–129.

Boyce, J., 2008, *Van Diemen's Land*. Melbourne; Black Inc.

Brock, P., 1993, *Outback ghettos: Aborigines, institutionalisation, and survival*. Cambridge; Cambridge University Press

Brown, T., & Dickson, K., (eds.), 2013, *Needwonnee*. Hobart; Dixie Designs.

Buchanan, A. M., 1994, *Index to Tasmanian Deaths / Burials, 1797–1840*. Hobart; A.M. Buchanan.

Calder, G., 2010, *Levee, Line and Martial Law: a History of Dispossession of the Mairremmener people of Van Diemen's Land 1803–1832*. Launceston; Fullers Bookshop.

Cameron, P., 2011, *Grease and Ochre*. Launceston; Fullers Bookshop.

Carruthers, S. W., 1957, *Three Centuries of the Westminster Shorter Catechism*. Fredericton; Beaverbrook Foundations / University of New Brunswick.

Choo, C., 2001, *Mission girls: Aboriginal women on Catholic missions in the Kimberley, Western Australia, 1900–1950*. Crawley; University of Western Australia Press.

Church of England, 1968, *The book of common prayer and administration of the sacraments, and other rites and ceremonies of the church according to the use of the Church of England, together with the psalter or psalms of David, pointed as they are to be sung or said in churches, and the form and manner of making: ordaining and consecrating bishops, priests, and deacons*. London; W. Clowes by Eyre & Spottiswoode.

Clark, J., 1988, 'Devils and Horses: Religious and Creative Life in Tasmanian Aboriginal Society', in Roe, M., (ed.), *The Flow of Cultures*. Canberra; Australian Academy of the Humanities.

Currey, J., (ed), 2005, *Knopwood's Hobart Town Diary*. Malvern; Colony Press.

Dammery, S., 2001, *Walter George Arthur A Free Tasmanian?* Clayton; Monash Publications in History.

D'Arcy, J., 2010, 'Child of the metropolis: George Augustus Robinson in London', *History Australia*, 7 (3), pp. 55.1 to 55.18. DOI:10.2104/ha100055.

Davis, R., & Petrow, S., (eds.), 2004, *Varieties of Vice-Regal Life*. Hobart; Tasmanian Historical Research Association.

Douglas, B., 2001, 'Encounters with the Enemy? Academic Readings of Missionary Narratives on Melanesians', *Comparative Studies in Society and History*, 43 (1), January 2001, pp. 37–64.

Duling, D.C., 2011, 'Memory, collective memory, orality and the gospels', *HTS Teologiese Studies/Theological Studies* 67 (1), Art. #915, 11 pages. http://dx.doi.org/10.4102/hts.v67i1.915.

Fels, M., 1982, 'Culture Contact in the County of Buckinghamshire, Van Diemen's Land 1803–1811', *Tasmanian Historical Research Association*, 29 (2), pp. 47–79.

Fowler, R. M., 1980, *The Furneaux Group*. Canberra; Roebuck.

Franklin, M.A., 1976, *Black and White Australians*. South Yarra; Heinemann.

Gondarra, D., 1988, ' "Father, You Gave Us The Dreaming …" Aboriginal Theology and the Future', in Dutney, A., (ed.), *From Here to Where? Australian Christians Owning the Future*. Melbourne; Uniting Church Press.

Gunson, N., 1974, *Australian reminiscences and papers of L. E. Threlkeld : missionary to the Aborigines, 1824–1859*. Canberra; Australian Institute of Aboriginal Studies.

Gunson, N., 2002, 'Reality, History, and Hands-on Ethnography: the Journals of George Augustus Robinson at Port Philip 1839–1852', *Aboriginal History*, 26, pp. 225–237. http://press.anu.edu.au/wp-content/uploads/2011/05/ch0937.pdf accessed 14.5.2014.

Hamilton-Arnold, B., (ed.), 1994, *Letters and Papers of G. P. Harris, 1803–1812: Deputy Surveyor-General of New South Wales at Sullivan Bay, Port Phillip, and Hobart Town, Van Dieman's Land*. Victoria: Arden Press.

Harris, J., 1990, *One Blood*. Sutherland: Albatross.

Harris, J., 1994, 'Robinson, George Augustus', in Dickey, B., (ed.), *The Australian Dictionary of Evangelical Biography*. Sydney; Evangelical History Association.

Hindmarsh, B., 1999, ' "My Chains Fell Off, My Heart Was Free" Early Methodist Conversion Narrative in England', *Church History*, 68 (4), pp. 910–929.

Hofmeyr, I., 2003, 'Portable Landscapes', in Trigger, D., & Griffiths, G., *Disputed Territories*. Hong Kong; Hong Kong University Press, pp. 131–153.

Hookey, M., 1929, *Bobby Knopwood and His Times*. Hobart; W.E. Fuller.

Horton, D., 1979, 'Tasmanian Adaptation', *Mankind*, 12, pp. 28–34.

Hull, H. M., 1859, *The Royal Kalendar and Guide to Tasmania from 1859*. Hobatt Town; William Fletcher.

Johnson, A., 2001, 'The Book Eaters: Textuality, Modernity, and the London Missionary Society', *Semeia*, 88, pp. 13-40.

Johnston, A., 2004, 'The Little Empire of Wybalenna: Becoming Colonial in Australia', *Journal of Australian Studies*, 81, pp. 17-31.

Johnston, A., & Rolls, M., 2008, 'Reading Robinson in the Twenty-First Century: An Introduction', in Johnston, A., & Rolls, M., (eds.), *Reading Robinson*. Hobart; Quintus.

Jones, R., 1970, 'Tasmanian Aborigines and Dogs', *Mankind*, 7 (4), pp. 256-271.

Jones, R., 1977, 'The Tasmanian Paradox', in Wright, R. V. S., *Stone Tools as Cultural Markers: Change, Evolution and Complexity*. Canberra; Australian Institute of Aboriginal Studies, pp. 189-204.

Juster, S., 1989, 'In a Different Voice: Male and Female Narratives of Religious Conversion in Post-Revolutionary America', *American Quarterly*, 41 (1), p. 34-62.

Kenny, R., 2007, *The Lamb Enters the Dreaming*. Melbourne; Scribe.

Kidd, M. J., 2006, *The Sacred Wound of Australia*. Nimbin; Ohlah Publishing,

Lehman, G., 1998, *Narrative and Identity*, Honours Thesis, Hobart; University of Tasmania.

MacFarlane, I., 2008, *Beyond Awakening*. Launceston; Fullers Bookshop.

Mallett, M., 2001, *My Past — Their Future*. Hobart; Blubber Head Press.

McGoogan, K., 2005, *Lady Franklin's Revenge*. Melbourne; HarperCollins.

McGrath, A., 1995, 'Contested ground: what is 'Aboriginal history'?' in McGrath, A. (ed.), *Contested Ground: Australian Aborigines under the British Crown*. St Leonard's; Allen and Unwin, pp. 359-397.

McKay, T., 1992, *Van Diemen's Land Early Marriages 1803-1830* Vol 1. Kingston; T. McKay.

Miller, L., 2006, *Isness, the Terrain of Aboriginal Being*, School of Philosophy Thesis, Hobart; University of Tasmania.

Miller, R. S., 1985, *Thomas Dove and the Tasmanian Aborigines*. Melbourne; Spectrum.

Moneypenny, M., 1995-6, 'Going Out and Coming In: Co-operation and Collaboration Between Aborigines and Europeans in Colonial Tasmania', *Tasmanian Historical Studies*, 5, pp. 64-75.

Morgan, A., 1986, *Aboriginal Education in the Furneaux Islands (1798-1986)*, Unpublished Thesis, Department of Education, Hobart; University of Tasmania.

Muhlhausler, P., 1991, 'Overview of the pigdin and creole languages of Australia', in Romaine, S., (ed.), *Language in Australia*. Melbourne; Cambridge University Press, pp. 159-173.

Murray-Smith, S., (ed.), 1987, *Mission to the Islands*. Launceston; Foot & Playsted.

Muysken & Smith, 'Study of Creole and Pidgin Languages'
http://semantics.uchicago.edu/kennedy/classes/sum07/myths/creoles.pdf Accessed 11 May 2014.

Nanni, G., 2012, *The Colonisation of Time: Ritual, Routine and Resistance in the British Empire*. Manchester; Manchester University Press.

Nicholls, M., (ed.), 1977, *The Diary of the Reverend Robert Knopwood 1803-1838*. Launceston; Foot & Playsted.

Nixon, F. R. 'Charge delivered to the Clergy of the Diocese of Tasmania, 22nd May 1855', pp. 8 &15 http://www.anglican.org.au/docs/archive/72.pdf Accessed 14/3/2013.

Nixon, Rev Francis, R., DD, Bishop of Tasmania, 1857, *The Cruise of the Beacon, a narrative of a visit to the islands in Bass's Straits*. London; Bell and Daldy.

Paulson, G., & Brett, M., 2012, 'Five Smooth Stones: Reading the Bible through Aboriginal Eyes,' in author's possession.

Perkins, R., & Langton, M., (eds.), 2008, *First Australians An Illustrated History*. Melbourne; Miegunyah Press.

Peyer, B., 1997, *The Tutor'd Mind: Indian Missionary Writers in Antebellum America*. Amherst; University of Massachusetts Press.

Pike, B., 2013, *A River Dreaming*. Melbourne; Aboriginal Catholic Ministry.

Pilkington, D., 2002, *Follow the Rabbit Proof Fence*. St. Lucia; University of Queensland Press.

Plomley, N. J. B., 1966, *Friendly Mission*. Kingsgrove; Halstead Press.

Plomley, N.J.B., 1973, *An Immigrant of 1824*. Hobart; Tasmanian Historical Research Association.

Plomley, N. J. B. 1976, *A Word List of Tasmanian Aboriginal Languages*. Launceston; Foot and Playsted.

Plomley, N. J. B., 1987, *Weep In Silence*. Hobart; Blubber Head Press.

Plomley, N.J.B. & Henley, K.A., 1990, 'The Sealers of Bass Strait and the Cape Barren Island Community', *Tasmanian Historical Research Association*, 37 (2 & 3), pp. 37–127.

Powell, M., 2002, 'Rhetorics of Survivance: How Native Americans use Writing', *College, Composition and Communication*, 53 (3), pp. 396–434.

Pratt, M., 1991, 'Art in the Contact Zone', *Profession*, pp. 33–40.

Purtscher, J., 1993, *Children in Queen's Orphanage 1828–1863*. New Town; Schaffer.

Purtscher, J., 1993, *Infants at Queen's Orphanage, 1851–1863*. Hobart; Van Diemen's Land and Norfolk Island Interest Group.

Rainbow Spirit Elders, 1997, *Rainbow Spirit Theology*. East Melbourne; Harper Collins.

Rae-Ellis, V., 1976, *Trucanini Queen or Traitor?* Hobart; O.B.M.

Rae-Ellis, V., 1988, *Black Robinson*. Carlton; Melbourne University Press.

Reynolds, H., 1995, *Fate of a Free People*. Ringwood; Penguin.

Ricoeur, P., 1992, *Oneself as Another*. Chicago; Chicago University Press.

Robson, L., 1983, *A History of Tasmania*, Vol I. Melbourne; Oxford Univesity Press.

Rose, M., (ed.) 1996, *For the Record: 160 years of Aboriginal Print Journalism*. St Leonards; Allen and Unwin.

Roth, H. L., 1898, 'Is Mrs. F. C. Smith the "Last Living Aboriginal of Tasmania"', *The Journal of the Anthropological Institute of Great Britain and Ireland*, 27, pp. 451–454.

Roth, H. L., 1899, *The Aborigines of Tasmania*. Halifax; King & Sons; facsimile of second edition, 1968, Hobart; Fullers Bookshop.

Ryan, L., 2001, *The Aboriginal Tasmanians*. Sydney; Allen & Unwin.

Ryan, L., 2012, *Tasmanian Aborigines A History Since 1803*. Sydney; Allen & Unwin.

Sagona, A., 1994, 'The Quest for Red Gold', in Sagona, A., (Ed.), *Bruising the Red Earth*. Melbourne; Melbourne University Press, pp. 8–38.

Sandywell, B., 2013, *Reflexivity and the Crisis of Western Reason*, Vol. 1. Hoboken; Taylor & Francis.

Scott, J., 1990, *Domination and the Arts of Resistance*. New Haven; Yale University Press.

Skira, I., 1997, 'I hope you will be my friend': Tasmanian Aborigines in the Furneaux Group in the nineteenth century — population and land tenure, *Aboriginal History*, 21 (30), pp. 30–45.

Skye, L., 2007, *Kerygmatics of the New Millenium*. Delhi; ISPCK.

Stokes, J., 1846, *Discoveries in Australia*, Vol. 2. London; T & W Boone.

Summers, R., 2009, *Ronnie: Tasmanian Songman*. Broome; Magabala Books.

Tolar Burton, V., 2001, 'John Wesley and the Liberty to Speak: the Rhetorical and Literary Practices of Early Methodism', *College, Composition and Communication*, 53, (1), pp. 65-91.

Van Diemen's Land: Copies of All Correspondence between Lieutenant Governor Arthur and His Majesty's Secretary of State for the Colonies on the Subject of the Military Operations Lately Carried on against the Aboriginal Inhabitants of Van Diemen's Land (Including Minutes of Evidence Taken before the Committee for the Affairs of the Aborigines, 1830), 1971, Hobart; Tasmanian Historical Research Association.

Van Toorn, P., 2002, 'Before the Second Reformation: Nineteenth Aboriginal Mediations of the Bible in Van Diemens Land', *Semeia*, 88, pp. 41-69.

Van Toorn, P., 2006, *Writing Never Arrives Naked*. Canberra; Aboriginal Studies Press.

Watson, B., 2011/12, 'The Man and the Woman and the Edison Phonograph: Race, History and Technology Through Song', *Australasian Journal of Ecocriticism and Cultural Ecology*, 1, pp. 1-8.

Wesley, J., 'Reasons Against a Separation from the Church of England by John Wesley A. M., printed in 1758 with Hymns for the Preachers among the Methodists (so called) by Charles Wesley A. M. http://anglicanhistory.org/wesley/reasons1760.html accessed 14/5/2014.

West, I., 1987, *Pride Against Prejudice*. Canberra; Australian Institute of Aboriginal and Torres Strait Islander Studies.

West, J., 1852, *The History of Tasmania*. Launceston; Henry Dowling.

Widowson, H., 1829, *Present State of Van Diemen's Land Comprising an Account of its Agricultural Capabilities with Observations on the Present State of Farming &c. Pursued in that Colony and Other Important Matters Connected with Emigration*. London; Robinson.

Woolmington, J., 1985, 'Missionary Attitudes to the Baptism of Australian Aborigines Before 1850', *The Journal of Religious History*, 13 (3), pp. 283-293.

Websites cited

http://anglicanhistory.org/wesley/reasons1760.html accessed 14/5/2014.

http://www.austlii.edu.au/au/legis/tas/num_act/tcbira19123gvn16334/tcbira19123gvn16334.pdf accessed 8/2/2013.

http://www.austlii.edu.au/au/legis/tas/num_act/cbira19459gvn14312/ accessed 8/2/2013.

http://www.bartleby.com/224/1417.html accessed 2/3/2012.

http://www.companyofangels.net/evbiomth.html accessed 17/5/2014.

http://www.govhouse.tas.gov.au/governor/previous-governors accessed 10/5/2014.

http://www.methodist.org.uk/who-we-are/history/separation-from-the-church-of-england accessed 16/5/2014.

http://www.sydneybethelunion.com.au accessed 12/5/2014.

http://trove.nla.gov.au/work/36699062?q=Perkins+and+Nephew+Emporium+Hobart&l-availability=y&l-australian=y&c=picture&versionId=47644210 accessed 11/2/2014.

APPENDIX A

Church baptism records of Aboriginal children baptised in Van Diemen's Land[1]

Hobart Town Baptisms 1803 — by Reverend Knopwood

When Baptised	When Born	Child Name
1810 43 baptisms including...		
25th June 1810		Jacob
22nd September 1810		George John
1811 41 baptisms including...		
4th January 1811		Ann
4th January 1811		Mary
4th January 1811		Lucy Murray
14th January 1811		Mary Tilchett Farum
15th July 1811	Aged 6 years	George Weston
23rd September 1811		Sarah May
1812 41 baptisms including...		
27th August 1812		Arabella
28th August 1812		Sombruna
1813 40 baptisms including...		
1st January 1813		Robert McCauley
28th February 1813		Celia Margaret Walpole Bush
28th February 1813		Charles Henry Walpole Bush
16th June 1813		Lorennah
26th June 1813		John Clarence
21st October 1813		James Martin
24th December 1813		Van Diemen

Parents	Abode	Quality / Profession	By Whom
A Native of Van Diemen's Land			R Knopwood *B
A Native Boy 7 years old			R Knopwood *B
A Native wo man of V D Land			R Knopwood *B
A Native woman of V D Land			R Knopwood *B
A Daughter of Ann Le a Native Woman of V D Land			R Knopwood *B
A Native woman of V D Land			R Knopwood *B
A Native Boy V D Land			R Knopwood *B
A Native Girl	Hobart Town		R Knopwood *B
A Native Girl	7 years old of V D Land		R Knopwood
A Native of V D Land			R Knopwood
A Native V D Land			R Knopwood
A Native V D Land	10 years old		R Knopwood
A Native V D Land	5 years old		R Knopwood
A Native of V D Land	8 years old		R Knopwood
A Native of V D Land			R Knopwood
A Native Boy			R Knopwood
A Native Boy			R Knopwood

When Baptised	When Born	Child Name
1817 71 baptisms including...		
8th September 1817	About 8 years old	Catherine Van Diemen

When Baptised	When Born	Child Name
1818 85 baptisms including...		
12th January 1818	9 years old	Christian Marsh
9th March 1818	About 18 years	Charles Frederick Van Diemen
4th May 1818	8 years old	Marie Campbell

When Baptised	When Born	Child Name
1819 161 baptisms including...		
17th February 1819	About 17 years	Thomas
23rd February 1819	7 years old	Mary Dempsey
4 April 1819	8 months	Joshua Van Diemen
18th April 1819	About 7 years	George Van Diemen
18th April 1819	5 years	William Thomas
14th June 1819	7 years old	James Jenkins
14th June 1819	7 years old	Charles
24th August 1819	15 years	David Derwent
24th August 1819	20 years	Robert New Norfolk

When Baptised	When Born	Child Name
1820 105 baptisms including...		
12th May 1820	About 15 years	Maria Davis

When Baptised	When Born	Child Name
1833 PARISH OF CLARENCE PLAINS 24 baptisms including...		
11th March	13th March 1821	Rebecca

When Baptised	When Born	Child Name
LAUNCESTON		
1811 43 baptisms including...		
18th March 1811		Charles Mountgarrett
18th March 1811		William Lyttleton Quamby

Parents	Abode	Quality / Profession	By Whom
A Native Girl V D Land	? Hogan's, Servant Girl		R Knopwood

Parents	Abode	Quality / Profession	By Whom
A Native Boy			R Knopwood
A Native Boy of V D Land	E Lord's boy		R Knopwood
A Native Girl V D Land			R Knopwood

Parents	Abode	Quality / Profession	By Whom
A Native Boy V D Land			R Knopwood
A Native Girl Van Diemen's Land			R Knopwood
A Native Boy V D Land			R Knopwood
A Native Boy V D Land	Hobart		R Knopwood
A Native Boy V D Land			R Knopwood
A Native Boy V D Land			R Knopwood
A Native Boy V D Land	Hobart		R Knopwood
A Native of V D Land			R Knopwood
A Native of V D Land			R Knopwood

Parents	Abode	Quality / Profession	By Whom
A Native of V D Land			R Knopwood

Parents	Abode	Quality / Profession	By Whom
A Native Girl of Van Diemen's Land			R Knopwood AM

Parents	Abode	Quality / Profession	By Whom
A Native boy V D L			Robert Knopwood
A Native boy of V D L	Lyttleton was Magistrate in Launceston		Robert Knopwood

When Baptised	When Born	Child Name
1814		
18th March 1814		Dalrymple
18th March 1814		Hannah
1820		
January twelvth (sic) One thousand eight hundred and twenty. Baptized at Norfolk Plains	About eleven Years of Age	Fanny Hardwick
May twenty fifth, One Thousand eight hundred and twenty	About Seven Years of Age	John
1830		
No. 309 June 2nd	DOB 'About 1827'	Ben
1832		
No. 521 Dec 25th	Born 1822	Robert adopted Aboriginal
1835 (Wesleyan Church)		
11th January 1835	Born Unknown	Thomas Harman
Repeated in St John's Register on same day No 804 Jan 11th	DOB Unknown	Thomas Harman
1836		
No. 859, Baptised Feb 16th	About 1822	Nanny Allan
No. 1006, Baptised Dec 28th	About 1830	Sophia
GEORGE TOWN		
1821 51 baptisms including...		
Bpt. 9th October 1821	B. 24th Sept 1816	Charles
Bpt. 9th October 1821	B. 12th Aug 1817	George

Parents	Abode	Quality / Profession	By Whom
A Native Girl			Robert Knopwood
			Robert Knopwood
A Native Black Child			By me John Youl Chaplain
Native Black Boy			By me John Youl Chaplain
No first name of parents 'Lomond' (Surname)	Kingston	Aboriginal	W.H.Browne
by John Bromley	River Tamar	Sawyer	W.H. Browne
Aboriginal Natives			J. A. Manton
Native Names unknown	Abode Uknown		This entry is made on the certificate of the Rev Ja Manton Wesleyan Minister
Native of Kangaroo Island	Quality		W.H. Browne Chaplain
William Dutton & Sarah 'an aboriginal'	Launceston	Mariner	W.H.Browne
Patrick Morrison & Elizabeth (A Native)	George Town	Born at King Is	John Youl
Patrick Morrison & Elizabeth (A Native)	George Town	Born at King Is	John Youl

When Baptised	When Born	Child Name
1823		
July 5th 2 G'Town	Aged 7 years	Margaret
1824		
November 1st 1824 LAUNCESTON	About 7 years old	Mary Ann
1826		
No. 10 April 26th	Dec 5th 1825	Fanny
No. 22	About 6 years of age	Susannah an Aborigine of V.D.Land
CAMPBELL TOWN		
1834		
25th Nov	About 10 years old	John Batman
25th Nov	23 years of age	John

Marriage Register — Launceston

Aug 3 1830 No. 152 Black Bill otherwise (William Ponsonby) of Kingston and Catherine Kennedy of Kingston were

Married in this Church by Banns. This sixteenth day of August in the year 1830. By me W.D. Browne LLD Chaplain

This marriage was solemnized between us   : William Ponsonby his X mark

                                              : Catherine Kennedy her X mark

In the presence of William Appleyard of Launceston. And William Elliott of Launceston

111. The Banns of Marriage were published between Black Bill and Catherine Kennedy Aboriginals at Kingston.

1st time   18th July 1830

2nd "   25th " "

3rd "   1st Aug   by WD Browne

Parents	Abode	Quality / Profession	By Whom
Daughter an Aborigine of Van Diemens Land			By me John Youl Chaplain
An Aborigine			By me John Youl Chaplain
Charles & Elizabeth Hardwicke	Norfolk Plains	Settler	John Youl Chaplain
Charles & Elizabeth Hardwicke	Norfolk Plains	Settler	John Youl
Aboriginal Native	Benlomond		William Bedford
Sydney Native, Pidgeon	Native		William Bedford

APPENDIX B

Aboriginal children listed in Hobart Orphan School Register

* Indicates died at the school [2]

GIRLS SCHOOL REGISTER				
Name of Child	Age	Mother Name	Father Name	Admitted
Pungerawallah		Aborigine		6 Feb 1835
Mowana		Aborigine		6 Feb 1835
Walkenny		Aborigine		6 Feb 1835
Tully		Aborigine		6 Feb 1835
Tina		Aborigine		(6) 9 Feb 1835
Mary Ann Thomson	10y	Aborigine		28 Feb 1839
Mary Sherwood	8y	An Aborigine, native of Adelaide		27 Dec 1841
Fanny	8y	Aborigines from Flinders Is		9 Dec 1842
Martha	7y			9 Dec 1842
Fanny, Martha and Jessie		Aborigines from Flinders Is		
Mathina Flinders	6y	An Aborigine		14 Jul 1843
Mathina	12y	Aborigine		28 Dec 1847
Martha	12y			28 Dec 1847
Nannie*	10y			28 Dec 1847
Hannah	7y			28 Dec 1847

Discharged	Page	Religion	Remarks
30 Sep 1835	6	P [Protestant]	Removed to Flinders Island
27 May 1835	6	P	
18 Jun 1835	6	P	
17 Jun 1835	6	P	Died of the measles
15 Jun 1835	6	P	Removed to Flinders Island
10 Dec 1839	12	P	to Flinders Island by Com^n of Gov'r
27 Sept 1843		P	Died in hospital
8 Feb 1843	19	P	Discharged to Mr Clarke by order of Gov'r
2 Mar 1843	19	P	Died in Hospital
			Admitted by Command of Lieutenant Governor
1 Feb 1844	21	P	Delivered to Dr Milligan
5 Aug 1851	31	P	Delivered over to Dr Milligan
18 Dec 1849	31	P	Discharged to her mother by order Dr Milligan
25 Apr 1849	31	P	Died of inflammation of the lungs
20 May 1850	31	P	Discharged to the service of Dr Smith Flinders Island by command of the authority of the Lieut Governor

BOYS SCHOOL REGISTER				
Name of Child	Age	Mother Name	Father Name	Admitted
Thomas Bunce	7y	An Aborigine		2 Aug 1828
Daniel	10y	Aborigine		17 Aug 1832
Peter	9y			17 Aug 1832
Arthur	11y	Aborigine		30 Nov 1832
Friday	10y			30 Nov 1832
Duke	6y			30 Nov 1832
William		Aborigine		3 Sep 1834
George				3 Sep 1834
Frederick*				3 Sep 1834
Samuel		Aborigine		3 Sep 1834
Charles*		Aborigine		3 Sep 1834
Beamanrook		Aborigine		6 Feb 1835
Tommierick				6 Feb 1835
Menow (Mendou)				6 Feb 1835
Fireboke*				6 Feb 1835
Thomas Thompson	4y	Parents unknown, Half Caste		9 May 1836
Teddy	7y	An Aborigine		27 Feb 1839
Billy Lannie	8y	Aborigines		28 Dec 1847
Adam	7y			28 Dec 1847
Morriarty*	6y	Aborigine		28 Dec 1847
William Clark	10y	Orphans of the late Mr Clark Storekeeper Aborigine		20 Apr 1850
Sandford Clark	4y			20 Apr 1850
Clark, Alexander (M)	13y	Dead Aborigine Storekeeper		30 Apr 1850

Possibly ... Tamar Joe				28 June 1836

Discharged	Page	Religion	Remarks
16 Nov 1836	1	P	Removed to Flinders Island
30 Sep 1835	3	P	Removed to Flinders Island
30 Sep 1835	3	P	Removed to Flinders Island
26 May 1835	3	P	Removed to Flinders Island
26 May 1835	3	P	
4 Feb 1840	3	P	
26 Apr 1835	5	P	Removed to Flinders Island
26 Apr 1835	5	P	
30 Sept 1835	5	P	Died in Hosp
26 Apr 1835	5	P	Removed to Flinders Island
26 Nov 1839	5	P	Died in Hospital
9 Jun 1835	6	P	Sent to Flinders Island
30 Sep 1835	6	P	Sent to Flinders Island
30 Sep 1835	6	P	
2 Jun 1835	6	P	Died
26 Aug 1847	8	P	Removed to Flinders Island
30 Dec 1839	11	P	Removed to Flinders Island
13 Jan 1853	23	P	Col. Funds. Discharged to the order of Joseph Milligan Esq.
13 Jan 1853	23	P	
5 Mar 1852	23	P	Died of inflammation of the lungs
2 Nov 1832(52)	27	P	
1 Jul 1837(51)	27	P	Removed to Infant School
14 Jan 1852	27	P	
			[See Plomley, 1987, p. 847]

APPENDIX C

Bible translation by Wilkinson at Wybalenna 1833
Genesis 1
Walker's diary, Plomley's rendering[3]

Genisana — First chaptera	**Genesis 1 Chap.**
1 Trota Godna Pomale Hearana Coantana	1 In the beginning God created the heavens and the earth
2 Lewara Crackne	2 and darkness was upon the face of the deep
3 Godna carne Tretetea Tretetea Crackne	3 God said let there be light and there was light
4 Godna capie Tretetea narra coopa Godna dividena Tretetea lewara	4 And God saw the light that it was good. And God divided the light from the darkness
5 Godna carne coantana mingane Rotharia Rothana tibre	5 God said let the earth bring forth Grass and it was so
16 Godna pomale Cathabowa Tretetea Lackrana Wakalenna Tewara, Narra Pomale	16 God made two great lights, the greater light to rule the day, the lesser light to rule the night.
Purbanna	he made the stars also
17 Godna propara nerra weaticata Tringane Wetetea	17 God set them in the firmament of heaven to give light upon the earth
21 Godna promale Lackrana Penangana cardea Penugana	21 God made great whales + every living creature that moveth which the waters brought forth abundantly
25 Godna pomale Paccala, Illa, Pabela, Theepasia, Godna lapra narra coopa	25 And God made the beast of the earth and he saw that it was good
26 Godna carne mena pomale Wiba, lika mena	26 And God said let us make man in our image after our own likeness
27 Godna pomale Wiba lika mena	27 So God created man in his own image
31 Godna lapra cardea narra pomale narra carne narra coopa! coopa!	31 And God saw everything that he had made and behold it was very good

Walker's diary, Grant Finlay's rendering

10/12 third day in the forenoon I spent some time at the house of Thomas Wilkinson who favoured me with a copy of the translation of the 1 Chap of Genesis which is as follows

V1 In the beginning God created the heavens and the earth
    troteh Godneh pomleh heavenneh coentanneh

V2 And darkness was over the face of the deep
    lyeverreh crackneh

3 God said let there be light and there was light
    Godneh kany trytittyeh trytittyeh crackny

4 And God saw the light that it was good
    Godne lapr- - - trylittyeh — narreh coopeh

5 God divided the light from the darkness
    Godneh dyvidneh trytittyeh bywerreh

11 God said let the earth bring forth grass and it was so
    Godneh kany coentanneh ninginneh rothinneh tibreh

16 God made two great lights the greater light to rule the day
    Godneh pomleh cathehbyweh trylittyeh lackrenneh wakehlenneh

and the lesser light to rule the night
    tyrverreh (moon)

and he made the stars also
    marreh pomleh pullennah

17 God set them in the firmament of heaven to give light upon the earth
    Godneh propre togehticketteh   tringinneh trylittyeh

21 And God made great whales and all living creatures that moveth
    Godneh pomleh lackrenneh (*off page edge*) pynungyneh (fish)

which the waters brought forth abundantly
    gadyeh (plenty) pynungyneh

25 And God made the beast of the earth and saw that it was good
    Godneh pomleh packilleh (bullock), illa (bush kangaroo) &c. &c Godneh lapreh narreh coopeh

26 And God said let us make man in our own image, after our own likeness
    Godneh kany myneh pomleh wibeh   likeh myneh

27 So God created man in his own image
    Godneh pomleh wibeh likeh narreh

28 God saw everything that he had made and behold it was very good
    Godneh lapre gadyeh narreh pomleh narreh kany narreh coopeh coopeh[4]

King James Version of Genesis 1 with ~~strikethrough~~ the words omitted by Wilkinson

Genesis 1: 168 of 797 words used

¹In the beginning God created the heaven and the earth.

²~~And the earth was without form, and void;~~ and darkness was upon the face of the deep. ~~And the Spirit of God moved upon the face of the waters.~~

³And God said, Let there be light: and there was light.

⁴And God saw the light, that it was good: and God divided the light from the darkness.

⁵~~And God called the light Day, and the darkness he called Night. And the evening and the morning were the first day.~~

⁶~~And God said, Let there be a firmament in the midst of the waters, and let it divide the waters from the waters.~~

⁷~~And God made the firmament, and divided the waters which were under the firmament from the waters which were above the firmament: and it was so.~~

⁸~~And God called the firmament Heaven. And the evening and the morning were the second day.~~

⁹~~And God said, Let the waters under the heaven be gathered together unto one place, and let the dry land appear: and it was so.~~

¹⁰~~And God called the dry land Earth; and the gathering together of the waters called he Seas: and God saw that it was good.~~

¹¹And God said, Let the earth bring forth grass, ~~the herb yielding seed, and the fruit tree yielding fruit after his kind, whose seed is in itself, upon the earth:~~ and it was so.

¹²~~And the earth brought forth grass, and herb yielding seed after his kind, and the tree yielding fruit, whose seed was in itself, after his kind: and God saw that it was good.~~

¹³~~And the evening and the morning were the third day.~~

¹⁴~~And God said, Let there be lights in the firmament of the heaven to divide the day from the night; and let them be for signs, and for seasons, and for days, and years:~~

¹⁵~~And let them be for lights in the firmament of the heaven to give light upon the earth: and it was so.~~

¹⁶And God made two great lights; the greater light to rule the day, and the lesser light to rule the night: he made the stars also.

¹⁷And God set them in the firmament of the heaven to give light upon the earth,

¹⁸~~And to rule over the day and over the night, and to divide the light from the darkness: and God saw that it was good.~~

¹⁹~~And the evening and the morning were the fourth day.~~

~~²⁰And God said, Let the waters bring forth abundantly the moving creature that hath life, and fowl that may fly above the earth in the open firmament of heaven.~~

²¹And God created great whales, and every living creature that moveth, which the waters brought forth abundantly, ~~after their kind, and every winged fowl after his kind: and God saw that it was good.~~

~~²²And God blessed them, saying, Be fruitful, and multiply, and fill the waters in the seas, and let fowl multiply in the earth.~~

~~²³And the evening and the morning were the fifth day.~~

~~²⁴And God said, Let the earth bring forth the living creature after his kind, cattle, and creeping thing, and beast of the earth after his kind: and it was so.~~

²⁵And God made the beast of the earth ~~after his kind, and cattle after their kind, and every thing that creepeth upon the earth after his kind:~~ and ~~God~~ saw that it was good.

²⁶And God said, Let us make man in our image, after our likeness: ~~and let them have dominion over the fish of the sea, and over the fowl of the air, and over the cattle, and over all the earth, and over every creeping thing that creepeth upon the earth.~~

²⁷So God created man in his own image, ~~in the image of God created he him; male and female created he them.~~

~~²⁸And God blessed them, and God said unto them, Be fruitful, and multiply, and replenish the earth, and subdue it: and have dominion over the fish of the sea, and over the fowl of the air, and over every living thing that moveth upon the earth.~~

~~²⁹And God said, Behold, I have given you every herb bearing seed, which is upon the face of all the earth, and every tree, in the which is the fruit of a tree yielding seed; to you it shall be for meat.~~

~~³⁰And to every beast of the earth, and to every fowl of the air, and to every thing that creepeth upon the earth, wherein there is life, I have given every green herb for meat: and it was so.~~

³¹And God saw every thing that he had made, and, behold, it was very good. ~~And the evening and the morning were the sixth day.~~

APPENDIX D

Sermons by Aboriginal people, other than Walter Arthur and Thomas Brune

Noemy

Appendix B   No 1

Copies

The addresses delivered by the Abor at their meeting for prayer and mutual instruction at the Aboriginal Settlement Flinders Island on Saturday evening 24th Feby 1838

Noemy a Western Native

He first addressed his own tribe in their own language in the following terms as translated to me by the native girl Bessy Clark a Western

You ought to live peaceably together not steal from each other nor tell lies nor scold each other

He then addressed the entire assembly in the language of the Settlement of which the following is a translation

You men ought not scold one another — clean your houses early in the morning — do not be sulky — put your bad tempers away from you Love God — love Jesus Christ — Do not remain no longer in the bush when you go for firewood doing what is bad

---

No 2 The address delivered by the Aborigines at their meeting for prayer and mutual instruction at the Ab¹ Settlement Flinders Is on Saturday 10th March 1838

Noemy a Western Aboriginal

He addressed his own tribe in their native language as was translated to me by a native girl Bessy Clark He told them they acted improperly in not remaining on the Settlement and that they ought not be roving in the bush He afterwards spoke to the assembly generally in the language of the Sett^t of which the following is a translation

Women you are still continuing to do what is improper when you go to the bush for firewood God may take away your lives very soon for your wickedness You go about the settlement some of you living like dogs God does not like that — bad people will be sent to hell bad people are the Devils people Gods country is a fine place yes heaven is a good place Jesus Christ the Son of God is there Good men and women are there Jesus Christ came from heaven to save sinners every man is a sinner if you do not become good people you will all go to Hell to the Devils house You will never go to Heaven Gods country[5]

No 3

Report of the speeches delivered by the Abors at their weekly meetings for prayer and mutual instruction at Flinders I Ab^l Sett^t on Saturday 17th March 1838

Noemy a Western

God made us all both black men + women and white men and women Why do we not all love God God is very good He provides everything for us always Jesus Christ the Son of God loves us and is desirous to make us good men + women The devil can not make you good no never The devil is very bad and black men + women have bad hearts very bad and the Devil makes them worse But God is good and Gods country is a good country Heaven is a happy place put away the Devil Do not love the Devil do not make bad things Hell is the Devils country and a very bad place of great burning — You do too many bad things and you go to hell when you die You go to the Devils country — Jesus Christ is the Son of God What did he do for us He died on the cross to save sinners What shall we do to be saved Believe in the Lord Jesus Christ the world will be burned up by + by^6

No 4

Report of the speeches delivered by the Abo: at their meetings for prayer and mutual instruction at the Abn^l Settlement Flinders Island on Saturday evening 31st March 1838

The natives met this evening at the usual house and Neptune who was not expected from his being confined during the week by Opthalvia(?) would not remain at home he came with a cloth covering his face to shade the light from his eyes and had to sit on the floor between the forms during the service to save his eyes from the light of candles

---

Noemy a Western Native

He addressed his own country men in their own language and which was translated to me by the native females Clara and Bessy Clark He told them how he was first married to a little girl that he then did not know any thing about God on his country — He then asked several questions to the people [in] relation to the creation the coming of Jesus Christ into the world God loving the world &c. and then addressed them in the language spoken on the Settlement — We ought to learn about God more than we do — we ought to love God much more than we do — we do not love him enough God is very good to us and his country is a good country – God loves us and if we love him he will not put us away from him — God sent Jesus Christ his son to bring us to his country — there is no hunger there — no thirst there no no sickness there a great number of good ~~things~~ men and women are there — You black men and women are bad you scold too much & some then fight you steal from one another you show that you love the Devil for you do the Devils work God does not like that — You all dead people soon and where will you go to then — Is it to the Devils country there is much burning there many hungry + sick and crying a great deal — Oh it's a bad place why are you not like me I do not scold or fight I don't tell lies I love God a little and love him a big one by + by I pray to God + sing hymns to God every evening in my house and why do not you do so — many of you do not I love God — God loved me first — God so loved the world that [he gave] his only begotten son that whosoever believeth in him should not perish but have everlasting life[7]

Report of the addresses delivered by the Ab[ls] of Van Diemens Land at their weekly meeting for prayer and mutual instruction held the 14th April 1838

The service commenced by a native youth repeating the confession of the Church of England service and the Lords Prayer in which all the natives present join I then read the second chapter of Matthews Gospel and translated some of the leading facts into the language spoken on the Settlement after which we sang a hymn

---

Noemy a western native commenced

He spoke to his own tribe first in their own language which was translated to me by Bessy Clark a western girl You walk about too much why do you so you play to much also you will soon get sick again remain in your houses and learn you dont vissed(?) your book do not be lazy but work and learn to work He then addressed the assembly in the language of the Settlement Black men and black women do not forget God + son Jesus Christ do not forget him You do not love Jesus Christ as you ought but if you love him a little one more you will love him more by + by If you love the Devil you will go to Hell if you love Jesus Christ you will go to Heaven Hell is a bad place Heaven a good place a very good place — He then put the following questions which were answered by the people Who is Jesus Christ? the Son of God What is salvation? Forsake every bad thing Put away the Devil Love Jesus Christ Love God Love to go to Heaven[8]

The Rev T Dove Chaplain of the Settlement at the conclusion of the meeting expressed the high satisfaction and delight he felt at the observations which were made he said 'that Noemy was not merely an elegant but an eloquent speaker and that Alexander was a very sensible man'.

The Commandant who was likewise present stated why Alpha was not so far advanced as the others having been occupied with himself and his sons in the bush from the commencement of the mission[9]

The addresses delivered by the Aboriginals of Van Diemens Land at their weekly meetings for prayer and mutual instruction held on Saturday even[g] 21 April 1838

Alexander, Neptune then Noemy

Noemy a western He addressed his own tribe in their native language interpreted by Clara 'You talk too much of other people you should not talk bad things of each other when you are walking when you go in the bush you speak bad of each other and of other people in place of talking about God White men hunted you they were bad men You do not like to be here plenty of you die

He then addressed the assembly generally in the language spoken on the Settlement

In your own country you did not know there was a God all that you knew was to make spears and waddies and to kill one another by + by you came here Mr Clark read to you plenty No waddy no spear in heaven a fine country white men and black men there they are always singing about God In hell you cry you burn you cannot put it away But if you go to heaven you will not die any more – you will be there little boys Angels little girls to you old women there always young forever there you will always sing of God always have him in your mind I pray in my house do you pray do you sing of the bible Heaven a good place a good country of God of Jesus Christ do you love to go to Heaven[10]

     There were present at this meeting Mrs and Miss Robinson Mrs Clark Rev T Dove AM Chaplain who expressed himself highly pleased as did also the Commandant

The above is a faithful and correct report translated by me from the languages generally spoken on the Settlement and from notes taken at the time of the delivery of the address

               Signed Robt Clark
               Late Catechist[11]

Rrumathapana / **Druemerterpunner** / **Alexander**

No 4

Report of the speeches delivered by the Abo: at their meetings for prayer and mutual instruction at the Abn^l Settlement Flinders Island on Saturday evening 31st March 1838

The natives met this evening at the usual house and Neptune who was not expected from his being confined during the week by Opthalmia would not remain at home he came with a cloth covering his face to shade the light from his eyes and had to sit on the floor between the forms during the service to save his eyes from the light of candles

----

Noemy, Neptune spoke first
          Alexander a Big River Native

     I tell you men and women you are not good you do not learn the bible you do not learn none of Gods book heres the bible / taking hold of one on the desk / it tells us of Jesus Christ and of heaven Heaven is a good place Hell is a bad place You like to go there do you You like to have plenty plenty[sic] hungry plenty sick no good place that but Gods country a good country Heaven a fine place you like it no hunger there no thirst there no sick no bad people all are good there you like it there learn to be good You are not like me I dont tell lies I dont fight Jesus Christ tells us love one another You scold you tell lies you will not go to Gods country Jesus is there God is there plenty of good men are there you will never die there never be old you will love God always there

     Questions put to the Abo: by Alexander
To Rebecca: Where is God? In heaven everywhere
To Harriet Who is Jesus Christ? The Son of God
To Jane Who made you? God
To Flora What did Jesus Christ do for you? He died for our sins according to the scriptures
To Juliet What will you do to be saved Believe in the Lord Jesus Christ

The above correctly taken and translated by Rob.ᵗ Clark
Late Catechist

The Rev T Dove the Chaplain of the Settlement was present at these meetings and publicly expressed his pleasure and satisfaction at hearing them and stated that several of the addresses were both eloquent and elegant and their gestures particularly graceful

Signed Rob.ᵗ Clark
Late Catechist

The preceding appears to me to be faithful extracts of the addresses delivered by the Abo: whose names are appended to them

Signed T Dove
Chaplain of Flinders[12]

Alexander a Big River native

Put away your corroberries put away your bad things your wicked doings I say my friends why don't you love God — Mr Clark put a great many questions to you why do you not always pay attention to what he says to you — you play too much at marbles you walk about too much You don't love Jesus Christ enough like me I love God I love Jesus Christ I will go to Heaven when I die — No old men there all young boys there no sickness there God loves you if you are good you go to Heaven a happy place good place good people there[13]

There were present at this meeting Mrs and Miss Robinson Mrs Clark Rev T Dove AM Chaplain who expressed himself highly pleased as did also the Commandant

The above is a faithful and correct report translated by me from the languages generally spoken on the Settlement and from notes taken at the time of the delivery of the address

Signed Rob.ᵗ Clark
Late Catechist[14]

Wurati / Alpha

Report of the addresses delivered by the Ab.ˡˢ of Van Diemens Land at their weekly meeting for prayer and mutual instruction held the 14ᵗʰ April 1838

The service commenced by a native youth repeating the confession of the Church of England service and the Lords Prayer in which all the natives present join I then read the second chapter of Matthews Gospel and translated some of the leading facts into the language spoken on the Settlement after which we sang a hymn

Noemy, Neptune, Alexander, Leonidas, then Alpha

Alpha

He addressed the meeting in his native language / the Brune Island / interpreted by Wild Mary and by himself afterwards My brothers in our own country a long time ago we were a great many men a great number — but the white men have killed us all — they shot a great many — we are now only a few people here and we ought to be fond of one another we ought to love God God made everything the Salt water the bullock the horse the opossum the kangaroo and wombat Love him and you will go to him by + by[15]

The Rev T Dove Chaplain of the Settlement at the conclusion of the meeting expressed the high satisfaction and delight he felt at the observations which were made he said "that Noemy was not merely an elegant but an eloquent speaker and that Alexander was a very sensible man

The Commandant who was likewise present stated why Alpha was not so far advanced as the others having been occupied with himself and his sons in the bush from the commencement of the mission[16]

The addresses delivered by the Aboriginals of Van Diemens Land at their weekly meetings for prayer and mutual instruction held on Saturday even^g 21 April 1838

Alexander, Neptune, Noemy, Napoleon, Leonidas, then Alpha ...

Alpha — a Brune Island Native Interpreted by Sophie — you make your persons too filthy by putting grease and ochre on yourselves — you dirty your clothes you dirty yourselves — put it away you women — Jesus Christ loves you me and every body

To Juliet Who made you? God
Where is God? Everywhere[17]

There were present at this meeting Mrs and Miss Robinson Mrs Clark Rev T Dove AM Chaplain who expressed himself highly pleased as did also the Commandant

The above is a faithful and correct report translated by me from the languages generally spoken on the Settlement and from notes taken at the time of the delivery of the address
        Signed Robt Clark
        Late Catechist[18]

No 2 The address delivered by the Aborigines at their meeting for prayer and mutual instruction at the Ab^l Settlement Flinders Is on Saturday 10th March 1838

Noemy and Neptune first, then Leonidas the only other one.

      Leonidas — a Big River Native

Love the Bible it is a good book it is Gods Book why do you not all learn to read Gods book it tells you plenty about God about Jesus Christ you are too lazy to learn

  A correct translation taken by me
  Signed/ Robt Clark
  Late Catechist[19]

Report of the addresses delivered by the Ab^{ls} of Van Diemens Land at their weekly meeting for prayer and mutual instruction held the 14th April 1838

The service commenced by a native youth repeating the confession of the Church of England service and the Lords Prayer in which all the natives present join I then read the second chapter of Matthews Gospel and translated some of the leading facts into the language spoken on the Settlement after which we sang a hymn

Leonidas a Big River Native

Gentlemen and Ladies you play too much you tell too many lies of each other you put away God God loves you do not let God go from your minds Let Jesus Christ jump up in your hearts then you are good and you are on your road to heaven God made everything the sea the sun the moon the kangaroo the emu the whale the wombat the pacalla(?) /bullock/ the pacoothina /horse/ all God made very good[20]

The addresses delivered by the Aboriginals of Van Diemens Land at their weekly meetings for prayer and mutual instruction held on Saturday even^g 21 April 1838

Alexander, Neptune, Noemy, Napoleon, then Leonidas...

Leonidas a Big River Native

Ladies and Gentlemen you look out too much for bad things you are not good at all you have bad hearts You see(?) pray to God to give you good hearts why do you lose(?) him too much You black women you been to play too much white woman don't play at balls and win(?) about like you You do not like God by + by God wont like you Pray to God in your houses pray to him that Jesus Christ may spring up in your hearts You go to heaven a good place that you did not make Heaven God made it God made the trees the salt water the moon the stars the kangaroo the porky the Pacoother the Shup(?) the wallaby — God make everything sing plenty to God in your Librussa(?) pray to him every night to passaway the Devil and sickness Look out for God and he will look out for you and take care of you[21]

There were present at this meeting Mrs and Miss Robinson Mrs Clark Rev T Dove AM Chaplain who expressed himself highly pleased as did also the Commandant

The above is a faithful and correct report translated by me from the languages generally spoken on the Settlement and from notes taken at the time of the delivery of the address
        Signed Robt Clark
        Late Catechist[22]

Piway / **Napoleon**

The addresses delivered by the Aboriginals of Van Diemens Land at their weekly meetings for prayer and mutual instruction held on Saturday even^g 21 April 1838

Alexander, Neptune, Noemy, then Napoleon...

Napoleon a Ben Lomond Native

Blackman Blackwoman why do you forget God Jesus Christ came into the world to save sinners He then put the following questions to the natives around him

To Harriet
        What shall we do to be saved? Believe in the Lord Jesus Christ

To Clara
        What did Jesus Christ do for us? He died for our sins according to the Scriptures

To Caroline
>Where was Jesus Christ born? In Bethlehem[23]

Followed by Leonidas, Alpha and Robert (Ben Lomond)

There were present at this meeting Mrs and Miss Robinson Mrs Clark Rev T Dove AM Chaplain who expressed himself highly pleased as did also the Commandant

The above is a faithful and correct report translated by me from the languages generally spoken on the Settlement and from notes taken at the time of the delivery of the address
>Signed Robt Clark
>Late Catechist[24]

Appendix B   No 1

Copies

The addresses delivered by the Abor at their meeting for prayer and mutual instruction at the Aboriginal Settlement Flinders Island on Saturday evening 24th Feby 1838

>Neptune a Western Native
>*In margin "this is an error of the catechist he is from N coast of VDL GAR"*

You man and woman do not be lazy attend your School why do you remain sitting at home you learn a great deal of good things at school why do you forget them so soon Why do not the old women come to school — I do not stay at home — I come to School I pray to God in my house every night — You people why do you have to walk about at night it is very bad — I remain in my house why don't you remain at home recalled what the parson / the catechist / has told you if you remember it you will become good people He has told you about God You learn to love God that will make you good people if you are not good the Devil will take you by + by

The above is a correct report taken by me
>/signed/ Robt Clark
>Late Catechist[25]

No 2 The address delivered by the Aborigines at their meeting for prayer and mutual instruction at the Ab^l Settlement Flinders Is on Saturday 10th March 1838

>Neptune a Western Native

He addressed his tribe in their own language which was translated to me by the western woman Clara and Bessy Clark *GAR says Neptune is north coast, but he's being translated by western women, whose language is he speaking?* In your own country you were bad people and a great many of you died God did not love what you were doing — God sent you from your own country Why are you continuing those bad things — after a little time you will all die You ought to love God for God is very good to us all — He then addressed them in the language of the Settlement of which the following is a translation God loves all men He sent Jesus Christ his Son into the world to save us we should always love God — but we do not know God at first God made the white man come to tell us of Jesus Christ the Son of God He came from Heaven to save sinners — God made man first of the dust of the ground and he breathed into his nostrils the breath of life and man became a living soul — Do not be a bad people love God — God loved us first — you did a great deal of wickedness you did not love God and you soon will know that God does not love wicked people always He loves good people and brings them to Heaven bad people who tell lies and scold and steal they do not love God but go to Hell by + by love Jesus Christ and you will be good people[26]

Drinene / Neptune

No 3

Report of the speeches delivered by the Abors at their weekly meetings for prayer and mutual instruction at Flinders I Ab^l Sett^t on Saturday 17th March 1838

Neptune a Western Native

My brothers and sisters why do you forget God You do not remember him always and you are too fond of doing what is bad Women you go into the bush too often you are like the dogs — God does not love bad black men or black women He cannot love what is bad if you are bad if you are bad you are the Devils people Gods people are good people they love God they love Jesus Christ the Son of God he died for our sins bad men will not walk in Gods country that is a good country no sickness there you do not like God I love God No people who do bad things are there no bad things not all there — learn to read the bible it is a good book it is Gods book Love God for that book Love God for Jesus Christ the Son of God — He came into the world to save sinners A very long time since a great number of people were drowned they were bad people they do too much evil and God put them away By + by God burn up the world Will you like to go to the Devil then If you are bad men and women God will send you to the Devils country But if you love God he will keep you in heaven — His country a very fine place where you will remain forever God will look out for you there and take care of you and you will not fall down from him

>The above a correct translation
>/signed/Robt Clark
>Late Catechist[27]

No 4

Report of the speeches delivered by the Abo: at their meetings for prayer and mutual instruction at the Abn^l Settlement Flinders Island on Saturday evening 31st March 1838

The natives met this evening at the usual house and Neptune who was not expected from his being confined during the week by Opthalvia(?) would not remain at home he came with a cloth covering his face to shade the light from his eyes and had to sit on the floor between the forms during the service to save his eyes from the light of candles

Noemy's speech first

Neptune — a Western Native

What prevents you my friends to love and to know God — You did not know God in your own country — you were evild[sic] me there — the white men hunted you and shot you there are a great many white men bad and a great many black men bad too God sent the white man Parson/Catechist and he has instructed us about God and Jesus Christ the Son of God we now know that Jesus Christ made the trees the salt water the sun and moon and the kangaroo and the emu and every thing God loves every thing that is good and he loves good men and good men love God — God gives us everything The parson/Catechist reads it in the Bible and he tells us there are a great many black men in another country who read Gods book about Jesus Christ the son of God — We all are bad people let us put away the devil for he will bring us to Hell it is a bad place no good there do you like to go there you men and women then why will you not learn to read the Bible and love Jesus Christ You are not like me I learn to read Gods book by + by learn about Jesus Christ not to tell lies nor steal but love God the Bible tells us plenty about Gods country — you old men when you die by + by you love Jesus Christ you will not be old in Heaven you will always be young men — there are no old men there — you will never die there never sick there never hungry and no bad people there no wicked white men there — God and Jesus Christ + angels and good men there – if you do not love God now when you die you travel to the Devils country — look out and learn about God — love God love Jesus Christ always and you will always be happy pray to him every night and he will take care of you[28]

Report of the addresses delivered by the Ab[ls] of Van Diemens Land at their weekly meeting for prayer and mutual instruction held the 14th April 1838

The service commenced by a native youth repeating the confession of the Church of England service and the Lords Prayer in which all the natives present join I then read the second chapter of Matthews Gospel and translated some of the leading facts into the language spoken on the Settlement after which we sang a hymn

---

Noemy first (as usual!)

Neptune a western

He addressed the tribe he belongs to in their own language translated to me by Bessy Clark

Every woman should mind her own house and not be going to other peoples homes keep your blankets clean carry plenty of wood to your houses for your fires take care of your clothes and sew them when they are old or torn do not throw them away when you go to the bush a hunting as you used to do You men you ought to work do not be idle Do as much good as you can and God will love you He then addressed them in the language of the Settlement — Gentlemen and Ladies you love God you love Jesus Christ In your own country you did not know Jesus Christ no you were like the kangaroos you went about every place the white man came to your country they kill your countrymen a great many of them you then came to live in this place and good white men came to teach you about God about Jesus Christ you are not bad now the white men does not kill you now not never Put away the Devil he makes every thing bad God makes every thing good Praise God always[29]

The addresses delivered by the Aboriginals of Van Diemens Land at their weekly meetings for prayer and mutual instruction held on Saturday even[g] 21 April 1838

Alexander first, then Neptune

Neptune a western

He spoke in his own language to his tribe which was interpreted by the native woman Clara

Do not laugh do not talk whilst I am speaking you should not laugh in this house God does not like it you are a lazy people — don't love work — I tell you again look out your things wash them and mend them and take care of them

He then addressed the assembly in the language of the Settlement — Do not forget Jesus Christ he came into the world to save sinners You are sinners I am a sinner Look at the Bible down here you love God no Parson/Catechist teach you plenty forget it too soon why do you forget it Remember God and Jesus Christ learn to read quickly What is salvation / answered by the whole assembly / put away wickedness put away the devil Love Jesus Christ and love God and love to go to Heaven[30]

There were present at this meeting Mrs and Miss Robinson Mrs Clark Rev T Dove AM Chaplain who expressed himself highly pleased as did also the Commandant

The above is a faithful and correct report translated by me from the languages generally spoken on the Settlement and from notes taken at the time of the delivery of the address
        Signed Robt Clark
        Late Catechist[31]

Malboy / Robert (*Son of Rolepa / George and Luggenemenener / Tuery, and brother of Walter Arthur*)

The addresses delivered by the Aboriginals of Van Diemens Land at their weekly meetings for prayer and mutual instruction held on Saturday even^g 21 April 1838

Alexander, Neptune, Noemy, Napoleon, Leonidas, Alpha,

Robert a Ben Lomond Native

This man spoke in tolerably good English

Plenty of women here — why do you come here — to learn about God — you know nothing in your own country but to fight plenty you learn plenty of good things from the white man You could not make a house no you make a breakwind You sleep in a break wind not in a warm house The Commandant make a fine house for the black man You cant make glass for a window You wild people all every one When you come here you know nothing you go about naked but you kill kangaroo you no make stone houses you only make a break wind all round

There were present at this meeting Mrs and Miss Robinson Mrs Clark Rev T Dove AM Chaplain who expressed himself highly pleased as did also the Commandant

The above is a faithful and correct report translated by me from the languages generally spoken on the Settlement and from notes taken at the time of the delivery of the address
        Signed Robt Clark
        Late Catechist[32]

APPENDIX E

The Aboriginal or Flinders Island Chronicle and other writings by Walter Arthur and Thomas Brune

Robinson Papers A7074 (Reel CY 825 Mitchell Library) and Plomley, N. J. B., 1987, *Weep in Silence*. Hobart; Blubber Head Press, Appendix IV: C,

Aboriginal
or
Flinders Island Chronicle
Under the Sanction of the Commandant

The object of this journal is to promote
Christianity civilization and Learning amongst
the Aboriginal Inhabitants at Flinders Island.
The chronicle professes to be a brief but accurate
register of events of the colony Moral and religious
This journal will be published weekly on Saturdays
the copies to be in ~~Aboriginal~~ Manuscript and written
exclusively by the Aboriginals the Size half foolscap
and price two pence.
The Profit arising from the Sale of the journal
to be equally divided among~~st~~ the writers
which it is hoped may induce Emmulation
in writing excite a desire for useful knowledge
and promote Learning generally.
Proof sheets are to be Submitted to the
commandant for correction before publishing
Persons out of the colony may Subscribe
  Thomas Bruney
  Walter Juba Martin[33]

Prospectus

I certify that this Copy was written by one of the Aboriginals at Flinders Island whose signature is herewith attached

Aboriginal	G A Robinson
Settlement	Commandant
Flinders Island	
10th Sept 1836[34]	

The Aboriginal
or
Flinders Island Chronicle
Under the Sanction of the Commandant

The object of this journal is to promote
Christianity Civilization and Learning amongst
the Aboriginal Inhabitants at Flinders Island.
The chronicle professes to be a brief ^{but} accurate
register of events of the colony Moral and Religiou^s
This journal will be published weekly on Saturdays the copies
to be in Manuscript and written exclusively by the Abori^{gines}
the Size half foolscap and price two pence.
The Profit arising from the Sale of the journal to be
equally divided amongst the writers which it is hoped
may induce Emmulation in writing excite a desire
for useful knowledge and promote Learning generally.
Proof sheets are to be Submitted to the commandant
for correction before publishing Persons out of the
colony may Subscribe

Walter Juba Martin   Thomas Bruney[35]

I certify that this copy was written by one of the Aborigines at Flinders Island
Flinders Island   G A Robinson
10th Sept 1836   Commandant[36]

The Aboriginal
Flinders Island Chronicle
Under the Sanction of the Commandant

The object of this journal is to promote Christianity
Civilization and Learning amongst the Aborigines Inhabita^{nts}
at Flinders Island.
The chronicle professes to be a brief ^{but} accurate register
of events of the colony Moral and Religious This
Journal will be published weekly on Saturdays the
copies to be in Manuscript and written exclusively by the Aborigines
the size half foolscap and the price two pence.
The Profit arising from the Sale of the Journal
to be equally divided amongst the writers it ^{which} is hoped
may induce Emmulation in writing Excite a desire for

useful knowledge and promote Learning Generally.
Proof sheets are to be Submitted to the commandant
for correction before publishing
Persons out of the colony may Subscribe
    Walter Juba Martin
    Thomas Bruney[37]

I certify that this Copy was written by one of the Aboriginals at Flinders Island
Flinders Island   G A Robinson
10 Sept 1836   Commandant[38]

          The Aboriginal
                or
      Flinders Island Chronicle
    Under the Sanction of the Commandant

The object of the journal is to promote christianity
Civilization and Learning amongst the Aboriginal Inhabitants at Flinders Island.
The chronicle professes to be a brief but accurate
register of events of the colony Moral and Religi^{ous}
This journal will be published weekly on
Saturdays the copies to be in Manuscript and
written exclusively by the Aborigines the Size
half foolscap and the price two pence.
The Profit arising from the Sale of this
journal to be equally divided amongst
the writers which it is hoped may induce
Emmulation in writing Excite a desire for
useful knowledge and promote Learning
Generally.
Proof sheets are to be Submitted to the
commandant for correction before published
Persons out of the colony may Subscribe
    Thomas Brun[sic][39]

Prospectus

I certify that this Copy was written by one of the Aboriginals at Flinders Island
Flinders Island   G A Robinson
10 Sept 1836   Command^{t}[40]

The Aboriginal
or
Flinders Island Chronicle
Under the Sanction of the Commandant

The object of the journal is to promote christian^{ity} civilization and Learning amongst the
Aboriginal Inhabitants at Flinders Island.
The chronicle professes to be a brief but accurate
register of events of the colony Moral and Religious
This journal will be published weekly on Saturdays
the copies to be in Manuscript and written exclusiv^{ely}
by the Aborigines the Size half foolscap and the
price two pence.
The Profits arising from the Sale of this journal
to be equally divided amongst the writers which it
is hoped may induce Emmulation in writing
excite a desire for useful knowledge and promote
learning generally.
Proof sheets are to be Submitted to the command^{ant}
for correction before publishing. Persons out of the
colony may Subscribe
   Thomas Brune[41]

I certify that this Copy was written by one of the Aboriginals at Flinders Island
Flinders Island   G A Robinson
10 Sept 1836   Commandant[42]

The Aboriginal
or
Flinders Island Chronicle
Under the Sanction of the Commandant

The object of the journal is to promote christianity
civilization and Learning amongst the Aboriginal
Inhabitants at Flinders Island. The chronicle
professes to be a brief but accurate register of
events of the colony Moral and Religious this
journal will be published weekly on Saturdays
the copies to be in Manuscript and written
exclusively by the Aboriginals the Size half
foolscap and the price two pence. The Profits

arising from the Sale of this journal to be equally divided amongst the writers which it is hoped may induce Emmulation in writing excite a desire for useful knowledge and promote Learning generally. Proof sheets are to be Submitted to the comm^{andant} for correction before publishing. Persons out of the colony may Subscribe
   Thomas Bruney[43]

  The Aboriginal or Flinders Island Chronicle under the sanction of the Commandant

The object of this journal is to promote Christianity civilisation and learning amongst the Aborigines, inhabitants at Flinders Island. The Chronicle professes to be a brief but accurate register of events of the colony moral and religious. This journal will be published weekly on Saturdays the copies to be in manuscript and written exclusively by the Aborigines the size half foolscap and the price two pence.

The profits arising from the sale of the journal to be equally divided amongst the writers which it is hoped may induce emulation in writing, excite a desire for useful knowledge, and promote learning generally. Proof sheets are to be submitted to the Commandant for correction before publishing. Persons out of the colony may subscribe.

Walter Juba Martin   Thomas Bruney[44]

   The Aboriginal
     or
  Flinders Island Chronicle
 Under the Sanction of the Commandant

N° 1   Saturday 10th Sept 1836   price 2^d

In commencing our Journal agreeable to the Prospectus we cannot look back on the Events Connected with our history this we leave with the Divine blessing to the heart and head that Has been instrumental in uniting us together and providing us with Instruction and guiding us into the habits of civilized life. ^{and} the enjoyment of security from the oppression of bad men we date our history of events from the Month of October 1835 when our beloved father made his appearance among us dispelling the darkness and cheering us with a dawn of hope freedom and happiness we had been in a deplorable

state. we looked for a better day and it has arrived
what a contrast between the present and the past
A market was established on the Settlement in
August last for the sale of articles which we
require and to purchase our shins and mariners
after the market we were regaled with a dinner
of Mutton and pudding. We are learning the use
of money. Events of the week. H. M. Colonial
Schooner Eliza arrived at Green Island and the
[page 14]
Commandant is to proceed in her to Hobart Town
we feel even his loss for a day from us and hope he
will soon come back again
    published at the Cathechists for the writers
      Flinders Island

I certify that this Copy was written by one of the
Aboriginal Youths at Flinders Island
GAR
Thomas Brune[45]

      The Aboriginal
        or
    Flinders Island Chronicle
  Under the Sanction of the Commandant

N° 1   Saturday 10th Sept 1836   price 2d

In commencing our Journal agreeable to the
Prospectus we cannot look back on the events
connected with our history this we leave with the
Divine blessing to the heart and head that has
been instrumental in uniting us together and providing
us with instruction and guiding us into the habits of
civilized life & the enjoyment of security from the
oppression of bad men We date our history of
events from the Month of October 1835 when our
beloved father made his appearance among us
dispelling the darkness and cheering us with a dawn
of hope freedom and happiness. We had been in
a deplorable State we looked for a better day
and it has arrived what a contrast between
the present and the past. A market was established
on the Settlement in August last for sale

of articles which we require and to purchase our
skins and Mariners after the market we were
regaled with a dinner of Mutton and pudd^{ing}.
We are learning the use of money.
        Events of the week.
H. M. C. Schooner Eliza arrived and the com
[page 16]
mandant is to proceed in her to Hobart Town we
feel even his loss for a day from us and hope he will
Soon come back again

Published for the writers at the Cathechists
        Flinders Island[46]

    The Aboriginal or Flinders Island Chronicle under the sanction of the Commandant

No. 1 Saturday 10 September 1836 [=1837]   price 2d.

In commencing our Journal agreeable to the prospectus we cannot look back on the events connected with our history; this we leave with the Divine blessing to the heart and head that has been instrumental in uniting us together and providing us with instruction guiding us into the habits of civilised life and the enjoyment of security from the oppression of bad men. We date our history of events from the month of October 1835 when our beloved father made his appearance among us dispelling the darkness and cheering us with a dawn of hope freedom and happiness. We had been in a deplorable state. We looked for a better day and it has arrived. What a contrast between the present and the past. A market was established on the settlement in August last for the sale of articles which we require and to purchase our skins and mariners. After the market we were regaled with a dinner of mutton and pudding. We are learning the use of money. Events of the week. H.M. Colonial schooner Eliza arrived at Green Island and the commandant is to proceed in her to Hobart Town. We feel even his loss for a day from us and hope he will soon come back again.

Published at the catechist's for the writers   Flinders Island[47]

        The
    Flinders Island
    Weekly Chronicle
    28th September 1837

    The Natives people of Van Diemen's Land is gone
out hunting and some of their men his got some books out
with them and they are singing and reading out
in the bush and praying to God every night I suppose
and they behave themselves under the Directions of the
Commandant The people of Van Diemen's Land

which I speak of; My friends which are here
now and my people is well off in Flinders Island
The men which his now out hunting they will come again
on the Settlement in a short time the Settlement boat
is gone to the Island to get some geese and the boat
is coming back to the Settlement

        The Natives people his learning about God
and learning to read and learning about Jesus Christ
and the way that we should go to heaven when we
dies and if we be bad men we will go down into
everlasting burning. It is better for us to Look after God
and he will take us up to heaven were[sic] we cane [sic] enjoy
happiness.

        For it is good for us to look out for him now
then is time for us to go to hell hereafter always
singing in heaven no hunger no thirst we will
have everything that is good in heaven, Natives
of Van Diemen's Land is health and soberly
in Flinders Island were[sic] they dwelt and the
people of Van Diemen's Land about have some
reason about God in their hearts

        And I can tell you my friends that
their[sic] is a great God over you and me and
 when we look to him for blessings and new
hearts and new Spirits within all these things
that we must ask for my friends[48]

Flinders Island
Weekly Chronicle
28th September 1837

        The ^Natives people of Van Diemen's Land is ~~the~~
gone out hunting and some of them his got some
books out with them and they are singing out
in the bush and praying to God every night
I suppose; and they behave ~~themself~~ themselves
under the Directions of the Commandant
The people of Van Diemen's Land
which I speak of; ~~his;~~ My friends which are here
now and my people his well off in Flinders
Island the men which his now out huntting
they will come again on the Settlement
in a short time the Settlement boat is gone
to the Island to get some ~~geeses~~^geese and the boat
~~th~~ is coming back to the Settlement

The Natives people his learning ~~boat~~ about God
and learning to read and learning about
Jesus Christ and the way that we should
go to heaven when we dies and if we be
bad men we will go down into
everlasting burnings.
It is better for us to ~~Look~~ seek after
God and he will take us up to heaven
were[sic] we cane [sic] enjoy ~~the~~ happiness
      For it is good for us to look out
for him now, then, is time for
us to go to hell ~~up with~~ hereafter
Thomas Brune Aboriginal
Youth[49]

      The Copy which I wrote his forwarded to
the Natives School and the Natives were hereing[sic]
of it and the people were carrying wood
This morning and the Native women
were carrying grass
      The New Holland women
and a sealers boat man and two children
and he came to the Commandants Office and
ask the Commandant for Time for mend
his boat and he had to sleep at one of the
prisoners huts and then he had to go away
      The people which are in Hobart Town
They ~~works at tared~~ trade manufacturing[sic] Shoemakers
Carpenters Joiners Blacksmiths Gunsmiths
These are works which they do in V.
D. L. They is now which I could
tell You my black people you could
not do these things the native people of Van
Diemen's Land are ~~his~~ well off in there[sic]
Situation where they are and I hope
God will protect them in every place
were[sic]ever they go
      The Brig Tamar hast been here with flour and she hast forwarded
us the flour to Settlement the sheeps ~~his~~ are
well off on these Island they are increasing
very much we get some to eat and
white people Distributed to the Natives
and they have as much as they like The
Commandant don't like them ~~th~~ to have
Saltmeat always Mutton his always

Provided for them the people which
his in Van Diemen's Land hast got the
government property[50]

                                    The
                              Flinders Island
                              Weekly Chronicle
                              2 October 1837

The Native people of Van Diemen's Land is not
only people of Devil there are the people of God
is not them the people of God very good yes
it is my friends very good the School is going to
be put up for them as the Commandant directed
them in a short time we will sing in that
School it is most important and Delight it is to
learn about God and about is ways and How
dreadful it is to go on the way to the Devil and
how can we enjoy the happiness; and if we go on the
ways of God it is good for us and then we can have
God for our father the Native people of Van Diemen's
Land is the people of God and it is good for us
to look out for him now, and then it is certain
that ʷᵉ cane[sic] have happiness hereafter
        The people gose[sic] to the church and the people
Hears about God the Aboriginal Youths Walter
and Thomas Bruney Assisting Mr Clark in the
Church of Sundays then Mr Clark tells
them about God and about Jesus Christ who
came down from heaven into our world to save
sinners and then he was crucified and the cross
was in form of a T and then was buried and on the
third day he arose from the dead and now
is interceeding [sic] fro them that come unto God
but him
        We learn these from the Officers
From Mr Clark from Mr Dickenson and
Mr Dockercillen(?) and from Commandant and
from Mr William we should thank these
Gentlements[sic] for it and love them as You
would your own self
        Thomas Brune Aboriginal Youth[51]

The Flinders Island
Weekly chronicle
the 2 October 1837

Now my Dear friends you know that is but one
God only. The God who made the sun, and moon, and stars
and every thing that you can see round about you
would you like to pray if you would my friends
that I know some of you which now can read and
can spell words of four or five siylailb[sic] and you know
that some of them can read out of the Bible it
was was to try Because of the Bible which
is God Book and that is best Book which we
call the Bible and that of book of books and they
all understand they all know how to sing hymns
and some of them can read also
and now my friends I want to tell you
one thing what a thing it is to die without haveing
the love of God in our hearts you seen the
other day a man die which of hope is gone to Glory
Because my friend we all got to die you all got
to die some time or a another perhaps you mite[sic] die
by and by Don't tell when days shall come
You can't tell it of myself when I have got to die

> that our hearts may be fixed up God for God
> careth you
> may we learn more and more of God and of his
> Son Jesus Christ
> And now and when we are in school I always see
> Mis Thomas Brune Laughting[sic] and playing away
> in the middle of School
> The Natives of Flinders Island have being some
> time ago have being makeing[sic] themselves
> their own garden and sowing their own fruit and
> made their own fences and also other things which
> cannot express now
> and as them want to the Sisters to hunt and
> also for skins and when before returning from the
> Sisters we met some of the Native women and
> their Names were Flora and Louisa
> You said that God made you and me and the Sea
> the Mountains and the tree and the salt waters the
> hearts of them Shall say to my Soul where is
> now thy God   Trimus Wader(?)
> Walter George Arthur[52]

The Flinders Island Weekly Chronicle the 2 October 1837

Now my dear friends you know that there is but one God only, the God who made the sun and moon and stars and everything that you can seen [sic] round about you. Would you like to pray? If you would my friends that I know some of you which now can read and can spell words of four or five syllables and I know that some of them can read out of the Bible if was to try, because of the Bible which is God Book and that is best book which we call the Bible and that of book of books and they all understand and they all know how to sing hymns and some of them can read also.

And now my friends I want to tell you one thing, what a thing it is to die without having the love of God in our hearts. You seen the other day a man die which I hope is gone to glory. Because my friends we all got to die, you all got to die some time or another, perhaps you might die by and by. I can't tell when days shall come; I can't tell it of myself when I have got to die. O, that our hearts may be fixed up God, for God careth you. And may we learn more and more of God and his son Jesus Christ.

And now and when I am in school I always see Mr Thomas Brune laughing and playing away in the middle of school.

The natives of Flinders Island have been some time of go have being making themselves their own gardens and sowing their own fruit and made their own fences and also other things which cannot express now. Nine of them went to the Sisters to hunt and also for skins, and when were returning from the Sisters we met two of the native women and their names was Flora and Louisa.

You said that God made you and me and the sea and the mountains and the tree and the salt waters. The hearts of them shall say to my soul, where is now thy God.

Walter George Arthur   Thinks Walter[53]

The
Flinders Island
Weekly Chronicle
6th October 1837

The people knows that there is but one God and
over them and the people may put their trust in him
always. O what a blessing it is if we hear in words
speaking from heaven God made man he made him
like unto himself he made him holy and perfect
and happy and put him into the garden of Eden
to dress it and keep it
      My friends you are not the Children
of God by Nature we are born to sin and come forth
the short of the glory of God the people of Van D.

L. their work is Delight in their working you
must pray to God with all your hearts and
with all your soul and with all your Mind
and with all your strenght[sic]
      And now my friends you shall
see the son of man shall come in his Glory
and all the holy Angels with him then he sets
the sheep on his right and the wicked
on his left which of you think my friends
think now of yourselves would you be the
wicked one my friends you would not say now
you cannot serve two masters and when he takes
you up before is barr what will you say then you
would not say nothing at all he knows every thing
in your thoughts you ought to pray to God to give
you new hearts and a new right sprits within
you the Aboriginal male Noemy has got the love
of God shead[sic] abroad in his heart he tells them about
you and Jesus Christ and everything that is good for
them and for every body and now my Dear
brothers and sisters will you lissen[sic] to these things
whats told to you and keep it in your hearts
you knows that God made you and you knows
that Jesus Christ came into the world to die for sins
according to the scriptures and you know that
God made every things
      The commandant his magistrate over the
Flinders Island and that God may prosper him in all
is[sic] ways and that God may protect him may were[sic]
ever he goes the people of this Island may pray
to God and serve him Blesst[sic] the Lord & our souls
all that is within us blesst[sic] his holy name
the people with are in Hobart Town they are
working at Shoemakers, Taylors, blacksmiths and
gunsmiths carpenters, joiners musence(?) patimakers(?)
      Thomas Brune Aboriginal
Youth & writer & Editor[54]

The
Flinders Island Chronicle
6th of October

The people of Flinders Island have been learn about God a little but eagerly(?) must
and they are learning to read now as fast as they can but they all even a
way into the bush and get sick and they stay they will never come hom

again no they all say their [sic] is to much work for them to do
The Native women says to much work to do carring(?) grass you all day that's too much carry a little grass
I haplthy learn of God and of his Jesus Christ every day and every night when you are agoing to bed and pray to him that he may bless you in your hearts you say our father which are in heaven that you is like the God that made you because of you look what God hast told you in the Bible God wont like you nay God would like you no more he will cast you from his presentes[sic] and if and if he did God forbid. May they all love him and that when they die they go to him to be with him for ever.
And now my dear friends what was it kept you out so long a time my friends Cant you tell what it was kept you out so long a time thanks they were looking out for the sick
The people who are at the settlement they and the commandant used to give them sing(?) cabbages
You thank[sic] that you can find those things on the top of the ---ope Flinders and you thank[sic] was you can find tea and sugar upon tea tree and they can they can[sic] find the Rackar Grawning[?] upon the Gum tree as you have heard the Commandant tell you a long time up go [sic ?ago?] God who made sun and moon and stars and the all the living creatures that walketh wherein there is life which you would now ruin(?) do God is not like you or me God is a spirit and a spirit has no flesh and bones a spirit is an invisible being who is like unto him there is but one God the God who made you and me and that God would call you or me to on and in a moment of time.
That God who shall judge the [sic] (thee or them) in righteousness and in the proceeding of time God looked down from heaven to see if there were any one who was nay one that was seeking after God. And there was none no not one they were all gone a astray and they all lost the love in their hearts
And now my dear friends if there was a Gentlemen down from Hobart Town and ask among people as you Where is God in what manner would you answer them you would taught (?laught?) you would you
A Now dear my friend learn how to love God because when you die You may go up to God to be with him for ever and Sing glory to God on high and the lamb that was slayn[sic] for us and that -----
to read in this book and understanding it because there is no other to God to God[sic] but by learning out of this book because there is no other book better than this Bible
Because the Bible came from God and if it came from God it must be a good book and those who learn of that book and understand it is a far better thing than into the bush and hunt for those things which is not up much good

                Walter George Arthur
                Editor and writer[55]

The Flinders Island
Weekly Chronicle
The sixth of October 1837

The natives who are now in the settlement are learning about God and of
his son Jesus Christ they all know who to pray why don't you pray pray while
it is time because you mite fall to when you know not from whence you
are how can a man tell from whence his
The Lord is good to Black Native and he shall judge the Quick and the
dead you did not know these things when you were in your native
words no I know that you did not know nothings at all but have
the Commandant as being so kind as to gather you and now you are
learning of God and by and by ^{and} when you get to learn more and more becau^{se}
if you don't learn about God and about Jesus Christ God would like
you at all he will hid his face from you for ever wont like
you any more well then you should try to learn of God when
it is time you should try and ^{ask} yourselves where shall my soul
go to when I die why if good it go up God who give it if bad
it will sink down and there God as forsaken you will then
you should not say eyes when you are asked a question to you
how any of ^{them} people who were cast into the hell for their bad behaver[sic][56]

The
Flinders Island ~~Weekly~~ Chronicle
11th Oct 1837

The natives who are on the Settlement having
learning of God why don't you try to learn for
God is good who is like unto him — What are
the chief truths of the Christian religion One we
first to acknowledge the only God What is God +
what are his perfection — God is a spirit infinite
and eternal without beginning + without
and creator of all things and in unity of this Godhead
have but three persons of one substance pomer(?)
and authority Father Son + Holy Ghost and now
my friends God loves you all white + black of
the truth I perceive God is no respector of
persons the Lord is to all attentive and he is
present in this house now and are from hover(?)
he is Lord of all he judged the quick + the
dead you did not know anything of him
when you were in your own country in your
native woods well then you should try to learn
of God when it is done you ask yourselves
where shall my soul go when I die why if good

it will go to God if bad it will go + ^will live with
the Devil for ever + ever and there shall
be no end and the Lord said come unto me
all you that are heavy laden + will give
you rest unto your soul and when you like
to do this — perhaps you like your prayers said
to you but you never knew about prayer before
God is the father of prayer — Now my friends
you know that God loves nothing that is bad
The Settlement was not like which it now is
before the Commandant came down no but it is
another one altogether now the Comm^dt came down
see how good he is to you not like a long time
ago when there was the other people who are gone
away long since you know you had not much
to eat when the other Comm^dt was down before
You know that God made the world and stars
mountain the seas the small trees the big gum
trees the tea trees and the sand which is up on
the sea shore because you know you would
not do good thing except God be with you For
God all powerful he died the just for the
unjust that he might bring us home to God +
when you go to bed pray that he may
bless you in all your ways for God don't love
people that are wicked and who are sinful No
God does not This things my dear friends wh
don't you love the God who cause ^your corn
field ~~to grow~~ when it is ripe falleth to the ground
and then you are done away with + are gone
forever and ever and are done away with for here
is your portion There were two people one said some
words like this God be merciful unto me a
sinner and the other stood + prayed + said
God I thank thee I am not as other sin-
-ners are

    Walter George Arthur Ab^nl Youth
    Editor + Writer[57]

The Flinders Island Weekly Chronicle

The brig Tamar arrived on the 16th of October 1837

I can't tell yet what brig it is. It arrived on the 16th of October but by and by we shall hear all about what things have occurred in the neighbouring islands and now my dear friends what was that kept you out so long; now you, what good, what was you doing in the bush, such a long time ago in the bush and now you see what good have you got by stopping out so long. If you had come home sooner along with Alexander you would had plum pudding.

It was a long time ago since you first left the settlement. Thomas Brune sung out and said hullo, here comes four copper bushmen coming in from the bush. It will be a long time before the commandant will let you go again, I am certain of that, and I went outside of the commandant's office and I looked towards Mount Franklin and I behold the men aploughing in a field that in the direction of Mount Franklin on [eight?] of October 1837.

You did know nothing at all about their ploughing the ground or any thing at all. Now you see there is none of the good people alive. No, they are dead and gone, which I hope is all gone to glory and when any of you are dead perhaps you might see them again which have gone before you. If that when I die I should like to see my brothers and sisters which have gone before us to glory. And now I seen this afternoon some of the copper coloured natives have arrived again to this settlement, and I saw two people agoing shooting; and Thomas Brune has got a way of bringing dogs to the commandant's office and the clerk is always making a noise, and I saw Mr Thomas Brune come this morning to get a wheelbarrow and I asked him where he was agoing to, boy, but he would not take any thing at all, he was sulky. I think he was because Mrs Clark sent him for the wheelbarrow that was on the settlement. And I also seen Neptune scrubbing his bed tick at the lumber yard the other evening, and the people was told to go to the saw pit for to get some boards and met the sawyer on the road. Mr Walter asking him how is it that there is no boards cut. He said they shall if you all come this afternoon you can have them then, and now you heard that you that the [commandant] has being always tell you not to sleep on the ground and not sleeping upon the bed berths and where you have heat all round that's the way to the grave. May people out of the colony subscribe.

Walter George Arthur
Aboriginal youth
Editor and writer[58]

The Flinders Island Weekly Chronicle
the 24th of October 1837

And now my dear friends I want to tell you and I saw some women carrying woods upon Sunday so I want to ask Mr Clark if it right to carry wood upon Sunday. I don't think it is right to carrying wood on Sunday. No, I don't think it is right to carry woods on God's day. No, that I am sure it is not right for any one to do such a thing on his day. You should not play or work on that day. You should not do any thing on God day, you not growl, you should not kill the little robin redbreasts or the swallows or the martins for they are God's favourite birds. And also another thing, you should now throw about the soap; they have too much Mr Clark because when I am about the place I always see plenty of soap laying about. I only want to put it down that you all may know that the soap is fine thing to wash yourselves with and yet they don't care for it, no they would sooner put on that there clayey stuff what they have being always used and they like it better than they would have soap to wash they faces. And now you see all your houses are getting finished now and you will be amusing yourselves every day, and then you will be playing at all sorts of games and then you be amusing yourselves every day, and then you will not have to go for wood no more, and grass too. You will like that, yes you will like that, they will I know that well; and on Sunday last week as I was taking a walk round the field, two of us we stood and two was me and Washington, and Washington said to me, why is it that the wheat rise up itself, it don't up by itself jump up, it no but the Great God that would living you and me to an end of a moment of time.

And I seen the native women and what they was doing I cant tell, and I saw a man carrying a ringtail possum. And I also saw the native men at work in the garden and I think they at gathering the thistles that was growing in the garden. There was about 10 or 11 there was and I also saw some of the women awalking around the stockyard, and I also saw a running race between two boys this morning; I seen them run as fast as they would and their names was Teddy and John Franklin, and Franklin meant Teddy begin to fight; and I also saw Charlie Clark kill a redbreast.

Walter George Arthur
editor and writer[59]

The Flinders Island Weekly Chronicle
28th October 1837

On the 25th October Commandant was given us a lecture upon Pneumatics. The people were drest up as in the same as we was going to church the white people also they were drest up as well as them and the Officers and the militaries and they were all assemble together in the school houses.

Then the commandant took a shilling and feather was put on a ruler and commandant let them down and one fell down as quick as the other and what caused the feather swim so long in the air because the feather is much lighter than this shilling if there was no air at all we could not live and the feather and a shilling would fall down both in the same time.

The commandant took a glass in his hand and put water in it then afterwards he put on his hand and turned the glass upon the paper and what caused the paper to keep the water in between the glass and the paper because the pressure of the air was under it and that keeps the water up.

The birds swim in the air just in the same way of the fishes swim in the water. You say the same that bird is go wing. Well, just in the same way of the fishes they got fins the birds make use of their wings and the fishes make use of their fins and their tails.

Some times see then large pelicans flying over the settlement with their wings stretched out and what makes them pelicans fly so easily because the air keeps them up.

What is the cause of the success drawing immense wheat my friends dont you see that success draws immense wheat.

And now my friends you must learn all these things and when these things was told you on the 25th October you ought to keep these things in your heads and remember it.

And you knows who made all these things.

Thomas Brune
Aboriginal youth
editor and writer[60]

The Flinders Island Weekly Chronicle
9th November 1837

The natives is making road in the forest in the rear of the commandant's quarters and women also carrying grass this morning and the native men also they were carrying wood they are working all day. The settlement is a fine situation. I say that the people is very well off on the settlement they get every thing and what more can they want. My good friends you must not take one another's things and you must not steal from one another. You know that the commandant don't like it and when you are agrowling the Devil is there it is the Devil that makes you fight. God does not love people who steal.

I saw the native women going to work at making their gowns. They was getting crawfish yesterday on the pig island.

The people is very good but the people are not good in Jesus Christ. I saw Edward come in the Commandant's office and I give him pen and paper and he began to write on the paper.

And he began to laugh at me. I before give paper to Achilles and he began to laugh and I seen the native men playing spears today. Some of the people love to put on red ochre and grease which is very bad work.

Thomas Brune
Aboriginal youth
Editor and writer[61]

The Flinders Island Weekly Chronicle
the 16th of November 1837

And now you see that all your houses are getting finished they will be done in a very short time.

And when the houses are all finished I hope you will have prayers always and when you can learn to read books and mind what your teachers say to you and you should try to spell in your lessons and try to ask each other you ask the parson when you see him he always goes down and see how you are all getting on there are but three houses at present and they will be very soon done and now you see how kind the commandant is to you you ought to try to learn much because if you do not learn it will be the worse for you my friends but you cannot learn a bit too much no my friends that you cannot.

And the white men are making a fence to the barley field and 2 of the aborigines native boys are eng[??] and the brig arrived at Green Island on the 26th of November 1837 and the native aboriginal Ajax when to hunt after the rats and mouses and would sooner he would go after them things than he would take up a book and began to try to learn and read no but he would sooner rather go and hunt for to fill his belly he think that there is not enough to eat at the settlement to fill his belly but if he was to take that fine books which is Gods book and if Ajax would read he would not be so fond of hunt as he is liking.

Walter George Arthur
Editor and writer[62]

Sermon May 1838

My friends I want to tell you there is but God over you and me that God who made the heaven and the earth the seas and all that are in the world and if you pray to him you will have eternal life if you dont pray you will have eternal punishment and when Jesus Christ come again into the world and shall set good on his right hand and the wicked on his left and when the last sentence comes upon you if you are bad then you will be in Hell for ever and ever in pain and torment O my friends pray while it is time draw nigh to God and he will draw nigh to you.

Now my friends would you like to be good if you would be good pray night and day it will bring you to a place of happiness if you like to pray God will hear you when you offer up your prayers and supplications and to make other people pray too as well as yourself.

There will be a great day of judgment when all the people arise up before the great God who made the heaven and the earth when all the people gives an account of all the things that are done in our bodies whether they be good or bad.

Now my friends let us love the Lord they God with all our hearts with all our souls and with all our strength love thy neighbour our selves if we do not we have eternal punishment and there we will be in torment where the fire is not quenched for ever. Dont you think my friends their a God all yes my friends God is over all blessed be his name this morning Jesus Christ is the same yesterday and today and forever.

And now my friends swear not at all for God knoweth the hearts of men whether they be good or bad there will a day of judgment when all the people whell before him.

Thomas Brune Editor and writer
at the Commandants Office[63]

(Plomley's Note: This sermon seems quite unreal, a mere copy of the words of G.A. Robinson or Robert Clark. Other sermons are dated 16 December 1837, 1 January and 6, 20 February 1838, and are signed by either Walter George Arthur or Thomas Bruney).[64]

ENDNOTES APPENDICES

1. Hobart, TAHO RGD 32. Launceston, George Town and Campbell Town, TAHO NG 748/1-5.
2. TAHO SWD 28/1/1.P
3. Plomley, N. J. B. 1976, *A Word List of Tasmanian Aboriginal Languages*. Launceston; Foot and Playstead, pp. 41, 42.
4. ML Walker Papers, G W Walker 9 Dec 1833, B727, CY1408, p. 313.
5. ML Robinson Papers, A7044 CY548, pp. 39-40.
6. ML Robinson Papers, A7044 CY548, p. 41.
7. ML Robinson Papers, A7044 CY548, pp. 43-44.
8. ML Robinson Papers, A7044 CY548, pp. 47-48.
9. ML Robinson Papers, A7044 CY548, pp. 49-50.
10. ML Robinson Papers, A7044 CY548, pp. 51-52.
11. ML Robinson Papers, A7044 CY548, p. 54.
12. ML Robinson Papers, A7044 CY548, pp. 45-46.
13. ML Robinson Papers, A7044 CY548, p. 48.
14. ML Robinson Papers, A7044 CY548, p. 54.
15. ML Robinson Papers, A7044 CY548, pp. 49-50.
16. ML Robinson Papers, A7044 CY548, pp. 49-50.
17. ML Robinson Papers, A7044 CY548, pp. 53-54.
18. ML Robinson Papers, A7044 CY548, p. 54.
19. ML Robinson Papers, A7044 CY548, p. 40.
20. ML Robinson Papers, A7044 CY548, p. 49.
21. ML Robinson Papers, A7044 CY548, pp. 49-50.
22. ML Robinson Papers, A7044 CY548, p. 54.
23. ML Robinson Papers, A7044 CY548, pp. 51-52.
24. ML Robinson Papers, A7044 CY548, p. 54.
25. ML Robinson Papers, A7044 CY548, pp. 38-39.
26. ML Robinson Papers, A7044 CY548, p. 40.
27. ML Robinson Papers, A7044 CY548, p. 42.
28. ML Robinson Papers, A7044 CY548, pp. 44-45.
29. ML Robinson Papers, A7044 CY548, p. 48.
30. ML Robinson Papers, A7044 CY548, p. 51.
31. ML Robinson Papers, A7044 CY548, p. 54.
32. ML Robinson Papers, A7044 CY548, p. 54.
33. ML Robinson Papers, A7074 CY825, p.1.
34. ML Robinson Papers, A7074 CY825, p. 2.
35. ML Robinson Papers, A7074 CY825, p. 3.
36. ML Robinson Papers, A7074 CY825, p. 4.
37. ML Robinson Papers, A7074 CY825, p. 5.
38. ML Robinson Papers, A7074 CY825, p. 6.
39. ML Robinson Papers, A7074 CY825, p. 7.
40. ML Robinson Papers, A7074 CY825, p. 8.
41. ML Robinson Papers, A7074 CY825, p. 9.
42. ML Robinson Papers, A7074 CY825, p. 10.
43. ML Robinson Papers, A7074 CY825, p. 11.
44. Plomley, N. J. B., 1987, *Weep in Silence*. Hobart; Blubber Head Press, Appendix IV: C, p. 1009.
45. ML Robinson Papers, A7074 CY825, p. 13 & 14.
46. ML Robinson Papers, A7074 CY825, pp. 15 & 16.
47. Plomley, 1987, p. 1009.
48. ML Robinson Papers, A7074 CY825, p. 17.
49. ML Robinson Papers, A7074 CY825, p. 19.
50. ML Robinson Papers, A7074, CY825, p. 20.
51. ML Robinson Papers, A7074 CY825, p. 22.
52. ML Robinson Papers, A7074, CY825, p. 23.
53. Plomley, 1987, p. 1010.
54. ML Robinson Papers, ML7074, CY 825, p. 25.
55. ML Robinson Papers, ML7074, CY 825, p. 27 (page 26 is blank)
56. ML Robinson Papers, ML7074, CY 825, p. 29.
57. ML Robinson Papers, A7044 CY548, pp. 118-120.
58. Plomley, 1987, p. 1011.
59. Plomley, 1987, p. 1011.
60. Plomley, 1987, p. 1012.
61. Plomley, 1987, p. 1012.
62. Plomley, 1987, p. 1013.
63. Plomley 1987, p. 1014.
64. Plomley, 1987, p. 1014.

APPENDIX F

Wybalenna Chronology

1831	October–December Robinson in Big River
1831	November 10th Settlement moved from Gun Carriage Island to "The Lagoons" [Plomley, 1987, p. 57]
1832	February–November Robinson in North west
1832	March 1st W J Darling replaced Wight as Commandant [Plomley, 1987, p. 57]
1832	Backhouse and Walker's first visit [Plomley, 1987, p. 57]
1832	Government 'awards' 100 ewes and 3 rams to the Aborigines involved in the 'conciliatory mission' [ML Robinson Papers A7074 CY548]
1832	September 22nd Mr William Budd appointed to take charge of stores [ML Robinson Papers A7062 CY549 p. 10]
1832	October 16th Darling went to north west to get Aborigines captured by George Robinson, plus brought four women from among the sealers returned in November [Plomley, 1987, p. 62]
1832	November 25th Darling visited Hobart, left Maclachlan in charge, taking 9 Aborigines and 1 half-caste boy a son of a sealer. Of the 9 only 4 (1 girl & 3 boys) could speak English, the 3 boys taken to Orphan School [Plomley, 1987, p. 63]
1832	December–1833 October Robinson at Macquarie Harbour
1833	January 10th Darling arrived back at "the Lagoons" [Plomley, 1987, p. 63]
1833	February 10th Settlement moved from "The Lagoons" to Wybalenna [Plomley, 1987, p. 57]
1833	May Budds left the settlement [Plomley, 1987, p. 68]
1833	June 1st & 4th Mr & Mrs Wilkinson appointed to instruct Aborigines on Flinders Island [ML Robinson Papers A7062 CY549 pp. 27, 29–30]
1833	June Thomas Wilkinson arrived with Louisa and four children [Plomley, 1987, p. 69]
1833	June 18th Mr & Mrs Dickenson appointed as storekeeper on Flinders Island [ML Robinson Papers A7062 CY549 p. 39]
1833	August Loftus Dickenson arrived to become storekeeper in place of Budds [Plomley, 1987, p. 68]
1833	September Wilkinson wrote to Arthur with translation of principal parts of Genesis
1833	October conflict between Darling and Wilkinson
1833	October 13th William Budds and wife arrive as store keeper, on same boat as Backhouse and Walker's second visit [Plomley, 1987, p. 62] re: Wilkinson's translation and conflict

78 natives and 4 infants in a total of 111 total settlement population.

1833	November 20th Fifteen Aborigines from the neighbourhood of Port Davey who surrendered to Mr Robinson and his party to be transported to Flinders Island [ML Robinson Papers A7062 CY549 p. 51] These would have come from Macquarie Harbour area Dec '32–Oct '33
1833	December Allen replaced McLachlan as surgeon [Plomley, 1987, p. 71] Allen later (Sept 1837) reported there were eighty-seven Natives and fifty Europeans at the time [ML Robinson Papers A7066 CY551 pp. 201–221]
1833	December–1834 August Robinson doing 'last remnant on west coast'
1834	January 10th Governor approved 50 heifers and 700 sheep to be at adjacent islands [ML Robinson Papers A7062 CY549 pp. 57–58]
1834	January Backhouse and Walker report to Arthur re: Wilkinson, Darling arguments [ML GW Walker Papers]
1834	January 12th Moriarty (Port Officer) to Nickolls Commandant re: supply of a new whale boat for transporting sheep from islands to the settlement [ML Robinson Papers A7062 CY549 pp. 59–60]
1834	March 19th Governor approved Brickmaker, labourer and two shoemakers to the Settlement [ML Robinson Papers A7062 CY549 p. 73]
1834	April 14th Wilkinson left the settlement [Plomley, 1987, p. 70]
1834	July 11th Robert Clark appointed as catechist [ML Robinson Papers A7062 CY549 p. 79]
1834	July 24th Darling left Wybalenna and James Allen put in charge until new Commandant arrived [Plomley, 1987, p. 78]
1834	July 27th Darling (63rd Regiment) left Flinders Island, J Allen (Surgeon) in charge until 23rd September 1834 [Robinson Papers A7066 CY551 p. 227]
1834	August Robert Clark appointed as catechist [Plomley, 1987, p. 71]
1834	August 12th Montague (CSO) requesting Darling to provide monthly rather than 3-monthly returns for the Settlement [ML Robinson Papers A7062 CY549 p. 83]
1834	September 6th audit of stock by Dickenson, supplies are desperately low [ML Robinson Papers A7062 CY549 p. 89]
1834	September 24th Henry Nickolls arrived, with wife and five children, to take up position of Commandant [Plomley, 1987, p. 78] until 9th November 1835 [Robinson Papers A7066 CY551 p. 227] This date in November is after Robinson arrived
1834	October 1st Nickolls Settlement Order 4, Natives going to Green Island for muttonbird will be issued with biscuit in lieu of flour [ML Robinson Papers A7074 CY825 Settlement Order 4]
1834	October 7th Montague to 'Commandant' re: Jackey an Aborigine from NSW sent to VDL under sentence for life for murder [ML Robinson Papers A7062 CY549 p. 91]
1834	November 7th Montague to Nickolls Esq 'quantity of flour as will prevent scarcity' [ML Robinson Papers A7062 CY549 pp. 93–96]
1834	November 12th Supply of stores [ML Robinson Papers A7062 CY549 p. 97]

1834	November 15th Rations issued: Monday Aborigines 10 o'clock, Military 12 o'clock; Every Saturday Civil Officers 10 o'clock, Prisoners 12 o'clock [ML Robinson Papers A7074 CY825 Settlement Order 8]
1834	November 25th Settlement Order: on advice of surgeon ration of beef for Aborigines increased from 12 oz to one pound per diem [ML Robinson Papers A7074 CY825 Settlement Order 10]
1834	November 29th Daily scale of rations Civil Officers: Meat 1 lb fresh or salt, flour 1 lb, sugar 2 oz, tea 1/4 oz, salt 1/2 oz, soap 1/2 oz, vinegar 1/4 quart, candles 2 oz, oil 1/2 gill(?), spirits may be issued in lieu of tea, sugar, soap and salt. Aborigines: meat 1 lb fresh or salt, flour 1-5-3/7, spirits 1/28 gallon, vinegar 1/4 quart, 1/6 oz candles. (Same rations for officers, Aborigines, prisoners), some wives of military received additional allowance [ML Robinson Papers A7062 CY549 pp. 107–108]
1834	December 3rd Clark appointed to distribute rations of the Aborigines [ML Robinson Papers A7074 CY825 Settlement Order 11]
1834	December 15th Montague to Commandant, whole of rations approved "with the exception of full rations to the Catechist's children who are only entitled to half rations which under case of age"[ML Robinson Papers A7062 CY549 p. 115]
1834	December 18th Montague to the Commandant, Lieut Gov does not approve of your employing the Aborigines in boats and wishes that you should discourage the practice, instructions given to Principal Superintendent to furnish four men as crew [ML Robinson Papers A7062 CY549 pp. 111–112]
1834	December 20th Montague to Commandant, Lieut Gov most likely method of bringing the natives to habits of civilisation and industry will be by gradually withdrawing them from their former customs in doing so however much caution and circumspection is evidently necessary and the carrying [of] such a measure into effect must mainly depend upon the manner of supplying the means within your power ... Lieut Gov never objected to provision of live stock... Lieut Gov disapproves of practice of issuing to the Natives a week's rations at a time [ML Robinson Papers A7062 CY549 pp. 119–126]
1834	December 20th Montague to Commandant Catechist's wife to be involved in instructing the native women and children, "to make herself as useful as possible by affording them every instruction and assistance in her power" [ML Robinson Papers A7062 CY549 p. 127]
1834	December 20th Cask of rum sent to the settlement to be returned [ML Robinson Papers A7062 CY549 pp. 129–130]
1835	February 11th Settlement Order 'not any prisoner is allowed to come to that part of the Settlement occupied by the natives unless especially addressed to do so by the Commandant ... any dealings of any kind between the natives and the prisoners is strictly prohibited ... white house holders are generally requested and prisoners ordered to discourage the visits of the natives to their small dwellings ... if civil officers are desirous of the services of the natives the Commandant will be happy to allow the same but expects, indeed requests, to be applied to for such indulgence [ML Robinson Papers A7074 CY825 Settlement Order 13]

1835	February 19th Letter from Commandant [Nickolls] to CSO re: (five?) children removed to Orphan School but no explanation about why [ML Robinson Papers A7062 CY549 p. 161]
1835	April 28th Clark letter reports servants one a prisoner and the other a 14 year old girl "coming to a knowledge of the truth", reading Bible to her parents each evening, attending Clark's day school, beginning of Sabbath School, Aboriginal people [ML Robinson Papers A7062 CY549 pp. 165-169]
1835	May 21st Governor approved a "hospital" at Flinders Island for sick Aborigines [ML Robinson Papers A7062 CY549 p. 181]
1835	May 28th Col Sec to Commandant "You ought not have undertaken additions to buildings without previous authority" [ML Robinson Papers A7062 CY549 pp. 185-186]
1835	May Catechist's Report re: conflict between two main tribes [ML Robinson Papers A7074 Part 6 CY825]
1835	May 28th & 31st Col Sec to Commandant re: undertake post mortems "if not likely to cause alarm amongst Aborigines. [ML Robinson Papers A7074 Part 6 CY825] [Robinson Papers A7062 CY549 pp. 187-190]
1835	June 20th Appointment of convicts James Littleton Lotus as baker and Isaac Mendoza John on loan for six months [ML Robinson Papers A7062 CY549 p. 203]
1835	July 30th Col Sec received letter about "scenes of a disgusting nature that have taken place among the Aborigines in Mr Dickenson's presence", statement is imperfect, cannot understand [ML Robinson Papers A7062 CY549 pp. 205-206]
1835	July 30th Col Sec to Commandant, Lieut Gov will approve whatever additions are necessary to the buildings for the officers but nothing more [ML Robinson Papers A7062 CY549 p. 209]
1835	October W Nickolls reports that sheep flock is now 199 [ML Robinson Papers CY548]
1835	October Robinson leaves Hobart to become Commandant
1835	October 17th Robinson arrives at Settlement on Tamar [ML Robinson Papers A7044 Vol 23 CY548]
1835	October 24th Clark to Robinson re: schools, Clark seeking permission to address the Congregation [ML Robinson Papers A7062 CY549 p. 215]
1835	October 27th Clark to Robinson Class report progress from Alphabet Class to words [ML Robinson Papers A7062 CY549 p. 233f]
1835	October 28th Clark to Robinson re: removal of prisoner from his (Clark's) service [ML Robinson Papers A7062 CY549 p. 217]
1835	October 29th Clark to Robinson re: deaths in recent months [ML Robinson Papers A7062 CY549 p. 221]
1835	October 29th Clark to Robinson re: Ben Lomond people out hunting, sometimes returning to the Settlement [ML Robinson Papers A7062 CY549 p. 223]
1835	October 20th Allen to Robinson re: causes of deaths, suitability of housing, suitability of current site

1835	November 2nd Catechist report of absentees from Divine Service [ML Robinson Papers A7062 CT549 p. 235]
1835	November 2nd Nickolls with location as "Wybalenna Flinders Island" — all others use "Flinders Island Settlement"[ML Robinson Papers A7062 CY549 p. 241]
1835	November 2nd Nickolls — reception of 100 ewes, Native rations at one hundred and twenty requiring 100 ewes and 20 cows [ML Robinson Papers A7063 CY549 p. 243]
1835	November 9th Clark to Robinson re: capabilities of Natives in receiving instruction including request that Thos Brunsey be brought from Hobart Town [ML Robinson Papers A7062 CY549 pp. 255-258]
1835	November 11th Robinson to Allen to mark out ground for Government Garden, Soldiers Garden, select double Native hut for School and Chapel (consult with Catechist), these huts will be abandoned due to unsuitable for habitation; examine Catechist's quarters and plan for the Native children accommodated there; should Natives be encamped in the bush or in cottages at present on Settlement; whether the two flocks (Government and Aborigines) be placed on same island, similar for sheep; Should Aborigines be in more sheltered abode? [ML Robinson Papers A7062 CY549 pp. 263-265]
1835	November 11th Settlement Order Mrs Clark to superintend the Native Women [ML Robinson Papers A7062 CY549 p. 267]
1835	November 11th Prisoners are not permitted to keep dogs, tobacco no longer a ration but Commandant reserves right to issue it as he thinks deserving as stimulus to industry and good conduct [ML Robinson Papers A7062 CY549 pp. 267, 269]
1835	November 11th Public Service on the Sabbath will commence at o'clock in the morning and o'clock in the afternoon and the bell will toll until such time as the service commences [ML Robinson Papers A7062 CY549 p. 267]
1835	November 11th Settlement Order banning any seducing or bartering between prisoners and Aborigines [ML Robinson Papers A7062 CY549 p. 269]
1835	November 12th Return of fresh meat distributed Oct 1834–Nov 1835 [ML Robinson Papers A7062 CY549 p. 273]
1835	November 16th Allen to Robinson plots of ground for Gardens, most northerly of Native huts selected for School and Chapel require fireplace and chimney in south end, a window on each side and in the gable, floor with sugar mats with plastering and whitewash be sufficient for the present, berth in one of the rooms of the kitchen for boys to sleep in. Pigs on Isabella Is; Goats on any; Aborigines' sheep (largest flock) Prime Seal; Gov sheep Green or Kangaroo Is; Aborigines need sheltered huts, ought not be confined to those presently used [ML Robinson Papers A7062 CY549 pp. 277-279]
1835	November 25th Clark to Robinson re: Allen on Kangaroo Island with Aborigines collecting mutton bird eggs when boat from Launceston 2 men and 1 boy collecting bird eggs [ML Robinson Papers A7062 CY549 p. 285]
1835	December 2nd Roll of Aborigines School — Boys from 1st Nov 1835 with Catechist's comments on each boy [ML Robinson Papers A7062 CY549 pp. 292-4]
1835	December 4th School moved from house next to Commandants to the upper house[ML Robinson Papers A7062 CY549 p. 300]
1835	December 4th *Manalakina* died

1835	December 11th Clark to Robinson with requisition for materials for Adult school, and thanks for writing papers for Boys School [ML Robinson Papers A7062 CY549 p. 303]
1835	December 14th Clark to Robinson, weekly school report [ML Robinson Papers A7062 CY549 p. 305]
1835	December 14th Clark to Robinson, sharing his unused rations of beef and pork since the Aborigines went hunting the previous July [ML Robinson Papers A7062 CY549 p. 307]
1835	December 14th Allen states Bullock Driver Daniel Murrell stole potatoes from paddock [ML Robinson Papers A7062 CY549 pp. 308-314]
1835	December 15th Clark to Robinson re: people falling asleep in Divine Worship [ML Robinson Papers A7062 CY549 pp. 315-317]
1835	December 19th Catherine Clark to Robinson report of Aboriginal women making gowns [ML Papers A7062 CY549 pp. 319-320]
1835	December 23rd death of woman, Nobic-? [ML Robinson Papers A7062 CY549 p. 323]
1835	December 23rd Several charges against Daniel Murrell stealing potatoes, neglect of duty, insolence. Statements by James Clarkson re seeing Aborigines taking potatoes during funeral "parmatta apples" and statement by Frederick Phipps not seeing them[ML Robinson Papers A7062 CY549 p. 327-329] John Webb charged with gross violation of Settlement Order, on 25th Dec gave native women milk in Commandant's kitchen[ML Robinson Papers A7062 CY549 p. 330]
1835	December 24th Death of Aboriginal man, Noura [ML Robinson Papers A7062 CY549 p. 335]
1836	January 1st Settlement Order for hoisting the flag when vessel appears, anchored, and on Sabbath day, sun up to sun set [ML Robinson Papers A7062 CY549 p. 331]
1836	January 6th Western Natives returned from hunting, served with flour and tobacco for the day [ML Robinson Papers A7062 CY549 Vol 42 p. 5]
1836	January 6th Cranky Dick left Settlement alone to go hunting, face Big River tribe [ML Robinson Papers A7062 CY549 p. 7]
1836	January 7th Hector left Settlement alone to go hunting, meet two Natives who left yesterday [ML Robinson Papers A7062 CY549 p. 9]
1836	January 15th Robinson gives new names to some Aborigines when they are at a separate table at his house for tea [Plomley, 1987, p. 336]
1836	January 18th-28th series of charges against convicts by Dickenson and others [ML Robinson Papers A7062 CY549 pp. 17-22]
1836	January 30th Report of two Native girls and Clark's daughter (5 years of age) accosted by Hawker and Bullock Driver who wanted eldest girl to "go into the bush" [ML Robinson Papers A7062 CY549 p. 25]
1836	February 8th Schools Committee established for the instruction of Aboriginal people [ML Robinson Papers A7064 Vol 43 CY550 p. 295]

Coincided with Robinson's completed list of new names for all Aboriginal people [Plomley, 1987, p. 344]

1836	February 16th Mrs Clark report to Robinson re: Native women [ML Robinson Papers A7062 CY549 pp. 25-37, 63-64] Instructions for the overseers of the female natives [ML Robinson Papers A7062 CY549 pp. 73-74] Inventory of articles in new cottages, Lalla Rookh, Queen Elizabeth and King Romeo [ML Robinson Papers A7062 CY549 p. 75]
1836	February 22nd Dickenson receives supplies including 24 slates and 1000 slate pencils [ML Robinson Papers A7062 CY549 p. 65-68]
1836	February 24th Governor orders that six month's supplies be always on hand at the Settlement [ML Robinson Papers A7062 CY549 p. 87]
1836	February 26th Report by Clark on the students in his class [ML Robinson Papers A7062 CY549 p. 87 100]
1836	February 29th Mrs Clark report to Robinson re: native women, soldier's wives in charge; saw natives making their dampers on Sabbath [ML Robinson Papers A7062 CY549 pp. 111-113]
1836	February Attendance of teachers [ML Robinson Papers A7064 Vol 43 CY550 p. 181]
1836	March 1st Clark's report re: first month of Sunday and weekday schools [ML Robinson Papers A7062 CY549 pp. 145-146]
1836	March 2nd Letter Robinson to his son, George re: Aborigines "still at large". 9 Aborigines on way to Launceston from Charles Robinson [ML Robinson Papers A7062 CY549 pp. 147-150]
1836	March 3rd inventory of items in Aboriginal people's houses [ML Robinson Papers A7062 CY549 pp. 154-155]
1836	March 13th Robinson & Natives departed for Launceston in Isabella [ML Robinson Papers A7044 Vol 23 CY548]
1836	March 2nd Rations to the Aborigines, to such Aborigines as are averse to salt meat, one pound of flour, a quarter an ounce of tea and two ounces of sugar will be substituted in lieu thereof but on the occasion of fresh meat being allowed the committed allowance will not be found [ML Robinson Papers A7062 CY549 p. 123]
1836	March 7th Bell will toll at six and convicts expected to make themselves in orderly manner to attend the service [ML Robinson Papers A7062 CY549 p. 124]
1836	March 7th J Allen, Memo ophthalmic infection contagious 16 to 20 days, no security against a new attack, fever [ML Robinson Papers A7062 CY549 pp. 167-168]
1836	March Attendance of pupils and teachers at weekday evening and Sabbath schools [ML Robinson Papers A7064 Vol 43 p. 182]
1836	March 29th Report of Major Ryan on the state of the Aborigines at the Settlement Clark speaking in "their language" and in English [ML Robinson Papers A7062 CY549 pp. 213-257]
1836	April 9th Robinson to J Montague CSO re: "probably expenses of Aboriginal Settlement 1st January-31st December 1837 [ML Robinson Papers A7044 Vol 23 CY548 pp. 1-3]Probably in response to Ryan's report
1836	April 9th etc Robinson in Hobarton writing some letters, [he was away while Ryan visited and reported] including appreciation to certain gentlemen in Bothwell who are endeavouring to arrange a suitable appreciation of Robinson's labours. Also letter

to Major Ryan "Soldiers wives are not suitable to work among Aboriginal females, I expect to leave Hobarton in about a fortnight" [ML Robinson Papers A7044 Vol 23 CY548]

1836 April 6th Clark report to Robinson re: schools [ML Robinson Papers A7062 CY549 pp. 291–293]

1836 April 11th Statements from Clara and Big Bett re: Phipps and Webb 'connecting' with (raping) them [ML Robinson Papers A7062 CY549 pp. 297–311]

1836 April 17th Ryan to Robinson re: two prisoners Phipps and Webb's 'cohabiting' with two native women [ML Robinson Papers A7062 CY549 pp. 295-297]

1836 April Letters from Jorgenson to Robinson, in jail wanting to borrow two dollars [ML Robinson Papers A7062 CY549 pp. 323–326]

1836 April Attendance of pupils and teachers at weekday evening and Sabbath schools [ML Robinson Papers A7064 Vol 43 pp. 182–183]

1835 April Return of absent days at Sabbath and weekday evening schools for March and April [ML Robinson Papers A7062 CY549 p. 337]

1836 May 16th Commandant appointed Magistrate Flinders Island [ML Robinson Papers A7062 CY549 pp. 349–350]

1836 May 20th List of Stores (extensive!) [ML Robinson Papers A7062 CY549 pp. 359–367]

1836 May Attendance of pupils and teachers at weekday evening and Sabbath schools [ML Robinson Papers A7064 Vol 43 p. 183]

1836 June 4th Request for list of prisoners at Settlement [ML Robinson Papers A7062 CY549 p. 383]

1836 June 17th Commandant and family arrived at Wybalenna on Tamar [ML Robinson Papers A7044 Vol 23 CY548]

Victualling list of Aborigines proceeding to Flinders Island aboard the Government Brig Tamar 28th May to 18th June 1836 being 22 days: Thomas Brune (spelling is somewhat unclear, the ru could be ui), Thomas Thomson Marone, Mary Ann Thomson Moana [ML ROBINSON Papers A573 CY940 p. 93]

1836 June 27th Robinson to Captain Moriarty re: note accompanying Native canoe [ML Robinson Papers A7062 CY549 pp. 407–408]

1836 June Attendance of pupils and teachers at weekday evening and Sabbath schools [ML Robinson Papers A7064 Vol 43 p. 183]

1836 July 1st Robinson to Montague re: first report since arriving at the Settlement after 16 days at sea [ML Robinson Papers A7044 Vol 23 CY548 pp. 11–14]

1836 July 1st Robinson to Montague re: shipments of birds and sheep to Launceston [ML Robinson Papers A7044 Vol 23 CY548 pp. 14–15]

1836 July 1st Robinson to Montague re: possibility of sourcing sheep and cattle for Flinders Island from Sydney due to high prices in V D L [ML Robinson Papers A7044 Vol 23 CY548 p. 15]

1836 July Robinson to Montague re: inferior quality of cloth supplied to the Settlement [ML Robinson Papers A7044 Vol 23 CY548 p. 16]

1836	July Robinson to Montague re: requesting a flagellator because of the increasing number of convicts supplied to the Settlement [ML Robinson Papers A7044 Vol 23 CY548 p. 17]
1836	July Robinson to Montague re: Settlement launch Harmony so badly damaged as to require a man to continually employed to bale her out [ML Robinson Papers A7044 Vol 23 CY548 pp. 17-19]
1836	July Robinson to Dickinson (storekeeper) to remit to the Aborigines the amounts owed for skins purchased prior to Robinson arriving [ML Robinson Papers A7044 Vol 23 CY548 p. 22]
1836	July Robinson to Montague re: remaining amount of £50 owed to his son for services rendered in pursuit of the hostile natives in 1831. Of the £71 promised, only £21 so far paid [ML Robinson Papers A7044 Vol 23 CY548 p. 23]
1836	July Robinson to Montague re: 3 deer that arrived in April are progressing, request a buck of the same species; also request a hive of bees and fruit trees and vines for an orchard [ML Robinson Papers A7044 Vol 23 CY548 p. 23]
1836	July Robinson to Montague re: punishment of prisoners Webb + Phipps "the only evidence of criminal connexion was the (Native) woman herself ... Catechist could not instruct them in nature of an oath" [ML Robinson Papers A7044 Vol 23 CY548 pp. 24-25]
1836	July Robinson to Spode Esq Prin: Supt re: payment of 1/- per diem to prisoner Overseer and Constable [ML Robinson Papers A7044 Vol 23 CY548 p. 26]
1836	July Attendance of pupils and teachers at weekday evening and Sabbath schools [ML Robinson Papers A7064 Vol 43 p. 184]
1836	July 12th Mr Clark appointed Acting Storekeeper while Dickinson leaves with sick wife [ML Robinson Papers A7064 Voc 43 CY550 p19] [ML Robinson Papers A7044 Vol 23 CY548 p. 23]
1836	July 26th Montague to Robinson re: "insurmountable problems in removing Aborigines from Flinders Island to coast of New Holland" Lt Gov hopes to accede to your employment in Port Philip [ML Robinson Papers A7064 Vol 43 CY550 pp. 45-48]
1836	July 27th Robinson to Montague re: receiving 50 wethers via Shamrock as a supply of fresh meat for Aborigines [ML Robinson Papers A7044 Vol 23 CY548 p. 44]
1836	July 27th Robinson to Mr Neale, George Town requesting two or three Cape of Good Hope geese [ML Robinson Papers A7044 Vol 23 CY548 p. 47]
1836	July 30th Montague to Robinson requiring 3 month advance requirement for ordinance and providing for full examination of ordinances [ML Robinson Papers A7064 Vol 43 CY550 pp. 51-53]
1836	July Robinson to Montague re: extensive report on the Settlement (health, school, etc) [ML Robinson Papers A7044 Vol 23 CY548 p. 26-40]
1836	August 1st Hopkinson to Robinson re: sheep at Prime Seal and requirements for stores [ML Robinson Papers A7064 Vol 43 CY550 p. 55]
1836	August 3rd Dickenson to Col Sec (while in Hobart) re: request increase in remuneration [ML Robinson Papers A7064 Vol 43 CY550 pp. 57-59]

1836	August 3rd Robinson to Montague et al re: four convicts broke into the store, then stole the two whale boats and absconded [ML Robinson Papers A7044 Vol 23 CY548 pp. 47-50]
1836	August 4th Whitcomb to Robinson re: Robinson's house improvements in New Town Road and busts of Robinson and *Wurati* and his wife; 'no word yet on new Governor's name' [ML Robinson Papers A7064 Vol 43 CY550 pp. 61-64]
1836	August 12th Mr Miller to Robinson report following inspection of sheep at Prime Seal Island [ML Robinson Papers A7064 Vol 43 CY550 p. 79]
1836	August 17th Robinson to Clark re: daily ration to juvenile Aborigines; also "Oil and cotton does not form a component of the daily ration" [ML Robinson Papers A7044 Vol 23 CY548 p. 50]
1836	August 17th Robinson to Mrs Clark re: clothing made for the Aboriginal women, seeking list of names of those to receive the clothing [ML Robinson Papers A7044 Vol 23 CY548 p. 52]
1836	August 17th Robinson to Allen and Clark re: Mr Budds complaint about the quality of mutton birds supplied in Launceston [ML Robinson Papers A7044 Vol 23 CY548 p. 52]
1836	August 22nd Robinson to Capt Davis to bring half the sheep from Prime Seal to prevent them all dying for lack of food [ML Robinson Papers A7044 Vol 23 CY548 p. 52]
1836	August 28th & 29th Surgeon Allen and Catechist Clark flurry of notes and letters to Robinson complaining about each other's lack of supply of rations or suitable bedding for the Aborigines, particularly the children [ML Robinson Papers A7064 vol 43 CY550 pp. 110-130] [ML Robinson Papers A7044 Vol 23 CY548 pp. 53-55]
1836	August 31st Names of Aborigines listed [ML Robinson Papers A7064 Vol 43 CY550 p. 131] 178 Adults: 59 men and 119 women
1836	August 31st Ceasing giving salted meat to Aborigines in favour of fresh meat only, and flour in lieu of salted meat, salt meat to white inhabitants only. Robinson 'very humble servant' to Montague CSO [ML Robinson Papers A7064 Vol 43 CY550 p. 133] [ML Robinson Papers A7044 Vol 23 CY548 p. 61]
1836	August Attendance of pupils and teachers at weekday evening and Sabbath schools [ML Robinson Papers A7064 Vol 43 p. 184]
1836	August Robinson to Allen Weekly market (on Tuesdays) instituted for the Aborigines, Allen required to be present since he is in member of the Committee of Management of the Native property [ML Robinson Papers A7044 Vol 23 CY548 p. 53]
1836	September 2nd Muster of Convicts 14 listed [ML Robinson Papers A7064 Vol43 CY550 p. 133]
1836	September 8th Dickenson seeks salary increase from Lieut Governor for responsibility at the Settlement [ML Robinson Papers A7064 Vol 43 CY550 p. 145]
1836	September 8th Robinson to Montague re: report on health etc of Aborigines [ML Robinson Papers A7044 Vol 23 CY548 pp. 62-66]
1836	September 9th Return of number of deaths 1834, 1835 & 1836 [ML Robinson Papers A7064 Vol 43 pp. 147-150] [ML Robinson Papers A7044 Vol 23 CY548 p. 62]

1836	September 12th Letter from G A Robinson to son, George, re: his offer of appointment to New Holland with Lord Glenelg, "Eliza" leaving Flinders Island "tomorrow" [ML Robinson Papers A7064 Vol 43 CY550 pp. 153–155]
1836	September 12th Letter from G A Robinson to son George, 'you should write more often …' Family arrived at Fl Is 20th June 'your mother likes the place,' 4 births within last 6 months and not a single death, Charles went to Kents Group and Wilsons Promontory [ML Robinson Papers A7064 Vol 43 CY550 pp. 155–160]
1836	September 13th Names of the Aborigines incl explanation of name changes by Robinson [ML Robinson Papers A7064 Vol 43 CY550 pp. 161–168]
1836	September 14th Letter from Robinson to Northam re: *Wurati* [ML Robinson Papers A7064 Vol 43 pp. 169–170]
1836	September 14th Letter from Major Ryan in Launceston to Robinson 50 wethers, 4 work bullocks, bound for the Establishment [ML Robinson Papers A7064 Vol 43 CY550 pp. 171–176]
1836	September 15th Robinson leaves Flinders Island sailed to Hobart [Plomley, 1987, p. 381], returned to Launceston 24th November by coach [Plomley, 1987, p. 396], George Town 2 Dec [Plomley, 1987, p. 397], left 4th Dec and arrived Flinders 6 Dec 1836 [Plomley, 1987, p. 398]
1836	September 26th Letter from Bramwell (Catechist at Glenorchy Gang) to Robinson offering to become Catechist at the Establishment [ML Robinson Papers A7064 Vol 43 CY550 pp. 179–180]
1836	October 3rd Extract of petition from Gilbert Robertson to House of Commons [MLRobinson Papers A7064 Vol 43 CY550 pp. 187–190]
1836	October 7th 3 men drowned while attempting to swim ashore to beach at Wybalenna [ML Robinson Papers A7064 Vol 43 CY550 pp. 197–198]
1836	October 7th Loss of sloop Harmony near Prime Seal Island taking rations to shepherds, bales for wool, Allen wrote to Robinson 7th December [ML Robinson Papers A7064 Vol 43 CY550 p. 305]
1836	October 8th Letter from Montague CSO and Wedge to Robinson re: some Native women taken from south coast of New Holland by sealers and requesting Robinson to take action [ML Robinson papers A7064 Vol 43 CY550 pp. 201–203]
1836	October 18th Tuesday Letter from Robert Clark to Doctor Allen re: fire in Catechist's residence and burning of many books and other items for the school [ML Robinson Papers A7064 Vol 43 pp. 204–206] Allen to Robinson 7th December 1836 [ML Robinson Papers A7064 Vol 43 CY550 p. 309]
1836	October 24th boy named George died, 'one of the most promising boys' in the school [ML Robinson Papers A7064 Vol 43 CY550 p. 297]
1836	October 26th Robinson to Gov Arthur nearing end of his term as Governor, Robinson 12 months since plan re: Aborigines of New Holland; Robinson plan to permanently remove VDL Aborigines to south coast of Australia [ML Robinson Papers A7064 Vol 43 pp. 207–214]
1836	October 28th Robinson to Northam re: rejection of SA offer

1836	October 29th Robinson to Col Sec re: establish central station south coast New Holland and success of VDL establishment in getting an erratic nation to a civilized mode of life [ML Robinson Papers A7064 Vol 43 pp. 219-221]
	Arthur finished as Governor
1836	November 2nd Robinson to Hindmarsh Robinson appointment to South Australia "post poned". Robinson "deeply interested in the amelioration of the Aborigines of New Holland, should exist in distinct communities apart from the whites [ML Robinson Papers A7064 Vol 43 pp. 223-224]
1836	November 8th Hobart Town Robinson to Gentlemen re: letters of testimony appreciating Robinson's services to the colony [ML Robinson Papers A7064 Vol 43 CY550 pp. 225-227]
1836	November 10th Robinson to Montague CSO Request shoemaker as Birch absconded with other convicts several months ago. None available [ML Robinson papers A7064 Vol 43 CY550 pp. 236, 237]
1836	November 10th Robinson to Montague CSO Settlement in destitute condition and requires immediate stores [ML Robinson Papers A7064 Vol 43 CY550 p. 236]
1836	November 11th Hobart Town Robinson to Rev Mr Dowling, G C Clark Esq, T Anstey Esq re: letters of testimony appreciating Robinson's services to the colony [ML Robinson Papers A7064 Vol 43 CY550 p. 239]
1836	November 16th Thomas Bunce / Bruny discharged from Hobart Orphan School [TAHO SWD 28/1/1]
1836	November 17th Robinson to various gentlemen re: appreciation for services [ML Robinson Papers A7064 Vol 43 CY550 pp. 253-254]
1836	November 21st Robinson to son George, from Hobart Town (he had been there eight weeks), succeeded in acquiring land for him and Charles, "I have always thought that Col Arthur had a prejudice to you and your brother, will fetch at least one pound per acre (for you £1000) ought to be thankful to Almighty God for his mercy to you
1836	November 28th Major Ryan (Launceston) to Robinson, embarkation of sheep for Flinders Island.
1836	November 29th Surveyor General to Robinson re: allotments sold by Robinson to Thomas Hace(?) one of which was originally part of what is now the Burial Ground for Trinity Parish. No measure of allotment in Surveyor General's office [ML Robinson Papers A7064 Vol 43 CY550 p. 277]
1836	December 1st R Clark Catechist report to Commandant Robinson for services 1st Sept to 1st Dec 1836 [ML Robinson Papers A7064 Vol 43 CY550 p. 303]
1836	December 2nd List of 24 prisoners discharged to public works and rationed Flinders Island [ML Robinson Papers A7064 Vol 43 CY550 p. 305]
1836	December an additional award of one hundred ewes and three rams was made by the Government to the friendly natives for their subsequent services [ML Robinson Papers CY548]
1836	December 6th Tamar arrived with Commandant and sheep from Launceston [ML Robinson Papers A7044 CY548 Vol 23] having left 15th September

1836	December 8th Allen to Robinson requesting more medical supplies [ML Robinson papers A7064 Vol 43 CY550 p. 311]
1836	December 9th (Friday) fire broke out in kitchen of Catechist's house [ML Robinson Papers A7064 Vol 43 CY550 p. 317]
1836	December 11th Tamar left Settlement (arrived on 10th) with Robinson and Benjamin (an Aborigine) to go to Launceston to join Mr Robinson Jnr (Charles) and his party [ML Robinson Papers A7064 Vol 43 CY550 p. 317]
1836	December 10th Charles Robinson to Robinson requesting disposing of 500 acres granted to him by Governor and appropriate the land[ML Robinson Papers A7064 Vol 43 CY550 p. 315]
1836	December 13th Clark to Robinson re: no knowledge of private property held by the Aborigines prior to the market in August. [ML Robinson Papers A7064 Vol 43 CY550 pp. 323-324]
1836	December 16th Eliza left to convey Commandant to Port Philip, returned January 1837 no date [ML Robinson Papers A7044 Vol 23 CY548]
1836	December 17th Clark to Robinson report 'lack of stationery' using leaves from my books [ML Robinson Papers A7064 Vol 43 CY550 p. 329]
1836	December 17th Allen, Dickenson and Clark to Robinson re: Rolepa's son with Batman at Ben Lomond, seeking his return and that of another boy Leuimeerinna(?) [ML Robinson Papers A7064 Vol 43 CY550 pp. 331-332]
1836	December 17th Samuel Hopkinson (convict shepherd) to Robinson re: sheep flock on Prime Seal Island, 330, 25 bags @ 30 pounds wool per bag [ML Robinson Papers A7064 Vol 43 CY550 p. 335]
1836	December 19th Mr & Mrs Humphrey appointed Master and Matron to Flinders Island Settlement by Thomas Ryan Commandant, Launceston [ML Robinson Papers A7064 CY550 Vol 43 p. 367]
1836	December 19th Thomas Ryan Commandant, Launceston to Dr Arthur Hobart re: replacing Dr Allen at Flinders Island during his leave of absence [ML Robinson Papers A7064 Vol 43 CY550 p. 365]
1836	December 22nd Robinson to Forster C. V. Magistrate re: convicts Phipps and Webb (a Baker) being retained at the Settlement after the conclusion of their sentences in August and Sept. Difficult to get people to the settlement [ML Robinson Papers A7064 Vol 43 CY550 pp. 341-342]
1836	December 22nd Robinson travelled to Port Phillip with several Aboriginal people [Plomley, 1987, p. 405] Parnabuke, Hector, David and one female Maria, or Matilda [ML Robinson Papers CY549 pp. 13-15] returned 8th January 1837 [Plomley, 1987, p. 414]
1836	December 23rd Samuel Hopkinson (convict shepherd) to Robinson re: sheep on Green Island, new sheep dead, request build a shed with some tobacco [ML Robinson Papers A7064 Vol 43 CY550 pp. 341-343]
1836	December 26th Clark to Robinson re: house inspections [ML Robinson Papers A7064 Vol 43 CY550 p. 357]

1836	December Return of attendance at Sabbath and week day school [ML Robinson Papers A7064 Vol 43 CY550 p. 373]
1837	January 5th John Franklin arrives in VDL becomes Governor (until 21st August 1843)
1837	January while Robinson at Port Philip Mother of Noemy died and Kangaroo Billy (Ray?) during influenza epidemic, boat crew of six men drowned at sea between Settlement and Green Island, making nine drowned in a few months[ML Robinson Papers CY549 p. 14]
1837	January 8th Robinson and others returned from Port Phillip [Plomley, 1987, p. 414]
1837	January 9th Clark to Robinson, visited Native houses, swept out, beds made. Many have gone to live in breakwinds, greater portion hunting, Noemy's mother interred Sat evening [ML Robinson Papers A7065 CY550 p. 41]
1837	January 11th Peter (Bruny) refuses to work with Tailor "on any account" [ML Robinson Papers A7065 CY550 p. 43]
1837	January 12th Clark writes to Rural Dean seeking increase in his salary [ML Robinson Papers A7065 CY550 p. 47]
1837	January 14th Clark to Robinson reporting on Walter absent from School, Peter not at Tailors, children going bush since not sleeping in his house and under his constant supervision, wants new dormitory and children back residing at his house when repaired from fire. Thomas Bruny and Walter teaching in breakwind next to Clark's house [ML Robinson Papers A7065 CY550 pp. 65-70]
1837	January 14th Clark to Robinson, death of child of Maria, interred 16th Jan. Some of Gohannah's friends with her husband returned from bush where they've been for a length of time [ML Robinson Papers A7065 CY550 pp. 71-73]
1837	January 16th Clark to Robinson re: Robinson's directive that 6d be given to those attending the School to learn singing [ML Robinson Papers A7065 CY550 p. 75]
1837	January 23rd Clark re: attendances at Sunday worship, prisoners, natives, officers, soldiers, free persons [ML Robinson Papers A7065 CY550 p. 83]
1837	January 23rd Clark's count of number of dogs with Aboriginal people, 79, and how many for each named Aboriginal person [ML Robinson Papers A7065 CY550 p. 85] Noemy has the most, 6.
1837	January 23rd Clark reporting to Robinson, Louisa has again separated from her husband and has gone to live with King George, also Native women delivered 115 'back loads' of grass [ML Robinson Papers A7065 CY550 p. 87]
1837	January 24th Clark reported King George separated from wife Agnes, now living with Flora. Catechist asked George to take back wife, but he refused, asked Flora to leave but she also refused. This "unlawful connexion are a disturbance to the portion of the Settlement they reside in" [ML Robinson Papers A7065 CY550 p. 89]
1837	January 24th Market held and cash paid for work by Aborigines [ML Robinson Papers A7044 CY548 pp. 124-127]
1837	January 24th Book of accounts of market from 18th Oct to 31st Dec closed and audited by Mr Surgeon Allen. Large number of the vouchers perished in fire on 18th Oct. Also payments to Aborigines as inducement for learning hymn singing [ML Robinson Papers A7065 CY550 pp. 101-103]

1837	February 16th Market held and cash paid for work by Aborigines, threshing packing barley, skins, apprehending prisoner who had absconded, and those whose dogs were killed [ML Robinson Papers A7044 CY548 pp. 128–129]
1837	February 22nd Big dinner, over 100 present, Commandant at head, officers, Big River, then the rest [Plomley, 1987, p. 426]
1837	March 6th and various dates throughout March, Cash paid to women regularly attending Mrs Dickinson's house, men regularly attending school, women carrying grass, men carrying wood, men digging potatoes, women gathering potatoes, men and women making new road [ML Robinson Papers A7044 CY548 pp. 130 – 132]
1837	April 17th–27th Cash paid to women employed collecting mutton birds from Chalky Is, men navigating the boats while at Chalky [ML Robinson Papers A7044 CY548 p. 133]
1837	April 29th Several men, mostly clan leaders "address each other in own languages" during Saturday prayer meeting [Plomley, 1987, p. 439]
1837	May 1st Monthly catechetical examination by Allen and Dickenson [ML Robinson Papers A7066 CY551 pp. 3–30]
1837	May 3rd Clark to Robinson re: first language addresses and Allen's reply "No restriction, Clark unable to make himself understood"[ML Robinson Papers A7066 CY551 p. 49–53]
1837	May 6th Allen to Robinson re: strongly opposing Clark's statement re: the potato crop, "impugn my character" "flies in the face of truth" 4 pages [ML Robinson Papers A7066 CY551 p55–58] probably related to Allen's comments re: Clark's ideas of teaching in first language or the 'language of the settlement' Robert Miller 50th Regmt re: Frederick Phipps gardening experience planting potato crop [ML Robinson Papers A7066 CY551 pp. 59–60]
1837	May 8th Rations for Aboriginal children living with Clark's [ML Robinson Papers A7066 CY551 p. 65]
1837	May 8th inspection of children living with Clark [ML Robinson Papers A7066 CY551 p. 71]
1837	May 8th Mrs Clark to Robinson re: bands knitted by Jemima and Flora, are they approved by Robinson? If so, will make more [ML Robinson Papers A7066 CY551 p. 73]
1837	May 8th Court of Justice Assembled King George and King William Presidents, Peter Bruny charged [ML Robinson Papers A7066 CY551 p. 75]
1837	May 9th–21st Quarterly Catechetical Examinations Leonidas, Albert, Washington, Noemy, Eugene, James, Joseph, Andrew, Francis, Hector, Bonaparte, Romeo, Christopher, Alexander, Tippo Saib, Alexander, Alphonso, Frederick, Rodney, G Robinson, W Robinson, Peter Pindar, Edmund, Phillip, Augustus, Henry, Constantine, Ajax, Milton, King George, Thomas, Neptune, Teddy Clark, Alfred, Achilles, Hannibal, Prince Walter, Thomas Bruny Thomas Thompson, Peter Brune, Charles Clark, Mary Ann, Sabina, Mary Ann Thompson, Sarah, Moama, Betsy, and others [ML Robinson Papers A7044 CY548 pp. 265–309] also in [ML Robinson Papers A7066 CY551 pp. 81–149]
1837	May 17th Clark to Robinson re: unsuitability of whale boat used between Settlement and Green Island "I have been reared in boats and shipping in a large sea port"

	[ML Robinson Papers A7066 CY551 p. 161], Dickinson same opinion [ML Robinson Papers A7066 CY551 p. 163]
1837	May 24th Mrs Dickenson unable to instruct female Aborigines [ML Robinson Papers A7066 CY551 p. 181]
1837	May 24th Robinson to Medical Officer, in response to MO request for a person acquainted with the language of the Aborigines to accompany you on your visits to the Natives, I have to state that I have no person under my command acquainted with the language of the Natives [ML Robinson Papers A7066 CY551 pp. 185–186]
1837	May 25th Walsh to Robinson re: man severely burned, request someone to attend him as wife unable to [ML Robinson Papers A7066 CY551 pp. 189–190]
1837	May 27th Robinson payment to Clara 1 s and Daphne 2 s for bands made under direction of Mrs Dickenson[ML Robinson Papers A7066 CY551 p. 191]
1837	May 27th Walsh Return of weekly Medical Report sick civilians, military, Aborigines, Servants, Men in Government employ [ML Robinson Papers A7066 CY551 p. 193]
1837	May 29th Clark to Robinson deficiency in rations for Natives [ML Robinson Papers A7066 CY551 p. 211]
1837	May 30th Principal's Office, tracts for distribution among prisoners [ML Robinson Papers A7066 CY551 p. 217]
1837	May Nominal list of convicts that have been employed in Public works at Flinders Island, Sept 1833 to May 1837 [ML Robinson Papers A7066 CY551 pp. 224–226]
1837	May Cash paid to men employed collecting wattle for thatching, making road at rear of Commandants quarters, road to stone quarry, second road at rear of Commandants quarters, men working in bush clearing strawberry garden all paid in Pounds, shillings, pence. Attendance at School in May paid in "dollars" [ML Robinson Papers A7044 CY548 pp. 133–135]
1837	June 1st Sarah arrived from sealers and was interviewed by Robert Clark [ML Robinson Papers A7044 CY548 pp. 291–293]
1837	June 2nd Catherine Clark to Robinson, three worsted stockings manufactured by the following Native females, Harriet, Louisa, Patty [ML Robinson Papers A7066 CY551 p. 237]
1837	June 2nd Clark: Storekeeper required to attend Government and Native stores to assist in removing the old and new barley belonging to the Natives and to measure those barley and also the wheat and to make out a return of their respective quantities. RClark, Clerk of the Native Market [ML Robinson Papers A7066 CY551 p. 239]
1837	June 2nd Corporal Miller visited Woody Is with Coxswain and two Aborigines (females), met sealer, 2 Aboriginal women and 3 children (2 of them his), Miller brought one woman and her son to the Settlement the next morning [ML Robinson Papers A7066 CY551 pp. 243–245]
1837	June 3rd Aboriginal woman, Sarah, interviewed by Clark, she was from Kangaroo Island [ML Robinson Papers A7044 CY548 pp. 391–392][ML Robinson Papers A7066 CY551 pp. 247–249]

1837	June 8th Clark to Robinson monthly catechetical examination "pupils not improving but the reverse" [ML Robinson Papers A7066 CY551 p. 265]
1837	June 8th conflict between Clark, Robinson, Storekeeper about Clark's keeping of Natives' accounts of the market, problem of 6 pounds not accounted for, Clark disputed this [ML Robinson Papers A7066 CY551 pp. 267–270]
1837	June 12th Letter of sale of barley of the Aborigines taken into store, 37 bushels of barley, 5 bushels of wheat [ML Robinson Papers A7066 CY551 p. 281]
1837	July 1st Died this morning the native woman called Rheinhoop [ML Robinson Papers A573 CY 940 p. 137]
1837	June 14th Weekly return of Medical report by Walsh with number of sick civilians, Military, Aborigines, Servants and Men in employ of the Government [ML Robinson Papers A7066 CY551 p. 283]
1837	June 20th Gift of £19/9/4 (added to earlier £100) from various men of Campbell Town to Robinson "from your services in the removal of the Aborigines" [ML Robinson Papers A7066 CY551 p. 303]
1837	June 22nd Medical Attendant Report on accident in which "Daniel" was badly burned, his treatment [ML Robinson Papers A7066 CY551 pp. 317–320]
1837	June 23rd Sentries at the store, store window broken [ML Robinson Papers A7066 CY551 p. 321]
1837	June 23rd Sparkes to Robinson, turnip paddock fencing post and rail stake, six hundred and seven yards, whole of posts, rails were brought by the Aborigines [ML Robinson Papers A7066 CY551 p. 325]
1837	June 23rd Clark to Robinson re: 9 roads made by the Aborigines and paddocks sown with vegetables, crops, etc [ML Robinson Papers A7066 CY551 pp. 331–333]
1837	July 15th Reallocation of 'huts' to other Aborigines when some, chosen by Robinson, went into new brick houses [Plomley, 1987, p. 461]Brick houses are the "terraces"
1837	July 18th Allocation of brick houses (terraces) with names of those in each (No 4: Sara, child [Fanny Cochran-Smith], Eugene; Margaret and Philip) [Plomley, 1987, p. 463]
1837	July 20th Ryan to Alfred ____(?) re: causes of decline of population of Aborigines [ML Robinson Papers A7066 CY551 pp. 40–42]
1837	July 22nd Received upon the strength of this Establishment from the 21st Inst inclusive Ten Adult Aborigines they having arrived from the Main per the Tamar on 20th inst. Robinson [ML Robinson Papers A573 CY 940 p. 137]
1837	July 31st List of sick people at the Settlement [ML Robinson Papers A7066 CY551 p. 77]
1837	July 31st List of names of Aborigines at the Settlement, 116 with 20 names crossed out [ML Robinson Papers A7066 CY551 p. 79]
1837	August 9th List of Aborigines attending Sabbath and week day evening schools listing classification in alphabet, spelling, testament, reading, Bible, Catechetical question, Writing, and Arithmetic. Pupils names: Leonidas, Albert, Washington, Napoleon, Benjamin, Robert, Isaac, Edward, Noemy, Eugene, James, Joseph,

Francis, Andrew, Alexander, Tippo, Arthur, King Alpha, Frederick, Peter Pindar, Augustus, Philip, Henry, Christopher, Bonaparte, G Robinson, Hannibal, Milton, Alpha, Ajax, Thomas, King George, Rodney, Romeo, Henry, Hector, Walter, Tho Brune, Tho Thompson, Peter Brune, David Brune, Charley Clark, R Clark, John Franklin, Teddy, 44 men.

Adelaide, Amelia, Agnes, Ann, Clara, Catherine, Deborah, Daphne, Evelyn, Elizabeth, Emma, Flora, Fanny, Henrietta, Harriet, Helen, Juliet, Jemima, Jane, Kitty, Louisa, Lucy, Lalla Rookh, Margaret, Matilda, Maria, Wild Mary, Petuck, Patty, Paulina, Pillap, Eliza Robinson, Rose, Sarah, Sophia, Sabina, Susan, Semiramus(?), Tarchemineric(?), Mary Ann, M A Thompson, Nomymircric(?), Caroline, Rebecca, Bessy [ML Robinson Papers A7044 CY548 pp. 387–390] 45 women.

1837	August 16th Died this morning the Native woman Andromache [ML Robinson Papers A573 CY 940 p. 137]
1837	September 1st Robinson to Capt (Port Officer) provision of preferred boat not possible as it needs full crew of seven men, but have acquired a lesser boat [ML Robinson Papers A7066 CY551 p. 177]
1837	September 2nd Clark to Robinson re: native language and lingua franca sermon by Noemy [ML Robinson Papers A706 CY551 p. 183]
1837	September 16th Robinson to Montague (Col Sec) re: letter from Gilbert Robertson to House of Commons seeking compensation for his efforts in searching out Aborigines [ML Robinson Papers A7066 CY551 pp. 233–241]
1837	September J Allen to Robinson extensive report re: diseases [ML Robinson Papers A7066 CY551 pp. 201–221]
1837	September 22nd Charles Robinson seeks permission to pasture sheep on Chappell Island [ML Robinson Papers A7066 CY551 p. 273]
1837	October 6th Robinson to Montague Col Sec Office, discontinue salt meat on recommendation of Mr Allen Medical Officer who sees it as cause of the increased mortality among the Aborigines [ML Robinson Papers A7044 CY548 p. 393]
1837	October 13th Montague to Robinson, fresh meat has been supplied via sheep etc to the Settlement [ML Robinson Papers A7044 CY548 p. 394]
1837	November 7th Died a female Aborigine Jemima [ML Robinson Papers A573 CY940 p. 199]
1837	November 13th Died a female Aborigine Pondam------- (?)[ML Robinson Papers A573 CY940 p. 199]
1837	November 17th Died this morning the female Aborigine Elizabeth [ML Robinson Papers A573 CY940 p. 199]
1837	November 21st Rewards for those showing improvement in examinations, paniccans, handkerchiefs and pipes [ML Robinson PapersA7066 CY551 p. 149]
1837	November Clark to Archdeacon: Return of Oct–Dec attendance at Sabbath day and evening schools and Divine Services [ML Robinson Papers A7066 CY551 p. 169]
1837	December 18th Died last night the female Aborigine child William(?) being just under four years of age [ML Robinson Papers A573 CY940 p. 213]

1837	December 23rd Robinson to Walsh (Medical Officer) authorised to inspect the children domiciles at the Catechist's home, bedding, preparation of diet, etc. [ML Robinson Papers A7044 CY548 pp. 396-397]
1837	December 27th Walsh to Robinson [ML Robinson Papers A7066 CY551 pp. 209-211]
1837	December 29th Died the male Aborigine Benjamin [ML Robinson Papers A573 CY940 p. 213] Post Mortem examination 30th Dec [ML Robinson Papers A7066 CY551 p. 227]
1837	December 29th Died the male Aborigine Constantine [ML Robinson Papers A573 CY940 p. 213] Post Mortem examination 30th Dec [ML Robinson Papers A7066 CY551 p. 225]
1837	December 31st Nominal return of Free persons, Military and Prisoners Oct 1835 to Dec 1837 [ML Robinson Papers A7066 CY551 pp. 231-237]
1837	Sheep flock comprised 1026 [ML Robinson Papers A7044 CY548]
1838	January 25th (same day as Governor but on board the Shamrock)[ML Robinson Papers A7044 Vol 23 CY548] Mr Dove had arrived to take charge of the spiritual concerns of the settlement. Mrs Dove was on board of the vessel. Mr Dove and Mr Wilson visited the settlement and then returned to the cutter for his wife and luggage (Plomley, 1987, p. 523. Preached first sermon 28th January 1838 [Miller, 1985, p. 26]
1838	January 25th-28th Sir John and Lady Franklin visited Wybalenna [Plomley, 1987, pp. 523-530]; arrived on Eliza on 25th January [ML Robinson Papers A7044 Vol 23 CY548] listed after arrival of Shamrock so probably occurred later in the day.
1838	30th January Robinson to Clark, appointment of Rev T Dove to permanent spiritual charge of the Aborigines ... your appointment as Catechist in consequence superseded [ML Robinson Papers A7044 CY548 p. 397]
1838	January last edition of the Flinders Island Chronicle published, perhaps coinciding with visit of Governor Franklin and/or arrival of Thomas Dove to become catechist. Also Walter Arthur went with Mary Ann to Chalky Island after their marriage in mid-March 1838 until January 1839.
1838	February 9th-16th Annual Examination of the Aboriginal School [ML Robinson Papers A7044 CY548 pp. 60-95]
1838	February 24th Saturday first language sermons by Noemy and Neptune, translated by Bessy Clark to Robert Clark [ML Robinson Papers 7044 CY548 pp. 38-39]
1838	March 6th-12th various reports Robinson, Clark, Dickinson, Dove and Walsh regarding road to Grass Tree plains, now 5 miles 520 yards, and road to Stony Castle 4 English miles, built by the Aboriginal men under supervision of Charles Robinson [ML Robinson Papers A7044 CY548 pp. 120-123]
1838	March 10th Saturday Sermons by Noemy, Neptune and Leonidas, translated by Clara and Bessy Clark to Robert Clark [ML Robinson Papers A7044 CY548 pp. 39-40]
1838	March 16th Walter Arthur and Mary Ann married by Rev T Dove [ML Robinson Papers A7044 CY548 p. 114] Three days after this Walter and Mary Ann went to Chalky Island for almost 9 months, then went to Prime Seal. Walter is not named as one of the signatories of the petition (11/8/1838) about going to Port Philip with Robinson. They came back to the Settlement on 25th January 1839.

1838	March 17th Saturday Sermons by Noemy & Neptune [ML Robinson Papers A7044 CY548 pp. 39-40]
1838	March 20th Robinson to Clark, 21st Clark to Robinson re: capabilities of Aborigines, incl Clark's biographies of several deceased Aborigines [ML Robinson Papers A7044 CY548 pp. 102–113]
1838	March 31st Walsh (Medical Officer) reporting to Robinson re: opinion on health of Aborigines. More prone to inflammations of the lungs [ML Robinson Papers A7044 CY548 pp. 55-60]
1838	March 31st Saturday Sermons by Noemy, Neptune, Alexander [ML Robinson Papers A7044 CY548 pp. 43-46]
1838	April 14th Saturday Sermons by Noemy, Neptune, Leonidas, Alpha [ML Robinson Papers A7044 CY548 pp. 47-50]
1838	April 21st Saturday Sermons by Alexander, Neptune, Noemy, Napoleon, Leonidas, Alpha, Robert [ML Robinson Papers A7044 CY548 pp. 50-54]
1838	June 16th Analysis of the Aborigines of Van Diemen's Land [ML Robinson Papers A7044 CY548 p. 21]
1838	June 21st Robinson note regarding the disturbance of cremation sites for several deceased persons, note includes a map of the locations of several 'incinerated' sites in relation to particular paddocks [ML Robinson Papers A7044 CY548 p. 450 approx]
1838	June 30th Obituary of Aborigines 30th Sept 1837–30th June 1838 [ML Robinson Papers A7044 CY548]
1838	July 1st New chapel opened [the one still standing] as the grounds on which the old place of worship had been pronounced to be injurious to the health of the Aborigines, no longer existed [Miller, 1985, p. 42]
1838	August 13th Robinson to Hobart Town, got Dove to write glowing reference about his behaviour towards the Aborigines [Plomley, 1987, p. 576]
1838	August 18th Robinson offered Chief Protector in Port Phillip [Plomley, 1987, pp. 576–577] Dove's reference seems to have helped
1838	August 22nd Robinson set out for Sydney [Plomley, 1987, p. 577]
1838	August 31st Robinson landed in Sydney [Plomley, 1987, p. 582]
1838	December 16th Died the female Aborigine Paulina [ML Robinson Papers A573 CY940 p. 267]
1839	January 10th Robinson returned to Settlement [Plomley, 1987, p. 611]
1839	January 25th Walter and Mary Ann return from Prime Seal Island after their 10 months away from the Settlement [Plomley, 1987, p. 776 from Settlement Journal]
1839	February 12th Doves leave Settlement "taking" Mary Ann Thompson with them [Plomley, 1987, p. 615]
1839	February 16th Departure of chaplain and family, the military (five in number) and their families, the coxswain and family, the overseer and family, twenty-three convicts, two aboriginal boys and also one half caste girl [Mary Ann Thompson] (the brother of the girl accompanied me to Port Phillip as a domestic and it had

been Mrs Robinson's intention to have taken the girl also) taken without my consent by Mrs Dove. The number of aborigines that will remain after deducting those who accompany me to Port Phillip will be (all ages and sexes) about sixty (Plomley 1987) [Plomley, 1987, p. 785]

1839   February 24th George Robinson leaves for Port Philip [Plomley, 1987, p. 112] and George Robinson Jnr becomes Commandant until 15th April

1839   April 16th Malcolm Laing Smith arrived to become new Commandant but G Robinson uncooperative, so delayed start until 24th April [Plomley, 1987, p. 121]

1841   June 10th Board of Inquiry critical of Dove, seek to reduce funding [Plomley, 1987, p. 129]

1841   August 10th Peter Fisher appointed Commandant and Catechist [Plomley, 1987, p. 131]

1842   February 6 children sent to Orphan School, against parent's wishes [Plomley, 1987, p. 132]

1842   April 12th Jeanneret appointed Commandant, but he wanted separate teacher for the children and delayed leaving Hobart to take up the appointment [Plomley, 1987, p. 135]

1842   June 15th Fisher handed Commandant role to Jeanneret, but didn't leave Flinders until 16th July [Plomley, 1987, p. 133]

1842   July 6th Jeanneret reports that he 'persuaded' parents to send children to Orphan School and six are sent [CSO 8/157/1166, pp. 59–60; 16 Nov pp. 117–4] Parents reluctant because due to 'the large number of deaths there'[Plomley, 1987, p. 136– CSO 15 Sept 1842 8/157/1166, pp. 174–209]

1842   July 16th Jeanneret reports return of Aboriginal people from Port Phillip, *Wurati* had died on voyage and was buried on Green Island. Fourteen from VDL / Tasmania, two from South Australia had gone with Robinson, plus John Allen who'd gone with Batman. The two from South Australia stayed in Port Phillip, those from VDL / Tasmania returned, some in July, some in Oct: two were hanged, four died in accident/sickness/old age, Peter Bruney stayed and died Port Phillip Dec 1843, Thomas Thomson may have remained in Victoria [Plomley, 1987, p. 136]

1842   October 10th Letters from Walter George Arthur to Walker [ML Robinson Papers CY3695]

1843   August John Franklin replaced by Eardly-Wilmot as Governor of VDL [Plomley, 1987, p. 165]

1843   November 12–14th possibly, Franklin, Bishop Nixon, and others, visited Settlement on Franklin's way to Port Phillip (and back to England)[Plomley, 1987, p. 165] Nixon Report CSO 8/183/3099; Hobart Town Advertiser 9 May 1845, Hobart Town Advertiser 1 & 24 Nov 1843; Hobart Town Courerier 10 & 17 Nov 1843; Examiner 27 Sept, 11, 18, 22 Nov, 2 & 13 Dec 1843; Port Phillip Herald 17 Nov 1843; CSO 8/110/2311 pp. 5–8; CSO 11/26/378 pp. 13–15]

1844   February 4th Joseph Milligan replaced Jeanneret [Plomley, 1987, p. 134], and Robert Clark reappointed as Catechist [Plomley, 1987, p. 143] and brought back 3 children from the Orphan School [Plomley, 1987, p. 144] See preamble of Milligan's appointment, Aborigines have a 'natural right to their land' [Plomley, 1987, p. 144]

1844	July 31st Milligan's wife, Eliza, died the day after giving birth to a son [Plomley, 1987, p. 146]
1844	second half of year, Milligan visiting other islands with Aborigines tending the boat [Plomley, 1987, p. 146]
1845	August 11th Jeanneret petitions Lord Stanley and is compensated by restoring him to his former office or some other lucrative position [Plomley, 1987, p. 148](GO 1/58, pp. 61–34)(CSO11/10/242, p. 229)
1845	December 30th Walter Arthur's letter to G W Walker [Plomley, 1987, p. 148], Aborigines want to support themselves.
1846	February 17th Petition to Queen [CSO 17 Feb 1846 11/26/378 pp. 13-15; p. 12; pp. 5-8; pp. 3-4; CSO 24/8/824, p. 243][Plomley, 1987, p. 166]
1846	February 18th Clark report to Milligan on conditions at the Settlement from Feb 1844-Jan 1846 [Plomley, 1987, p. 149]
1846	March Jeanneret replaced Milligan [Plomley, 1987, p. 134]
1846	April 3rd Further letter from petitioners to Col Sec [CSO11/26/378 pp. 16, 17] [Plomley, 1987, pp. 150, 167]
1846	June 10th Mary Ann writes to Col Sec [CSO 11/26/378 pp. 20-1] [Plomley, 1987, p. 167
1846	June 12th Jeanneret rebuts the petition[CSO11/26/378 pp. 53-89][Plomley, 1987, p. 151]
1846	June 15th WG Arthur to Governor [CSO 11/26/378 pp. 35–41][Plomley, 1987, p. 167]
1846	June 16th John Allen (Jacky) to Governor [CSO 11/26/378 pp. 29-30][Plomley, 1987, p. 167]
1846	June 16th Washington to Governor [CSO 11/26/378 p. 31-32][Plomley, 1987, p. 167]
1846	June 17th WG Arthur to Governor [CSO 11/26/378 p. 22-24][Plomley, 1987, p. 167]
1846	June 18th Davey Bruney to Governor [CSO 11/26/378 p. 25-27][Plomley, 1987, p. 167]
1846	June 19th Alphonso and Alexander to Governor [CSO 11/26/378 pp. 33-34] [Plomley, 1987, p. 167]
1846	June 29th Jeanneret to Clark re: 'bad influence over natives' [CSO 11/26/641 pp. 323-324][Plomley, 1987, p. 167]
1846	July 15th WG Arthur to Col Sec [CSO 11/26/378 p. 174–177][Plomley, 1987, p. 167]
1846	August 5th Jeanneret to Col Sec complaints about Clark [CSO 11/26/641 pp. 293-296] [Plomley, 1987, p. 167]
1846	August 6th Clark to Col Sec responding, including letters of support from Noemy Mewerick [this is Noemy's additional name], Mary Ann Arthur, and Fanny Cochrane [CSO 11/26/641 p301-315][Plomley, 1987, p. 167]
1846	Sept–Oct Eardly-Wilmot recalled as Governor but still in VDL. Charles La Trobe Superintendent of Port Phillip in charge of VDL [Plomley, 1987, p. 156]
1846	October 6th-27th Matthew Curling Friend investigates the Settlement [CSO11/27/658 pp. 3-7; 13-14; 35-192][Plomley, 1987, p. 168]
1846	October 25th Jeanneret suspended Clark as Catechist [CSO11/27/658 p. 277][Plomley, 1987, p. 168] and travelled to Hobart to meet La Trobe

1846	December 'early' Jeanneret returned to Flinders Island
1846	December 12th Clark to Friend protesting suspension [Plomley, 1987, p. 157]
1846	December 16th Clark to Col Sec protesting suspension [Plomley, 1987, p. 157]
1847	January 7th Col Sec to Jeanneret ordering restoration of Clark [Plomley, 1987, p. 157]
1847	January 14th Friend to Col Sec, restore Clark or remove him from the island [Plomley, 1987, p. 157]
1847	January 27th Denison became Governor
1847	March 27th Clark visited Hobart, (Jeanneret did not allow Aborigines to accompany him) met Denison and large number of papers [Plomley, 1987, p. 158]
1847	March 31st Jeanneret sent report to Governor [Plomley, 1987, p. 158]
1847	May 5th Jeanneret ordered to reinstate Clark [Plomley, 1987, p. 160], dismiss Jeanneret and replace him with Milligan [Plomley, 1987, p. 160]
1847	May Clark returned to Settlement
1847	May 27th Jeanneret issued warrant for arrest of Clark and family [CSO 24/7/101 p. 45, statement by Aboriginal parents p. 30][Plomley, 1987, p. 169]
1847	June 9th Milligan replaced Jeanneret [Plomley, 1987, p. 134] and Jeanneret sought to disrupt the Settlement
1847	July & August arguments between Milligan and Jeanneret
1847	July 14th plans underway for removal to Oyster Cove, influenza epidemic. 14 men, 23 women and 10 children [Plomley, 1987, p. 162]
1847	October 18th Milligan supervised removal to Oyster Cove but did not live there [Plomley, 1987, p. 134], Clark made Superintendent [Plomley, 1987, p. 162]
1848	February Jeanneret left Flinders Island [Plomley, 1987, p. 163]

INDEX

Aboriginal Chronicle	*See Flinders Island Chronicle*
Alexander	*See* Druemerterpunner
Arthur, Mary Ann	92, 103, 113, 115, 118, 165, 170, 172–73, 176–80, 257, 264, 267–9, 271
Arthur, Walter	47, 56, 70–73, 81, 92–107, 112–16, 118–20, 122–24, 127–29, 131–32, 157, 164–65, 168, 171–77, 180, 184–85, 229–48, 263–64, 267–71
Beeton, Lucy	139–47
Bell and Lancaster	48, 90, 92–93, 112
Bromby, Bishop	147–49, 157
Brownrigg	146–50
Bruny, Thomas	5, 45–48, 71, 81, 97–98, 104–05, 115, 185, 212, 229–48, 261
Bunce, Thomas	*See* Bruny, Thomas
Catechism	6, 71–72, 88–89, 93 – 94, 98–104, 119, 130, 140, 169
Clark, Robert	47, 65, 67, 74–75, 78–82, 88–107, 111–33, 164, 166–68, 175–77, 211–12, 222–25, 228, 238, 245, 251–72
Crackney	67, 84, 130, 214
Creation story	9–11, 17–29, 43, 51–53, 67–69, 77, 80, 96–99, 126–27, 129–30, 219
Darling	64–66, 68, 72–75, 250–51
Dowwringgi	80, 116, 130
Drinene	219–28, 245, 264, 268–69
Druemerterpunner	80, 116, 120, 129–130, 221
Fereday, Reverend	141, 143–45, 147–48
Fire	9–10, 17–21, 27–29, 51–54
Flinders Island Chronicle	71, 81, 91, 104–06, 113–116, 132
Hardwicke, Fanny	58, 60, 206
Hobart Orphan School	34, 41, 44–49, 55–56, 65, 67, 70–71, 77, 82, 95–99, 105, 115, 132, 135, 165–66, 170, 172, 177, 180, 183, 210–13
Kennedy, Catherine	208
King's Orphan School	*See* Hobart Orphan School
Knopwood, Robert	14, 35–40, 42, 202–07
Leonidas	*See* Dowwringgi
Luggenemenener	47, 56, 71, 72, 77, 92, 119, 128, 228
Macauley, Robert	30, 42–44, 159
Manalakina	16, 19, 22, 28, 54, 69, 92, 94, 128, 254
Mannalargenna	*See Manalakina*

Mathinna	45, 70, 165, 210
May, Robert Hobart	6, 36–38, 41
Milligan, Joseph	164–69, 178, 211, 213, 270–72
Naming	vi, 6, 21, 23–24, 25–26
Napoleon	See Piway
Neptune	See Drinene
Nicholls Rivulet Methodist	152, 179, 181–86
Nixon, Bishop	140–43, 145, 171–74, 178, 270
Noemy	102, 106, 112–13, 116, 118–21, 123–25, 128, 130–31, 218, 220–24, 226–28, 241, 263–64, 266–69, 271
Oyster Cove	See putalina / Oyster Cove
Piway	116, 120, 223–24, 228, 266, 269
Ponsonby, William	208
putalina / Oyster Cove	48, 138, 140, 145, 152, 164–86
Queen's Orphan School	See Hobart Orphan School
Reibey	143–48, 181
Rolepa	47, 56, 71, 77, 92, 102, 114, 118–20, 128, 228, 262
Sermons	22, 27, 50–53, 71, 79–80, 94, 99, 103, 111–16, 122–32, 172, 175, 185, 218–28, 248, 267, 268, 269
Smith, Fanny Cochrane	6, 165, 166, 168, 170–72, 176–85, 210, 266–67, 271
Smith, William	168, 172, 176–85
Truganini	See Trukanini
Trukanini	1, 16, 27, 100, 127–28, 170–71, 178, 182
Tuery	See Luggenemenener
Tanaminawayt	See Piway
Tunnerminwerwait	See Piway
Wilkinson, Thomas	47, 65–74, 76, 77, 79, 89–90, 92, 94–96, 102, 105, 111, 118, 214–17, 250–51
Wurati	15 16, 20–22, 25–27, 42–44, 51–52, 69, 77, 80, 82, 92, 97, 99, 116, 118, 120, 123–25, 128, 130, 222, 259–60, 270
Wooraddy	See Wurati

www.ingramcontent.com/pod-product-compliance
Lightning Source LLC
Chambersburg PA
CBHW080245030426
42334CB00023BA/2710